# Energy, Wealth and Governance in the Caucasus and Central Asia

In 1991 the eight countries of the Caucasus and Central Asia (CCA) became independent from the former Soviet Union. Although a region rich in natural resources, the transition toward a market economy has not gone smoothly for the CCA countries. Drawing upon recent progress in development economics and political science, the book provides fresh analysis of the CCA countries' transition by tracing the impact of the natural resource endowment. The book examines the synergies between energy-rich and energy-poor states and highlights the practical consequences of both well-managed and poorly-managed energy revenue deployment.

The region has been a relatively slow reformer, its governments have become more authoritarian, and the contributors argue that despite recent growth spurts, further reform is required to sustain rapid GDP growth and nurture democracy. They suggest that unless CCA elites change the way in which they deploy natural resource revenues, regional development will fall short of its potential with possibly disastrous consequences. The contributors apply the experience of the developing market economies to demonstrate that the region still holds considerable potential to become an important stable supplier of raw materials and a source of industrial demand to the global economy. However, the CCA could become a threat to the global economy as a consequence of the misuse of energy revenues in promoting the interests of predatory political elites.

With contributions from prominent specialists on resource-driven economies *Energy, Wealth and Governance in the Caucasus and Central Asia* provides a systematic and integrated analysis of the political economy of resource-driven growth in the CCA region.

**Richard M. Auty** is Professor of Economic Geography at Lancaster University, UK.

**Indra de Soysa** is Associate Professor of Political Science at the Norwegian University of Science and Technology.

# Energy, Wealth and Governance in the Caucasus and Central Asia

Lessons not learned

**Edited by Richard M. Auty and Indra de Soysa**

Routledge
Taylor & Francis Group

LONDON AND NEW YORK

First published 2006
by Routledge
2 Park Square, Milton Park, Abingdon, Oxon OX14 4RN

Simultaneously published in the USA and Canada
by Routledge
270 Madison Ave, New York, NY 10016

*Routledge is an imprint of the Taylor & Francis Group*

Transferred to Digital Printing 2006

© 2006 Editorial matter and selection, Richard M. Auty and Indra de
Soysa individual chapters, the contributors

Typeset in Times by RefineCatch Ltd, Bungay, Suffolk

*British Library Cataloguing in Publication Data*
A catalogue record for this book is available from the British Library

*Library of Congress Cataloging in Publication Data*
Energy, wealth & governance in the Caucasus & Central Asia: lessons
not learned / edited by Richard Auty and Indra de Soysa.
p. cm — (Central Asia research forum)
Simultaneously published in the USA and Canada by Routledge.
Includes bibliographical references and index.
1. Caucasus — Economic conditions.   2. Asia, Central—Economic
conditions—1991–   3. Energy policy—Caucasus.   4. Energy policy—
Asia, Central.   5. Caucasus—Politics and government.   6. Asia,
Central — Politics and government — 1991–   I. Title: Energy, wealth
and governance in the Caucasus and Central Asia. II. Auty, R. M.
(Richard M.) III. De Soysa, Indra.
IV. Series: Central Asia research forum series.
HC415.16.E64 2005
333.79′09475′09049—dc22
2005001292

ISBN10: 0–415–37206–2 (hbk)
ISBN10: 0–415–40577–7 (pbk)

ISBN13: 978–0–415–37206–0 (hbk)
ISBN13: 978–0–415–40577–5 (pbk)

# Contents

# Figures

# Tables

# Acknowledgements

This project was conducted under the auspices of the National Bureau of Asian Research. We gratefully acknowledge the financial support of the MacArthur Foundation, which got the project started, and subsequent financial assistance from ZEF (University of Bonn), the US Army War College, the PNNL Center for Global Security and REECAS/Jackson School. Gael Tarleton demonstrated outstanding organisational flair in setting up stimulating conferences in Seattle and Washington DC at which the findings were presented and debated. Meanwhile, all of the contributors showed great discipline in adhering to the tight deadlines of our schedule and they accepted suggestions for revision with grace and good humour. But this book would not have been completed without Erica Johnson, who conceived of the project, marshalled the funding and displayed diligence, determination, encouragement and intellectual curiosity of the highest order.

# Contributors

**Dr Roy Allison** has been head of the Russia and Eurasia Program at the Royal Institute of International Affairs (Chatham House), London, since 1993. He is also currently a senior associate member of St Antony's College, Oxford University and a senior research fellow of the Centre for International Studies at the university, where he directs a project on Russian and Iranian policy in Central Asia and regionalism.

**Dr Richard M. Auty** is Professor of Economic Geography at Lancaster University. During 1998–99 he was senior research fellow and project director for the Helsinki-based UNU/WIDER project on resource abundance and economic development. His books include: *Resource Abundance and Economic Development*, OUP, 2001; *Sustainable Development in Mineral Economies*, with R.F. Mikesell, OUP, 1998 and *Resource-Based Industrialisation: Sowing the Oil in Eight Developing Countries*, OUP, 1990.

**Robinder S. Bhatty** is a private consultant working on military and political risk issues in the Caucasus, Central Asia and South Asia. Since 1996 he has been a Senior Associate with Cambridge Energy Research Associates, a leading consulting firm to the global energy industry, working on political, commercial and security risk assessments in Kazakhstan, Azerbaijan, Georgia and Turkey.

**Dr Willem Buiter** is Professor of European Political Economy at the LSE. He has held academic appointments at Princeton University, the University of Bristol, the London School of Economics, Yale University and the University of Cambridge in 1994–2000. He has been a consultant and advisor to the International Monetary Fund, World Bank, Inter-American Development Bank, the European Communities and a number of national governments and government agencies. He served for three years 1997–2000 on the Monetary Policy Committee of the Bank of England. He has published widely on open economy macroeconomics, monetary and exchange rate theory, fiscal policy, social security, economic development and transition economies.

**Dr Cevdet Denizer** is senior economist and program team leader for the Europe and Central Asia Region at the World Bank. Previously, he served as senior economist and regional strategist for Central Asia, the Middle East and North Africa at the International Finance Corporation. He has published extensively on the economic transition.

**Dr Indra de Soysa** is Associate Professor of Political Science, Trondheim University, Norway. He was previously at the Center for Development Research (ZEF), University of Bonn and the International Peace Research Institute in Oslo. His principal research interests are in democracy and development, democracy and governance, globalization and the causes of civil and political violence. He has published widely in the political science literature and his latest book is *Prepared for the 21st Century? Globalization, Localization and Development*, Routledge, 2003.

**Akram Esanov** is a Ph.D. candidate at Kansas State University, where he specializes in economic development, macroeconomics, political economy, monetary economics and econometrics. Most recently, Mr Esanov served as an economist at the European Bank for Reconstruction and Development, doing country risk analysis. He has held positions at the International Monetary Fund, the World Bank and the Regional Office of the UN in Uzbekistan.

**Dr Clemens Grafe** lectures in the Department of Economics at Birkbeck College, University of London. From 1999 to 2002, Dr Grafe was the principal economist for Russia and Central Asia at the European Bank for Reconstruction and Development, and from 1994 to 1996 served at the Russian European Centre for Economic Policy (RECEP). He has published numerous articles in the fields of international macroeconomics and monetary economics.

**Erica Johnson** is a Ph.D. candidate at the University of Washington where she specializes in the politics of the former Soviet Union. Before resuming her graduate studies she worked for a number of years as a project director for the National Bureau of Asian Research.

**Dr Mark N. Katz** is Professor of Government and Politics at George Mason University in Fairfax, Virginia. He is the author of several books, including *Russia and Arabia: Soviet Foreign Policy toward the Arabian Peninsula* (1986), *Revolutions and Revolutionary Waves* (1997), *Middle Eastern Sketches* (1997), and *Reflections on Revolutions* (1999). He is also the editor of a collection of readings entitled, *Revolution: International Dimensions* (2001).

**Dr Anil Markandya** is Lead Economist for East Europe and Central Asia at the World Bank, and Professor of Economics at Bath University. He is an environmental economist who has published widely on climate change, environmental valuation, green accounting, macroeconomics and trade.

His books include *Blueprint for a Green Economy*, *Green Accounting in Europe*, *Reconciling Trade and Development* and *Cleaning the Ganges*. He was a lead author for one of the chapters of the *Third Assessment Report on Climate Change*, published by Cambridge University Press in 2001.

**Dr Richard Pomfret** is Professor of Economics at the University of Adelaide. He has specialized for some years on Central Asia and most especially Uzbekistan. His publications include *The Economies of Central Asia*, Princeton University Press, 1995 and numerous journal articles, most recently in *Economic Development and Cultural Change* and *World Economy*.

**Dr Martin Raiser** is senior economist and resident representative in Uzbekistan for the World Bank. He was formerly at the European Bank for Reconstruction and Development in London. He has published widely on the economic transition, including fields as varied as social capital, structural change, privatization and natural resource use.

**Dr Charles E. Ziegler** is Professor and Chair of the Department of Political Science at the University of Louisville, where he specializes on foreign relations and policy, and domestic politics, of the former Soviet Union, North-east Asia, China, Japan, South Korea and the Russian Far East. His publications include: *Russia's Far East: A Region at Risk*, co-edited with Judith Thornton, University of Washington Press, 2002; 'Environment, Soviet Union' in *International Encyclopedia of the Social and Behavioral Sciences*, 2001; *The History of Russia*, Greenwood Press, 1999; and *Environmental Policy in the USSR*, University of Massachusetts Press, 1987.

# Part I

# Introduction

# 1 Transition to mid-income democracies or to failed states?

*Richard M. Auty*

## The context

The eight countries of the Caucasus and Central Asia (CCA), which became independent from the former Soviet Union (FSU) in 1991, are experiencing a difficult transition toward a market economy. We now know that initial conditions are an important cause of this. The legacy of a long exposure to central planning is one important reason for the difficult transition (de Melo *et al.* 2001), and remoteness from dynamic market economies is another (Kopstein and Reilly 2000). This book explores the CCA transition by tracing the impact of a third key initial condition, namely the natural resource endowment. This third factor has been relatively neglected by the transition literature probably because that literature initially focused on the higher-income Central and East European (CEE) countries, for which the primary sector (and therefore natural resources) is relatively unimportant. But for the lower-income transition countries in the CCA region the primary sector remains large relative to GDP. Recent research on the developing market economies indicates that differences in the natural resource endowment affect the nature of the political state (Ross 1999; Auty and Gelb 2001) and the development trajectory in important ways (Sachs and Warner 1995 and 1997; Wood and Berge 1997; Auty 2001).

Four of the CCA countries account for two-thirds of the region's population and generate unusually high levels of revenue from their natural resources (primarily energy, but not exclusively so), relative to GDP.[1] This natural advantage could help expedite the transition by raising the rate of investment and imports to accelerate the required restructuring of the economy, as well as by strengthening safety nets to ease the social cost of unemployment. Yet the CCA region has been a relatively slow reformer, its governments have become more authoritarian and despite recent growth spurts in seven of the eight CCA countries, further reform is required to sustain rapid GDP growth and nurture democracy. It is the thesis of this book that regional welfare will fall well short of its potential, possibly disastrously so, if the CCA elites do not change the way in which they deploy the natural resource revenues. The book draws upon the experience of the developing market economies to explain why.

The experience of the developing market economies and also the more successful CEE transition economies suggests that effective economic reform sustains growth in per capita income, which in turn nurtures political accountability and democracy. This virtuous development trajectory reflects the positive association between rising per capita income and the strengthening of three key sanctions against anti-social governance, namely increasing pressure for political accountability as sources of taxation diversify away from trade toward profit, income and sales taxes (Ross 2001); evolving social capital and civic voice (Woolcock *et al.* 2001); and growing demands by private firms for improved institutions such as secure property rights and the rule of law (Li *et al.* 2000). However, reform has decelerated in most CCA countries.

At independence, the CCA elites were unchallenged by new social forces and they have relied heavily on a subset of revenues, which we will term rent, to replace lost subventions from Moscow to consolidate their political power. Rent is defined here as revenues in excess of those required by an efficient enterprise to remain in business after covering all costs of production, including a risk-related return on capital. In theory, this economic rent can be extracted from a producer (say by a windfall tax) without impairing the incentive to invest and produce. Economic rent therefore represents a bonus for the economy, which in the case of natural resource rents can be viewed as a gift of Nature.[2] The natural resource rents in developing market economies typically range between 10 and 22 per cent of GDP (Auty and Gelb 2001: 131), with outliers at either end of the spectrum. The resource rent of the four resource-abundant CCA countries has been above this range, and substantially so in some cases, ranging up to 60 per cent of GDP (see Chapter 3).

Rent can accrue not only from the extraction and processing of natural resources, but also from managerial innovation, a technological lead and a government or private monopoly. In addition to natural resource rent, two other forms of rent have been important in the CCA region, namely geopolitical rent and contrived rent. Geopolitical rent comprises aid and other forms of external assistance, which Chapter 6 shows have been sizeable in the resource-poor CCA countries (10–20 per cent of GDP annually). Contrived rents are extracted by governments using their power to change relative prices within the domestic economy (Tollison 1982). Contrived rent can be viewed as revenue generated in excess of that required for effective developmental public spending.

Economic theory suggests that increased natural resource rents and the foreign exchange obtained from resource exports should raise investment and boost a country's capacity to import capital goods, so that if the rents are efficiently invested they will accelerate economic growth. Economic theory does not, however, offer a full explanation for what happens in practice because it has tended to neglect the political dimension of policy formation (Auty and Mikesell 1999: 13–31). The political elite in resource-rich developing countries often acts with a different rationale from the developmental political state that is assumed in economic theory. According to Lal (1995), the developmental political state has two basic characteristics: first, sufficient autonomy to pursue a coherent economic policy and, second, the aim of maximizing broad social welfare over time. Many developing countries, especially resource-abundant ones, engender predatory political states that lack one, or both, of these characteristics.

Unfortunately, the experience of the resource-rich developing market economies in recent decades cautions that a benevolent outcome is far from assured. As a group, the resource-rich countries have experienced significantly less robust economic growth than the resource-poor countries since the 1960s (Figure 1.1). The oil-exporting countries have performed especially poorly. Most became overly dependent on revenue windfalls during the 1974–78 and 1979–81 oil booms and were unable to sustain economic growth when oil prices subsequently fell (Gelb and Associates 1988). Even after oil prices collapsed in the mid-1980s, the energy-rich countries continued to generate the highest natural resource rent in relation to GDP out of six categories of country, classified by their natural resource endowment, but they experienced the slowest per capita GDP growth (Auty 2001).

Nor have high energy revenues been associated with favorable political developments (Eifert *et al.* 2003). Rather, the oil-exporting countries tend to repress democracy and nurture brittle political states, which are associated with relatively high rates of violent regime change (Ross 2001). Certainly, within the CCA region, authoritarian forms of government have consolidated their position as the regional norm, despite some initial experiments with more pluralistic systems. In recent years, for example, oil-rich Azerbaijan

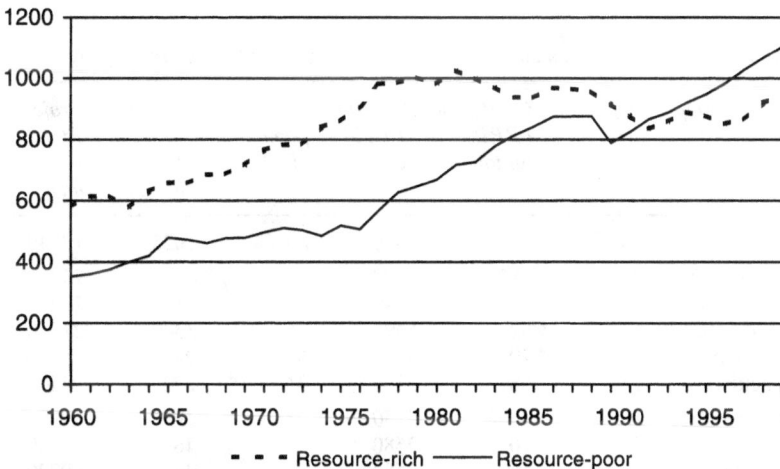

*Figure 1.1* Median GDP per capita (constant 1995 US$) of resource-rich and resource-poor developing countries.

*Source:* World Bank (1999).

and Kazakhstan have drifted towards the less accountable forms of government that were already favored by resource-rich Uzbekistan and Turkmenistan. The resource-poor CCA countries show a more varied pattern, but as a group they too have been characterized by relatively authoritarian regimes.

At first sight this gloomy prognosis seems to be contradicted by the fact that by 2003 the CCA countries formed one of the most dynamic global economic regions (Aslund 2003), in marked contrast to the sustained growth collapses that characterized their initial years of transition reform. Yet the economic dynamism that emerged in seven of the eight CCA countries (Uzbekistan's sluggish growth is the exception) during the late 1990s is fragile. It largely rests on high energy prices and associated foreign direct investment (FDI) in the three energy-exporting countries of Azerbaijan, Kazakhstan and Turkmenistan; and on worker remittances and sizeable foreign aid (geopolitical rent) in resource-poor Armenia, Georgia, Kyrgyzstan and Tajikistan. Closer inspection reveals that such rapid growth is likely to prove ephemeral in the absence of continuing economic reform to improve incentives for wealth creation. But economic reform weakens the rent-extracting system of the patronage networks that sustain the CCA elites, which therefore seek to retard reform.

Some idea of the potential loss of welfare to the region as a consequence of inadequate reform and a growth collapse can be gained from Table 1.1, which projects per capita income, assuming that high GDP growth rates diffuse across the entire region and are sustained. Such rapid growth would quadruple the real per capita income of the CCA region within two decades, lifting it to levels equivalent to those of Spain or Taiwan in the mid-1990s. In addition, the CCA region could become an important and stable source of

*Table 1.1* GDP projections 2000–2020, Caucasus and Central Asian Region

| Country group | Population 2000 | GDP 2000 (PPP$ billion) | PCI 2000 (PPP$/ hd) | Projected population 2020 | Projected GDP 2020 (PPP$ billion) | Projected PCI 2020 (PPP$/ hd) |
|---|---|---|---|---|---|---|
| CCA Region | 73 | 225 | 3080 | 85 | 1023 | 12040 |
| Resource-rich | *53* | *182* | *3430* | *62* | *830* | *13390* |
| Azerbaijan | 8 | 22 | 2740 | 10 | 110 | 10960 |
| Kazakhstan | 15 | 82 | 5490 | 15 | 334 | 21960 |
| Turkmenistan | 5 | 20 | 3800 | 6 | 94 | 15200 |
| Uzbekistan | 25 | 58 | 2360 | 31 | 292 | 9440 |
| Resource-poor | *20* | *43* | *2150* | *23* | *193* | *8390* |
| Armenia | 4 | 10 | 2580 | 4 | 46 | 10320 |
| Georgia | 5 | 13 | 2680 | 5 | 49 | 10720 |
| Kyrgyzstan | 5 | 13 | 2540 | 7 | 67 | 10160 |
| Tajikistan | 6 | 7 | 1090 | 7 | 31 | 4360 |

*Source:* World Bank 2002.

energy resources for the global economy in 2020. Were the regional states to overcome obstacles to integration, the CCA region could also function as a dynamic market with a combined purchasing power of $1 trillion, only slightly less than that of Brazil or the Russian Federation at the end of the twentieth century. Even though different starting conditions mean that the resource-poor countries would lag the energy-rich countries, and the real per capita income of Tajikistan might still be barely one-third the regional average, all countries would experience sizeable welfare gains from such an arrangement.

## Principal aims and basic approach of the research

Rent can be deployed by a developmental political state to promote wealth creation for the polity, but it can also be used by predatory political elites for purely personal or political ends. This book analyzes how the scale of the rent and also its extraction and redistribution have adversely affected both economic and political reform in the CCA countries, and then goes on to justify more viable patterns of rent deployment. A distinctive feature of this research is therefore the rectification of past neglect of the role of natural resources in shaping the transition in the low-income countries. The research focuses not only upon the political economy of the dominant resource-rich countries, however, but also on the synergy between those countries and the region's resource-poor countries.

The capture and deployment of rents plays a central role in the political economy of most developing countries. Each of the three basic forms of rent can comprise tens of per cent of GDP and because they are fungible (i.e. easily switched from one account to another), developing country governments can use them either to accelerate economic development or to enrich themselves and their political clients. The rents are also potentially volatile and therefore destabilizing. Competition for the rent nurtures rent-seeking behavior in the form of political lobbying (and bribery) that absorbs effort at the expense of directly productive activity like investment to raise productivity and create extra wealth (Krueger 1974). Rents therefore offer siren-like temptations to brittle and/or factional political states to use them to shore up their political position, often at the expense of sustained economic growth and political reform. Large-scale maladroit use of rent can severely distort an economy in a few years, or it can do so cumulatively over a decade or more. In either case, the economy is rendered vulnerable to a growth collapse from which recovery may take a generation or more because such a collapse depletes all forms of capital (produced, human, social and natural). Rent-seeking is a pronounced feature of the CCA region, and both the economic and political consequences of rent-seeking are invariably grim.

A second distinctive aspect of this research is the use of models to complement the richly textured narrative analyses that characterize much of the political science literature (Ebel and Menon 2000; Olcott 2002). The research distils the experience of the developing market economies into political economy models of resource-driven development. The models are adapted to take account of specific initial conditions in the CCA countries after the collapse of the USSR. The models generate predictions regarding the pace of economic and political reform. Explanations for departures from these predictions are sought in country-specific factors such as leadership qualities or chance events. In other words, the models first filter out the plethora of historical detail in order to identify the basic forces at work in all the countries, but then draw upon historical descriptive analyses to add the nuances that furnish the fullest explanation.

In this context, the research presented in this book has four basic aims, which are to:

1   Establish how the differing natural resource endowments of the CCA countries have affected progress with economic reform to stabilize the macro-economy and restructure the economy in order to maximize sustainable economic growth;
2   Determine how the extraction and deployment of the rent has shaped the incentives of the region's political elite to pursue economic and political reform;
3   Analyze how the region's political economy has hampered co-operation in mutually beneficial policies regarding trade, environmental management and military security;
4   Assess the potential for leading external political powers to wield economic and political influence to promote the long-term welfare of the CCA region.

## The structure of the book

The book is structured in five main Parts:

  I. The aims of the study and the resource-driven models,
 II. Progress with economic reform within each of the eight CCA countries,
III. Political constraints on economic and constitutional reform,
 IV. Prospects for co-operation in trade, environmental management and security and
  V. Political levers available to external countries with which to influence events within the CCA region, and policy recommendations.

The aims and content of each Part are described in more detail below.

### The analytical framework

Chapter 2 introduces two resource-driven political economy models with which to structure the analysis, namely the competitive industrialization economic model with endogenous democratization (the CIEN model) that tends to be associated with resource-poor countries, and the staple trap economic model with exogenous democratization (the STEX model), which is associated with resource-abundance. The two models draw on the experience of the developing market economies, which is adapted to the transition economies by taking account of the impact of initial conditions on their political economy. Chapter 2 establishes that initial conditions in the CCA countries were among the least propitious for economic and political reform.

The basic insight that drives the two models emanates from differences in the motivation to provide the public goods and efficiency incentives that are required to sustain economic growth. In the absence of sizeable resource rents, the political states in resource-poor countries have a strong incentive to create wealth by providing public goods and incentives for efficient investment. If government income is a percentage of total output, then the government must increase output in order to boost its income. Low resource rents therefore place a premium upon the efficient use of scarce resources to promote sustainable economic growth. Moreover, in this way low rents align the interests of the government with those of the population at large to render the political state both benevolent and developmental.

In contrast, the political state in the resource-rich country has an alternative source of income (from natural resource rents), which the elites can extract and deploy to benefit themselves and key political supporters. Rent extraction has the added political attraction of conferring immediate political benefits whereas the gains from wealth creation accrue through the longer term. Natural resource abundance is therefore more likely to nurture non-developmental political states, which have less incentive than their counterparts in the resource-poor countries to provide public goods and maintain incentives for efficient investment. The models are not deterministic, however, and a handful of countries including Botswana, Chile, Indonesia and Malaysia show that resource-rich countries can sustain long periods of rapid economic growth.

Differences in the natural resource endowment affect the development trajectory as well as the motives of the political state. Resource-poor economies rely relatively briefly on primary product exports because they embark on competitive industrialization early (i.e. at a low per capita income) in order to generate the foreign exchange with which to import the goods that they cannot produce themselves. The resulting CIEN development trajectory accumulates produced, human and social capital faster than with the STEX trajectory, as explained in detail in Chapter 2. Per capita income therefore rises rapidly and incrementally strengthens sanctions against anti-social governance. Basically, rapid per capita GDP growth expands a capitalist class that challenges authoritarian governance (O'Loughlin *et al.* 1998). The result is that rising per capita income brings an incremental transition from autocratic regimes via an oligarchy, which dissolves into a democracy that is consensual, as autonomous urban interest groups proliferate. The CIEN model therefore suggests that the resource-poor CCA countries face superior prospects to those of the resource-rich countries for political development as well as for economic development.

The resource-rich countries tend to engender non-developmental political states that generate a development trajectory that leads to a staple trap, characterized by increasing dependence on a primary sector with declining competitiveness. A longer reliance on primary product exports postpones competitive industrialization and heightens income inequality so that social tension intensifies. This encourages governments to deploy rent to expand employment in protected industry (that cannot compete) as well as the bureaucracy, creating a burgeoning parasitic sector whose demand for subsidies outstrips the rent. The resulting staple trap development trajectory exhibits a sustained decline in investment efficiency so that economic growth slows and without economic reform growth collapses (Auty 2001). The process of a growth collapse also weakens sanctions against anti-social governance. In fact, the collapse of the USSR exhibits features of the STEX model, yet the CCA countries appear to have learned little from that experience.

However, a growth collapse discredits the regime in power and creates scope for democratization under favorable external conditions (such as democratic neighbors or western assistance with recovery). This 'exogenous' democratization therefore tends to occur abruptly and it also tends to be more vulnerable to reversal than the endogenous democratization associated with low resource rents and the CIEN model. The STEX model clearly has resonance for the four resource-abundant CCA countries.

### Regional differences in economic reform and economic growth

Part II examines how differences in the natural resource endowment within the CCA region have affected the pace of economic reform and therefore progress in macroeconomic stabilization and economic restructuring. Chapter 3 provides an overview of the performance of resource-rich and resource-poor countries during the first decade of transition. It estimates the natural resource rents and shows that they have been unusually large not only in oil-rich Azerbaijan and Kazakhstan, but also in Turkmenistan and Uzbekistan. Chapter 3 also shows how differences in the reliance of the elites on external capital (for investment in order to access the rents) in the resource-rich countries or aid in the case of resource-poor countries have affected the initial pace of economic reform and the strength of the post-transition economic rebound.

Chapters 4 and 5 examine the transition prospects of the resource-rich countries in more detail. Chapter 4 focuses upon the oil-rich states of Azerbaijan and Kazakhstan, noting significant differences in the relative size and duration of the *potential* oil rent streams. Azerbaijan faces the more problematic rent stream because it is projected to be larger relative to non-oil GDP than that of Kazakhstan, and also of considerably shorter duration, peaking during 2009–13 compared to the 2020s for Kazakhstan. The chapter then constructs optimistic forecasts for rent deployment and sets out the principal conditions required to achieve them. It finds that both countries lack basic institutional requirements for effective oil rent deployment. Consequently, pessimistic scenarios are developed, which are all too easy to construct from the experience of the developing market oil-exporting economies.

Chapter 5 explains why resource-rich Uzbekistan and Turkmenistan depended less on external capital to expand their resource rents than the two oil-exporting countries. It notes the implications of a reduced dependence on assistance from the international financial institutions (IFIs) and also describes how each country generates rent from the non-energy sector (principally irrigated agriculture). These countries are the slowest reformers in the region. The Turkmen regime assumes that expanding natural gas exports removes pressure for economic reform. Uzbekistan claims to be pursuing gradual reform, but both its strategy and the results differ significantly from those of successful gradual reformers in East Asia, like China and Vietnam.

Finally in Part II, Chapter 6 analyzes the four resource-poor countries. It notes that any pro-reform bias arising from the limited nature of resource rents and the associated high dependence on IFI assistance has been offset by civil strife that retarded reform in three countries (Armenia, Georgia and Tajikistan) and, in particular by the extremely steep compression of GDP following the collapse of the USSR. The four resource-poor countries have relied heavily on international aid, which has sharply increased their rates of debt to GDP, especially in Tajikistan and Kyrgyzstan, which are experiencing difficulty with debt service. Yet despite their dependence on IFI assistance both economic and political reform has slowed in the resource-poor countries, which has retarded the required competitive restructuring of their economies.

### The political economy of reluctant reform

Part III explains the incomplete nature of economic and political reform by examining the socio-political constraints on the CCA elites. A body of research is beginning to address the role of social capital in economic development. Basically, social capital is reflected in trust within both the public and private sectors, and the higher it is in an economy, the lower are transaction costs and the fewer the impediments to investment in wealth creation. Little work has been done on the social capital of the CCA states. Chapter 7 starts to address this omission by establishing that the relationship between per capita income and social capital formation is positive, so that rising per capita incomes are associated with improving social capital that finds expression in the strengthening of civic associations (which give vent to the concerns of the wider populace) and the decline in corruption.

A corollary is that a decline in per capita income, such as followed the demise of the Soviet Union, is likely to be associated with a decline in social capital and increased obstacles to effective investment in wealth creation (Treisman 2002). Chapter 7 identifies self-locking vicious circles in the CCA countries as falling public revenues squeeze the real incomes of public sector employees and encourage civil servants to resort to petty corruption in order to augment their incomes. Chapter 7 shows how the self-locking cycle of corruption deters investment and encourages businesses to retreat into the gray economy, while more extreme reactions include recourse to violent crime linked to narcotics and terrorism. The net effect is to discourage investment in economic restructuring and undermine security.

Chapter 8 analyses the political states in the CCA region in order to understand why the elites condone these obstacles to economic restructuring. It classifies the eight regimes in the region, which range from the autocracies of Turkmenistan and Uzbekistan, through the concentrated oligarchies of Azerbaijan and Kazakhstan to the fractured oligarchies that rule Tajikistan and Kyrgyzstan and the diffusing oligarchies of Armenia and Georgia. The chapter argues that in all four regime types the patronage networks benefited initially from economic reform because partial privatization increased the access of the elite to rents. However, ongoing reform increases competition, which reduces rents and jeopardizes these patronage networks, so the elite impedes reform. Moreover, rent-seeking also occurs at the regional and local levels as well as the national level and in contrast to Suharto's Indonesia, for example, it is weakly controlled, so even if a central government embraced accelerated reform it would encounter difficulty in implementing it. Rent-seeking therefore remains a pronounced feature of the CCA region.

Chapter 8 goes on to analyze patterns of rent-seeking in each of the four sets of political states. It concludes that by hampering reform, patronage jeopardizes long-term growth and with it the long-term survival of the regimes in most CCA countries. Consequently, in order to avoid the political risks of a growth collapse elites with dynastic pretensions may find it more prudent to take advantage of the current economic booms to build their legitimacy by reforming to increase wealth creation. Uzbekistan, which has been growing slowly and whose rent extraction is liquidating the physical assets that deliver the rents, has the most pressing incentive to reform, not least because of the implications for security and political power of a growth performance that lags far behind that of Kazakhstan, its principal regional rival. More optimistically, the two resource-poor Caucasian countries are near the tipping point that could reinvigorate economic reform and transform their diffusing oligarchies into democracies.

### *Prospects for beneficial co-operation between resource-rich and resource-poor*

Part IV examines how the political economy described in Parts II and III affects the potential synergies among the resource-rich and resource-poor CCA countries regarding trade, the environment and security. It also explores the prospects for improvement through regional co-operation. Chapter 9 examines three forms of closer economic integration:

- increased trade among the eight countries of the Caspian Basin themselves,
- expanded trade with their nearest neighbors (including China, Iran, Russia and Turkey) and,
- increased commerce with the global economy.

As remote and mostly landlocked states the Caspian Basin countries are especially disadvantaged if their immediate and/or near neighbors are hostile or have moribund economies. For example, dynamic neighboring markets create demand for energy exports that incur far lower transport costs (and higher profit margins) than distant markets outside the region. It might be hypothesized that intra-regional trade could prove attractive, given the potentially unfavorable global trading conditions for most regional products other than energy. For instance, expanding oil exports strengthen the real exchange rate in the energy-rich countries and thereby open up opportunities for the resource-poor countries to export bulky manufactured goods and perishable agricultural products to their neighbors.

However, recent trends have seen the repression of trade between neighboring countries, which is particularly detrimental to the smaller economies. This is because economic autarky becomes less viable the smaller the size of the economy, so that small economies have most to gain from the specialization in their comparative advantage that trade allows. However, while trade restrictions do negatively impact growth prospects, the similarity of the principal exports of countries in the CCA region combines with their remoteness from the largest global markets to render trade with larger near neighbors such as China, Russia, Iran and Turkey potentially more stimulating for regional growth. But capturing these benefits also depends on regional co-operation to construct low-cost transport links to these markets.

Chapter 10 establishes the slow progress in resolving the very severe environmental problems that are an important legacy of the Soviet era. It first focuses on the Caspian Sea as an example of a common resource that continues to be blighted in the absence of effective regional agreements concerning not only the control of pollution and protection of species, but also the allocation of mineral resources among the littoral states. The disputed mineral allocation has already provoked one military confrontation, but not yet an outbreak of armed hostilities. The final section of Chapter 10 addresses the Aral Sea Basin and shows how current policies extract rents at the expense of exacerbating environmental damage and liquidating the irrigation network, on which the Uzbek regime in particular depends for its political survival.

Chapter 11 addresses regional security threats. It first evaluates in broad terms the perceived characteristics and likelihood of military threats and conflict in the CCA region. The core threat perceptions of local states and elites are identified and compared with what appear to be the most likely actual risks of traditional and non-traditional threats and conflicts. The chapter concludes by identifying the serious constraints and obstacles that have limited attempts at multilateralism and co-operative security in the region.

### Scope for applying external leverage on CCA governments

Part V analyzes geopolitical issues. Chapter 12 examines the prospective impacts of Russian–Iranian relations and interventions on developments in the greater CCA region. Specifically, it first compares how Russia and Iran currently measure (or view) their respective economic, political and security priorities in the CCA region. It then goes on to discuss the role that Iran plays in Caspian energy development and to explore how an Iranian–American rapprochement and also rapid democratization in Russia might affect the regional influence of both Iran and Russia.

China is a quiet but major player in the region, especially in Kazakhstan's energy sector. As China deals with growing demand for energy and increased reliance on imports to satisfy consumption, the resources of the Caspian (and China's own western regions) are of growing importance. China's contract to develop two large oil fields in Kazakhstan, which was won by outbidding US and Russian companies, is an indication of its long-term goals and also of the geopolitical significance that China assigns to gaining access and influence in the CCA region. In this context, Chapter 13 examines the relationship between China and Russia and Central Asian oil and gas. It first reviews Russia's energy resources, and then assesses China's energy needs and goes on to discuss East Asian participation in Russian and Central Asian projects.

Chapter 14 considers the scope for western powers to exert leverage within the CCA region, focusing mainly on the IFIs. Western engagement increased after the United States gained a military presence in Central Asia in connection with the war on terrorism, and both US and EU energy firms are developing the region's oil and gas infrastructure. The rebuilding of Afghanistan also has important implications for CCA regional development. Western involvement in the region aims to help the newly independent CCA countries to assert independence from Russia and discourage greater reliance on Iran, while also promoting democracy and market economies.

Western leverage is often undermined, however, because hard trade-offs are frequently entailed between rewarding security co-operation and criticizing human rights, while reform is invariably thwarted by the patronage systems, which sustain the national and local elites. Nevertheless, Chapter 14 uses the rent-driven political economy models to demonstrate the incompatibility of the patronage system with the long-term survival of the elites as well as with raising broad-based social welfare. It then sets out a four-pronged strategy to curb those aspects of the patronage system that repress wealth creation and nurture those that advance it. Finally, Chapter 15 summarizes the thesis and its policy implications. The rent-driven political economy models are at the heart of both the thesis of the book and also its policy recommendations, so we now proceed to explain them in more depth in Chapter 2.

## Notes

1 These countries are Azerbaijan, Kazakhstan, Turkmenistan and Uzbekistan. The resource-poor countries of the region are Armenia, Georgia, Kyrgyzstan and Tajikistan.
2 Used in this sense the entire rent is a windfall, but the term 'windfall rent' is sometimes applied more specifically to the extra revenues derived from a sudden but temporary boost to the price of a commodity, as during the 1974–78 and 1979–81 oil price booms (see Gelb *et al.* 1988).

## References

Aslund, A. (2003) Sizing up the Central Asian economies, *Journal of International Affairs* 56(2), 75–87.

Auty, R.M. (2001) *Resource Abundance and Economic Development*, Oxford: Oxford University Press.

Auty, R.M. and Gelb, A.H. (2001) Political economy of resource-abundant states, in: Auty, R.M. (ed.) *Resource Abundance and Economic Development*, Oxford: Oxford University Press, 126–144.

Auty, R.M. and Mikesell, R.F. (1999) *Sustainable Development in Mineral Economies*, Oxford: Clarendon Press

De Melo, M., Denizer, C., Gelb, A. and Tenev, S. (2001) Circumstance and choice: The role of initial conditions and policies in transition economies, *World Bank Economic Review*, 15(1) 1–31.

Ebel, R. and Menon, R. (2000) *Energy and Conflict in Central Asia and the Caucasus*, Lanham MD: Rowman and Littlefield.

Eifert, B., Gelb, A.H. and Tallroth, N.B. (2003) The political economy of fiscal policy and economic management in oil-exporting countries, in: Davis, J.M., Ossowski, R. and Fedelino, A. (eds.) *Fiscal Policy Formulation and Implementation in Oil-Producing Countries*, Washington DC: IMF, 82–122.

Gelb, A.H. (1988) *Oil Windfalls: Blessing or Curse?* New York: Oxford University Press.

Kopstein, J.S and Reilly, D.A. (2000) Geographic diffusion and the transformation of the postcommunist world, *World Politics* 53, 1–37.

Krueger, A.O. (1974) The political economy of the rent-seeking society, *American Economic Review* 64(3).

Lal, D. (1995) Why growth rates differ. The political economy of social capability in 21 developing countries, in: Koo, B.H. and Perkins, D.H. (eds.) *Social Capability and Long-run Economic Growth*, Basingstoke: Macmillan, 310–327.

Li, S., Li, S. and Zhang, W. (2000) The road to capitalism: Competition and institutional change in China, *Journal of Comparative Economics* 28, 269–292.

Olcott, M.B. (2002) *Kazakhstan: Unfulfilled Promise*, Washington DC: Carnegie Endowment for International Peace.

O'Loughlin, J., Ward, M.D., Lofdahl, C.L., Cohen, J.S., Brown, D.S., Reilly, D.,

Gleditsch, K.S. and Shin, M. (1998) The diffusion of democracy 1946–94, *Annals Association of American Geographers* 88(4), 545–574.

Ross, M.L. (1999) The political economy of the resource curse, *World Politics* 51, 297–322.

Ross, M. (2001) Does oil hinder democracy? *World Politics* 53(3), 325–361.

Sachs, J.D. and Warner, A.M. (1995) Economic reform and the process of global integration, *Brookings Papers on Economic Activity* 1, 1–118.

Sachs, J.D. and Warner, A.M. (1997) Natural resource abundance and economic growth, mimeo, Cambridge MA: HIID.

Tollison, R.D. (1982) Rent-seeking: A survey, *Kyklos* 35(4), 575–602.

Treisman, D. (2002) The causes of corruption: A cross-national study, *Journal of Public Economics* 76(3), 399–458.

Wood, A. and Berge, K. (1997) Exporting manufactures: Human resources, natural resources, and trade policy, *Journal of Development Studies* 34, 35–59.

Woolcock, M., Pritchett, L. and Isham, J. (2001) The social foundations of poor economic growth in resource-rich countries, in: Auty, R.M. (ed.) *Resource Abundance and Economic Development*, Oxford: Oxford University Press, 76–91.

World Bank (2002) *World Development Indicators 2002*, Washington DC: World Bank.

# 2 Resource-driven models of the development of the political economy[1]

*Richard M. Auty*

## Introduction

This chapter describes and explains the CIEN and STEX resource-driven political economy models, which are constructed from the recent experience of the developing market economies. The models are then adapted to analyze the constraints upon economic reform in the centrally planned countries in transition to a market economy, with particular reference to the Caucasus and Central Asian (CCA) countries.

It may be recalled from Chapter 1 that the resource-rich developing market economies have under-performed compared with the resource-poor economies since the 1960s. Table 2.1 shows that the rate of per capita GDP growth in all four resource-rich categories of developing market economy[2] collapsed during the years of heightened trade shocks in 1973–85, causing the median PCGDP of the resource-rich countries to fall below that of the resource-poor countries. Despite this empirical evidence, economic theory provides no convincing explanation as to why resource-abundance should be inherently disadvantageous. In fact, during the first golden age of economic growth from 1870 to 1913, resource-abundant countries experienced rapid growth, and in many cases out-performed the resource-poor countries of that period (Lewis 1978; Maddison 1995). Moreover, the fact that the median per capita income of the resource-rich countries was around 50 per cent higher than that of the resource-poor countries during the 1960s (Figure 1.1) suggests that resource-abundance was not detrimental before that period.

Nevertheless, numerous recent studies confirm that since the 1960s, resource-abundant developing countries have experienced much slower growth in PCGDP than resource-poor countries (Sachs and Warner 1995, Lal and Myint 1996, Ross 1999, Auty 2001a). This conclusion is robust in light of both sensitivity tests (Sachs and Warner 1997a) and differences in how the natural resource endowment is classified (Wood and Berge 1997).

The recent experience of the developing market economies therefore suggests that the current expansion of oil rents in the CCA countries has the potential to be a curse if it is mismanaged. For example, the oil booms of 1973–78 and 1979–81 each transferred around 2 per cent of gross world

Table 2.1 Investment, GDP growth and investment efficiency, six natural resource endowment categories 1960–1997

| Resource endowment category | Investment (% GDP) (1) | GDP growth (%/Year) (2) | ICOR (3) | PC GDP growth (%/Year) (4) | Population growth (%/Year) (5) | Number of countries (6) |
|---|---|---|---|---|---|---|
| Small non-mineral resource-rich[1] | | | | | | |
| 1960–73 | 14.8 | 4.2 | 3.5 | 1.6 | 2.6 | 24[a)] |
| 1973–85 | 20.5 | 3.4 | 6.9 | 0.7 | 2.7 | 29[b)] |
| 1985–97 | 21.9 | 3.5 | 6.0 | 0.9 | 2.6 | 27[c)] |
| Small oil-exporting resource-rich | | | | | | |
| 1960–73 | 24.5 | 6.6 | 3.7 | 4.0 | 2.6 | 8[d)] |
| 1973–85 | 31.0 | 6.5 | 5.7 | 2.3 | 4.2 | 8[d)] |
| 1985–97 | 23.9 | 1.9 | 12.4 | -0.7 | 2.6 | 8[d)] |
| Small ore-exporting resource-rich | | | | | | |
| 1960–73 | 17.5 | 4.9 | 5.7 | 2.2 | 2.7 | 10[e)] |
| 1973–85 | 21.8 | 3.0 | 7.3 | 0.1 | 2.9 | 10[e)] |
| 1985–97 | 17.1 | 2.3 | 7.5 | -0.4 | 2.6 | 10[e)] |
| Large resource-rich[2] | | | | | | |
| 1960–73 | 20.3 | 5.4 | 4.0 | 2.7 | 2.7 | 8[f)] |
| 1973–85 | 21.8 | 3.1 | 7.1 | 0.7 | 2.4 | 10 |
| 1985–97 | 20.1 | 4.0 | 5.0 | 1.9 | 2.1 | 10 |
| Small resource-poor | | | | | | |
| 1960–73 | 18.8 | 6.1 | 3.2 | 3.5 | 2.6 | 8[g)] |
| 1973–85 | 24.8 | 4.0 | 6.2 | 1.8 | 2.2 | 8[h)] |
| 1985–97 | 23.0 | 4.4 | 5.2 | 2.4 | 2.0 | 8[h)] |
| Large resource-poor | | | | | | |
| 1960–73 | 17.7 | 5.0 | 4.2 | 2.4 | 2.6 | 7 |
| 1973–85 | 25.5 | 5.8 | 4.4 | 3.7 | 2.1 | 7 |
| 1985–97 | 26.3 | 6.0 | 4.4 | 4.7 | 1.3 | 7 |

Source: Derived from World Bank 1999.

Notes
1. Resource-rich = 1970 cropland/head > 0.3 hectares.
2. Large = 1970 GDP > $7 billion.

product from the oil-importing market economies to the oil-exporting econ-omies. This additional rent and foreign exchange should have accelerated economic growth in the oil-exporting countries by permitting higher levels of investment and greater capacity to import capital goods. In fact, although the oil-exporting economies did boom through the late 1970s the majority of them subsequently experienced a severe and protracted growth collapse through the mid–1980s from which most, like Nigeria, Saudi Arabia and Venezuela, have yet to recover. Table 2.2 shows that during 1985–97 the oil-exporting countries experienced negative growth in PCGDP, and the lowest rate among six categories of natural resource endowment. Yet the oil-exporters continued to generate the highest natural resource rents relative to GDP.

However, the historical experience of the market economies cautions that the so-called resource curse is not a deterministic law. Moreover, the resource curse has recently attracted dissenting voices. For example, Lederman and Maloney (2003) challenge Sachs and Warner (1995 and 1997a) by finding a mild positive link with primary product exports and economic growth. How-ever, the Sachs and Warner data cover 1970–90 when most resource-rich developing countries experienced a growth collapse, whereas Lederman and Maloney cover the years 1980–2000 by which time many countries were pur-suing economic reforms under IFI guidance aimed at correcting previous economic mismanagement. Moreover, Lederman and Maloney separate out the effect of over-specialization in export commodities from the overall export dependence effect. They find export over-specialization does nega-tively impact economic performance. Over-specialization is a feature of the

*Table 2.2* Share of rents in GDP 1994 and GDP growth 1985–1997, by natural resource endowment

| Resource endowment | PCGDP growth 1985–97 (%) | Total rent (% GDP) | Pasture and cropland rent (% GDP) | Mineral rent (% GDP) |
|---|---|---|---|---|
| Resource-poor[1,2] | | | | |
| Large | 4.7 | 10.56 | 7.34 | 3.22 |
| Small | 2.4 | 9.86 | 5.41 | 4.45 |
| Resource-rich | | | | |
| Large | 1.9 | 12.65 | 5.83 | 6.86 |
| Small, non-mineral | 0.9 | 15.42 | 12.89 | 2.53 |
| Small, hard mineral | −0.4 | 17.51 | 9.62 | 7.89 |
| Small, oil exporter | −0.7 | 21.22 | 2.18 | 19.04 |
| All countries | | 15.03 | 8.78 | 6.25 |

*Source:* Derived from World Bank 1999.

*Notes*
1. Resource-poor = 1970 cropland/head < 0.3 hectares.
2. Large = 1970 GDP > $7 billion.

STEX model that, as shown in this chapter, explains growth collapses in resource-abundant countries.

A second challenge to the resource curse suggests that institutions are more important than geography (Acemoglu *et al.* 2002). Whereas Sachs and Warner (1997b), for example, estimate that environmental factors (that include primary product export dependence, tropical diseases, remoteness and being land-locked) account for most of the under-performance in PCGDP growth of sub-Saharan Africa compared with East Asia, institutionalists reject this analysis. The institutionalists point instead to colonial legacies and whether they spawned extractive institutions, such as plantations and mines, or institutions that created local wealth, like yeoman farming systems (Acemoglu *et al.* 2002). However, Glaeser *et al.* (2004) convincingly show that the statistical analysis of Acemoglu *et al.* (2002) is flawed and that their thesis under-estimates the importance of human capital and policy choice, both of which variables are incorporated into the CIEN and STEX models outlined below.

Within this broader context, the present chapter explains the CIEN and STEX political economy models and adapts them to the CCA countries. The STEX model offers a plausible explanation for why natural resource abundance can adversely affect the political economy (Auty 2004). It shows that in recent decades high natural resource rent has tended to have three adverse effects on the developing market economies. First, it has fostered predatory political states by encouraging political and economic agents to divert effort into rent extraction at the expense of wealth creation so that the efficiency of investment has declined. Second, a longer dependence on primary products has retarded industrialization and slowed labor absorption, heightening income inequality. Governments respond by deploying rent to subsidize employment, typically by over-expanding the bureaucracy and protecting infant industry, which proves counter-productive, however, because it reverses competitive diversification of the economy and increases the vulnerability of the economy to a growth collapse (Figure 2.1). Third, the political state has tended to regress during the events preceding a growth collapse because sanctions against anti-social governance (political accountability, social capital and the rule of law) are progressively weakened.

The corollary is that low rent confers three beneficial effects upon the evolution of the political economy. First, low rent tends to foster developmental political states because it strengthens government incentives to promote wealth creation in the absence of opportunities for rent extraction and distribution. Second, low rent shortens the period of dependence on the primary sector so that industrialization is early (i.e. it occurs at a relatively low per capita income). In consequence, manufacturing is initially labor-intensive (Figure 2.2). It is also competitive because it is the principal source of the foreign exchange needed to purchase the capital goods required to build the infrastructure of a modern economy. The resulting low-rent development trajectory triggers virtuous economic and social circles that sustain

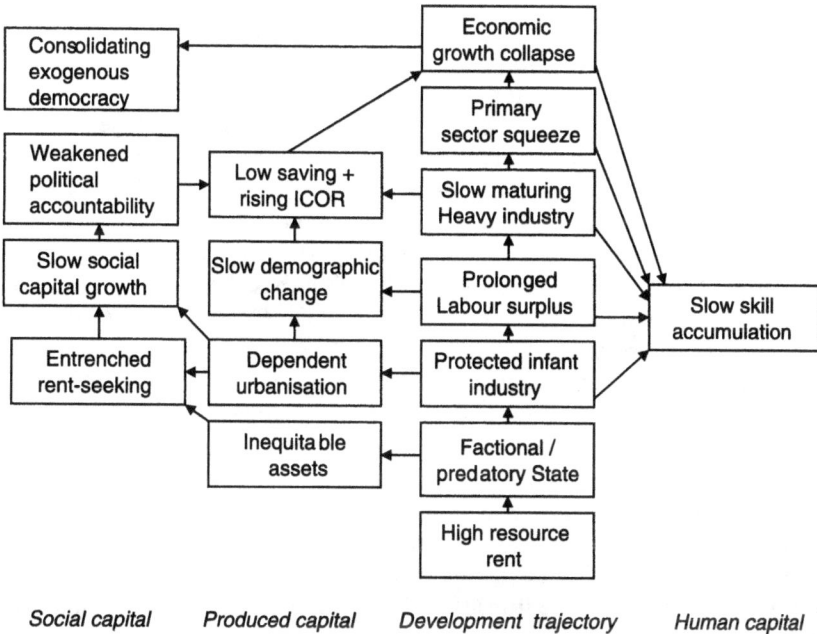

| Social capital | Produced capital | Development trajectory | Human capital |

*Figure 2.1* Staple trap and exogenous democratization model (STEX).

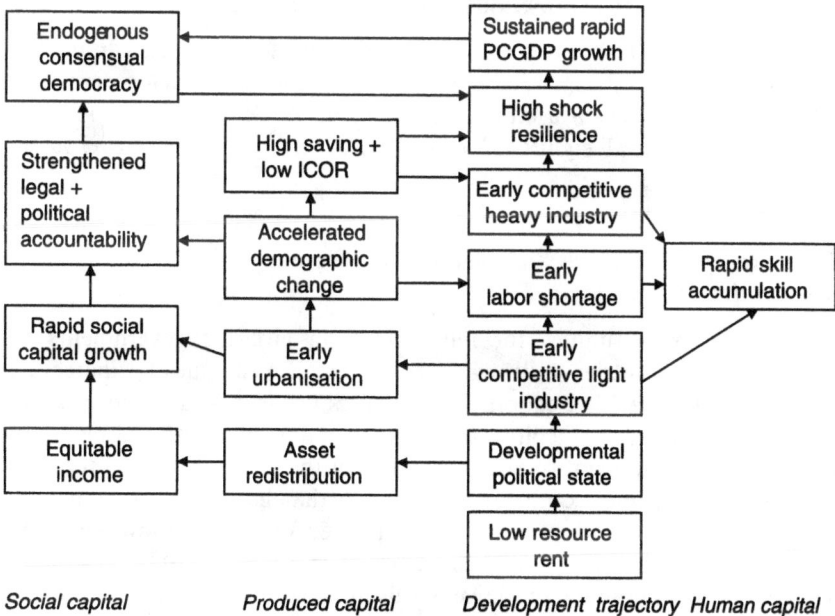

| Social capital | Produced capital | Development trajectory | Human capital |

*Figure 2.2* Competitive industrialization and endogenous democratization model (CIEN).

rapid PCGDP growth. Finally, rapid PCGDP growth strengthens all three sanctions against anti-social governance to promote endogenous democratization, which tends to be incremental. The CIEN model explains very well the development of a low-rent political economy.

The chapter is structured as follows. The next section, pages 22–27, explains the two models in more depth. The models are presented as stylized facts models rather than mathematical ones in order both to achieve greater flexibility than more reductionist mathematical models and to enhance their accessibility. It is important to stress once again, however, that the models are not deterministic: they reflect strong probabilities based on the experience of the developing market economies since the 1960s. Consequently, reforming countries like those of the CCA region can learn from previous experience and improve their management of natural resource rents. The following Section, on pages 27–29, deploys the STEX model to explain the particularly disappointing performance of the oil-exporting economies. The final section adapts the models to the CCA countries in transition to explain the collapse of the resource-rich USSR and how the natural resource endowment and three other initial conditions (specifically, the length of exposure to central planning, remoteness from dynamic market economies and the scale of GDP compression caused by the transition shock) have constrained economic and political reform.

## Modeling rent-driven transitions to high-income democracy

The STEX and CIEN resource-driven political economy models capture the essential features of, respectively, high-rent and low-rent development. The CIEN model provides a useful counter-factual to the STEX case. It holds positive lessons for all eight CCA countries, but especially the four resource-poor ones.

### Low rent: competitive industrialization and endogenous democratization model

Constrained opportunities for rent extraction give the governments of resource-poor countries a strong incentive to raise revenues by increasing output through wealth creation. This requires prudent taxation in order to provide public goods to facilitate trade and to maintain incentives for efficient investment. This imperative aligns the aims of the government and the governed in resource-poor countries more broadly than has usually been the case in resource-abundant countries of late. Expressed another way, low rents tend to nurture a developmental political state, which is benevolent because, after Lal (1995), it has both the objective of raising broad-based social welfare and also the autonomy to pursue a coherent economic policy.

A developmental political state seeking to raise output over the long term will adhere to the comparative advantage of the economy. The limited scope for commodity exports in low-rent countries means that advantage lies in competitive industrialization that commences at a relatively low per capita income (Figure 2.2). Cheap labor implies that this stage is also labor-intensive and it rapidly absorbs surplus rural labor, putting upward pressure on real wages. Rising wage costs must be offset by higher productivity, which propels diversification into capital-intensive and skill-intensive products, which must also be competitive in the absence of subsidies from natural resource rent. A second consequence of early industrialization is early urbanization, which accelerates passage through the demographic cycle so that population growth slows, the dependent/worker ratio falls and savings rise, all at a relatively low PCGDP level (Bloom and Williamson 1998). When combined with the incentive to invest efficiently that a competitive economy confers, this sustains rapid PCGDP growth.

The CIEN economic trajectory also creates a virtuous social circle because the elimination of surplus rural labor puts a floor under the wages of poor workers while the rapid accumulation of human capital during industrial diversification caps the skill premium (Londono 1996; Birdsall *et al.* 2001), so that income distribution tends to be more egalitarian and lowers social tension. Moreover sustained rapid rises in PCGDP strengthen three sanctions against anti-social governance. First, the tax base shifts early from relying on rent and commodities to dependence on income, sales and profits taxes, which steadily intensifies demand for political accountability in public expenditure (Ross 2001). There is some evidence, however, that this effect may be lagged because citizens have been prepared to trade off economic success for political accountability (Auty 2004). Second, early competitive urbanization replaces bonding social capital that can stifle initiative (Stiglitz 1995) with linking social capital that strengthens civic associations and curbs corruption (Woolcock *et al.* 2001; Treisman 2002). Third, the proliferation of competitive entrepreneurs brings demands to strengthen property rights and the rule of law in order to protect their gains.

The net effect of the CIEN low-rent political economy trajectory is to diffuse political power to a widening set of social groups. The process can be modeled by a three-stage shift (Table 2.3, rows 1–3). The initial state is assumed to be an autocracy, which is given an incentive to be benevolent by low rent, as explained above. The second stage is an oligarchy whose power diffuses because rapid industrialization and urbanization diversify the elite, which co-opts sections of the expanding middle class to balance rivals and reduce the risk of policy capture by a single group. Britain in the nineteenth century provides a clear example (Lizzeri and Persico 2003). A diffusing oligarchy therefore dissolves into the final political stage, which is a democracy that is likely to be consensual rather than polarized because sustained PCGDP growth builds a consensus for pro-growth economic policies. In such an environment, an election defeat does not bring dramatic change in policy and investor confidence is retained. In this way, sustained PCGDP growth *incrementally* propels the political state along the CIEN trajectory towards

Table 2.3 Evolution of political accountability, under political states with differing autonomy and aims

| Autonomy of state | Basic aims of state | Critical features | Rent pattern | Strength of sanction against anti-social governance | | |
| --- | --- | --- | --- | --- | --- | --- |
| | | | | Political accountability | Social capital | Rule of law |
| *Developmental* | | | | | | |
| Benevolent autocratic nation builder | Secure rapid GDP growth to sustain compact elite + build social unity | Low rent; external threat; poor have low opportunity cost | Modest rent-siphoning; efficient diffuse rent-raising + dispersal | Weak; but predation curbed by priority for social unity | Bonding s.c. dominant; slow expansion of bridging + linking | Nominal; elite dispense justice, at times arbitrarily |
| Diffuse factional oligarchy | Expand elite to deter policy capture and sustain rapid GDP growth | Low rent; intra-elite (land/ethnic/army) rivals; rapid GDP growth | Low diffuse rent extraction for public goods + (skewed) wealth creation | Moderate: growing parliament power v. executive | Competitive urbanization builds autonomous linking + bridging s.c. | Strengthening legal protection; common law fairer > civil law |
| Consensual factional democracy | Growth then equity via providing basic social entitlements | Low rent; middle-class growth saps elite + shrinks poor | Diffuse extraction + dispersal for growth > redistribution | High: independent parliament + second chamber | Autonomous linking + bridging s.c.; risk of Olson effects | Legal independence cuts transaction costs + risk |
| *Non-Developmental* | | | | | | |
| Predatory autocratic dictator | Maximize elite rent siphoning through force if necessary | High rent; violent predation; staple trap trajectory | Point rent extraction by elite slows GDP growth | None: power held by violence, which only elite contest | Weak: intense elite rivalry; weak bond s.c. of poor v. elite | None: elite controls by force; poor rely on custom |

| | | | | | | |
|---|---|---|---|---|---|---|
| Concentrated Factional oligarchy | Dominant faction captures policy to sustain rent + power | High rent; unequal asset share; staple trap trajectory | Point extraction but some public goods benefit mainly elite | Minimal; puppet legislature run by oligarchy | Dependent on elite; repressed civic associations | Skewed to favor elite > poor |
| Polarized Factional democracy | Capture policy to benefit tribal clients even if slows long-term GDP growth | Democracy polarized on tribal lines; retarded GDP growth | Rent extraction + skewed distribution to tribal clients > GDP growth | Fragile: parliament liable to wild policy swings + some dictator risk | Polarized civic associations feed polarized democracy | Judiciary subject to capture + biased to tribal clients |

*Note:* Moving down the table, political accountability strengthens incrementally and endogenously under developmental political states (associated with low rent). It is retarded for non-developmental political states, but after a growth collapse exogenous democratization can occur abruptly if neighborhood effects are accommodated.

the status of a high-income consensual democracy. Mauritius, Singapore, South Korea and Taiwan provide examples.

### High rent: the staple trap and exogenous democratization model

In recent decades rent-rich states have tended to exhibit predatory motives rather than developmental ones, reflecting the strong political attraction of rent extraction and distribution compared with wealth creation (Auty 2001a). A high ratio of rent/GDP offers the political state the option of increasing revenue through rent capture rather than wealth creation. The political attraction of this option is strengthened by the fact that it confers immediate gain whereas the reward from wealth creation is long-term. High rents also provide a strong incentive to capture the political state for self-enrichment, underpinned by the assurance that some rent can be diverted to placate political opponents, if necessary.

A second impact of high rent is to lengthen dependence on the primary sector so that the economy skips the labor-intensive manufacturing stage of the CIEN model and loses the beneficial economic and social effects of that stage (Figure 2.1). This perpetuates surplus rural labor and amplifies income inequality and social tension, which prompt the government to use rent to create jobs by over-extending the bureaucracy and protecting infant industry that has little incentive to mature and become internationally competitive. The growth of this rent-dependent parasitic sector lowers investment efficiency, so that PCGDP growth slows. Yet rent recipients block reforms designed to restructure the economy and boost investment efficiency, so the government finds it politically easier to perpetuate the system by extracting the return to capital from the primary sector as well as the rent. But this policy weakens the primary sector, corrodes incentives for wealth creation and reverses competitive diversification so the economy is vulnerable to shocks and a growth collapse. Moreover, recovery from a growth collapse is protracted (as Table 2.1 documents) because when an economy is deflected from its comparative advantage, all forms of capital (social, human and environmental, as well as produced) decay.

The distortion of the economy that precedes a growth collapse also weakens sanctions against anti-social governance. First, expanding social entitlements enhance the rent dependence of both government and economic agents, rather than diminishing it, reducing pressure for political accountability. Moreover, as movement along the STEX trajectory shrinks rent-fuelled patronage, the government concentrates the dwindling rent on its strongest supporters and represses erstwhile favored political groups that lose out. Second, rent-driven urbanization yields a rent-dependent civil society rather than one with autonomous civic associations that confer voice and lower transaction costs. Third, businesses lobby the government to retain a share of the declining rent stream because such lobbying is potentially more lucrative than efforts to strengthen the rule of law (Li *et al.* 2000). In addition, a growth collapse reduces incomes and thereby expands corruption to the detriment of both social capital and the rule of law (Treisman 2002).

The stylized evolution of the political state under high rent is therefore likely to start from a predatory autocracy that pursues rent extraction over wealth creation (Table 2.3, row 4). Rivalry within the elite may spawn a concentrated oligarchy that has a broader encompassing interest than the autocracy. However, the promise of rapid enrichment (with low risk of sanction) devalues wealth creation and confers a strong incentive to resist the diffusion of group power and defend the rent patronage system, by force if necessary. This feature has strong relevance for many CCA countries.

Yet, exogenous democratization may occur after a growth collapse, given favorable external factors like western assistance that is conferred on condition that the *political* economy is reformed and/or a democracy-friendly neighborhood effect. Even so, such an endogenous democracy is likely to be polarized rather than consensual. One reason is that, as noted earlier, high rent tends to heighten income inequality, which polarizes political parties between the pursuit of income redistribution and the defense of wealth (Table 2.3, row 6). In addition, the new political state requires a lengthy period of consolidation during which it is vulnerable to regression. Recent examples of the STEX trajectory include Argentina, Ghana, Indonesia, Peru, Venezuela and Zambia.

In summary, the rent-rich STEX development trajectory is likely to stall and experience a growth collapse, accompanied by political regression. Changes in government tend to be abrupt and erratic after a growth collapse, rather than incremental. Democratization is likely to depend on external factors and to be fragile, requiring a period of consolidation during which it may regress. Not surprisingly, the PCGDP of rent-rich countries is much more weakly linked than that of rent-poor countries to the strength of sanctions against anti-social governance (Auty 2004). But the corollary is that the CIEN model suggests that resource-poor economies engender virtuous economic and social circles that sustain rapid PCGDP growth and endogenous democratization. The next section adapts the STEX model to energy-exporting economies, because such countries dominate the CCA region.

## Adjusting the staple trap model for oil-exporting countries

The distortion of the economy and the associated deterioration in all forms of capital are potentially greater where the natural resource has 'point' socio-economic linkages, like minerals, than with resources that generate diffuse socio-economic linkages such as peasant crops *within a developmental political state*. In the case of mining and oil extraction, the capital-intensive production function concentrates revenues on one or two large multinational firms, a small labor aristocracy of mineworkers and the government. Taxation therefore dominates domestic socio-economic linkages. This is because domestic expenditure by factors of production is small due to the small energy sector workforce, while the specialized nature of production inputs constrains backward linkage by favoring imports over domestic supplies. Forward linkage is similarly stunted because resource-processing is often most competitive if located in overseas markets. The resulting dominance of rent flows by taxation increases the role of the government and, consequently, it amplifies the probabilities of predatory behavior, of policy failure and of economic distortion due to maladroit rent deployment. In contrast, the diffuse socio-economic linkages associated with peasant cash crops spread the rents across a wider set of economic agents who exhibit greater capacity than do governments to treat windfalls as temporary phenomena and to invest efficiently (Baldwin 1956; Bevan *et al.* 1987).

Of particular concern with regard to Azerbaijan, Kazakhstan and Turkmenistan, the extreme resource abundance of oil-rich countries (Table 2.2) sustains the transfer of rents even longer, so that the distortion of the political economy risks being greater. This section therefore considers policies to reduce the risk. During oil booms, political pressures encourage governments to adopt levels of investment and consumption that are difficult to rein back during a downswing. The over-rapid domestic absorption of the rents causes the real exchange rate to strengthen, triggering Dutch disease effects by weakening competitiveness in the non-mining tradeables sector (agriculture and manufacturing) and leading to their premature contraction. A common policy response is to protect tradeable activity by closing the economy to international trade, which also increases the scope for rent capture and distribution. This has occurred in Turkmenistan and Uzbekistan, and more recently in Kazakhstan.

Although trade policy closure is strongly associated with growth collapses in resource-rich countries, it is not a necessary condition for a collapse and is less likely to occur in the *capital-surplus* oil-exporting countries (Sachs and Warner 1997a). Capital-surplus oil-exporters are those with high ratios of oil reserves per capita that produce rents too large to be absorbed within the domestic economy. The initial scale of rent to GDP in the three energy-rich CCA countries qualified them as capital surplus. Saudi Arabia is an example of a capital-surplus oil-exporting country that maintained a more open economy during the oil booms, but it too experienced a severe growth collapse when oil prices fell in the early 1980s. Rather, growth collapses occur because the resource rents facilitate a relaxation of market discipline and proliferate rent-dependent activity, compound economic distortions and entrench vested interests, which make it politically difficult to execute the necessary economic reforms. As Part II shows, several CCA countries quickly encountered this undesirable set of circumstances.

The macroeconomic effects of chronic excess demand caused by the over-rapid domestic absorption of the energy rents and deficient demand during a downswing are not symmetric. Excess demand causes inflation and high import leakages; deficient demand causes real activity to contract, unemployment to rise and real incomes to fall. Over a price cycle of boom and bust, the economy progressively moves towards stagflation (Gelb and Associates 1988). It is therefore desirable to keep spending levels stable, or growing at moderate rates.

A growth collapse is not inevitable in energy-rich countries and it is possible to sustain rapid economic growth from a finite resource. Basically, the government of an energy-rich country needs to invest a sufficient amount from the rent stream in alternative wealth-generating assets (for example, produced or human capital) such that when the mineral is exhausted the same income stream as emanated from mineral extraction is sustained in perpetuity (Auty and Mikesell 1998). There are three basic requirements to maintain the income component of the mineral and minimize Dutch disease effects (the premature contraction of the non-mining tradeables, notably agriculture and manufacturing). First, sterilize the mineral windfalls (in an offshore capital development fund) in order to slow the domestic absorption of the rents and thereby limit the Dutch disease effects. Second, buffer public expenditure from a possible rent collapse (with a mineral revenue stabilization fund that smoothes out domestic rent absorption). Third, invest a sufficient fraction of the natural capital in alternative wealth-producing assets (using a project evaluation unit to ensure the efficiency of public sector investment). But such policy prescriptions touted by the IFIs have in the past often neglected the risk that economic policy will be captured by the political elite and subverted to sustain its patronage networks, a problem that Part III argues is at the heart of faltering reform in the CCA region.

## Natural resources and the transition to a market economy

### *The STEX model and the collapse of growth in the Soviet bloc countries*

The growth collapse of the Soviet bloc severely affected the eight CCA countries and echoes the STEX model. In pursuit of autarky, central planners closed the economy and transferred resources from sectors of comparative advantage like mining into sectors like heavy industry and agriculture in which few Soviet bloc countries held a strong comparative advantage, least of all the CCA countries. After some initial success that reflected the ability of a command economy to rapidly mobilize under-used inputs, the efficiency of capital sustained a steady decline. From the late 1950s the growth rate decelerated despite an increase in the rate of investment relative to GDP: the increased investment failed to offset diminishing returns (World Bank 1996: 3). The rise in oil prices in 1974 inflicted a shock that was positive for the USSR, which was a net oil exporter, but negative for most of the Central and East European (CEE) countries, which imported oil.

The oil shock of 1974 appears to have eased reform pressure in the USSR (Lavigne 1999: 60 and 92), whereas it provided the oil-importing CEE countries with an incentive to experiment with economic reform. Moreover, the

Soviet Union compounded the impact of extra rent from higher oil prices by expanding oil exports to the market economies, which more than doubled during 1975–85 to 3.2 million barrels per day (BP 1986). This implies annual rents in excess of $17 billion, assuming an oil price of $25 per barrel and extraction costs of $10. However, the Soviet rent stream abruptly evaporated when oil prices plummeted in 1985 and annual growth in NMP, which was already low, more than halved to barely 1 per cent 1986–89 (Lavigne 1999: 58). The collapse of the USSR was therefore triggered not just by diminishing returns to investment and the mismanagement of Perestroika but also by the sudden loss of oil rent.

### Initial conditions and economic reform in the CCA countries

The deceleration of economic growth within the Soviet bloc occurred earlier in the higher-income countries, like those of Eastern Europe, and was less pronounced among the lower-income republics like the CCA. However, the pricing system that governed exchange within the USSR left the CCA countries in receipt of substantial geopolitical rent, often to a significant degree, with the exception of Turkmenistan. Consequently, the collapse of the Soviet Union not only exerted a profound trade shock on the CCA countries when demand from trade partners collapsed, but it also abruptly shrank their public finances as well.

The IFIs urged rapid reform because many economists initially believed that the transition to a market economy required rapid and comprehensive ('big bang') economic reform. This conclusion appeared to be supported by evidence from the mid-1990s for twenty-five transition economies (de Melo *et al.* 1996). The benefits of 'big bang' reform arise from rapid stabilization of the economy and swift reduction in fiscal deficits to squeeze down inflation, along with rapid realignment of prices to speed economic restructuring. Swift and comprehensive reform limited the absolute decline in both GDP and government revenue. In contrast, most late reformers like the CCA countries merely slowed the decline in output prior to reform even as their economies disintegrated (ibid.). Their output then contracted at an accelerating rate and after three years it was lower than that of the advanced reformers and still falling, while inflation was far more severe. Aslund *et al.* (1996), Havrylyshyn *et al.* (1998), Berg *et al.* (1999) and Fischer and Sahey (2000) all confirm the economic advantages of early and vigorous reform. Those economic advantages are buttressed by political advantages, not least the avoidance of 'reform' fatigue, which risks causing the reform effort to stall, as it did in the Russian Federation in the mid-1990s.

More recently, however, researchers like Roland (2000) have championed the case of gradual reform. Gradual reform is better described as dual-track reform in which the government encourages the emergence of a dynamic market track or sector (that might comprise agriculture, manufacturing or services or some combination of these) that grows fast enough to absorb surplus labor from the moribund plan sector. Over time, this allows the gainers in the dynamic sector to compensate losers in the plan sector, so that an orderly contraction of the latter occurs. From a political perspective, whereas rapid reform distributes the social costs unevenly and heightens the risk that the reforming government will be swept from power, dual-track reform minimizes such risk. These potential benefits from a dual track reform strategy help to inform the policy recommendations made for the CCA countries in Part V of this study.

Yet the debate during the initial decade of transition surrounding the pace of reform proved too simple because the choice of reform strategy and policy is sensitive to initial conditions (de Melo *et al.* 2001). It may be recalled that the four key initial conditions are length of exposure to central planning, remoteness from dynamic market economies, the natural resource endowment and the scale of GDP compression caused by the USSR's growth collapse.

Taking each of the principal initial conditions in turn, the longer the exposure to central planning then the more distorted the macro-economy (ibid.), the greater the corrosion of market-friendly institutions and social capital (Raiser *et al.* 2001) and the stronger the vested interests opposed to reform (Aslund 2000). With regard to proximity to dynamic market economies, the literature suggests that the more the remoteness, the lower the foreign investment available to facilitate economic restructuring (Kopstein and Reilly 2000) and the lower the concern for political accountability and civic voice (Raiser *et al.* 2001). In the low-income transition countries like the CCA countries, which have relatively large primary sectors, resource abundance is associated with predatory political states with weak incentives to provide public goods and invest efficiently (Auty 2001b), reluctance to reform (see Chapter 3), strong Dutch disease effects that retard economic restructuring (Rosenberg and Saavalainen 1998) and high levels of rent-seeking and corruption (Mauro 1995; Leite and Weidmann 1999). Finally, the greater the degree of GDP compression caused by the transition shock, the greater the corrosion of social capital and the higher the rent-seeking and corruption (Treisman 2002).

Based on these differences in initial conditions, the transition economies can be classified into four geographical groups (Table 2.4). *Effective rapid economic reform builds on an initial political disposition for change that arises out of relatively modest economic distortion* (so there is significant memory of market institutions), proximity to market economies, limited distraction of economic and political agents by resource rents and modest GDP compression. The least favorable reform prospects arose in the countries of the FSU due to high levels of distortion by central planning, coupled with high resource rents in many countries and remoteness from markets, especially in Central Asia.

The dominant energy-rich CCA countries have tended to use their rents to consolidate autocratic regimes and defer reform, albeit after a more

*Table 2.4* Initial conditions and transition trajectories, by geographical region

| Pre-condition outcome | Index | CEE Rapid reform[a] | NCIS + SEE Faltering reform[b] | CCA Faltering reform[c] | East Asia Gradual reform[d] |
|---|---|---|---|---|---|
| History | Years central plan | 45 | 59 | 71 | 34 |
| | Macro distortion (1 high) | −0.70 | 0.29 | 1.02 | −0.96 |
| | Over-industrialized (% GDP) | 10.2 | 11.7 | 3.9 | −2.0 |
| | Farm employment (% total) | 14 | 26 | 32 | 63 |
| | PCGNP (1989 US$ at PPP) | 7,495 | 5,592 | 4,354 | 950 |
| Geography | Per capita cropland (ha) | 0.46 | 0.59 | 0.47 | 0.18 |
| | Political state[e] | CD | PD | PA/CO | BA |
| | Market proximity (1 near) | 1 | 2 | 4 | 2 |
| | Institution quality (10 high) | 5.0 | −3.6 | −8.1 | −5.8 |
| | Social cohesion (3 strong) | 2.88 | 0.54 | 1.24 | n.a. |
| Reform outcomes | Reform index (4 complete) | 3.9 | 3.2 | 3.0 | 2.1 |
| | 89/02 GDP ratio | 1.01 | 0.70 | 0.74 | 2.99 |
| | 92/98 Govt. expenditure ratio | 1.04 | 0.74 | 0.53 | 0.93 |
| | Mid-90s income gini | 0.31 | 0.37 | 0.51 | 0.38 |
| | True saving (% GDP) | 10.9 | 1.4 | −2.8 | 10.8 |

*Source:* Auty 2001b.

*Notes*

a. Croatia, Czech Rep., Estonia, Hungary, Latvia, Lithuania, Poland, Slovak Rep., Slovenia.
b. Belarus, Bulgaria, Moldova, Romania, Russia, Ukraine.
c. Armenia, Azerbaijan, Georgia, Kazakhstan, Kyrgyzstan, Tajikistan, Turkmenistan, Uzbekistan.
d. China and Vietnam.
e. CD consensual democracy; PD polarized democracy; BA benevolent autocracy; PA predatory autocracy; CO concentrated oligarchy.

promising start in Azerbaijan and Kazakhstan, both of which reformed in order to attract large inflows of foreign direct investment with which to revive their oil sectors (see Chapter 4). Yet three of the energy-rich CCA countries (the exception is war-stricken Azerbaijan) were also able to use their rents to ease the scale of GDP compression, whereas the resource-poor countries, three of which were afflicted by civil strife, could not. Consequently, GDP compression averaged 66 per cent in the resource-poor CCA countries compared with 44 per cent in the resource-rich CCA countries and 29 per cent in the CEE countries. Offsetting this effect somewhat, geopolitical rent increased steadily in the resource-poor CCA countries and evinced a faster pace of economic reform than in the resource-rich countries as a group. However, as Part III demonstrates, even if a national government favored reforms, it would have difficulty implementing them because regional and local governments have shown more concern for maintaining the patronage networks by which they extract and distribute rent than for reform to create wealth (Collins 2004; Jones Luong forthcoming).

In contrast, the low-income East Asian countries in transition, as a group, faced the most propitious conditions for reform. Their shorter exposure to central planning left a less distorted economy, with a much smaller legacy of obsolete state industry compared with the CCA countries and a correspondingly higher fraction of the workforce in agriculture (Table 2.4, column 6), which responded swiftly to simple changes in incentives and strongly impacted GDP growth. In particular, the coastal states (and the coastal provinces in the case of China) were well placed to attract manufacturing with declining competitiveness from adjacent market economies like Japan and Taiwan. Moreover, as the CIEN model suggests, resource-poor China and Vietnam engendered benevolent autocracies that reformed earlier than resource-rich Cambodia and Myanmar, with Laos occupying an intermediate position. China also opted for dual-track reform, rather than rapid reform, and its experience provides useful lessons for sustaining reform in the CCA countries.

## Conclusions

The resource-driven political economy models help to explain the recent under-performance of the resource-rich developing market economies. Encouraged to intensify their level of economic intervention by fashionable post-war policies, most governments in resource-rich countries deployed their rents in ways that cumulatively transferred inputs from competitive activity to uncompetitive activity. This progressively lowered the efficiency of investment and locked the economy into a staple trap that aborted competitive diversification and caused economic growth to decelerate. This rendered the economy increasingly vulnerable to external shocks and a growth collapse. The advocates of interventionist policies had failed to anticipate the extent to which the deployment of rents would feed predatory political states that repressed sanctions against anti-social governance. The STEX model shows that these adverse characteristics tend to be heightened in energy-rich countries, which has ominous implications for the CCA region. In this context, central planning can be viewed as an extreme form of excessive intervention and the legacy of high macro-economic distortion, remoteness from offsetting western influences and substantial GDP compression compound the adverse consequences of resource abundance.

The CIEN model suggests that, paradoxically, the resource-poor countries may face more auspicious development prospects. It shows that the absence of rents increases the incentive for the political state to be developmental and to align its interests with those of the majority population in order to create wealth. The resulting sustained rapid growth in PCGDP may be expected to strengthen sanctions against anti-social governance to achieve an incremental and endogenous democratization. However, on a more optimistic note, the establishment of a benevolent state in resource-rich countries can achieve a similar outcome, albeit with more political challenges arising from a slower rate of employment creation. These challenges call for astute management of the natural resource rents to *competitively* diversify the economy first into an expanding range of primary commodities and then into an expanding set of manufactured exports as, for example, in Indonesia during 1965–95 and also Malaysia.

Yet the resource-poor countries are affected by initial conditions other than the scale of the rent, including long exposure to central planning, remoteness from dynamic market economies and compression of GDP on a scale that exacerbated negative features of their social capital. These other conditions have offset to varying degrees the potential beneficial incentives from low resource rent, but perhaps less so in the western Caucasus where Armenia and Georgia exhibit positive effects from their closer proximity to Western Europe (se Chapter 6). The next four chapters analyze in detail how initial conditions affected the pace of economic reform in the eight CCA countries and also their future development prospects, beginning with an overview of the four energy-rich countries in Chapter 3.

## Notes

1   The constructive comments of Erica Johnson are gratefully acknowledged, but any errors remain the responsibility of the author.
2   The countries are classified according to their size (using GDP in 1970 as an index of domestic market potential for industrialization) and their cropland per capita in 1970. Most countries fall into the small resource-abundant category so this is further sub-divided to identify the mineral economies (with oil or ore at least 40 per cent of exports).

## References

Acemoglu, D., Johnson, S. and Robinson, J. (2002) Reversal of fortune: Geogrqaphy and institutions the making of the modern world income distribution, *Quarterly Journal of Economics* 117, 1231–1294.

Aslund, A. (2000) Why has Russia's economic transformation been so arduous?, in: Pleskovic, B. and Stiglitz, J.E. (eds.) *Annual World Bank Conference on Development Economics 1999*, Washington DC: World Bank, 399–424.

Aslund, A., Boone, P. and Johnson, S. (1996) How to stabilise: Lessons from post-Communist countries, *Brookings Papers on Economic Activity 1*, 217–314.

Auty, R.M. (2001a) *Resource Abundance and Economic Development*, Oxford: Oxford University Press.

Auty, R.M. (2001b) Transition reform in the mineral-rich Caspian region countries, *Resources Policy* 27(1), 25–32.

Auty, R.M. (2004) Patterns of rent-extraction and deployment in developing countries: Implications for governance, economic policy and performance, paper presented at the Poverty Reduction and Economic Management Unit (PREM) Seminar, World Bank, Washington DC, April 27 2004.

Auty, R.M. and Mikesell, R.F. (1998) *Sustainable Development in Mineral Economies*, Oxford: Clarendon Press.

Baldwin, R.E. (1956), Patterns of development in newly settled regions, *Manchester School of Social and Economic Studies* 24, 161–179.

Berg, A., Borensztein, E., Sahay, R. and Zettelmeyer, J. (1999) The evolution of output in transition economies: Explaining the differences, IMF Working Paper 99/73, Washington DC: IMF.

Bevan, D., Collier, P. and Gunning, J.W. (1987) Consequences of a commodity boom in a controlled economy: Accumulation and redistribution in Kenya, *World Bank Economic Review* 1, 489–513.

Birdsall, N., Pinckney, C. and Sabot, R. (2001) Natural resources, human capital and growth, in: Auty, R.M. (ed.) *Resource Abundance and Economic Development*, Oxford: Oxford University Press.

Bloom, D.E. and Williamson, J.G. (1998) Demographic transitions and economic miracles in emerging Asia, *The World Bank Economic Review* 12, 419–455.

BP (1986) *BP Statistical Review of World Energy 1986*, London: British Petroleum.

Collins, K. (2004) The logic of clan politics: Evidence from the Central Asian trajectories, *World Politics* 56, 224–261.

De Melo, M., Denizer, C. and Gelb, A. (1996) Patterns of transition from plan to market, *World Bank Economic Review* 10, 397–424.

De Melo, M., Denizer, C., Gelb, A. and Tenev, S. (2001) Circumstance and choice: The role of initial conditions and policies in transition economies, *World Bank Economic Review* 15, 1–31.

Fischer, S. and Sahay, R. (2000) The transition economies after ten years, IMF Working Paper 00/30, Washington DC: IMF.

Gelb, A.H. and Associates (1988) *Oil Windfalls: Blessing or Curse?* New York: Oxford University Press.

Glaeser, E.L., La Porta, R., Lopes-de-Silanes, F. and Shleifer, A. (2004) Do institutions cause growth? NBR Working Paper 10568, Cambridge MA: National Bureau of Economic Research.

Havrylyshyn, O., Izvorski, I. and van Rooden, R. (1998) Recovery and growth in transition economies: A stylized regression analysis, IMF Working Paper 98/141, International Monetary Fund, Washington DC.

Jones Luong, P. (Forthcoming) Economic 'decentralization' in Kazakhstan: Causes and consequences, in: Jones Luong, P. (ed.) *The Transformation of Central Asia: State-Societal Relations from Soviet Rule to Independence*, Ithaca NY: Cornell University Press.

Kopstein, J.S. and Reilly, D.A. (2000) Geographic diffusion and the transformation of the post-communist world, *World Politics* 53, 1–37.

Lal, D. (1995) Why growth rates differ. The political economy of social capability in 21 developing countries, in: Koo, B.H. and Perkins, D.H. (eds.) *Social Capability and Long-run Economic Growth*, Basingstoke: Macmillan, 310–327.

Lal, D. and Myint, H. (1996) *The Political Economy of Poverty, Equity and Growth: A Comparative Study*, Oxford: Clarendon Press.

Lavigne, M. (1999) *The Economics of Transition*, London: Macmillan.

Lederman, D. and Maloney, W.F. (2003) Trade structure and growth, World Bank Policy Research Working Paper 3025, Washington DC: World Bank.

Leite, C. and Weidmann, J. (1999) Does Mother Nature corrupt – Natural resources, corruption and economic growth, IMF Working Paper 99/85, International Monetary Fund, Washington DC.

Lewis, W.A. (1978) *Growth and Fluctuations 1870–1913*, London: Allen and Unwin.

Li, S., Li, S. and Zhang, W. (2000) The road to capitalism: Competition and institutional change in China, *Journal of Comparative Economics* 28, 269–292.

Lizzeri, A. and Persico, N. (2003) Why did the elites extend the suffrage? Democracy and the scope of government with application to Britain's Age of Reform, Working Paper, University of Pennsylvania: Philadelphia.

Londono, J.L. (1996) *Poverty, Inequality and Human Capital Development in Latin America, 1950–2025*, Washington DC: World Bank.

Maddison, A. (1995) *Monitoring the World Economy 1820–1992*, Paris; OECD.

Mauro, P. (1995) Corruption and growth, *The Quarterly Journal of Economics* 90, 681–712.

Raiser, M., Haerpfer, C., Nowotny, T. and Wallace, C. (2001) Social capital in transition: A first look at the evidence, EBRD Working Paper 61, London: European Bank for Reconstruction and Development.

Roland, G. (2000) *Transition and Economics: Policies, Markets, and Firms*, Cambridge MA: MIT Press.

Rosenberg, C.B. and Saavalainen, T.O. (1998) How to deal with Azerbaijan's oil boom? Policy strategies in a resource-rich transition economy, IMF Working Paper 98/6, IMF, Washington DC.

Ross, M.L. (1999) The political economy of the resource curse, *World Politics* 51, 297–322.

Ross, M.L. (2001) Does oil hinder democracy? *World Politics* 53(3), 325–361.

Sachs, J.D. and Warner, A.M. (1995) Economic reform and the process of global integration, *Brookings Papers on Economic Activity* 1, 1–118.

Sachs, J.D. and Warner, A.M. (1997a) Natural resource abundance and economic growth, Mimeo, Cambridge MA: HIID.

Sachs, J.D. and Warner, A.M. (1997b) Sources of slow growth in Africa, *Journal of African Economies* 6, 335–376.

Stiglitz, J.E. (1995) Social absorption capability and innovation, in: Koo, B.H. and Perkins, D.H. (eds.) *Social Capability and Long-Term Economic Growth*, Macmillan, Basingstoke, 48–81.

Treisman, D. (2002) Postcomminist corruption, Working Paper, Los Angeles: Department of Political Science, UCLA.

Wood, A. and Berge, K. (1997) Exporting manufactures: Human resources, natural resources, and trade policy, *Journal of Development Studies* 34, 35–59.

Woolcock, M., Isham, J. and Pritchett, L. (2001) The social foundations of poor economic growth in resource-rich countries, in: Auty, R.M. (ed.) *Resource Abundance and Economic Development*, Oxford: Oxford University Press, 76–92.

World Bank (1996) *World Development Report 1996: From Plan to Market*, Washington DC: World Bank.

World Bank (1999) *World Development Indicators 1999*, Washington DC: World Bank.

# Part II

# Transition trends and scenarios within the CCA region

# 3 Nature's blessing or nature's curse?

## The political economy of transition in resource-based economies

*Akram Esanov, Martin Raiser
and Willem Buiter[1]*

This chapter analyses the reform progress made in the energy-rich states of the Commonwealth of Independent States (CIS), Azerbaijan, Kazakhstan, Turkmenistan and Uzbekistan (AKTU for short) and contrasts their development to that in the resource-poor countries at the CIS periphery. The main argument of the chapter is that far from being a blessing that would have allowed energy-rich countries to cushion the impact of reforms and thus make faster progress, energy rents have often been wasted or appropriated by the ruling elites. Progress in key structural reforms has in some cases lagged even behind other CIS countries and significant policy challenges need to be addressed if natural resource wealth is not to turn into a curse for the region.

## Introduction

This chapter analyses reform progress during the first decade of transition in the energy-rich CIS states of Central Asia and the Caucasus, Azerbaijan, Kazakhstan, Turkmenistan and Uzbekistan (AKTU for short)[2] and contrasts their development to that in the resource-poor countries in that region. While agricultural land, minerals and hydrocarbon reserves are all part of a country's resource endowment, we focus on the availability of energy resources as the key differentiating factor in explaining transition paths in the CIS. This is because energy resources have tended to generate far larger resource rents than minerals or agriculture. Resource rents are here understood to be pure profits generated by the extraction of natural resources, once all factors of production have been remunerated at their opportunity cost and the costs of transport to market has been subtracted.

The main argument is that far from being a blessing that would have allowed energy-rich countries to cushion the impact of reforms and thus make faster progress, resource rents have often been wasted or appropriated by the ruling elites. Progress in key structural reforms has in some cases lagged behind even that in other CIS countries and significant policy challenges need to be addressed if natural resource wealth is not to turn into a lasting curse for the region.

The attempt to find a common explanation for the transition patterns observed across the resource-rich countries immediately faces the problem that along certain dimensions these patterns have differed quite dramatically between, say, Kazakhstan on the one hand and Turkmenistan on the other (Gürgen *et al.* 1999; Kalyuzhnova *et al.* 2001; Pomfret 2002). However, we propose a political economy explanation that can account for these differences, while at the same time pointing towards key common challenges for all resource-rich transition economies.

At the center of our argument is the idea that the presence of natural resource wealth allowed incumbent elites to remain in power and shut out reformers. This was the case in Turkmenistan and Uzbekistan. Where natural resources required expanded infrastructure – as in Azerbaijan and Kazakhstan – and the country depended on outside investment, an initial phase of liberalization was succeeded by a phase of increasing national assertiveness. What all four countries have in common is the lack of turnover among ruling elites and economic policies discouraging entry and entrepreneurship. The control over resource rents and policies aimed at limiting economic and political competition are the pillars of the political economy of reform in the resource-rich countries. In the resource-poor countries, the absence of resource rents meant that incumbent elites had less largesse with which to bolster their position. The associated insecurity, exacerbated by greater GDP compression, initially made the countries more receptive to economic reform, reinforced by IFI conditionality.[3]

The arguments in this chapter are related to the large literature investigating the impact of natural resources on economic performance (Sachs and Warner 1995; Auty and Mikesell 1998; Tornell and Lane 1999; Gylfason 2001). Most relevant here, Dalmazzo and de Blasio (2001) develop a model in which reform leads simultaneously to a reduction in rent appropriation by the elites and an expansion of private business opportunities. The results are that natural resource abundance reduces the incentives to reform and hurts growth. The combination of self-interested autocratic rule and access to resource rents is what drives the political economy of reform in this model, in line with the argument we outlined above. Political competition leading to more 'voice' in decision making by interest groups not associated with the elites can help to bring about liberalization.

The structure of the chapter is as follows. The first section (pages 41–47) provides an overview of reform progress in the resource-rich countries to date and compares it with the rest of the CIS. It shows that resource rents have typically been large in the AKTU countries but much of it has been dissipated in energy subsidies, rather than used to accelerate reform through taxation and redistribution to potential losers. As a result, the resource-rich Central Asian and Caucasus countries have actually lagged behind the rest of the CIS in some dimensions of reform. The second section (pages 48–52) tries to explain the patterns observed with reference to the disincentives to reform faced by elites as they continued to enjoy access to resource rents. It also shows that – as expected – political turnover in the resource-rich countries has been low. The final section (pages 52–54) examines possible ways out of excessive resource dependence for the countries in the region.

## Reform and structural change: the role of resources rents[4]

The degree of energy dependence in the four energy-rich countries of Central Asia and the Caucasus was particularly high under central planning and hence availability of energy resources was a particularly important source of potential subsidies. The beneficiaries of such subsidies were principally the inefficient old industrial dinosaurs throughout the Soviet Union. In trying to understand how the availability of resource rents influences the propensity to reform, the focus on energy rents is useful, since industrial dinosaurs were a critical constituency for incumbent political elites. We will show that energy rents in the energy-rich transition economies have indeed been largely consumed by implicit subsidies, rather than being used to support social safety nets and investment in public infrastructure and human capital to ease the process of adjustment.

### *How large are energy rents?*[5]

Table 3.1 shows that by the end of the 1990s, the AKTU countries had a dependence on oil and gas revenues in exports and government revenues similar to Iran or Norway and considerably higher than, for instance, Mexico. For Azerbaijan and Kazakhstan, resource dependence has increased considerably since the start of reforms. The Caspian oil fields were left underexploited in Soviet times, both for strategic and technological reasons, as Russia felt safer and technologically better equipped developing its own vast west Siberian reserves. Gas from Turkmenistan and Uzbekistan was, however, extracted at high rates during Soviet times and Turkmenistan was for a brief period in 1992–93 granted access to non-CIS markets for its gas exports, generating around US$3 billion in early resource rents. This difference has had a bearing on reform patterns, as we will show below.

Commensurate with the high degree of dependence on energy resources as a source of foreign exchange and government revenues, oil and gas production in AKTU generates very significant rents. Rents in principle accrue on both exports and domestic sales, and are shared between producers, the owners of transport infrastructure, governments and domestic energy consumers. Table 3.2 shows the ratio of oil and gas rents to GDP and how this is distributed among exporters, domestic producers and domestic energy consumers. Transport rents accruing to domestic transport operators are not considered in this analysis, as this would considerably complicate the picture.[6] We do not distinguish between rents accruing to the government through

Table 3.1 Indicators of resource dependence, selected transition economies and other oil-producing countries (in per cent unless otherwise) indicated

| | Azerbaijan[1] | Kazakhstan[2] | Russia[3] | Turkmenistan[4] | Uzbekistan[5] | Venezuela[6] | Mexico[7] | Iran[8] | Norway[9] |
|---|---|---|---|---|---|---|---|---|---|
| Oil and gas export in per cent of total exports | 85.2 (78.2) | 46.8 (34.1) | 50.4 (60.2) | 81 (62.6) | 12.3 (13.3) | 69.8 | 9.8 (7.3) | 69.4 | 0.35 |
| Oil and gas export in per cent of GDP | 30.5 (17.6) | 24.7 (12.1) | 21.5 (16.3) | 68.7 (31.6) | 4.3 (3.6) | 25.4 | 0.7 (0.5) | 14.7 | 0.14 |
| Oil and gas revenues in per cent of total government revenues | 36.2 (22.1) | 27.5 (5.0) | 30.1 (24.2) | 42.0 | 14.8 (15.4) | 42.5 | 24.1 (29.8) | 45.9 | 0.16 |
| FDI in oil and gas sector in per cent of total FDI | 80.5 (71.0) | 69.7 (83.3) | 10.7 | na | na | na | na | na | na |
| *Memo* | | | | | | | | | |
| Oil production (mt) 2000 | 14.02 | 35.00 | 312.70 | 7.25 | 7.60 | 153.88 | 168.78 | 188.63 | 148.92 |
| Gas production (bcm) 2000 | 6.00 | 11.50 | 551.00 | 46.00 | 54.88 | 28.00 | 36.40 | 53.20 | 20.00 |

*Source:* For all transition economies oil and gas production is for 2001 and from *BP Energy Outlook* 2000. For other countries energy production is for 1999 and from the EIA.

1. Figures for Azerbaijan are all from the IMF *Staff Report*, June 2001. Figures are for 2000 and those in brackets for 1999. Figures for the share of the oil and gas sector in FDI were calculated from gross inflow data. Net FDI into the oil sector was negative in 2000, due to repayments on inter-company loans under the PSAs.
2. Figures are for 2000, in brackets for 1999. Figures for oil and gas exports and government revenues are from IMF. Exports are not corrected for under-invoicing.
3. Figures are for 2000, in brackets for 1999, except for the share of oil and gas in FDI, which is from UNCTAD *World Investment Report* 2000 and refers to 1999. For oil and gas exports revenues are for the first quarter only.
4. Figures refer to 2000, in brackets to 1999. Figures for oil and gas exports are from Interfax. Turkmenistan's US dollar GDP is an EBRD staff estimate based on a weighted exchange rate taking into the existence of a large parallel market premium. Data for the share of oil and gas in government revenues are based on oral communications from the Ministry of Finance. Data for FDI into the energy sector is unavailable, but may amount to anything between half and two-thirds of FDI inflows in recent years.
6. Data are for 1998 and from the IMF.
7. Data are for 2000, in brackets for 1999. All data are from the Mexican statistical office.
8. Data are for 1999 and all from the IMF.
9. Data for exports are for 1999 and from the Norwegian statistical office. The share of oil and gas in government revenues is for 1998 and from the EU (www.eubusiness.com).

Table 3.2 Energy rents in AKTU and Russia, 1992–2000 (in per cent of GDP)

| Gas rents (% of GDP) | Total potential rent | | Export rent | | Domestic subsidy | | Producer rent | |
|---|---|---|---|---|---|---|---|---|
| | 1992–2000 average | 2000 | 1992–2000 average | 2000 | 1992–2000 average | 2000 | 1992–2000 average | 2000 |
| Azerbaijan | 8.6 | 5.7 | 0.3 | 0.0 | 9.8 | 5.1 | -1.5 | 0.6 |
| Kazakhstan | 1.2 | 1.5 | 0.0 | 0.0 | -0.5 | -0.1 | 1.7 | 1.6 |
| Turkmenistan | 47.2 | 31.6 | 36.2 | 23.4 | 11.1 | 13.2 | -0.1 | -4.9 |
| Uzbekistan | 13.3 | 17.8 | 2.4 | 4.6 | -0.5 | -6.3 | 11.4 | 19.5 |
| Russia | 11.3 | 16.5 | 3.8 | 5.4 | 5.3 | 4.3 | 2.2 | 6.9 |

| Oil rents (% of GDP) | Total potential rent | | Export rent | | Domestic subsidy | | Producer rent | |
|---|---|---|---|---|---|---|---|---|
| | 1992–2000 average | 2000 | 1992–2000 average | 2000 | 1992–2000 average | 2000 | 1992–2000 average | 2000 |
| Azerbaijan | 30.7 | 50.5 | 6.9 | 28.1 | 1.6 | 7.2 | 22.2 | 15.2 |
| Kazakhstan | 13.0 | 27.2 | 9.5 | 22.6 | 1.5 | 2.8 | 2.0 | 1.9 |
| Turkmenistan | 13.6 | 31.6 | 3.9 | 18.1 | 7.1 | 8.7 | 2.6 | 4.9 |
| Uzbekistan | 5.6 | 15.6 | 0.3 | 1.6 | 1.5 | 1.0 | 3.8 | 12.9 |
| Russia | 8.7 | 16.2 | 3.6 | 7.5 | 0.0 | 0.0 | 5.1 | 8.7 |

Sources: National statistical offices, International Energy Agency, Interfax Petroleum Report, PlanEcon.

Notes
Export rents are calculated as actual export revenues minus transportation costs, minus production costs.
Total rents are calculated as total production times export price minus production and transportation costs.
Domestic consumer subsidies are domestic consumption times the difference between domestic prices and import prices.
Domestic producer rent is total rent minus export rent, minus domestic consumer subsidies, minus producer rents.

taxes and royalties and those accruing to the owners of oil and gas resources (which in some cases are state-owned enterprises). Total rents are calculated by multiplying total production (TV) by the export price (EP) net of lifting (PC) and transportation costs (TC) per unit of output:

(1) $TR = TV*(EP - PC - TC)$

These total rents do not accrue entirely to the country if there are constraints on transport and thus a gap is introduced between domestic prices and net export prices. Actual export rents can thus be calculated analogously but using only actual export volumes (EV):

(2) $ER = EV*(EP - PC - TC)$

Domestic subsidies (DS) are calculated using import prices (IP) as the opportunity cost of energy, subtracting domestic prices (DP) and multiplying the resulting expression by domestic consumption (DV). Consumer subsidies do not include collection arrears, assumed to be zero in these calculations. When domestic prices exceed import prices, subsidies become negative.

(3) $DS = DV*(IP - DP)$, where $DV + EV = TV$

Domestic producer rents (DR) are total rents minus export rents and domestic consumer subsidies:

(4) $DR = TR - ER - DS = DV*(EP - PC - TC - IP + DP)$

Assuming export prices minus transportation costs are always higher or equal to import prices, domestic producer rents will be positive whenever domestic prices are above production costs. The difference between net export prices and import prices contributes to domestic producer rents by construction, although it does not generate an actual resource flow as exports are constrained by the availability of transport. The numbers in Table 3.2 therefore reflect largely hypothetical domestic producer rents, whereas export rents and consumer subsidies are estimates of actual resource flows.

Table 3.2 reveals that total energy rents during 1992–2000 have ranged between 15 per cent of GDP in Kazakhstan and over 60 per cent in Turkmenistan, which is high by any standards. Export rents have typically been less than half of the total, although they are higher in oil than in gas and have increased over time as new transport capacity from the Caspian has come on stream. Domestic rents have been shared among producers and consumers in different ways across the four countries. In Turkmenistan and to a lesser extent in Azerbaijan, domestic rents have gone mainly to domestic consumers in the form of across the board price subsidies. The same is true in the gas sector in Russia and Uzbekistan.[7] In Kazakhstan, energy prices are closest to opportunity costs and domestic subsidies have been relatively small, although noticeably increasing in the oil sector (as reflected, for instance, in recurrent export bans for domestic fuel products). In all countries a large share of domestic producer rents is also lost due to payment arrears or non-payment of domestic energy bills (Walters 2000).

### Energy rents and reform

In principle, governments can tax both export and domestic producer rents. In the transition context such tax revenue could help to smooth adjustment costs to the large supply and demand shocks resulting from transition for other sectors of the economy. However, rather than taxing available resources to cushion the costs of adjustment, AKTU governments have to various degrees chosen to maintain implicit transfers to special interest groups. In addition, in several instances, the leaders of the AKTU countries have appropriated export rents outside the state budget for the benefit of their closest entourage. This is most evident in Turkmenistan, where the US$1.5 billion foreign exchange reserves, largely earned from gas sales in 1992–93, remain under the direct control of President Niyazov.

Table 3.3 turns to the expenditure side of the budget and examines whether the stronger potential tax base of the AKTU countries has allowed them to spend more on investment in health and education. This might be an indication of attempts to ease the social costs of structural adjustment and make reforms politically more acceptable. The evidence in Table 3.3 reveals that this is not the case: Kyrgyzstan spends as much as Kazakhstan, Armenia almost as much as Azerbaijan and only Uzbekistan stands out as spending notably more than the average CIS country on health and education. These figures

*Table 3.3* Average expenditures on health and education

| | Health % GDP | | Education % GDP | |
|---|---|---|---|---|
| | Average 1991–2000 | 2000 | Average 1991–2000 | 2000 |
| *AKTU* | | | | |
| Azerbaijan | 1.5 | 0.9 | 4.2 | 3.8 |
| Kazakhstan | 2.4 | 2.2 | 4.1 | 3.9 |
| Turkmenistan | 2.6 | 3.6 | 4.6 | 2.8 |
| Uzbekistan | 3.6 | 3.0 | 8.2 | 7.3 |
| Russia | 3.3 | 3.1 | 3.7 | 2.8 |
| *CEE* | 5.5 | 5.4 | 4.7 | 4.7 |
| *CIS* | 3.1 | 2.3 | 4.9 | 3.6 |

*Source:* National authorities, IMF.

*Note:* Where data for 2000 were not available the number refers to the last available year. The average is computed using all available data during 1991–2000.

should not be over-interpreted, however, as the efficiency of expenditures and the quality of the services delivered in the social sector may vary.

What has been the effect of resource rents on economic reform? Table 3.4 shows the transition indicators for the eight dimensions scored by the EBRD in the first year of transition, in year 5 and in year 10, for AKTU and Russia, as well as averages for central and eastern Europe and the rest of the CIS. Compared with central and eastern Europe, the AKTU economies lag behind in most dimensions in year 5 and year 10. Compared with the rest of the CIS, this is the case only for foreign exchange liberalization in year 10, where the difference is statistically significant using a standard one-tailed t-test.[8] The AKTU countries do not significantly exceed the average for the rest of the CIS in any reform dimension. This is a remarkable result, if we remember the size of the rents available to these economies to cushion adjustment costs and thus the potentially much weaker feasibility constraint on implementing reform. However, it squares well with the political economy story sketched in the introduction: in countries with significant resource rents, incumbents can use these to fend off the pressure for reform.

Table 3.4 also reveals, however, that the above result is driven by Turkmenistan and Uzbekistan. Azerbaijan and Kazakhstan record reform progress similar to or even slightly above the CIS average in most dimensions. As mentioned above, Turkmenistan had early access to gas export rents in 1992–93. Moreover, Turkmenistan and Uzbekistan are important cotton producers. Cotton rents in both countries have accrued mainly to the government as a result of state trading in cotton exports and the persistence of the state order system in agriculture, whereby farmers receive only a fraction of the world market price for their produce. Some estimates indicate that agricultural sector rents were as high as 15 per cent of GDP in Turkmenistan in 1998 (Pastor and van Rooden 2000; Pomfret 2002). The early and easy availability of resource rents was arguably a key factor in allowing both countries to pursue much less reform-oriented policies than in the rest of the CIS.

By contrast, energy resources in Azerbaijan and Kazakhstan were not immediately available for exploitation and had to be developed first. This was done through a policy of opening up to foreign investment, exemplified by contracts with Chevron and Mobil for the Tengiz oil field in Kazakhstan (signed in 1993) and with a consortium led by BP for the Azeri-Chirag-Guneshli concession areas in Azerbaijan (signed in 1994). These international investors had to be convinced of the business-friendly intentions of the government – a key aspect of their risk calculations. Thus both countries were comparatively reform-minded during much of the 1990s. The presence of important foreign investment and the initial reliance on IFI funding has provided some support to economic reform policies, but how long this can last once major investments have been sunk and oil revenues increase substantially is an open question. The model would suggest that reduced dependence on foreign financial resources could cause the reform process to slow down or even reverse itself.

Table 3.4 Reform progress in energy-rich countries, compared to Eastern Europe and non-oil CIS average[1]

| Country | Year[2] | LSP | SSP | G&ER | PL | T&FES | CP | BR&IRL | SM&NB | ref1 | ref2 |
|---|---|---|---|---|---|---|---|---|---|---|---|
| Azerbaijan | t1 | 1.0 | 1.0 | 1.0 | 2.0 | 1.0 | 1.0 | 1.0 | 1.0 | 1.3 | 1.0 |
| Kazakhstan | t1 | 1.0 | 2.0 | 1.0 | 2.0 | 1.0 | 1.0 | 1.0 | 1.0 | 1.5 | 1.0 |
| Turkmenistan | t1 | 1.0 | 1.0 | 1.0 | 1.0 | 1.0 | 1.0 | 1.0 | 1.0 | 1.0 | 1.0 |
| Uzbekistan | t1 | 1.0 | 1.0 | 1.0 | 2.0 | 1.0 | 1.0 | 1.0 | 1.0 | 1.3 | 1.0 |
| Russia | t1 | 2.0 | 2.0 | 1.0 | 3.0 | 3.0 | 2.0 | 1.0 | 1.0 | 2.5 | 1.3 |
|  |  |  |  |  |  |  |  |  |  |  |  |
| CEE | t1 | 1.0 | 1.8 | 1.0 | 2.0 | 1.5 | 1.0 | 1.0 | 1.1 | 1.6 | 1.0 |
| CIS non-oil | t1 | 1.1 | 1.4 | 1.0 | 2.1 | 1.4 | 1.2 | 1.0 | 1.2 | 1.5 | 1.1 |
| AKTU (w/o Russia) | t1 | *1.0* | *1.3* | *1.0* | *1.8* | *1.0* | *1.0* | *1.0* | *1.0* | *1.3* | *1.0* |
| Azerbaijan | t5 | 1.0 | 2.0 | 1.7 | 3.0 | 2.0 | 2.0 | 2.0 | 1.0 | 2.0 | 1.7 |
| Kazakhstan | t5 | 3.0 | 3.3 | 2.0 | 3.0 | 4.0 | 2.0 | 2.0 | 1.7 | 3.3 | 1.9 |
| Turkmenistan | t5 | 1.0 | 1.7 | 1.0 | 2.0 | 1.0 | 1.0 | 1.0 | 1.0 | 1.4 | 1.0 |
| Uzbekistan | t5 | 2.7 | 3.0 | 2.0 | 3.0 | 2.0 | 2.0 | 1.7 | 2.0 | 2.7 | 1.9 |
| Russia | t5 | 3.0 | 4.0 | 2.0 | 3.0 | 4.0 | 2.0 | 2.0 | 3.0 | 3.5 | 2.3 |
|  |  |  |  |  |  |  |  |  |  |  |  |
| CEE | t5 | 2.3 | 3.5 | 2.2 | 2.8 | 3.6 | 1.8 | 2.4 | 1.8 | 3.1 | 2.1 |
| CIS non-oil | t5 | 2.4 | 3.0 | 1.8 | 3.0 | 3.1 | 1.9 | 1.7 | 1.6 | 2.9 | 1.7 |
| AKTU (w/o Russia) | t5 | *1.9* | *2.5* | *1.7* | *2.8* | *2.3* | *1.8* | *1.7* | *1.4* | *2.4* | *1.6* |
| Azerbaijan | T10 | 2.0 | 3.3 | 2.0 | 3.0 | 3.3 | 2.0 | 2.3 | 1.7 | 2.9 | 2.0 |
| Kazakhstan | T10 | 3.0 | 4.0 | 2.0 | 3.0 | 3.3 | 2.0 | 2.7 | 2.3 | 3.3 | 2.3 |
| Turkmenistan | T10 | 1.0 | 2.0 | 1.0 | 2.0 | 1.0 | 1.0 | 1.0 | 1.0 | 1.5 | 1.0 |
| Uzbekistan | T10 | 2.7 | 3.0 | 1.7 | 2.0 | 1.7 | 2.0 | 1.7 | 2.0 | 2.3 | 1.8 |
| Russia | T10 | 3.3 | 4.0 | 2.3 | 3.0 | 2.7 | 2.3 | 1.7 | 1.7 | 3.3 | 2.0 |
|  |  |  |  |  |  |  |  |  |  |  |  |
| CEE | T10 | 3.0 | 3.9 | 2.5 | 3.0 | 3.9 | 2.2 | 2.9 | 2.3 | 3.5 | 2.5 |
| CIS non-oil | T10 | 2.7 | 3.4 | 1.8 | 3.0 | 3.6 | 1.9 | 1.9 | 1.8 | 3.2 | 1.8 |
| AKTU (w/o Russia) | T10 | 2.2 | 3.1 | 1.7 | 2.5 | **2.3*** | 1.8 | 1.9 | 1.8 | 2.5 | 1.8 |

Notes

1. * indicates statistically significant difference in means of CIS oil and CIS non-oil at 10% level using a standard one-sided t-test.
2. The start of transition varies across countries: t1 = 1989 for Hungary and Poland, 1990 for Bulgaria, Czechoslovakia, Romania and former Yugoslavia 1991 for Albania and the Baltic states and 1992 for the CIS. t5 = t1 + 4 years; t10 = t1 + 9 years Results are not significantly changed if Russia is excluded from the group of CIS oil-rich economies.

## The political economy of resource dependence

Having established the importance of resource rents for the AKTU countries and highlighted the way in which these have been allocated, we now turn to a political economy interpretation of the observed patterns. First we show that already during Soviet times, AKTU served as a source of raw materials for the more industrialized western CIS. In return for selling their resources at prices far below world market values, these countries received considerable direct fiscal transfers from the Soviet center. We then provide a conceptual framework that analyses the consequences of the elimination of these implicit and explicit two-way transfers with the break-up of the Soviet Union.

### From soviet transfers to domestic rent appropriation

Under the Soviet system, the AKTU countries as well as other republics in the FSU specialized in the extraction of natural resources and the production of cash crops, while receiving manufactured goods from the western FSU. Because of the Soviet Union's biased pricing policy towards industry, the relative prices of raw materials and industrial goods were highly distorted. Producers of primary goods received lower prices compared with producers of industrial goods than they would have received had both traded at world prices. To compensate for these imposed unfavorable terms of trade the smaller FSU republics received large transfers from Moscow.

A number of papers have attempted to calculate the terms of trade shifts that resulted from the dissolution of the CMEA and the move to market prices in intra-republican trade (Tarr 1993; Orlowski 1993). Orlowski's calculations of implicit transfers in Soviet trade as of 1989 are shown in Table 3.5. It appears that Turkmenistan and Russia were net donors to all other republics, and that the biggest recipients of implicit transfers were the western FSU and the Caucasus, while the AKTU countries with the exception of Azerbaijan neither benefited nor lost much from this system of transfers. This is in part due to the relatively small net energy balances of AKTU, as their energy resources remained under-developed, and in part due to the significant production of final goods in countries such as Kazakhstan and Uzbekistan. The dead-weight loss associated with this distortionary system of taxes and subsidies did of course represent an unavoidable cost for all involved.

Yet, these numbers may be deceiving in two important respects. First, for many manufactured goods traded within the Soviet Union, a market reference price may not have existed. Orlowski's calculations are based on Goskomstat data, using their information of 'world market' prices rather than a true market benchmark.[9] Primary goods exporters are thus likely to have paid larger effective subsidies than would appear from Table 3.5. Second, with the exception of Turkmenistan, all AKTU countries were also importers of energy during Soviet times, reflecting the existing cross-border transport infrastructure. Some of this cross-border trade might not have taken place

*Table 3.5* Direct and indirect transfers in the Soviet Union

|  | *Indirect transfers* | *Direct transfers* |
|---|---|---|
| AKTU |  |  |
| Azerbaijan | 10.09 | 0.8 |
| Kazakhstan | 0.50 | 8.1 |
| Turkmenistan | −10.81 | 8.1 |
| Uzbekistan | 1.26 | 9.6 |
| Resource-poor Caspian |  |  |
| Armenia | 9.16 | 22.7 |
| Georgia | 16.02 | 2.0 |
| Kyrgyzstan | 2.72 | 6.9 |
| Tajikistan | 6.08 | 7.1 |
| Western CIS and Baltics |  |  |
| Belarus | 8.91 | −0.1 |
| Estonia | 12.08 | −0.2 |
| Latvia | 10.43 | 0.5 |
| Lithuania | 17.09 | −0.1 |
| Moldova | 24.05 | 0.6 |
| Ukraine | 3.61 | 0.3 |
| Russia | −3.67 | −0.4 |

*Source:* Orlowski 1993, 1995.

*Note:* Transfers are defined as positive for net recipients and negative for net donors.

under market conditions, and the AKTU countries may have borne an opportunity cost as a result.

The counterpart of being taxed through the system of distorted prices for traded goods was that the AKTU countries received among the largest subsidies from central transfers of any region in the FSU. Table 3.5 also shows the share of net fiscal transfers in GDP in 1989 based on Orlowski (1995). Armenia is an exception, driven by special support following the 1989 earthquake. Again with the exception of Azerbaijan, the AKTU countries received around 8 per cent of GDP in central transfers, with Kazakhstan and Uzbekistan benefiting the most. The western CIS and the Baltic states, by contrast, made moderate positive contributions into the central budget.

With the breakdown of the Soviet Union, both implicit and explicit transfers largely disappeared. Ruling elites in the CIS countries were thus faced with a serious challenge: how to replace implicit and explicit transfers in order to maintain their support base. It is in this respect that access to resource rents becomes crucial.

### Resource rents and economic policy during transition

Our basic framework follows Dalmazzo and de Blasio (2001). In their model, an autocratic government maximizes its revenue through rent appropriation by extracting resource wealth directly and by taxing business activity.

Economic reform reduces the ability of the government to appropriate rents through both mechanisms, while increasing production of non-resource output. In this set up, the presence of natural resources reduces reform incentives, because the direct effect on rent appropriation outweighs the indirect effect of increased business activity.[10] Dalmazzo and de Blasio also extend the model to the case of foreign aid and show how credible conditionality can lead to the adoption of reform policies, while non-conditional aid is equivalent to resource wealth in its negative effect on reform.

We extend this basic framework with an argument about government turnover at the start of transition. The incumbent government is closely associated with those interest groups that benefited most from the system of explicit and implicit transfers during Soviet times. As these transfers disappear with the break-up of the Soviet Union, incumbent elites will only remain in power if they can find a source of revenues to maintain transfers to their supporters. Natural resources are obviously a key potential source of revenues in this regard and we therefore would expect government turnover to be lower in resource-rich economies. Indeed, for the CCA countries, transition simply eliminated the 'Moscow loop' in the flow of resources, but did not have more fundamental distributional consequences aside from making some of the middlemen between Moscow and the republics redundant. We might expect this to be reflected in a higher degree of political cohesion and continuity with less of a challenge to the ruling elite than in resource-poor countries.

Looking at political turnover during the early transition period corroborates our general argument. Azerbaijan, Kazakhstan, Turkmenistan and Uzbekistan all have heads of state who were high communist officials during Soviet times. In the latter three countries these heads of state already stood at the helm of their country at the time of independence (Table 3.6). In all countries, moreover, the president has direct control over key natural resources. In contrast, the western CIS (and eastern Europe) were by and large characterized by a much higher degree of government turnover during the initial years of transition. Moreover, Table 3.6 reveals that the extent of political cohesion was also much higher in the AKTU countries, indicating the extent to which political preferences were aligned with the interests of the incumbent elites.

While this chapter does not try to offer a unified explanation for transition patterns in the whole of the CIS, it is worthwhile exploring the implications of the above arguments for the energy-poor CIS countries. There, implicit and explicit transfers were greatly reduced with no compensating gains from increased rent appropriation from the natural resources sector. This is reflected in higher turnover and less political cohesion. The only compensation for the loss of transfers was international support from IFIs and western donors. Since this support was conditional on implementing reform, we expect a higher degree of reform in resource-poor countries, even if their governments were not *per se* interested in economic reform. Indeed, the most rapid reform progress during the first four years of transition among the

*Table 3.6* Government turnover and social cohesion in transition economies

| | Government turnover (Mean tenure of government in months 1990–98) | Social cohesion (Share of seats held by ex-communists in first parliament) | (Share of seats held by largest non-communist party) |
|---|---|---|---|
| CEE | | | |
| Czech Republic | 25.5 | 16 | 55 |
| Estonia | 15.0 | 0 | 47 |
| Latvia | 20.8 | 9 | 43 |
| Lithuania | 15.0 | 14 | 80 |
| Hungary | 13.3 | 26 | 31 |
| Poland | 14.3 | 35 | 38 |
| Slovak Republic | 25.5 | 16 | 39 |
| Slovenia | 52.0 | 14 | 17 |
| Other CIS | | | |
| Armenia | 52.5 | 2 | 87 |
| Belarus | 52.5 | 79 | 21 |
| Georgia | 49.0 | 26 | 63 |
| Kyrgyzstan | 53.0 | 100 | 0 |
| Moldova | 26.5 | 38 | 35 |
| Tajikistan | 106.0 | 99 | 1 |
| Ukraine | 52.5 | 72 | 28 |
| Russia | 105.0 | 40 | 40 |
| AKTU | | | |
| Azerbaijan | 33.0 | 78 | 13 |
| Kazakhstan | 105.0 | 94 | 6 |
| Turkmenistan | 108.0 | 100 | 0 |
| Uzbekistan | 106.0 | 100 | 0 |

*Source:* EBRD 1999: Chapter 5.

former Soviet countries was made by the Baltic states, Kyrgyzstan and Moldova, while Armenia and Georgia made rapid headway once the regional conflict and instability in the Caucasus subsided.

One could ask, of course, why resource-rich countries would not reform as well in order to access western assistance and FDI. To the extent that this assistance outweighed the immediate loss to rent appropriation from reform, this would indeed be expected and we find that Azerbaijan and Kazakhstan chose this route during the early 1990s. As energy resources become more developed and the incumbents strengthen their hold on power, however, we would expect reform incentives to weaken, leading to less progress or even reversal in key reform dimensions. This phase is only beginning now but it points to the challenges ahead.

Finally, it is important to see this interpretation of the political economy of reforms in resource-rich transition economies not as a deterministic model of policy formation. A basic assumption of the model that underlies these stark conclusions is that governments in CCA countries are only interested in their revenues and do not care about society more generally. Once we allow for a government that cares for social welfare as well as for its own welfare, economic reforms become more likely even in resource-rich economies. This is why government turnover matters. Political competition increases the likelihood that a social welfare-maximizing government can assume power. Indeed, when the government is only concerned with social welfare it will always reform as long as reforms increase aggregate resources and welfare.

Governments thus always have real policy choices. With this in mind, the final section of the chapter looks at the experience of successful resource-rich economies around the world and draws some lessons for longer-term policy.

## Pathways out of excessive resource dependence

International evidence suggests that the AKTU countries will have to make special efforts to avoid the 'resource curse' of low growth and high volatility characteristic of many other resource-based economies (Sachs and Warner 1995; Auty and Mikesell 1998; Leite and Weidmann 1999; Dalmazzo and de Blasio 2001; Gylfason 2001). Four channels through which resource abundance may slow economic growth are typically highlighted in the literature: (a) the Dutch disease; (b) neglect of education; (c) rent seeking; and (d) poor economic policies or overconfidence.

These problems seldom occur in isolation. A typical sequence in a country failing to capitalize on its resource endowments could run as follows (see Auty and Mikesell 1998). High capital inflows during resource booms have a tendency to push up real wages and erode the competitiveness of the non-resource-based tradable goods sector. To some extent this is unavoidable and an efficient outcome of a resource windfall. However, it is often exacerbated by excessive public spending (i.e. in excess of what could be sustained over the long term by the additional resource-related income). The allocation of public resources is often on wasteful investment or bloated public sector employment in return for political loyalty, thereby distorting incentives. Large public spending further pushes up the real exchange rate, above its equilibrium level, causing external imbalances and increasing reliance on foreign borrowing to sustain public consumption once commodity prices fall or an important natural resource deposit becomes exhausted. Finally, macroeconomic instability results, investment is further discouraged and growth grinds to a halt (or turns negative).

The evidence presented in this chapter suggests that the problems of resource dependence may to some extent already have started to afflict the AKTU countries. They need not fall into the resource trap, however. The policy choices that must be made in order to turn natural resources into a blessing rather than a curse are not intellectually demanding – although they are likely to be politically difficult to implement. A small number of countries have actually made these choices, despite starting out as resource-dependent economies, and as a result have successfully developed. These countries are

Botswana, Chile, Malaysia and Thailand.[11] The experience of the successful resource-rich countries shows that management of resource windfalls and economic diversification are central to sustained economic growth. Indeed, in order to shelter itself from possible price swings and make best use of its resources, an economy can either diversify its asset portfolio or its economic production base, or both.

For an economy with exceptionally rich resource endowments, significant diversification of the production structure may not be a realistic aim. If returns to resource exploitation are very high, a high degree of specialization in production may be a natural outcome, in line with both short-run and long-run or dynamic comparative advantage. However, in such a case, financial portfolio diversification becomes of fundamental importance. Strong budgetary institutions and responsible fiscal policy are important prerequisites for successful portfolio diversification. Governments should only spend the share of resource revenues considered part of permanent income. Resource windfalls (which can be mediated either through the public or through the private sector) should be used to buy foreign assets, repay external debt or to invest in domestic projects with high and long-lasting social rates of return. For this a modern, well-regulated financial sector is needed that can effectively intermediate between domestic savings and international capital markets. In some cases, the creation of a government-owned but independently managed national savings fund can also provide an effective tool for portfolio diversification.[12]

For economies with a variety of production factors, economic diversification is feasible and resource rents could be partially used to lay the foundations to further the growth of the non-resource sector. It would appear that most AKTU countries, with the possible exception of Turkmenistan (which is very highly specialized in natural gas and cotton production) fall into the latter category. Economic diversification can be aided by complementary investments in physical infrastructure and human capital but is probably most directly linked to the investment climate for private business. Predictable government policies, low levels of red tape, stable tax rates and a level playing field for all businesses are the key ingredients of such a positive investment climate.

As the development of AKTU's substantial energy resources progresses, two further challenges will become ever more important. The first is to reform the domestic energy sector itself. Domestic energy producers will hardly be able to raise the external financing required, as long as they remain burdened with providing subsidies to domestic consumers by selling at below world market prices. These subsidies can be maintained because the government largely controls the transport infrastructure needed to access external markets. Yet, precisely this control also reduces the attraction of the AKTU countries to foreign investors. A policy to liberalize access to transportation while embarking on serious domestic price reform is thus needed. Again, Kazakhstan has moved furthest in this regard and with the Caspian Pipeline

Consortium now has the first non-state-owned pipeline from the Caspian to world markets in operation.

The second challenge will be to create the basis for prudent long-term fiscal management. Both Azerbaijan and Kazakhstan have established national stabilization funds to manage expected resource windfalls. Their independence from political interference remains yet to be tested. Moreover, such stabilization funds are likely to be ineffective if not embedded into an overall medium-term fiscal framework, which is still evolving in both countries. Kazakhstan has also introduced a funded pension system, which is expected to boost domestic savings over the medium term, and made progress in strengthening its financial system to better handle the required portfolio diversification. The other AKTU countries lag far behind. In the long run it is likely that fiscal prudence will only be achieved if the government becomes more accountable in all its operations to the population at large. This suggests that in addition to issues of economic management, the question of political reform is likely to force itself on to the agenda sooner or later.

## Conclusions

This chapter has drawn a link between the rather disappointing reform performance of the energy-rich transition countries and their natural resource wealth. We have argued that the incentives of governments to implement reforms in resource-rich economies are reduced, as this would lead to a reduction in their ability to appropriate resource rents. The larger the rents, the less likely are reforms. We find some evidence for this pattern in the experience of the AKTU economies compared with the remainder of the CIS to date.

However, it would be an exaggeration to see resource wealth, even during the past decade, purely as a curse for the AKTU countries. Their energy wealth has allowed them to attract far greater inflows of FDI than other CIS economies, with the corresponding positive impact on domestic suppliers, and technological and business standards. In Azerbaijan and Kazakhstan in particular, this together with the assistance of IFIs has provided an anchor for economic policy that has allowed reform progress to be made during the first decade of independence. Still, judged against its potential, the region's performance has been disappointing. More reform will be needed if the present economic upswing in the region is not to disappear with the next global downturn in oil and gas prices.

Looking ahead, the crucial challenge remains to improve the business climate for private enterprises in order to provide the basis for economic diversification. This issue has dominated during the first ten years and remains possibly the most prominent concern. All four AKTU economies could do more to liberalize foreign trade, simplify domestic licensing and business registration, strengthen financial institutions and improve tax collection practices to make it easier to set up new businesses. Kazakhstan is most advanced in this regard, while in Turkmenistan reforms have hardly begun.

# Notes

1 The views and opinions expressed in this paper are those of the authors: Akram Esanov, Martin Raiser and Willem Buiter. They do not reflect the views and opinions of the European Bank for Reconstruction and Development or the World Bank. Comments from Rick Auty, Sam Fankhauser, Clemens Grafe, Peter Sanfey and Yelena Kalyuzhnova on an earlier draft are gratefully acknowledged. The authors are also grateful to Natalya Shevchik and Katrin Tinn for research assistance on the calculation of resource rents.

2 We choose the slightly awkward acronym AKTU rather than the geographical label 'Caspian', since Uzbekistan does not actually lie on the Caspian Sea.

3 Unfortunately, initial instability of political elites in the resource-poor CIS countries gave way to retrenchment of the old guard with many reformers progressively squeezed out. IFI conditionality and initial reform outcomes have not been sufficient to consolidate a pro-reform constituency, although recent events in Georgia renew scope for change.

4 This section draws on work from Chapter 4 of the *Transition Report* 2001 (EBRD 2001).

5 The calculations in this section are highly tentative and based on partial information. A full account of the assumptions is given in the working paper version of this chapter (Esanov *et al.* 2002), which also compares our results with those in Chapter 4 of this volume. Detailed country-by-country calculations of resource rents and quasi fiscal deficits in the energy sector have been undertaken for Azerbaijan (EBRD 2001), Russia (Renaissance Capital 2002) and Uzbekistan (EBRD 2001).

6 Some transit countries, such as Belarus and Ukraine, have actually leveraged their control over export routes to extract very significant transit rents, which could explain their reform hesitation. To the extent that transit rents accrue to domestic pipeline operators, they can be treated analytically the same way as producer rents or export rents – that is as a source of tax revenue for the government.

7 The data on domestic oil and gas prices in Uzbekistan reported in EBRD (2001) are considerably below earlier estimates obtained from IMF Country Reports. For gas prices the difference is so large that we report only 2000 estimates for domestic subsidies and producer rents using World Bank data. Estimates presented in Esanov *et al.* (2002) suggest domestic subsidies were negative in the Uzbek gas sector, a finding that contradicts the received expert opinion in the country.

8 The difference between AKTU and CIS non-oil economies for price liberalization is marginally significant at the 12 per cent significance level.

9 The author notes these shortcomings himself and says his calculations are a 'plausibility test' (Orlowski 1993: 1002).

10 It is of course possible to imagine that reforms would increase effective tax revenues from the business sector and still encourage its growth. In this case, the effect of resources on reform might be immaterial, depending on the weight of the respective revenue sources.

11 Note, of course, that none of these countries is an important oil producer.

12 On the risks of political influence over national stabilisation funds, see IMF (2000).

# References

Auty, R. and Mikesell, R. (1998) *Sustainable Development in Mineral Economies*, Oxford University Press, Clarendon.

Dalmazzo, A. and de Blasio, G. (2001) 'Resources and incentives to reform: A model and some evidence on sub-Saharan African countries', IMF Working Paper No. 86, Washington DC.

EBRD (1999, 2001), *Transition Report*, London: EBRD.

Esanov, A., Raiser, M. and Buiter, W. (2002) Nature's blessing or nature's curse: The political economy of transition in resource-based economies, EBRD Working Paper 66, London: EBRD.

Gürgen E. *et al.* (1999) 'Economic reforms in Kazakhstan, Kyrgyz Republic, Tajikistan, Turkmenistan, and Uzbekistan', IMF Occasional Paper No. 183, Washington DC.

Gylfason, T. (2001) 'Nature, power, and growth', CESinfo Working Paper No. 413.

IMF (2000) Stabilization and savings funds for nonrenewable resources: Experience and fiscal policy implications, IMF Policy Paper, November 2000.

IMF (2002), Selected issues and Statistical Appendix, Country Economic Report 02/ 41, Washington DC: IMF.

Kalyuzhnova, Y., Jaffe, A., Lynch, D. and Sickles, R. (eds.) (2001) *Energy in the Caspian Region: Present and Future*, London, Palgrave.

Leite, C. and Weidmann, J. (1999) 'Does Mother Nature corrupt? Natural resources, corruption and economic growth', IMF Working Paper No. 85, 1999.

Orlowski, L. (1993) 'Indirect transfers in trade among Former Soviet Union Republics: Sources, patterns, and policy responses in the post-Soviet period', *Europe-Asia Studies* 45(6), 1001–1024.

Orlowski, L. (1995) 'Direct transfers between the Former Soviet Union Central Budget and the Republics: Past evidence and current implications', *Economics of Planning*, 58(1), 59–73.

Pastor, G. and van Rooden, R. (2000) 'Turkmenistan: the burden of current agricultural policies', IMF Working Paper No. 98, 2000.

Pomfret, R. (2002) 'Resource abundance, governance and economic performance in turkmenistan and Uzbekistan', University of Adelaide, School of Economics, mimeo.

Renaissance Capital (2002) *Gazprom: The Dawning of a New Valuation Era*, London: Renaissance Capital.

Sachs, J. and Warner, A. (1995) 'Natural resource abundance and economic growth', NBER Working Paper No. 5398.

Tarr, D.G. (1993) 'How moving to world prices affects the terms of trade in 15 countries of the former Soviet Union', Policy Research Working Paper No. 1074, World Bank.

Tornell, A. and Lane, P. (1999) 'The voracity effect', *American Economic Review* 89(1), 22–46.

Walters, J. (2000) 'Caspian oil and gas: Mitigating political risks for private participation', *The Centre for Energy, Petroleum and Mineral Law and Policy Journal*, 7, Article 5.

World Bank (2000) *World Development Indicators*, Washington, DC.

# 4 Optimistic and pessimistic energy rent deployment scenarios for Azerbaijan and Kazakhstan

*Richard M. Auty*

This chapter assesses the impact of increased energy rents on the two oil-rich CCA states, Azerbaijan and Kazakhstan. We have already established that oil rents can be a blessing or a curse, depending upon the nature of the political state. Under a developmental political state the natural resource rents from oil exploitation can facilitate economic reform by expanding the capacity to import and invest, and thereby accelerate the economic restructuring that will sustain rapid PCGDP growth.

However, the STEX model shows that rent-rich countries tend to nurture predatory states that deploy the oil rents so they may retard the transition to a market economy in three basic ways. First, rents allow predatory political states to consolidate their power by feeding rent-seeking patronage networks and corruption, which distort economic incentives and reduce the efficiency of investment and undermine wealth creation (Leite and Weidmann 2002). Second, the 'point' socio-economic linkages of oil production concentrate rents overwhelmingly on the government, which in the case of a predatory political state is likely to absorb them too rapidly (Bevan *et al.* 1987; Gelb and Associates 1988), rendering the economy vulnerable to a growth collapse. Third, economic restructuring will be retarded if the initial capital inflow to refurbish and expand oil production causes the post-transition rebound of the real exchange rate to quickly overshoot its equilibrium level (Rosenberg and Saavalainen 1998). This will expand the shares of capital-intensive mining and domestic services in GDP at the expense of agriculture and manufacturing (the Dutch disease effect), bringing recession through the short term and slowing economic growth over the medium and long term. Under these circumstances, PCGDP may be significantly lower in the long term than would have been the case without oil rent if the shrinking sectors, like manufacturing, exhibit positive externalities for the rest of the economy, like learning by doing. Nigeria provides a classic example of this.

This chapter develops both optimistic and pessimistic scenarios of the evolution of the political economy through the emerging oil booms in Azerbaijan and Kazakhstan. It begins in the next section (pages 58–63), by projecting the potential scale of the oil revenues in Azerbaijan and Kazakhstan relative

58    Richard M. Auty

to non-oil GDP. The third section (pages 63–66) then briefly summarizes the conditions required to optimize the benefits from the energy rents and projects optimistic scenarios for each country. The fourth section (pages 66–72) identifies existing institutional gaps that jeopardize the optimistic scenarios and considers whether they can be filled. The final section five (pages 72–74) speculates on pessimistic scenarios for the evolving political economy of each country.

## Projected oil revenues in Kazakhstan and Azerbaijan

Chapter 3 developed broad-brush estimates of the current scale of the potential energy rents, which are overestimates to the extent that Caspian production costs are relatively high and rent leakage is substantial. An additional complication arises from the fact that the scale of hydrocarbon reserves in the Caspian Basin remains uncertain. For example, BP (2003) records the proven oil reserves of Kazakhstan as 9 billion barrels compared with 7 billion barrels in Azerbaijan, while proven gas reserves are recorded as 1.84 trillion cubic meters and 0.85 trillion, respectively. Some upward revision in the BP figures can be expected because mineral companies tend towards cautious estimation. However, Azerbaijan is unlikely to see a substantial rise in its reserves because the south-western Caspian is a mature oil province and recent exploration has been disappointing. There is a much greater likelihood of a significant rise in Kazakh reserves. Wood McKenzie suggests reserves are several times larger than BP shows (Table 4.1). The IMF (2003a: 16) also puts the proved and potential oil reserves of Kazakhstan at 30 billion barrels, but in addition it recognizes the possibility that new discoveries (largely in the northern Caspian Sea) together with enhanced technology could double that figure. The sizeable difference in the scale of energy reserves between Kazakhstan and Azerbaijan generates contrasting oil revenue streams.

*Table 4.1* Estimated recoverable oil and gas, Caspian Sea region 2002

|  | Oil (bbls) | Gas (bcf) | Total (billion boe) | Gas % total |
|---|---|---|---|---|
| Azerbaijan | 6.63 | 21.34 | 10.384 | 36.2 |
| Kazakhstan | 29.84 | 93.31 | 46.262 | 35.5 |
| Russia[1] | 0.75 | 1.25 | 0.970 | 22.7 |
| Turkmenistan | 2.18 | 91.06 | 18.200 | 88.0 |

*Source:* McCutcheson and Osbon 2001.

*Note*
1. Caspian portion only.
Memo item: Uzbekistan possible reserves estimated at 1.2 bbls of oil and 32 bcf of gas (State Department (1997).

*Azerbaijan's brief intense boom*

In order to measure the potential rent from oil production, it is necessary to estimate the level of production, the price of oil and the rent per unit of production. The inherent uncertainty regarding predictions can be taken into account by projecting three scenarios (high, medium and low). Until recently, high case scenarios for Azerbaijan assumed that the Azeri International Oil Corporation (AIOC) might exploit two additional large oilfields and that one or more of nine other production-sharing agreements would prove fruitful. Rapid exploitation of these concessions would have boosted Azeri oil output to 3 million bpd by 2007 (Financial Times 1998). However, large new discoveries now look doubtful so it is more realistic to assume that for all three scenarios Azerbaijan relies on the 'early oil' that AIOC began to produce in 1998. In the absence of further discoveries or of improved extractive efficiency production will rise swiftly to peak at 1.3 million bpd during 2009–13, before falling to modest levels by 2020 (Table 4.2, row 1).

The three Azeri scenarios are therefore principally differentiated from each other on the basis of the international oil price, which is believed to fluctuate around a long-term cycle. The cycle is generated by the capital-intensive nature of oil production, which renders long-run investment lumpy so that global demand and supply are often out of balance. This causes over- and under-investment, which appear to drive a twenty-five-year price cycle. Briefly, high oil prices trigger over-investment that gluts the world market, which depresses prices and cuts investment. But lower prices also stimulate consumption, which steadily removes surplus capacity over a period of ten to fifteen years. Shortages then cause a price spike (as in 1999) that spurs renewed investment for around eight to ten years before surplus capacity creates another glut and the price cycle repeats itself. In this context, most oil price forecasts assume a fall towards a long-run price of $18/bl, with the

*Table 4.2* Azerbaijan: oil and gas fiscal revenues 1999–2000, with projections to 2020

|  | 1999 | 2000 | 2005 | 2010 | 2015 | 2020 |
|---|---|---|---|---|---|---|
| Production (m tons) | 13.8 | 14.6 | 17.9 | 66.7 | 48.6 | 27.9 |
| Production (mbpd: 7.33 bls/ton) | 0.277 | 0.293 | 0.359 | 1.339 | 0.976 | 0.560 |
| Oil prices (US$/bl) | 18.0 | 28.0 | 18.0 | 18.0 | 23.0 | 25.4 |
| Total oil revenue (US$ billion) | 0.165 | 0.320 | 0.591 | 1.557 | 1.095 | 0.920 |
| Estimated GDP (US$ billion) | 4.004 | 4.324 | 6.354 | 12.102 | 17.780 | 26.125 |
| Oil revenue share of GDP (%) | 4.1 | 7.4 | 9.3 | 12.9 | 6.2 | 3.5 |

*Source:* World Bank 2002a.

*Note*: Absent new finds, oil production will plateau 2008–13 and then fall sharply.

possibility of sharp gyrations caused by political shocks, such as the two Gulf Wars or a growth spurt in a large emerging economy like China. The downward pressure on prices reflects new oil discoveries (including those in the Caspian Basin), the ability of OPEC producers like Kuwait and Saudi Arabia to expand output and the expected return of Iraq to full production. Consequently, the oil prices used to develop the scenarios in this study are $18/bl for the medium case, and $24 and $12 for the high and low cases, respectively.

The rent per barrel is determined by the production costs and price, moderated by the production sharing agreement (PSA). The AIOC PSA front-loads capital recovery so that the AIOC can take up to 60 per cent of the oil price to recoup its operating costs and capital costs, including interest. The residual revenue is deemed 'profit oil' from which the government takes 35 per cent. Once cost recovery is complete (likely around 2010), the state oil company, SOCAR, takes 50 per cent of the profit oil and the government takes 15 per cent and the oil contractors 35 per cent, depending on prices and costs (Bagirov *et al.* 2003: 102–3). During the initial phase of heavy capital investment and capital recoupment the rent is squeezed because production costs are two to three times higher than those of more accessible fields in the Middle East (Table 4.3). The capital costs tend to be especially high in the Caspian Basin because substantial investments are required to regenerate the run-down Azeri oil extraction system and expand capacity, while remoteness from markets pushes up transportation costs. The costs of production in Table 4.3 may fall significantly once capital costs are recouped so that all else being equal the rent per barrel may rise significantly. In the mean time, however, the potential rent accruing to the government is smaller than in the Middle East and may be zero under the low price scenario.

*Table 4.3* Estimated cost of oil production, South-west Caspian Basin (US$/Barrel)

| Category | US$ |
|---|---|
| Finding[a] | 0.50 |
| Development (capital)[b] | 2.27 |
| Operating[c] | 2.00 |
| Pipeline tariffs[d] | 3.41 |
| Maritime shipping[e] | 1.03 |
| MNC + Local firm net income (75/25 equity)[f] | 1.32 |
| Corporate tax (25%) | 0.47 |
| Total production cost | 11.01 |

*Source:* After Planecon 1997, except c.

*Notes*
a. Based on 7 majors' world-wide average.
b. Based on estimates for 7 majors in FSU.
c. Bagirov *et al.* 2003, 180.
d. Estimates that assume minimal use of local material and skill inputs.
e. Based on rates from Black Sea to Europe.
f. Based on Tengizchevroil (TCO) Agreement.

In evaluating the economic impact of the rent, the absolute value is less critical than the size relative to GDP. Taking IMF (2002b) assumptions about the potential GDP growth rate (see footnote to Table 4.4), the *potential* rent across the low and high case Azeri scenarios ranges from zero to almost 50 per cent of GDP. At $18/bl the medium case scenario yields rents of around 10 per cent of GDP through the early part of the decade, rising sharply to 20 per cent in 2010 as production reaches the mid-point of its projected plateau. Revenues on this scale are double those that Venezuelan governments found so difficult to manage during the oil booms of 1974–78 and 1979–81 (Gelb and Associates 1988: 63–5). Using similar assumptions to those of the IMF but taking account of the impact of the PSA on oil rent distribution, the World Bank (2002a) estimates actual government oil revenues may average 6.2 per cent of GDP annually 2001–5 and 11.7 per cent of GDP 2006–10 (Table 4.2). The share of government revenue in total oil revenue will then jump substantially if, as expected, capital recovery is complete by 2010. The higher rent per barrel will offset to some extent the decline in oil output after 2013 to slow the fall in government revenue.

If prices collapse below $12/bl (the low case), the potential rents are eliminated although the PSA would still confer oil revenue on the government. Moreover, the build-up in oil investment would still propel GDP growth. The oil sector invested almost $3.5 billion in Azerbaijan from 1995–2000 and planned a further $13 billion for 2001–5. Most of this investment leaks out of the economy on imports, but AIOC estimates that one-fifth is expended domestically, currently equivalent to one-tenth of GDP annually.

*Table 4.4* Potential rent: Azerbaijan and Kazakhstan oil and gas, three price scenarios

| | Azerbaijan | | | Kazakhstan | | |
|---|---|---|---|---|---|---|
| | *2000* | *2005* | *2010* | *2000* | *2005* | *2010* |
| Unit rent ($/bl)[a] | | | | | | |
| 12.00 | – | – | – | – | – | – |
| 18.00 | 5.15 | 5.15 | 5.15 | 3.75 | 3.75 | 3.75 |
| 24.00 | 11.15 | 11.15 | 11.15 | 9.75 | 9.75 | 9.75 |
| Total rent ($ billion) | | | | | | |
| 12.00 | – | – | – | – | – | – |
| 18.00 | 0.550 | 0.675 | 2.517 | 0.973 | 1.838 | 2.565 |
| 24.00 | 1.192 | 1.461 | 5.449 | 2.530 | 4.779 | 6.669 |
| Total rent (% GDP)[b] | | | | | | |
| 12.00 | – | – | – | – | – | – |
| 18.00 | 12.7 | 10.6 | 20.8 | 5.3 | 7.0 | 7.0 |
| 24.00 | 27.60 | 22.3 | 45.0 | 13.9 | 18.2 | 18.1 |

*Notes*
a. Kazak oil price discounted by $2/bl due to impurities.
b. Azeri GDP = $4.004 billion in 1999 and grows 8%/year 1999–2005, then 40% in 2006 and 8%/year 2006–10.
  Kazak GDP $16.495 in 1999 and grows 9.5% 2000–01 and 7% 2001–2010.

Nevertheless, the vulnerability of the economy to a price collapse was shown in 1998, when prices fell below $10/bl and AIOC more than halved its investment expenditure. The sensitivity of the economy to oil price swings is shown by the estimate that a decline in the price of oil of $1/bl cuts slightly more than 0.5 per cent from GDP (and slightly less for Kazakhstan).

### Kazakhstan's relatively smaller, but more durable oil rent stream

Oil production in Kazakhstan is currently projected to peak a decade later than in Azerbaijan, at 3 million bpd in 2016, and to sustain a longer plateau (World Bank 2002b). This projection carries a relatively high degree of certainty because it reflects committed investments. It is taken as the basis for the low and medium case scenarios. However, the high case scenario assumes peak production is one-third higher, reflecting the greater probability of additional oil discoveries in Kazakhstan than Azerbaijan.

Oil extraction costs in the northern Caspian differ from Azerbaijan. Table 4.5 estimates Kazakh production costs assuming that oil is shipped through the CPC pipeline, which cut transport costs by $4/bl compared with earlier routes (ibid.). Extraction costs are lower than those of Azerbaijan but impurities in Kazakh oil trim the price by around $2/bl. Assuming these costs and the production volumes, Table 4.4 projects that by 2010 rents will range under the low and high cases from zero to 18 per cent of GDP, on a rising trend. Assuming 30 billion barrels of oil reserves and the need to maintain inter-generational equity the IMF (2002a) estimates that the reserves would be depleted over the years 2000–48. Under the medium case scenario, the net present value of the oil wealth to the government of Kazakhstan is $59 billion, whereas the total rent is $141 billion. Over half the rent accrues to private investors as a return to the specialized capital, technology and

*Table 4.5* Estimated cost of oil production, North Caspian (US$/barrel)

| Category | US$ |
| --- | --- |
| Finding Cost[a] | 0.50 |
| Development (capital) | 1.50 |
| Operating cost | 2.00 |
| Pipeline tariffs[b] | 3.40 |
| Maritime shipping cost[c] | 1.00 |
| MNC + Local firm net income (75/25 equity)[d] | 1.30 |
| Corporate tax (30%) | 0.55 |
| Total revenue requirement | 10.25 |

*Sources:* World Bank 2002a, Planecon 1997.

Notes
a. Based on 7 majors' worldwide average.
b. Completion of CTC pipeline cuts transport cost by $4/bl.
c. Based on rates from Black Sea to Europe.
d. Based on AIOC Agreement.

marketing services that they provide. This is a source of friction between the government and MNCs that seems likely to intensify, especially if the perceived risk of investment in Kazakhstan continues to fall (Ebel 2003).

As with Azerbaijan, the low case scenario eliminates the rents for Kazakhstan. The middle case scenario confers smaller rents relative to GDP than that for Azerbaijan, but the rent stream is projected to be less erratic and to last twice as long. Table 4.6 uses World Bank and IMF estimates, including PSA allocations, to project annual oil revenues for the government of around 4–6 per cent of GDP. Finally, the high case scenario assumes an oil price one-third above the medium case scenario and output one-third (1 million bpd) higher. This almost triples the potential rent stream (Table 4.4) and pushes peak production to 2022. It also implies that production may still exceed 1 mbpd in 2050 (IMF 2003a: 5). Even so, the high case scenario (like the low case) does not represent the upper (lower) extreme of the production scenarios. Consequently, both countries are vulnerable to strong price shocks, with Azerbaijan more at risk because of its briefer, more intense rent stream. The case for constructing effective institutions to mitigate risk is therefore strong.

## Policies and institutions for maximizing oil-driven social welfare

Basically, sustainable development from a finite resource like minerals calls for a developmental political state to invest sufficient rent in alternative

*Table 4.6* Kazakhstan: oil fiscal revenues 1999–2000, with projections to 2040

|  | 1999 | 2000 | 2005 | 2010 | 2015 | 2020 | 2030 | 2040 |
|---|---|---|---|---|---|---|---|---|
| Production (m tons) | 29.4 | 35.4 | 66.9 | 93.1 | 127.6 | 139.4 | 135.7 | 80.0 |
| Production (mbpd: 7.33 bls/ton) | 0.590 | 0.711 | 1.343 | 1.874 | 2.522 | 2.799 | 2.725 | 1.607 |
| Oil prices (US$/bl) | 18.0 | 28.0 | 18.0 | 18.0 | 23.0 | 25.4 | 30.0 | 37.7 |
| Total oil revenue (US$ billion) | 0.178 | 0.965 | 1.099 | 1.372 | 2.830 | 4.600 | 7.75 | 2.400 |
| Estimated GDP (US$ billion) | 16.49 | 18.25 | 26.31 | 36.91 | 51.76 | 72.60 | 142.82 | 280.96 |
| Oil revenue share of GDP (%) | 1.1 | 5.3 | 4.2 | 3.7 | 5.5 | 6.3 | 5.4 | 0.9 |

*Source:* World Bank 2002b for 1999–2010; IMF 2002a for 2015–2040.

*Note:* Absent further oil finds, oil production will plateau 2016–23 around 3 million bpd and then fall. Assumed post–2001 GDP growth rate of 7%.

wealth-generating assets to competitively diversify the economy. This will ensure that when the mineral is exhausted the same annual income stream that emanated from oil extraction is sustained in perpetuity. There are three basic institutional requirements to maintain the income component of the mineral stream (and also minimize distortion of the economy by Dutch disease effects). First, sterilize a fraction of the rent in a capital development fund, much invested abroad, in order to slow domestic absorption of the rents and thereby match the rent invested internally to domestic absorptive capacity. This will mute Dutch disease effects and evade the staple trap. Second, deploy a mineral revenue stabilization fund to smooth trends in public expenditure and buffer it from a possible rent collapse. Third, efficiently evaluate alternative public investment options to make sure that rent from the capital development fund is allocated to those projects with the highest social return so that the rent is deployed most efficiently to create alternative wealth-producing assets. The associated high level of transparency conferred by these three institutions lowers the risk of the rent being diverted into personal gain and capital flight.

Assuming a developmental political state that pursues appropriate economic and institutional reforms, then World Bank projections under the mid case scenarios allow for GDP growth rates of 8 per cent per annum for Azerbaijan, albeit with a higher spike around 2006 (Table 4.2) and slightly slower growth for Kazakhstan (Table 4.6). Both growth rates approximately double GDP each decade. *Per capita* GDP also doubles rapidly, given low population growth. Consequently, by 2020 the per capita income of Kazakhstan would reach that of Ireland or Israel in the mid-1990s, whereas Azerbaijan would match that of Greece (Table 4.7). Under the high case scenarios, the projected levels of per capita income might be as much as 50 per cent higher still if physical and human capital can be deployed as skillfully as in the East Asian dragon economies during 1960–90, for example.

Table 4.7 also traces changes in employment in the non-mining tradeable sectors of the two countries based on the norms for market economies with similar PCGDP (Raiser *et al.* 2001). The first two columns show change during the 1990s and include Russia for comparison with a mineral-driven economy at a higher PCGDP. The Kazakh economy already displays evidence of Dutch disease effects because employment in the tradeable sectors is barely two-thirds the norm and agricultural employment is especially weak. However, as in Russia, the oil price crash of 1998 led to a depreciation of the real exchange rate, by 20–30 per cent, which, when combined with state assistance, stimulated output in the non-oil tradeable sector (IMF 2003a: 40). If this stimulus persists, the projection to 2020 suggests that industrial employment may expand by almost 50 per cent during the years 2000–10 whereas agriculture retains a constant share of employment and then halves during 2010–20. Azerbaijan's lower per capita income means that it lags these trends by about one decade. It can also expect a sharper increase in industrial employment and a steeper contraction in agriculture due to the combination

Table 4.7 Structural change 1990–1999 and projections to 2020 (actual + norm % employment share)

| | Sector | Actual 1990 | Actual 1999 | Norm 1999 | Departure from norm in 1999 | Projected mid case norm 2010 | Projected mid case norm 2020 |
|---|---|---|---|---|---|---|---|
| Azerbaijan | PCI (US$ 1995) | 3,650 | 1,900 | 1,900 | | 3,900 | 8,000 |
| | Agriculture | 0.45 | 0.42 | 0.52 | −0.10 | 0.37 | 0.22 |
| | Industry | 0.23 | 0.12 | 0.19 | −0.07 | 0.23 | 0.26 |
| | Distortion | −0.01 | −0.17 | | | | |
| Kazakhstan | PCI (US$ 1995) | 5,400 | 3,400 | 3,400 | | 8,050 | 16,000 |
| | Agriculture | 0.22 | 0.22 | 0.38 | −0.16 | 0.22 | 0.11 |
| | Industry | 0.31 | 0.18 | 0.22 | −0.04 | 0.26 | 0.28 |
| | Distortion | −0.03 | −0.20 | | | | |
| Russia | PCI (US$ 1995) | 7,500 | 4,000 | 4,000 | | | |
| | Agriculture | 0.13 | 0.12 | 0.35 | −0.23 | | |
| | Industry | 0.42 | 0.29 | 0.23 | +0.06 | | |
| | Distortion | −0.07 | −0.17 | | | | |

Source: Raiser et al. 2001: 29 and 31.

of a strong legacy of Dutch disease effects from the first decade of transition and projected continued massive FDI inflows to rehabilitate the oil sector.

## Departure from optimum initial conditions

Such optimistic scenarios are projected on the existence of developmental political states, whereas Chapter 3 suggests that, after promising starts, both Azerbaijan and Kazakhstan have drifted towards more authoritarian regimes. Their political states function as concentrated oligarchies with considerable presidential power that has been directed at increasing wealth for the presidential family and associates. In the absence of reform to strengthen sanctions against anti-social governance, the long-term impact of energy rent on GDP is likely to be less beneficial, possibly significantly so, than is projected in Tables 4.2 and 4.6 (row 5).

### Distorted and weakened economies

Along with Turkmenistan, Azerbaijan and Kazakhstan experienced larger capital inflows relative to their GDP than other CIS transition economies. For example, per capita foreign direct investment (FDI) during 1989–2000 was $577 in Kazakhstan, $464 in Azerbaijan and $171 in Turkmenistan, the third highest (EBRD 2001: 68). This inflow of FDI was associated with a more rapid rebound in the real exchange rate compared with the resource-poor economies (Gürgen *et al.* 1999: 15; Pastor and van Rooden 2000: 7). Consistent with Dutch disease effects arising from massive investment and rapid oil expansion, Table 4.7 reveals that both economies were strongly distorted. However, since the 1998 oil price collapse the real exchange rate has softened significantly in Kazakhstan and Azerbaijan (and the resulting gains in competitiveness have not yet been wholly eroded), so that as in Russia, this has kick-started growth in agriculture, agro-processing and some machinery fabrication.

A sizeable reversal of the contraction of the non-oil tradeables must still occur, however if the staple trap is to be avoided. Table 4.7 shows that by 1999 employment in the tradeable sectors of Kazakhstan and Azerbaijan was one-quarter to one-third lower than that expected for a developing market economy at a similar level of development. In contrast, the four resource-*poor* Caspian Basin countries started the transition with a share of employment in the tradeable sector one-fifth *higher* than the norm but that gap halved to one-tenth higher to the late 1990s. This reflected a massive contraction in industry and a retreat into subsistence agriculture, which employed more than half the workforce in 1997 (Auty 2001). The oil rents helped the energy-rich countries to reduce the transition-linked contraction in government expenditure and allowed them to absorb a higher share of displaced workers in services, especially in government service in Kazakhstan (Table 4.8). But the weakened non-mining tradeable sector in both countries renders competitive diversification a critical requirement.

*Table 4.8* Revenue, expenditure and fiscal compression by reform group 1992–1998

| Pre-condition group | Income inequality (gini 1996–99) | Government expenditure (% GDP) | | | Fiscal gap 1992 (% GDP) | Fiscal gap 1998 (% GDP) |
|---|---|---|---|---|---|---|
| | | 1992 | 1995 | 1998 | | |
| Mid income | | | | | | |
| Central + E Europe | 0.31[a] | 42.7 | 44.7 | 44.3 | −3.3 | −2.7 |
| Northern CIS + SEE[b] | 0.37 | 50.5 | 41.0 | 37.1 | −12.9 | −3.1 |
| Russia | 0.49 | 57.9 | 39.6 | 39.5 | −18.4 | −8.0 |
| Low income | | | | | | |
| East Asia | 0.38 | 20.2 | 19.1 | 18.8 | −5.2 | −6.2 |
| Caspian Basin | 0.45 | 0.48 | 32.4 | 25.3 | −20.5 | −6.4 |
| Resource-poor Caspian | 0.49 | 50.1 | 35.3 | 24.4 | −32.1 | −8.8 |
| Mineral-rich Caspian | 0.40[c] | 45.9 | 29.4 | 26.2 | −8.6 | −3.9 |
| Azerbaijan | n.a. | 80.0 | 45.9 | 18.8 | −28.3 | −1.7 |
| Kazakhstan | 0.35 | 31.9 | 26.2 | 25.8 | −9.3 | −7.6 |

*Source:* Tanzi and Tsibouris 2001: 245–246, except column 1: World Bank 2004: 140, and row 1 ADB 2000: 264.

*Notes*
a. Excludes Slovak Republic.
b. South and East Europe.
c. Excludes Azerbaijan and Uzbekistan.

The Azeri economy is particularly dependent on rising oil rents and investment to sustain GDP growth. By 2002 the oil sector provided 89 per cent of exports, 29.5 per cent of GDP, 55 per cent of government revenues but only 1.1 per cent of employment (IMF 2003b). Whereas the oil sector grew at 20 per cent per annum in the late 1990s the non-oil sector grew at 6 per cent, mostly services. Oil dominated investment (World Bank 1998) and propelled the economy. Dutch disease effects created high levels of import dependence, including food, which may be harder to reverse than theorists like van Wijnbergen (1984) assume. By 2002 the public sector still generated over one-third of GDP and although two-thirds of jobs were in the private sector, many were in subsistence agriculture and help explain the high poverty rate, estimated at 50 per cent (World Bank 2002a). The Azeri energy-producing state-owned enterprises (SOEs) were still used for quasi-fiscal purposes, effectively subsidizing energy suppliers, industrial consumers and households to the tune of 11 per cent of GDP in 2002 (down from 27 per cent in 1999) through under-pricing, tolerance of payment arrears and theft (Petri *et al.* 2002: 24).

Yet after some backsliding on economic reform, in which tariff and non-tariff barriers increased and their degree of dispersal also rose (indicating rent-seeking activity), reform resumed in Azerbaijan in 2001. This may have reflected presidential efforts to curb the access of rivals to oil rents in order to boost the chances of Aleyev's son in the leadership succession. A start was also made on downsizing the civil service and strengthening a slimmer banking sector. In addition, the government began privatizing large SOEs, excluding the state oil firm, SOCAR. Whether the younger Aleyev has the political skill to maintain this momentum remains to be seen: the increased diversion of oil rents to consolidate presidential patronage is a distinct possibility.

In Kazakhstan, a dual economy developed during the 1990s as FDI flowed into capital-intensive intermediates like oil, steel and copper whereas labor-intensive non-mining tradeables oriented towards domestic demand, like agriculture, were starved of investment. In 2002 oil accounted for 17.5 per cent of GDP, 19.5 per cent of government revenue and 56 per cent of exports (IMF 2003a). But oil extraction employs less than 2 per cent of the workforce and most other exports are capital-intensive goods like metals, which employ few workers. However, evidence of a strong pick-up in employment emerged in 2000, notably in construction and services in response to higher incomes in the oil sector, although the energy sector multiplier in Caspian countries is a sieve-like 0.47, compared with 2.0 for north-east Scotland. Agricultural employment also began to expand, but reform remains blocked by vested interests and growth reflects government incentives and subsidies after a drift towards bankruptcy in 1998 (EBRD 2002). Manufacturing is also receiving assistance that encourages rent-seeking behavior. Consequently, the recent expansion of the employment-intensive tradeable sector (first agriculture and then machinery and food-processing) is consistent with the STEX model and is unlikely to be sustainable because it relies on state assistance (from the oil rent) via price support and/or import protection, which already induces crop surpluses and policy capture.

The projected pick-up in tradeable employment 1999–2010 shown for Kazakhstan in Table 4.7 assumes that oil rent absorption does not abort *competitive* diversification of the economy. Sustainable growth of the non-oil tradeables sector requires trade reform to eliminate the high dispersion of tariffs, increased competition to limit rent-seeking and a more investor-friendly environment. Moreover, Kazakhstan's dualistic development will further increase the income gap not only between workers in the capital-intensive export sector (mining and mineral-processing) and other sectors but also between rural and urban areas, mineral-rich and mineral-poor regions and between ethnic groups (Table 4.9). Meanwhile, privatization shifted responsibility for social welfare from SOEs to oblasts, and legislation in 1999 linked local social spending to various taxes raised within the oblasts. This implies that the regions most in need of social expenditure are the least able to afford it. Yet richer oblasts like Atyrau and Pavlodar resent the scale of the rent stream flowing to the center and fear it will be amplified by efforts to alleviate regional poverty (Olcott 2002). These regional resentments and income differentials in turn feed ethnic tensions, not only between Kazakhs in the south-west and the sizeable Russian populations in Almaty and the north-east, but also between the Small Horde of Kazaks in the west and the Great

*Table 4.9* Population and per capita income, principal economic regions of Kazakhstan 1999

|  | Population (millions) | Share ethnic Kazak (%) | Per capita income (US$PPP) | Economic activity |
|---|---|---|---|---|
| Almaty | 1.13 | 38.5 | 11,935 | Financial and commercial capital |
| West | 2.06 | 74.0 | 8,076 | Oil and gas production |
| North | 6.72 | 38.3 | 5,532 | Mining, heavy industry and wheat |
| South | 5.11 | 67.8 | 2,253 | Cotton and intermediate industry |

*Source:* Anderson and Pomfret 2002: 40 and 54, except column 2 from Olcott 2002: 247–248.

Horde who dominate the poor southern region. These clan tensions retard reform and hamper its implementation (Collins 2004) so that sustainable economic growth requires political and institutional reform.

### *Quality of institutions*

After modest initial efforts at political as well as economic reform designed to encourage IFI assistance and FDI, the governments of both Kazakhstan and Azerbaijan consolidated their power at the expense of nascent democratic institutions. The Azeri parliament's power to scrutinize the budget and impeach the president became nominal in 1995 when president Aleyev's supporters 'won' all but eight of the 125 seats in the election. The country's three high courts were made subservient to the president who 'won' re-election to a further term as president in 1998. Aleyev's son succeeded him in 2003. Similarly, the Kazakh government side-lined parliament in 1995 and 'won' the 1999 election with more than 80 per cent of the vote after banning its leading opponent. Kazakhstan is a 'submerging democracy' as the Nazerbaev family centralizes power on itself, key ministers (who are disgraced if they become too powerful) and several thousand Moscow-educated officials. Such concentrated oligarchies are brittle, however, because they lack legitimacy and can swing abruptly from strength to weakness if oil rents collapse. These features are reflected in the weak 'voice and accountability' scores for both countries in Table 4.10.

However, Khan and Jomo (2000) caution that rent-seeking need not conflict with welfare-enhancing growth, citing Indonesia during 1965–95 and South Korea as examples. On a more promising note, Central Asian countries established oil funds in 2001. In Kazakhstan the fund was greatly simplified and rendered more transparent in 2002. Inflows to the fund are expected to exceed domestic requirements after meeting investment needs to improve infrastructure across the country. Consequently, a substantial fraction of

Table 4.10 Index of Institutional Quality 2002, CCA and comparator countries and regions

| Country | PCGDP (US$PPP 2002) | Voice + accountability | Political stability | Effective governance | Regulation burden | Rule of law | Graft | Overall index |
|---|---|---|---|---|---|---|---|---|
| Energy-poor | 1,998 | -0.66 | -1.21 | -0.81 | -0.61 | -1.02 | -0.97 | -5.14 |
| Tajikistan | 930 | -0.95 | -1.19 | -1.23 | -1.29 | -1.27 | -1.07 | -7.00 |
| Kyrgyz | 1,560 | -0.96 | -1.21 | -0.81 | -0.46 | -0.83 | -0.84 | -5.11 |
| Georgia | 2,270 | -0.30 | -1.90 | -0.77 | -0.82 | -1.17 | -1.03 | -5.99 |
| Armenia | 3,230 | -0.42 | -0.53 | -0.42 | 0.13 | -0.79 | -0.44 | -2.47 |
| Energy-rich | 3,765 | -1.32 | -0.42 | -1.08 | -1.24 | -1.00 | -1.05 | -6.27 |
| Uzbekistan | 1,640 | -1.66 | -0.94 | -1.10 | -1.44 | -1.16 | -1.03 | -7.33 |
| Azerbaijan | 3,010 | -0.97 | -1.13 | -0.96 | -0.82 | -0.79 | -1.07 | -5.74 |
| Turkmenistan | 4,780 | -1.85 | -0.14 | -1.47 | -1.95 | -1.16 | -1.21 | -7.78 |
| Kazakhstan | 5,630 | -1.05 | 0.52 | -0.80 | -0.74 | -0.90 | -0.87 | -3.84 |
| Three comparators | 3,317 | -0.30 | -0.82 | -0.13 | -0.25 | -0.66 | -0.43 | -2.07 |
| Angola | 1,840 | -1.39 | -1.60 | -1.16 | -1.33 | -1.56 | -1.12 | -8.16 |
| Sri Lanka | 3,510 | -0.06 | -0.90 | 0.03 | 0.12 | 0.23 | -0.14 | -0.72 |
| Trinidad + Tobago | 6,440 | 0.56 | 0.03 | 0.47 | 0.66 | 0.34 | -0.04 | 2.02 |
| Four transition areas | | | | | | | | |
| CCA | 2,882 | -0.99 | -0.82 | -0.95 | -0.43 | -1.01 | -1.01 | -5.21 |
| East Asia | 3,410 | -1.03 | 0.14 | -0.30 | -0.73 | -0.46 | -0.47 | -2.85 |
| Northern CIS + SEE | 5,630 | -0.08 | -0.15 | -0.69 | -0.99 | -0.46 | -0.90 | -2.90 |
| C. + E. Europe | 12,280 | 0.97 | 0.60 | 0.43 | 0.50 | 0.55 | 0.40 | 3.45 |

Source: World Bank 2004a.

the fund is likely to be invested in foreign financial instruments. However, consideration is also being given to investing in the infrastructure of adjacent countries in order to enhance the growth prospects in the non-oil sector of the Kazakh economy (IMF 2003a: 14–15). Similarly, prospects improved for shrewd use of the oil fund to promote long-run development in Azerbaijan, although the Azeri president retains overall direction of the fund. The IMF made it a condition of a new three-year agreement that the oil fund is not to be used for loan guarantees and most of its receipts will be invested abroad for future generations, with only the interest available for government expenditure. Moreover, the oil fund must be managed within the budget, channel its revenue through the treasury and publish an annual audit along with quarterly reports (EBRD 2001).

Yet the beneficial use of the oil rent depends on rent-seeking being eliminated, or else more realistically, being coordinated so that it is directed more toward socializing risk and encouraging competitive investment that would not occur without 'extra' incentives. It also assumes that illicit levies imposed by rent-seeking on wealth-creating firms are not so onerous as to push those firms into the informal economy, as occurred in the case of two-thirds of Azeri GDP during the 1990s. However, corruption is high in both countries and flourishes at all levels. The accumulated wealth of each president may be $200 million for Aleyev and five times as much for Nazerbaev. In Kazakhstan, large sums are missing from the state budget, including $800 million and $450 million that Mobil and Chevron, respectively, expended to enter the Tenghiz partnership. Moreover, recorded oil export prices are below world prices, so that over $5/bl may have leaked into unofficial offshore accounts. In Azerbaijan, most of the estimated $3.75 billion potential rent generated from oil during 1996–2000 subsidized domestic consumers (Chapter 3) but two-fifths of the oil was exported and a fraction of this went into presidential assets that appear to be augmented by cuts on business deals. Without an impartial judiciary, ministries form lines of patronage whose ability to deliver rewards (like tax relief, relaxed regulation, preferential contracts and access to SOEs) depends upon proximity to the president and associates from his home region (Hoffman 2000).

Petty corruption also remains rife because the collapse of public revenue in the CCA region (Table 4.8) prompts civil servants to adopt 'grabbing-hand' tactics to supplement a public salary that may be one-fifth of basic subsistence. Moreover, partial reform creates scope for high-level officials to capture rents directly from opaque public institutions or indirectly by manipulating contrived rents. Such corruption raises the risk for investors, thereby lowering the efficiency of capital and discouraging long-term investment. Worse, as shown in Chapter 7, illicit imposts create a vicious circle that reduces the flow of legitimate tax revenue to the public sector so that wages remain too low, even as the same imposts repress investment in private sector employment so that public sector workers cannot escape from low-paid government jobs. However, the regime change in Azerbaijan in 2004 may improve prospects for the benevolent deployment of the oil rents, but recent positive moves are offset by the failure of either government to appreciate the risks of using rent to subsidize employment creation rather than promoting competitive investment to achieve that aim.

## Pessimistic rent deployment scenarios: the resource curse

Although there are mixed signals concerning government motives in both Azerbaijan and Kazakhstan, their regimes lack political legitimacy so they are vulnerable to economic and political shocks. This section applies the experience of the developing market oil exporters to construct plausible pessimistic scenarios of oil rent deployment for each country.

### A pessimistic Azeri scenario: political succession exacerbates the staple trap

A plausible pessimistic scenario might begin to unfold as follows. Lacking a democratic mandate and encountering high-level political opposition to its early efforts to harness oil rents for accelerated economic development, the new Azeri leadership succumbs to the temptation to build political support by accelerating the domestic absorption of the rents, by not only drawing directly on the oil fund (which still lacks adequate safeguards against such raiding (Bagirov *et al.* 2003)) but also bringing the rents forward by using the oil reserves as collateral for foreign loans. It uses the increased resources to lower taxes and expand consumption subsidies. Meanwhile, consumption also increases because faster domestic absorption of the rents further strengthens the real exchange rate, which makes foreign goods cheaper.

The high real exchange rate renders domestic products less competitive and thereby causes further contraction of the already emaciated non-mining tradeable sector. Rising unemployment (officially 13 per cent of the workforce in 2000) prompts the insecure new government to strengthen import protection by introducing 'temporary' higher tariffs and stronger para-tariffs. Moreover, fearing that rural poverty will accelerate rural–urban migration and heighten political tensions, the government also promotes improved rural infrastructure and provides grants to its supporters in business and local government for agriculture and agro-processing. These government interventions expand scope for rent extraction so that the real progress made in curbing corruption during the early 2000s is set back.

The construction sector booms and inflation accelerates, further sapping the already dubious efficiency of the new investment. The drive to legitimize the new regime therefore intensifies the staple trap into which Azerbaijan had fallen. Economic growth becomes ever more dependent on oil rents so the economy is acutely vulnerable to an external shock, which duly arrives in 2008, a decade after the start of the high price sequence in the long-run price cycle. Oil prices plunge due a glutted market, partly through investments like those in the Caspian coming on stream. But Azeri oil production is just beginning to level off so the resulting sharply lower rent stream turns the mortgaged future oil revenues into an acute debt service problem. Like its counterpart in Algeria in 1985, the Azeri government at first resists external pressure to cut public expenditure. Rather, it boosts external debt in the hope that the price downswing will be short-lived. This merely increases the harshness of the adjustment when international creditors force the government to turn to the international financial institutions (IFIs) for help in 2009.

The IFI-backed stabilization and structural adjustment programs demand sharp reductions in public expenditure and a depreciation in the real exchange rate. As with Algeria in the 1990s, stabilization is quickly achieved but the structural adjustment required to sustain rapid growth is far less successful. This is because the political uncertainty arising from the government's lack of legitimacy gives the domestic private sector little incentive to repatriate its capital and invest in long-term job creation. The stabilization package therefore abruptly reverses the employment gains made since the new leadership assumed power in 2004 and the associated recession halves per capita incomes to levels below those of 2000, further undermining the government.

### A pessimistic Kazakh scenario: dual economy stokes corruption and regional tension

In Kazakhstan, increased oil revenues threaten to intensify the regional and ethnic income differences and tensions, irrespective of whether the government opts to neglect them or to offset them. A pessimistic scenario for Kazakhstan may therefore run as follows. The ruling family continues to neglect income inequality and to turn a blind eye to corrupt behavior by leading ethnic figures at the national level, occasionally making an example of corrupt local officials in oblasts dominated by less favored clans or ethnic groups. The government initially sustains FDI in mining and mineral processing sectors by, in effect, conferring a fraction of the rents on investors to compensate for the higher costs of operation imposed by corruption. Yet FDI (mainly into Kashagan during the mid-2000s), and the rapidly expanding export revenues generated by earlier oil investment intensify the Dutch disease effects. Meanwhile, those tradeable sub-sectors that compete with importers but lack resource rent cannot absorb the illicit imposts from corruption so investors shun them and resort to importing goods or to capital flight.

Despite its diversified natural resource endowment, Kazakhstan becomes ever more firmly locked into the staple trap of high dependence on minerals. Yet total GDP expands briskly until the 2008 negative price shock. This event is less problematic for Kazakhstan than for Azerbaijan because the slower absorption of rents confers more scope for smoothing the adjustment. However, the gini coefficient for income distribution continues its inexorable rise towards Brazilian levels so the government responds by shifting still more responsibility for worker welfare on to foreign companies. The companies, which have for some time been chafing under government pressure to renegotiate PSA contracts, react by cutting their reinvestment and stepping up repatriation of their profits, effectively speeding liquidation of their investments (which are heavily front-loaded for just such an eventuality).

The deceleration in FDI exacerbates tension between the government and foreign investors. The government seeks to make foreign companies a scapegoat for the country's lop-sided economic development and threatens nationalization. This threat is carried out in 2010 as oil prices abruptly rebound in response to the overthrow of the Saudi government that had been fatally destabilized when oil prices plummeted in 2008. However, shorn of access to global technology, management skills and above all distribution chains, oil exports decline so that higher unit prices for oil only partly offset the effect of shrinking volume. After a brief recovery in popularity, government support collapses through 2011 as economic hardship worsens, opening the way for a military coup. The new military regime, like its Burmese counterpart during the 1990s, uses force to repress dissent in return for rents diverted to the army from the reviving oil sector, now under Chinese management, and also from participation in the lucrative international trade in smuggling drugs and weapons. Of course, neither of these specific scenarios will happen, but without changes in the nature of the political state a pessimistic outcome is a distinct possibility in both of the oil-rich CCA countries.

## Prospects for rectifying the institutional deficiencies

The scale of *potential* rent streams in Azerbaijan and Kazakhstan is substantial, and could exceed those of Algeria and Nigeria during the oil booms of the 1970s, whose mismanagement proved so damaging. However, absorption of the oil rents presents more problems for Azerbaijan than for Kazakhstan because the Azeri oil rents are likely to be larger relative to GDP and they will taper off more rapidly after a shorter but more intense peak 2009–13. With propitious conditions under a developmental political state, even the medium case scenario could double real per capita income each decade so that by 2020 Azerbaijan could reach the level of Greece in the mid–1990s and Kazakhstan the level of Ireland. Moreover, these outcomes would create diversified and resilient economies whose dynamic markets would benefit neighboring countries with less favorable natural resource endowments.

Unfortunately, the political states in both countries are concentrated oligarchies, which fall short of the requirements for successful rent deployment: they weaken political accountability, civic associations and institutions (Dosmukhamedov 2003). Both governments lack political legitimacy so that they are brittle and vulnerable to negative political and economic shocks. Moreover, the economies of Azerbaijan and Kazakhstan remain badly distorted and generate insufficient employment to alleviate poverty. Plausible pessimistic scenarios of oil rent deployment may be triggered by an unstable leadership succession, a price shock or social tensions arising out of dualistic development.

The pessimistic scenarios underline the primacy of the political state in determining the impact of energy rent deployment in the Caspian Basin region, a theme addressed more fully in Part III. Meanwhile, it is important to note that it is not just the population at large that will benefit from pro-growth reforms: the STEX model shows that ruling elites with dynastic ambitions also have much to lose from maladroit deployment of oil rent.

## References

Anderson, K. and Pomfret, R. (2002) Spatial inequality and development in Central Asia, Working Paper, Adelaide: University of Adelaide.

Auty, R.M. (2001) Transition reform in the mineral-rich Caspian Region countries, *Resource Policy* 27(1), 25–32.

Bagirov, S., Akhmedov, I. and Tsalik, S. (2003) State oil fund of the Azerbaijan Republic, in: Tsalik, S. (ed.) *Caspian Oil Revenues: Who Will Benefit?* New York: SOROS Foundation, 89–125.

Bevan, D., Collier, P. and Gunning, J.W. (1987) 'Consequences of a commodity boom in a controlled economy: Accumulation and redistribution in Kenya', *World Bank Economic Review* 1, 489–513.

BP (2003) *BP Statistical Review of World Energy 2002*, London: BP plc.

Collins, K. (2004) The logic of clan politics: Evidence from the Central Asian trajectories, *World Politics* 56, 224–261.

Dosmukhamedov, E.K. (2003) *Foreign Direct Investment in Kazakhstan: Politico-Legal Aspects of Post-Communist Transition*, Basingstoke: Palgrave.

Ebel, R. (2003) National fund of the Republic of Kazakhstan, in: Tsalik, S. (ed.) *Caspian Oil Revenues: Who Will Benefit?* New York: SOROS Foundation, 127–160.

EBRD (2001) *Transition Report 2001: Energy in the Transition*, London: EBRD.

EBRD (2002) *Transition Report 2002: Agriculture and Rural Transition*, London: EBRD.

Financial Times (1998) Kazakhstan: A survey, *Financial Times*, June 17.

Gelb, A.H. and Associates (1988) *Oil Windfalls: Blessing or Curse?* New York: Oxford University Press.

Gürgen, E., Snoek, H., Craig, J., McHigh, J., Izvorski, I. and van Rooden, R. (1999) Economic reforms in Kazakhstan, Kyrgyz Republic, Tajikistan, Turkmenistan and Uzbekistan, IMF Occasional Paper 183, Washington DC: IMF.

Hoffman, D.I. (2000) Azerbaijan: The politicisation of oil, in: Ebel, R. and Menon, R. (eds.) *Energy and Conflict in Central Asia and the Caucasus*, Lanham MD: Rowman and Littlefield, 59–77.

IMF (2002a) *Republic of Kazakhstan: Staff Report for the 2001 Article IV Consultation*, Washington DC: IMF.

IMF (2002b) *Republic of Azerbaijan: Staff Report for the 2001 Article IV Consultation*, IMF Country Report 02/40, Washington DC: IMF.

IMF (2003a) *Republic of Kazakhstan: Selected Issues and Statistical Appendix*, IMF Country Report 03/211, Washington DC: IMF.

IMF (2003b) *Republic of Azerbaijan: Selected Issues and Statistical Appendix*, IMF Country Report 03/130, Washington DC: IMF.

Khan, M.H. and Jomo, K.S. (2000) *Rents, Rent-Seeking and Economic Development: Theory and Evidence in Asia*, Cambridge: Cambridge University Press.

Leite, C. and Weidmann, J. (2002) Does Mother Nature corrupt? Natural resources, corruption and economic growth, in: Abed, G.T. and Gupta, S. (eds.) *Governance, Corruption and Economic* Performance, Washington DC: IMF, 159–196.

McCutcheson, H. and Osbon, R. (2001) Discoveries alter Caspian region energy potential, *Oil and Gas Journal* 99(51), 18–25.

Olcott, M.B. (2002) *Kazakhstan: Unfulfilled Promise*, Washington DC: Carnegie Endowment for International Peace.

Pastor, G. and van Rooden, R. (2000) Turkmenistan: The burden of current agricultural policies, IMF Working Paper 00/98, Washington DC: International Monetary Fund.

Petri, M., Taube, G. and Tsyvinski, A. (2002) Energy sector quasi-fiscal activities in the countries of the former Soviet Union, IMF Working Paper 02/60, Washington DC: IMF.

Planecon (1997) The sophisticated way to model earnings, mimeo, Washington DC: Meridian International Conference Center.

Raiser, M., Schaffer, M. and Schuchardt, J. (2001) Economic development, structural change and transition, Working Paper, Edinburgh: Department of Economics, Heriot-Watt University.

Rosenberg, C.B. and Saavalainen, T.O. (1998) How to deal with Azerbaijan's oil boom? Policy strategies in a resource-rich transition economy, IMF Working Paper 98/6, IMF, Washington DC.

State Department (1997) Caspian Region Energy Development Report, mimeo, Meridian International Conference Center, Washington DC.

Tanzi, V. and Tsibouris, G. (2001) Transition and the changing role of government, in: Havrylyshyn, O. and Nsouli, S.M. (eds.) *A Decade of Transition: Achievements and Challenges*, Washington DC: International Monetary Fund, 229–250.

Van Wijnbergen, S. (1984) The 'Dutch disease': A disease after all? *Economic Journal* 94, 41–55.

World Bank (1998) Update of the 1993 review of the energy sector, mimeo, Baku.

World Bank (2002a) *The Outlook for Oil and Gas Revenues in Azerbaijan*, Washington DC: World Bank.

World Bank (2002b) *The Outlook for Oil Revenues in Kazakhstan*, Washington DC: World Bank.

World Bank (2004a) *Governance Indices 2004*, Washington DC: World Bank.

World Bank (2004b) *World Development Indicators 2004*, Washington DC: World Bank.

WRI (1996) *World Resources 1996–97*, New York: Oxford University Press.

# 5   Resource abundance, governance and economic performance in Turkmenistan and Uzbekistan[1]

*Richard Pomfret*

This chapter analyses the connection between resource wealth, governance and economic performance in Turkmenistan and Uzbekistan. Since independence, both countries have remained heavily resource-dependent and they have had political stability, but, despite some similarities, their economic situations have been diverging since the transition shock in 1991. Although the two countries are resource-abundant, their resource endowments differ: both have energy resources and farmland suited to cotton-growing, but Turkmenistan's resource base is heavily skewed towards natural gas, with cotton and oil of lesser importance, and with very little other economic activity. Uzbekistan's major exports are cotton and gold, with energy endowments sufficient to cover domestic needs but without substantial energy exports. Both oil fields and cotton fields yield rents and this chapter estimates their scale and also examines how the different socio-economic linkages associated with each set of rents differentiates the capture of the rents and their deployment. The chapter argues that during the first decade of transition the rents from both sets of natural resources could be realized with little recourse to FDI so that both regimes were able to resist pressure for rapid reform. However, despite acknowledged policy errors, Uzbekistan managed its rents more effectively and responsibly than Turkmenistan and it faces the more promising future.

## Turkmenistan and Uzbekistan since independence

Both countries are fairly sparsely populated (Table 5.1) with large areas of desert, although Uzbekistan is the most populous Central Asian country with the region's metropolis, Tashkent, and with a large part of the densely populated Ferghana Valley in the east. In the late Soviet era, the Turkmen and Uzbek Republics had living standards similar to those in high or upper middle-income countries. Following a substantial decline in real income since the end of central planning and the dissolution of the Soviet Union, both are now low-income countries, according to World Bank estimates of GNP per capita in US dollars. Measuring gross national product (GNP) in US dollars has many conceptual problems, especially associated with determining the

*Table 5.1* Basic statistics, Turkmenistan and Uzbekistan 1992–2002

| | Population (millions) | | Area (thousand sq km) | GNP per capita (US$) | | Life expectancy (years) | | |
|---|---|---|---|---|---|---|---|---|
| | *1992* | *1999* | | *1991* | *2002* | *1991* | *2002* | |
| | | | | | | | *M* | *F* |
| Turkmenistan | 3.9 | 4.8 | 488 | 1,700 | 660 | 66 | 61 | 68 |
| Uzbekistan | 21.4 | 25.3 | 447 | 1,350 | 310 | 69 | 64 | 70 |

*Sources:* ESCAP 2002, World Bank 1993: 238–239; World Bank 2001: 274–279; World Bank 2004.

*Notes:* Turkmenistan's official statistics give GDP growth of 18% in 2001 and over 20% in 2002, but the EBRD has 'serious data concerns' over these figures. In the same report Turkmenistan's population is estimated at 5.2 million in 1999 and 5.8 million in 2002 (EBRD 2002b: 40).

appropriate exchange rate, and the estimates in Table 5.1 overstate the extent of the decline. Estimates based on output data indicate that Uzbekistan's real GDP in 2001 was 3 per cent higher than in 1989, while Turkmenistan's had fallen by 16 per cent since 1989 (EBRD 2002b: Annex 1.1). Measures of inequality and of poverty increased during the 1990s, but not by as much as elsewhere in the former Soviet Union (FSU), and these countries avoided the drop in life expectancy observed in Kazakhstan, Russia and other CIS countries.

Uzbekistan and, to a lesser extent, Turkmenistan contained the core areas of cotton production in the USSR. They were also the two largest producers of natural gas in Central Asia. For Turkmenistan, natural gas became the dominant economic sector in the 1980s and, at independence Turkmenistan was the fourth-largest gas producer in the world. The recent development of the gas fields meant that, unlike much of the region where energy production stagnated during the late Soviet era, Turkmenistan's gas exports to other former Soviet republics remained a major revenue earner in the years after independence. Uzbekistan's energy reserves were less developed before 1991 and, although exploitation increased after independence, it served to achieve self-sufficiency by 1995 rather than become a major export earner in the 1990s. Uzbekistan's second most important export after cotton is gold, whose value remains secret. An additional advantage arises from the character of the country's capital city, Tashkent, which, with over two million people, was the metropolitan center of Soviet Central Asia and home to a relatively developed manufacturing sector, abundant administrative and other skills, and relatively good transport infrastructure.

After independence both Turkmenistan and Uzbekistan aimed to sell their natural resource exports at world prices, although this was easier for cotton and gold than for either gas or oil, whose destinations were determined by the inherited pipeline system. Both governments tried to diversify their economies. In agriculture this centered on changing the crop pattern in favor of wheat, in part at the expense of cotton but also at the expense of forage and other crops. The outcome in both countries was to increase wheat production and reduce cotton output during the 1990s, although Uzbekistan was more successful in both increasing wheat output and limiting the decline in cotton, as well as in maintaining reasonable yields (Table 5.2).[2]

After 1991 Turkmenistan supplied natural gas to Ukraine and the Caucasus, charging world prices rather than the old plan prices and received the revenue, minus transit fees. Although substantial rents were earned on gas exports, maintaining them became increasingly difficult. The inherited pipeline system allowed transit states to levy high fees and final users to delay payment, knowing that Turkmenistan had no alternative outlets. In March 1997 Turkmenistan responded to the holdout problem by stopping gas exports to its main debtor, Ukraine. Supplies were only resumed, after protracted negotiations with Russia and with Ukraine and other importing countries, in January 1999 (Sagers 1999). That episode improved payments, although Ukraine only agreed to pay half of its bill in cash and the remainder in barter. The opening of a small pipeline to Iran in 1997 also helped to diversify outlets, but to date that pipeline has operated below capacity, apparently due to Iranian reluctance to purchase more gas from Turkmenistan.

The cotton sector of Turkmenistan also experienced problems. Rent extraction through a state order system left farmers with limited incentives. In addition, starting in the mid-1990s, the Turkmenistan government promoted import-substituting industrialization, mainly involving textile mills. It subsidized the cotton supply to the textile factories, which operated with low efficiency, possibly even negative value-added, and dissipated perhaps a third of the cotton rent (Pomfret 2001).

Through all of this, Turkmenistan's government has maintained its strategy of reform avoidance. Economic policy aimed to minimize change, while maintaining popular support through consumption subsidies (gas, water, electricity and bread were free to households). The simple economic structure permitted a quasi-planned economy to survive after the end

*Table 5.2* Cotton and wheat output and yield, Turkmenistan and Uzbekistan 1991–1998

|  | Seed cotton (1000 tonnes) | | Wheat (1000 tonnes) | |
|---|---|---|---|---|
|  | Turkmenistan | Uzbekistan | Turkmenistan | Uzbekistan |
| 1992 | 1290 (2.3) | 4128 (2.5) | 377 (1.9) | 964 (1.5) |
| 1994 | 1283 (2.3) | 3936 (2.6) | 675 (2.6) | 1362 (1.4) |
| 1996 | 436 (0.8) | 3350 (2.3) | 424 (0.7) | 2742 (2.1) |
| 1998 | 707 (1.2) | 3220 (2.1) | 600 (1.2) | 3094 (3.2) |

*Source:* Goletti and Chabot 2000: 50–52.

*Note*: Figures in parentheses are yields, in tons per hectare.

of Soviet planning. Controls were tightened in 1998 by foreign exchange restrictions, which created a black market, while domestic prices became ever more distorted and artificial. Performance is difficult to measure because national accounts data are the least credible in the CIS, but there has undoubtedly been a severe decline in output since independence. Poverty rates appear not to have risen as much as elsewhere in Central Asia, perhaps because, apart from the president and his immediate entourage, income distribution is fairly egalitarian.

Uzbekistan's situation at independence differed in that cotton and gold used more flexible transport systems and could be readily diverted to world markets. Chapter 3 argues that the immediate access to resource rents in Uzbekistan and Turkmenistan explains their resistance to economic reform, in contrast to Azerbaijan and Kazakhstan, which needed foreign assistance to develop their resources before the export revenue could flow in. Uzbekistan did, however, differ from Turkmenistan in that, although conservative, the government was not viscerally opposed to change. The official policy of gradual reform was not a euphemism for no reform. Housing and small-scale privatization were implemented rapidly, although large-scale privatization was not. Stabilization was delayed because the government initially resisted pressure for Big Bang reform, but, once convinced of the dangers from hyperinflation and of its causes, the Uzbek government, unlike Turkmenistan's, implemented a standard stabilization policy from January 1994. Uzbekistan also lodged a formal application for WTO membership, unlike Turkmenistan, which remains the only transition country not to have made such an application (Pomfret 2003).

By the mid-1990s the outstanding feature of the Uzbekistan economy was that, measured by GDP, its performance since 1989 was the best of all former Soviet republics and better than most eastern European transition economies. This was helped by the initial resource endowment, but also was a result of policies for public investment (Taube and Zettelmeyer 1998). Moreover, Uzbekistan had a good record of maintaining state revenues and public expenditures on education and health (Pomfret and Anderson 1997). Provision of targeted social services by innovative institutional change helped poverty alleviation (Coudouel and Marnie 1999). In sum, although Uzbekistan scored poorly on western-based transition indicators, it differed fundamentally from Turkmenistan's lack of any serious transition strategy, and its economic performance over the first decade after independence was superior.

In part, the differing outcomes between Turkmenistan and Uzbekistan can be attributed to differing leadership. Although both Niyazov and Karimov are orphans and technocrats who transformed from Gorbachev-appointed first secretaries of Soviet republics to presidents of new nation states, they differ in personality. Karimov is a trained economist, who takes pride in exerting competent management and in being a statesman on at least the regional stage. Karimov is encouraged to pursue economic development by competition with Kazakhstan for regional hegemony because he understands the close links between economic and political power. Although Karimov is clearly in charge, the image is of a team leader. Niyazov, by contrast, has established an extreme personality cult and, while he styles himself as leader of his people (Turkmenbashi), his actions show more concern for personal glorification and satisfaction than for economic development to improve the well-being of the population.[3] Niyazov's economic policies are simplistic: populist giveaways curry support while import substitution is pursued to diversify the economy, and his foreign policy asserts Turkmenistan's neutrality and abdicates responsibility for the give and take of diplomacy.

Two deeper determinants of the differences can be identified, however. First, Tashkent was the administrative, industrial and military center of Soviet Central Asia, the fourth largest city in the Soviet Union, and by far the most cosmopolitan metropolis in the region. In this setting, it is difficult to imagine an independent Uzbekistan tolerating the personality cult or simplistic policies of a Niyazov. Moreover, the presence of experienced administrators created the capacity for good administration that is evident in Tashkent and lacking in Ashgabat. Second, as discussed in Chapter 2, among resource-abundant countries, energy producers tend to have more appropriable rents and a greater propensity for state failure. Cotton requires maintenance of a structure of irrigation, provision of other inputs, processing and a marketing network; an organized state can extract rents from cotton, but it is harder for an individual despot to control without sharing some of the spoils (Pomfret 1995). Although despotic, Karimov has taken on board the concept of a developmental state, with Malaysia as a frequently mentioned model.[4]

Some regression in policy occurred, however. In 1996 a downturn in world cotton prices led to balance of payments problems for Uzbekistan and the government rejected market adjustment and instinctively turned to exchange controls, which were retained until late 2003. The gap between the official and market-determined exchange rates concealed the full extent of the tax on cotton growers and so was attractive to a government heavily reliant on rent from cotton. In most other respects, however, the wedge between world and domestic prices and the subsequent domestic distortions were recognized as harmful, and increasingly so as time passed. The government slowly acknowledged the costs of using controls and in 2000 began moving, albeit gradually, to undo the policy error, but even after the formal removal of exchange controls administrative obstacles to access to foreign exchange remained.

The Uzbek government continued with piecemeal reforms in the late 1990s, and the economy combined positive output growth with moderate inflation. By the early 2000s Uzbekistan still had the best performance record, measured by GDP relative to its pre-independence level, of any former Soviet republic.[5] This seems difficult to ascribe to initial conditions or favorable world prices for cotton, and seems to reflect competent governance (at least by the low standards of the FSU). The government also shows some flexibility over policy reform. Not only did it begin to loosen foreign exchange controls in 2000 but in 2001 it recognized the need to improve the environment for small and medium-sized enterprises, curbing bureaucratic controls and red tape.

This is not to claim that Uzbekistan has created a vibrant market economy like Poland's or a dynamic market sector as an engine of economic growth like China has achieved.[6] Nevertheless, although both Uzbekistan and Turkmenistan remain resource-dependent and have authoritarian regimes, they differ significantly. Both have exchange controls, but Uzbekistan's are being phased out. Cosmopolitan Tashkent is a far cry from the sterile center of Ashgabat. Foreign capital inflows have been modest, but their nature differs: in Turkmenistan foreign contractors build factories, monuments and hospitals for cash payment or barter (usually in cotton), whereas in Uzbekistan foreign investors invest their own capital in the expectation of future profits (most visibly the Daewoo joint venture).

## Energy and agriculture rents

### Estimating the energy rent

Turkmenistan's rents from natural gas and its use of natural gas revenues are non-transparent. Chapter 3 reports that $1.5 billion from natural gas sales in 1992–93 remains under President Niyazov's direct control. Revenues declined substantially in the mid-1990s as customers within the CIS stopped paying their bills. Gas exports at that time were recorded in the National Accounts at the contract price and arrears entered as capital outflows, but this foreign investment by Turkmenistan was largely a figment, and the value of actual receipts was hidden as they were deposited into secret funds.

In March 1997 Turkmenistan stopped supplying natural gas to delinquent customers, and only resumed supply after an agreement was reached in 1999. The income from gas exports was low during these years and there are signs that the president ran down the accumulated funds from past sales, so that by 2000 foreign debt was becoming an issue, although its magnitude was probably unknown given the complexity of the off-budget accounts. Export revenue from natural gas picked up again in 1999, but it remains unclear how diligent the CIS customers are in servicing their bills. In contrast to gas, oil exports have been less significant to Turkmenistan in recent years. By 1998 oil production had regained its 1990 level, but it was still only half of its 1975 peak. Exploitation of offshore oil is delayed by jurisdictional disputes over Caspian Sea boundaries and by indecision over new pipeline routes.[7]

Uzbekistan was a net energy importer in the Soviet era, importing oil and hydroelectricity and exporting small quantities of gas to south-eastern Kazakhstan and the Kyrgyz and Tajik republics. After 1991, however, Uzbekistan was sufficiently successful in developing domestic energy sources that it did not suffer from the shift to world prices on intra-CIS trade, and it ceased to be a net oil importer in 1995 (Table 5.3). The steady growth in output reflects in part the high degree of reliance on domestic demand,

Table 5.3 Hydrocarbon production and mineral rent 1990–2000

| | 1990 | 1991 | 1992 | 1993 | 1994 | 1995 | 1996 | 1997 | 1998 | 1999 | 2000 |
|---|---|---|---|---|---|---|---|---|---|---|---|
| **Turkmenistan** | | | | | | | | | | | |
| Oil (mbpd) | 120 | 115 | 110 | 90 | 85 | 85 | 90 | 110 | 130 | 145 | 150 |
| Gas (bcm) | 81.9 | 78.6 | 56.1 | 60.9 | 33.3 | 30.1 | 32.8 | 16.1 | 12.4 | 21.3 | 43.8 |
| Rent/GDP | na | na | na | na | 0.638 | 0.395 | 0.538 | 0.336 | 0.329 | 0.440 | na |
| **Uzbekistan** | | | | | | | | | | | |
| Oil (mbpd) | 70 | 70 | 80 | 95 | 125 | 170 | 175 | 180 | 190 | 190 | 175 |
| Gas (bcm) | 38.1 | 39.1 | 39.9 | 42.0 | 44.0 | 45.3 | 45.7 | 47.8 | 51.1 | 51.9 | 52.2 |
| Rent/GDP | na | 0.013 | 0.153 | 0.136 | 0.125 | 0.170 | 0.196 | 0.210 | 0.137 | 0.166 | na |

*Source*: BP and World Bank estimates reported in Auty 2002. Skagen 1997: 30 gives slightly lower estimates, but similar patterns for natural gas production 1991–6.

*Notes*: mbpd = million barrels per day; bcm = billion cubic metres.

which has been relatively stable due to Uzbekistan's relatively good GDP performance, and timely expansion of new fields (Skagen 1997: 25). Most of the gas production is taken up by domestic consumption. Uzbekistan exports to southern Kazakhstan, the Kyrgyz Republic and Tajikistan, although payments disputes disrupted supplies in 1998. Since the early 2000s Uzbekistan has also been exporting gas to Russia; in 2003 Uzbekistan exported 2.4 bcm to Russia, and a 2004 agreement with Gazprom envisaged rapidly increasing exports starting with 7.7 bcm in that year. As Chapter 3 demonstrates, the rent from Uzbekistan's oil and gas resources has been redistributed to consumers through domestic energy prices below world prices, while remaining rents go to general government revenue.

A detailed discussion of the estimated natural resource rents is available in Pomfret (2002). Delivered prices in the western CIS of around $2.25/mcf (compared to the world price of $2.5–3) and transport costs through the former Soviet network of about 40 cents/mcf per thousand kilometers would generate from 20 to 45 cents per mcf in rent.[8] Auty (2002) reports estimates of energy rents in Turkmenistan between 1994 and 1999 amounting to between 33 and 64 per cent of GDP. These are rough estimates, but they capture the widely held view that the Turkmenistan economy has been highly dependent on rents from natural gas. Similar estimates of energy rents in Uzbekistan range from 13 to 21 per cent of GDP over the 1994–99 period (Table 5.3).

### Agricultural rent: the cost of agricultural price controls

Turkmenistan and Uzbekistan have retained state procurement systems for cotton and wheat. In contrast, the neighboring Kyrgyz Republic eliminated state procurement in 1992 and Kazakhstan and Tajikistan did so in the mid-1990s. This is reflected in substantial differences in farm gate prices. Table 5.4 reports the local currency price of cotton for the 1997 harvest season, and the US dollar equivalent. Goletti and Chabot (2000: 55) estimate the average border parity price at $404 per ton, which is not far from the prices received by farmers in the Kyrgyz Republic, Tajikistan and Kazakhstan, but substantially above the prices that farmers receive in Turkmenistan or Uzbekistan.

*Table 5.4* Output price for cotton, 1997 harvest season

|  | Kazakhstan | Kyrgyz Republic | Tajikistan | Turkmenistan | Uzbekistan |
|---|---|---|---|---|---|
| In local currency units | 25,500 tenge | 7,100 som | 190,000 TR | 1,000,000 manat | 14,750 sum |
| USD at official exchange rate | $349 | $394 | $388 | $240 | $242 |
| USD at parallel exchange rate |  |  |  | $188 | $105 |

*Source:* Goletti and Chabot 2000: 55.

In their study of agricultural prices in eighteen developing countries, Krueger *et al.* (1988, 1992) found that overvalued exchange rates imposed a more serious burden on farmers than did trade barriers or other direct taxes.[9] Not surprisingly, the Uzbek foreign exchange controls of 1996 widened the black market premium. Goletti and Chabot (2000) calculate that at the parallel exchange rate the local currency price in Table 5.4 of 14,750 sum per ton translates into $105 per ton, or about a quarter of the border parity price. The burden of the overvalued exchange rate increased through the late 1990s. Turkmenistan's black market premium only became substantial in 1998 so that the effect of foreign exchange controls is not very great in Table 5.4, but has become a major source of price distortion since 1997.

In the regulated systems of Turkmenistan and Uzbekistan, farmers receive subsidized inputs and appear to benefit from more reliable supply of seed and fertilizers and better-managed irrigation than farmers in the Kyrgyz Republic, Kazakhstan or Tajikistan. Golettti and Chabot (2000) show differences in fertilizer prices (Table 5.5), and note the incentives to smuggle to neighboring countries, which benefits the farmers involved but is socially inefficient. Farmers in Turkmenistan and Uzbekistan also benefit from advanced interest-free partial payments, although it is unclear how promptly these and the final payments are made available and the extent to which farmers are free to use money credited to their bank accounts.

Table 5.6 summarizes the publicly available estimates of transfers out of agriculture in Turkmenistan and Uzbekistan during the 1990s. The distortions and transfers are significantly higher in Turkmenistan, and the gap between the two countries is likely to have widened since 2000 as the exchange rate distortion in Turkmenistan has increased while that in Uzbekistan is being reduced. The estimated transfers are not identical to the economic concept of rent, but they do provide a guide to the appropriable rent, or at least to what part has been expropriated.

### Agricultural rent: how is it used?

In Turkmenistan the difference between domestic cotton prices and world prices is divided between the cotton-marketing agency, the state budget, and the Agricultural Development Fund (ADF) 'in proportions that are

*Table 5.5* Cost per kilogram of nutrient (in US$)

|  | Kazakhstan | Kyrgyz Republic | Tajikistan | Turkmenistan | Uzbekistan |
| --- | --- | --- | --- | --- | --- |
| Nitrogen | 0.50 | 0.50 | 0.50 | 0.12 | 0.25 |
| Phosphorous | 1.50 | 1.50 | 1.00 | 1.00 | 0.50 |
| Potassium | 0.16 | 0.16 | 0.15 | 0.04 | 0.07 |

*Source:* Goletti and Chabot 2000: 60, citing data from an EU-Tacis 1995 report.

*Table 5.6* Estimated transfers out of agriculture

|  | Year | Coverage | Value | Reference |
|---|---|---|---|---|
| Turkmenistan |  |  |  |  |
| Lerman + Brooks | 1998 | Cotton + wheat | 1,565 billion manat | 11% GDP |
| Pastor + van Rooden | 1999 | Cotton + wheat | 2,880 billion manat | 15% GDP |
| Lerman + Brooks adjusted | 1999 | Cotton + wheat | 7,330 billion manat |  |
| Uzbekistan |  |  |  |  |
| Connolly + Vatnick | 1992 | Cotton | $367 million |  |
| Khan | 1995 | Agriculture |  | 10% ag. GDP |
| Herman | 1996 | Cotton + wheat | $1,533 million | 8% GDP |

*Source:* Pomfret 2002: Appendix.

not transparently displayed' (Lerman and Brooks 2001: 8). The residual difference between revenue from cotton sales, payments to cotton farmers and to the cotton-marketing agency, and transfers to the ADF should show up as state budget revenues. In the 1998 budget, cotton revenues are shown as $199 billion manat, which is much less than Lerman and Brooks' calculated residual (2030 revenue minus 700 to farmers minus 355 to the ADF minus marketing agency costs).

The most likely explanation of the gap is that cotton, or revenue from cotton exports, was channeled through the myriad off-budget funds directly controlled by the president. Prestige construction projects in the mid-1990s, such as the national airport, the presidential palace and the grandiose monuments in Ashgabat, were paid for in cash or in cotton. Later, in the early 2000s, Turkmenistan appeared to be accumulating foreign debt at commercial rates, but in the 1990s the foreign contractors were paid out of current income.

The net transfers from wheat were smaller than those from cotton and in Turkmenistan part of the rents went directly to consumers in the form of lower domestic prices for flour and bread. Such untargeted consumption subsidies are inefficient, compared to an alternative of higher wheat prices and tax revenue used to target the needy, but less socially wasteful than palaces and statues. Uzbekistan also transferred rents to consumers up until 1995, but subsequently shifted from general subsidies to a more targeted social security system.

In both Turkmenistan and Uzbekistan cotton mills benefited from input prices below world cotton prices. In Turkmenistan the distortion became larger as funds were used in the late 1990s and early 2000s to build up a substantial cotton textile and apparel industry. By the end of 2000 this industry was absorbing a third of the cotton crop and probably had negative value-added at world prices; the value of the finished cotton products may even have been less than the value of the raw cotton used in their manufacture (Pomfret 2001). Uzbekistan's promotion of its textile industry was less extreme and the costs were being acknowledged by 2001 when the government indicated a shift to a less dirigiste industrial policy. Most of the agricultural transfers in Uzbekistan appear to go to general government revenue, which will be addressed below.

### Summarizing the contrasting scale and deployment of the natural resource rents

Both Turkmenistan and Uzbekistan have enjoyed substantial resource rents over the decade since independence, but there are important differences in the magnitude, composition and use of the resource rents. In Turkmenistan the share of rents in GDP is much higher, the rents come primarily from natural gas, and their use has been less transparent than in Uzbekistan. Combining the estimates in Tables 5.3 and 5.6, Turkmenistan's energy and agricultural rents were in the region of 44 per cent of GDP in 1998 and 60 per cent of GDP in 1999. These are rough estimates, but they are very large and may still be underestimates due to the effects of foreign exchange controls.

In Turkmenistan the agricultural and energy rents have been used mainly to subsidize domestic consumers (of bread and gas) and producers (using cotton or gas) and to provide a treasure chest for the president's construction projects. Petri *et al.* (2002: 29) estimate that energy subsidies to consumers amount to 13 per cent of GDP. Turkmenistan has also levied transit rents on narcotics from Afghanistan. Elsewhere in the CIS such rents have accrued primarily to entrepreneurs/criminals, but for Turkmenistan there have been detailed allegations of President Niyazov's personal involvement in hashish convoys and heroin production.

Uzbekistan derives rents from energy, cotton and gold. The former, and part of the agricultural rents, are used to subsidize domestic consumers and producers. In the mid-1990s, prices to residential users of gas were 0.12–0.15 US cents per cubic meter, similar to Turkmenistan but much lower than the 4.2 cents in Kazakhstan or 15–18 cents in Turkey, and 1.84 cents per cubic meter to industrial users, compared to 0.24 cents in Turkmenistan and 8.37 cents in Kazakhstan (Skagen 1997: 51–2). Since 1995, however, the consumer subsidy element has been reduced and the rents have become part of the general government budget.

Uzbekistan emerges as one of the transition economies best able to maintain government revenues as a share of GDP. This is largely because resource rents have been recorded as public revenues, and Uzbekistan has used this situation to maintain public expenditure on education, health and social services. In 1998 expenditure on education accounted for almost 8 per cent of GDP, the highest share in any transition economy (World Bank 2002: 84–5).

## How sustainable are the resource rent flows?

Agricultural rents are vulnerable to adverse supply responses. There is considerable evidence that the negative supply response to state marketing of crops like cotton or cocoa is small in the short run, when the rents are a ready source of government revenue, but becomes larger. The most serious consequences of punitive taxation of an export crop are the long-run loss of sales and encouragement of illegal economic activities. The negative incentives will force the two governments to choose between current rent maximization and stagnating output, or allowing farmers to retain a larger share of the export revenue. Continuation of the current policies of rent extraction also provides incentives for smuggling cotton to neighboring states with freer markets, as from Uzbekistan across the porous border into Kazakhstan, where agricultural prices are less repressed.

Turkmenistan's energy rents seem to be more secure insofar as it has proven oil and gas reserves, which can be exploited at an increasing rate. The rate of exploitation may be influenced by national policies, which could affect the willingness of foreign firms to participate in the exploitation of the offshore reserves (for which Turkmenistan will require foreign assistance), but the revenue flows will depend upon exogenous factors such as world prices and the construction of new pipelines from the Caspian Basin. Uzbekistan's energy rents will be significant, but less important than energy rents are for Turkmenistan. Revenue from gold exports is also likely to be a steady income source for Uzbekistan.

The rents support differing regimes so their manner of capture and deployment depends on the evolution of those regimes. Turkmenistan has the most personalized post-Communist regime and probably the most mismanaged. The major change since independence has been in the use of the rents from energy and cotton. Otherwise, the economy is one of the least reformed. Economic performance has been poor. Despite these shortcomings, the required economic reforms are not especially drastic because Turkmenistan's comparative advantage for the foreseeable future will lie heavily in energy. Thus, the prime need is to replace the current abuse of the rents by a socially oriented husbanding, which requires a mix of economic diversification and portfolio diversification. Scope for efficient economic diversification is, however, limited and past emphasis on textile and apparel factories and on hotel building has been misplaced. A market-directed approach to small and medium-sized enterprises is preferable, although probably with limited impact, but that would reduce waste compared with the current strategy. Portfolio diversification would involve establishment of a capital fund, as reported for Azerbaijan and Kazakhstan in Chapter 4. The current situation in Turkmenistan is a pathological distortion of the fund concept where the resources are totally under the political control of the president. Changing that situation is a political rather than an economic matter.

The desirable cotton policy for Turkmenistan is more complex, because its reliance on the Karakum Canal for irrigation is a major cause of the desiccation of the Aral Sea, which is discussed more fully in Chapter 8. The Aral Sea problem is very difficult to address because the distribution of costs and benefits from any sensible policy would be unevenly distributed across countries, but reducing Turkmenistan's irrigated cotton production would help. Current policy is, however, heading in the opposite direction. The major construction project of the present decade involves a $4–5 billion artificial lake in the Karakum Desert to improve drainage and reduce salinization problems. The new lake has been criticized by practically all outside observers, but it has the president's support and hence there is no domestic opposition to the project.

Assessing the prospects for Uzbekistan is more complex because although the regime is despotic, it is less absolute and inflexible than Turkmenistan's. Gradual reform and occasional major policy reversals make it more difficult to predict future economic policy. Uzbekistan is relatively free from foreign debt, and political stability is not inconsistent with policy reform. Moreover, Uzbekistan cannot rely exclusively on resource rent extraction. Gold and energy offer less scope for rent extraction than cotton, which is likely to remain the dominant economic activity due to natural and inherited conditions, but the government is likely to acknowledge the advantages of reducing its rapacity in order to give farmers an incentive to increase yields.

Uzbekistan must diversify its economy and it has more scope to do so than does Turkmenistan. The strategy for this requires deepening reforms so that prices guide resource allocation in efficient directions. In the first half of the 2000s Uzbekistan appeared to be moving towards this with the adoption of a new attitude towards economic management aimed at helping small and medium-sized enterprises and loosening foreign exchange controls. Removing the latter would be a major step in reducing the rent extraction in agriculture and in improving operation of the domestic price system. As discussed in Chapter 8, both countries face a challenge in reversing the serious institutionalized corruption. According to Broadman and Recanatini (2001: 363) Turkmenistan is the joint-worst, with Tajikistan, of all transition countries, and Uzbekistan is in the next-worst group with Azerbaijan and Albania.[10]

Eifert *et al.* (2003) highlight the benefits for resource-rich countries of creating constituencies for the sound use of rents (through public information and education programs), the importance of transparent political processes and financial management, and the value of getting the political debate to span longer time horizons. Uzbekistan is far from ideal in these respects, but its government recognizes at least the first and last of the three points. Building on the classification of political states in Table 2.3, Eifert *et al.* (2003) develop a typology of rentier states with five categories: mature (consensual) democracies (e.g. Norway or Alberta), factional (polarized) democracies (e.g. Ecuador or Venezuela), paternalistic autocracies (e.g. Saudi Arabia or Kuwait), predatory autocracies and reformist (benevolent) autocracies. The first and last of these classes are developmental political states that provide institutions by means of which a country can avoid the resource curse, while the other systems will sooner or later suffer adverse consequences from misuse of rents, lack of transparency or short-termism.

In this classification Uzbekistan might be a predatory autocracy, but could be a reformist autocracy. Turkmenistan is not the paternalistic autocracy that it claims, but a predatory autocracy that focuses on administering rents, which it does unsoundly, without transparency and with no view to the future. Paradoxically, Turkmenistan with its potentially beneficial energy resources/population ratio has poor prospects because of the country's extremely predatory government. The major issue determining the country's future is the longevity of the president's rule. If he is overthrown or dies, a successor may well be motivated by capturing the rents rather than by avoiding the resource curse.

Uzbekistan's future is brighter and less dependent on regime change. The current regime provides competent governance, at least by the low standards of the FSU, which is reflected in its economic performance since independence. The country has a favorable resource endowment, which is not based solely on energy or mineral abundance. The government has relied heavily on resource rents, but has used the revenues reasonably well. Continuation of past policies could negatively impact long-term agricultural development, but the government is at least aware of the problems. The future will therefore depend in part on the world price for Uzbekistan's key exports, especially cotton, but even more on whether reforms are implemented which will allow the resource sectors to respond effectively to incentives and which will promote efficient diversification.

To date, the Uzbek government has provided public services and social policies reasonably efficiently, shifting from universal support in the early 1990s to more targeted social support in the second half of the decade, and this has helped to maintain public acquiescence despite the government's authoritarianism. If the government is serious in its proposals to re-establish currency convertibility and to reduce obstacles to small and medium-sized enterprises by liberalizing markets, then prospects are positive. But if the government refuses to loosen controls over economic activity, then the economy has little prospect of competitive diversification and the government will be forced to tighten rather than loosen its squeeze on the agricultural sector and risk killing the goose that lays the golden egg.

## Notes

1  I am grateful to Rick Auty for helpful comments on an earlier draft and to Alan Gelb for sharing his unpublished research. A longer version of this chapter (Pomfret 2002) is available from NBR at http://www.nbr.org
2  In the arid conditions in both countries output is volatile. The 1998 harvest was good in most districts due to exceptionally favorable rains, while 1996 was disastrous.

3 Niyazov routinely criticizes ministers in public and summarily dismisses them and officials. Although internal opposition is suppressed, there are frequent rumurs of plots (for example, surrounding a wholesale purge of the security force in April 2002). An assassination attempt in November 2002 was followed by a crackdown on suspected dissidents.

4 See Weinthal (2002) for how cotton rents and side payments are being used to curry favour in Uzbekistan and Luong (2004) for how differences in center–regional relations carried over from the Soviet era to determine power sharing in post-Soviet Central Asia.

5 According to the GDP estimates in the EBRD's May 2002 *Transition Report Update* Uzbekistan was the only former Soviet republic to have regained its 1989 output level.

6 The slow pace of reform underlies the frosty relationship with international financial institutions such as the IMF and World Bank, although Uzbekistan has also been relatively cautious about accepting loans from such sources. In 2004 the EBRD and the USA cut back their assistance to Uzbekistan due to the country's poor human rights record.

7 The southern Caspian appears to be less oil-rich than the northern Caspian, but oil exploration has been deterred by the major oil companies' concerns about property rights in Turkmenistan's jurisdiction.

8 This is based on an estimated cost of gas extraction of 50–55 US cents per thousand cubic feet (mcf). These costs and prices used by Auty (2002: 12n) are lower than those reported by Skagen (1997: 51–2), who estimated Turkmenistan's production costs in the mid-1990s to be 1.8 US cents per cubic metre.

9 In the sub-Saharan African countries in their study, for example, the direct tax burden on agriculture averaged 23 per cent while the indirect tax equivalent of exchange rate overvaluation was 29 per cent.

10 Measuring corruption is, however, difficult. Uzbekistan ranks as having relatively low corruption among transition countries, according to the BEEPS survey reported in the EBRD *Transition Reports* or the *Corruption Perceptions Index* compiled by Transparency International.

# References

Auty, R.M. (2002) Reform in Uzbekistan and Turkmenistan is minimal rather than gradual, Working Paper, Lancaster University, Department of Geography.

Broadman, H. and Recanatini, F. (2001) Seeds of corruption – do market institutions matter? *MOCT-MOST: Economic Policy in Transitional Economies* 11(4), 359–392.

Coudouel, A. and Marnie, S. (1999): From universal to targeted social assistance: An assessment of the Uzbek experience, *MOCT-MOST: Economic Policy in Transitional Economies* 9(4), 443–458.

EBRD (2002a) *Transition Report Update*, May 2002, London: European Bank for Reconstruction and Development.

EBRD (2002b) *Strategy for Turkmenistan* Document of the European Bank for Reconstruction and Development, approved by the Board of Directors on 10 July 2002 and posted on the website www.ebrd.org.

Eifert, B., Gelb, A. and Tallroth, N.B. (2003) The political economy of fiscal policy and economic management in oil exporting countries, in Davis, J.M., Ossowski, R. and Fedelino, A. (eds.) *Fiscal Policy Formulation and Implementation in Oil-Producing Countries*, Washington DC: IMF, 82–122.

ESCAP (2002) *Population Data Sheet*, August 1992.

Goletti, F. and Chabot, P. (2000) 'Food policy research for improving the reform of agricultural input and output markets in Central Asia', in Suresh, B. and Tashmatov, A. (eds.) *Food Policy Reforms in Central Asia*, Washington DC: International Food Policy Research Institute, 45–69.

Krueger, A., Schiff, M. and Valdes, A. (1988) Agricultural incentives in developing countries: Measuring the effect of sectoral and economy-wide policies, *World Bank Economic Review* 2(3), 255–271.

Krueger, A., Schiff, M. and Valdes, A. (eds.) (1992) *The Political Economy of Agricultural Pricing Policies*, 5 Volumes, Baltimore MD: Johns Hopkins University Press.

Lerman, Z. and Brooks. K. (2001) Turkmenistan: An assessment of leasehold-based farm restructuring, World Bank Technical Paper No. 500, Washington DC: World Bank.

Luong Jones, P. (ed.) (2004) *The Transformation of Central Asia*, Ithaca NY: Cornell University Press.

Pastor, G. and van Rooden, R. (2000) Turkmenistan – The burden of current agricultural policies, IMF Working Paper WP/00/98, Washington DC: International Monetary Fund.

Petri, M., Taube, G. and Tsyvinski, A. (2002) Energy sector quasi-fiscal activities in the countries of the Former Soviet Union, IMF Working Paper WP/02/60, Washington DC: International Monetary Fund.

Pomfret, R. (1995) *The Economies of Central Asia*, Princeton NJ: Princeton University Press.

Pomfret, R. (2000) Agrarian reform in Uzbekistan: Why has the Chinese model failed to deliver? *Economic Development and Cultural Change* 48(2), 269–284.

Pomfret, R. (2001) Turkmenistan: From communism to nationalism by gradual economic reform, *MOCT-MOST: Economic Policy in Transitional Economies* 11(2), 165–76.

Pomfret, R. (2002) Resource abundance, governance and economic performance in Turkmenistan and Uzbekistan, Working Paper, Seattle: National Bureau of Asian Research.

Pomfret, R. (2003) Trade and exchange rate policies in formerly centrally planned economies, *The World Economy* 26(4), 585–612.

Pomfret, R. and Anderson, K. (1997) Uzbekistan: Welfare impact of slow transition, WIDER Working Paper 135, United Nations University World Institute for Development Economics Research, Helsinki, Finland – revised version published in Aiguo, L. and Montes, M. (eds.) *Poverty, Income Distribution and Well-being in Asia During the Transition*, Basingstoke: Palgrave, 2002.

Rosenberg, C. and de Zeeuw, M. (2000) Welfare effects of Uzbekistan's foreign exchange regime, IMF Working Paper 00/61, Washington DC: International Monetary Fund.

Sagers, M. (1999) Turkmenistan's gas trade: The case of exports to Ukraine, *Post-Soviet Geography and Economics* 40(2), 142–149.

Skagen, O. (1997) *Caspian Gas*, London: Royal Institute of International Affairs.

Taube, G. and Zettelmeyer, J. (1998) Output decline and recovery in Uzbekistan: Past performance and future prospects, IMF Working Paper WP/98/132, Washington DC: International Monetary Fund.

Weinthal, E. (2002) *State Making and Environmental Cooperation: Linking Domestic and International Policies in Central Asia*, Cambridge MA: MIT Press.

World Bank (1993) *World Development Report 1993*, Washington DC: World Bank.
World Bank (2001) *World Development Report 2000/2001*, Washington DC: World Bank.
World Bank (2002) *Transition: The First Ten Years*. Washington DC: World Bank.
World Bank (2004) *World Development Indicators 2004*, Washington DC: World Bank.

# 6 Transition and economic development challenges in the resource-poor countries

*Cevdet Denizer*

## Introduction

Independence brought unprecedented challenges to the natural resource-poor countries of the former Soviet Union (FSU), the Kyrgyz Republic and Tajikistan in Central Asia, and Armenia and Georgia in the Caucasus. Since declaring themselves as independent states in late 1991 these countries have had to deal with a double transition, from a centrally planned to a market-based economy and from republics of the FSU to independent nations at the same time. In the process, Armenia, Georgia and Tajikistan suffered from either protracted regional conflicts or civil wars, which affected, and are still affecting, their economic and political transitions in important ways. Another important aspect of the independence of the resource-poor countries has been the loss of large transfers from the FSU, which combined with trade and payments disruptions after the Union dissolved to cause massive contraction in measured output and to push inflation to unprecedented peaks.

Although the reforms eventually restored economic growth and inflation was largely controlled, this improved performance has not offset the output contraction that took place during most of the 1990s. Current output levels are still on average 61 per cent of 1990 levels (Table 6.1). As a result, the four countries are the poorest in the FSU and poverty is widespread. It is also unclear whether they are yet on a sustainable development path because the structural reform agenda remains large and institutional deficiencies have become more apparent. Furthermore, new constraints, notably, the rapid build-up of large foreign debt in Kyrgyzstan and Tajikistan, have emerged as a problem. The large debt service requirements along with low tax collection ratios relative to GDP, raise serious concerns for both external and fiscal sustainability, which undermine economic growth prospects.

In this context, this chapter takes a fresh look at the economic prospects of the four resource-poor countries. Political factors heavily affected the reform process in all four countries and the speed and implementation of key policies depended on political stability and, for Armenia, Georgia and Tajikistan, on the achievement of peace. In fact, the overall governance and incentive structure has become the most important domestic constraint on private sector

Table 6.1 Reform and transition growth trajectories, by country and regional group

| Country group | First phase reform index | Second phase reform index | Cumulative GDP decline to low (%) | Year of lowest GDP | % Annual GDP growth from low | GDP 2003 compared to 1989 GDP (%) | Earnings Gini 2000 |
|---|---|---|---|---|---|---|---|
| Caspian Region | 3.1 | 2.1 | 55.1 | 1995 | 6.6 | 74 | 0.343 |
| Resource-rich | 2.5 | 2.0 | 44.2 | 1996 | 7.1 | 87 | 0.339 |
| Azerbaijan | 3.4 | 2.0 | 63.1 | 1995 | 8.4 | 64 | 0.365 |
| Kazakhstan | 3.2 | 2.3 | 40.0 | 1998 | 5.6 | 86 | 0.313 |
| Turkmenistan | 1.0 | 1.7 | 59.5 | 1997 | 11.3 | 91 | 0.408 |
| Uzbekistan | 2.2 | 2.0 | 14.4 | 1995 | 3.2 | 106 | 0.268 |
| Resource-poor | 3.6 | 2.1 | 66.0 | 1995 | 6.0 | 61 | 0.346 |
| Armenia | 3.6 | 2.4 | 65.1 | 1993 | 7.0 | 78 | 0.379 |
| Georgia | 3.9 | 2.3 | 74.6 | 1994 | 5.5 | 38 | 0.369 |
| Kyrgyzstan | 3.7 | 2.2 | 50.4 | 1995 | 4.8 | 70 | 0.290 |
| Tajikistan | 3.3 | 1.6 | 74.0 | 1996 | 6.6 | 57 | 0.347 |
| Memo Item | | | | | | | |
| CEE + BR | 3.9 | 3.3 | 28.9 | 1993 | 3.4 | 101 | 0.330 |

Source: Reform indices from EBRD 2003: 56; Gini from World Bank 2004; Rest from Fischer and Sahay 2000: 34.

Note: After EBRD 2002: 23. First phase reform includes price liberalization, trade and foreign exchange liberalization and small-scale privatization. Second phase reform involves large-scale privatization, governance and enterprise restructuring, competition policy, infrastructure reforms, banking and interest rate liberalization and non-bank financial institutions. Progress is measured from 1 (minimal) to 4 (virtually complete) according to criteria described in EBRD 2002: 21.

development and capital accumulation. We consider the structural reforms that are required to redefine the role of the state along with the attendant public administration reforms as a second key dimension of the political economy transition in the four resource-poor countries.

This chapter argues that domestic reforms by the resource-poor countries, although necessary for creating a market-based economy, are unlikely to be sufficient to recover the level of development attained under socialism and that long-term prospects are highly uncertain. The last decade has shown the significance of external factors, both regional and international, for a successful transition, and it is hypothesized that these factors will assume a larger role in shaping economic performance as well as political developments in future. In the absence of effective regional trading arrangements, both economic and political, that would enable the exploitation of the comparative advantage of the resource-poor countries and open the way for a degree of regional integration over the long term, the resource-poor countries will be confined to their underdeveloped and small domestic markets. It is possible, therefore, that the disappointing perception of wealth creation as long-term and distant, could channel the efforts of political and economic agents into rent-seeking at the expense of productive activities.

The rest of the chapter is organized as follows. The next section (pages 96–103) provides an overview of economic reforms and outcomes and discusses emerging issues. We also consider the impact of initial conditions in this section, which shed light on sources of growth in the medium term. The third section (pages 103–104) considers the domestic political constraints on further reform. The fourth section (pages 104–109) addresses the regional and international factors that are likely to affect development patterns and discusses the policy reforms required for growth, given the political economy. The chapter concludes with the fifth section (pages 109–110).

## Economic performance between 1991 and 2003: initial conditions and reforms

### The record: reform outcomes to date

Perhaps the most important initial condition was the onset of prolonged conflict early in the transition for three of the resource-poor countries. Soon after independence Armenia and Azerbaijan fought for control of Nagorno-Karabakh for almost four years, while Georgia faced secessionist movements in South Ossetia and later Abhkhazia, which triggered internal civil conflict until 1996. Tajikistan had a seven-year civil war that was not controlled until late 1997 (see Chapter 11). Only the Kyrgyz Republic was spared from conflict. These wars cost 10–20,000 thousand lives in the Armenia–Azerbaijan conflict and 50–70,000 thousand in the Tajik civil war.

The conflicts delayed reform and macroeconomic stabilization. During the conflicts public finances collapsed and monetary policy was out of control, with inflation reaching thousands of per cent. Output collapses were the largest in the FSU with Armenia and Georgia registering GDP falls around 42 per cent and 45 per cent, respectively, in 1992. Output declines were relatively smaller, but still large, in the Kyrgyz Republic (Table 6.1). Economic growth turned positive first in Armenia in 1994 after the end of the war, and in 1995 in Georgia (de Melo *et al.* 2001). The Kyrgyz Republic registered positive economic growth in 1996. Civil strife lasted longer in Tajikistan, and as a result, output declined steadily until 1997.

Table 6.1 shows that, once initiated, economic growth was rapid in Armenia, Georgia and the Kyrgyz Republic, averaging about 7 per cent in each country, but growth in Georgia and the Kyrgyz Republic then slowed in the late 1990s. Tajikistan exhibits a different pattern with slow initial GDP growth that steadily increased to average 9 per cent during 2000–3. While these growth rates are respectable, the level of output is still less than two-thirds the level in 1989, giving an idea of the development challenges and the need to sustain growth. Poverty increased drastically in all four countries, as measured by the poverty headcount index (i.e. percentage of people living under \$2.15/day).[1]

A new and worrisome development for all four resource-poor countries is a rapid accumulation of external debt to very high levels (Table 6.2), which raises concern about fiscal and balance of payments sustainability. In Kyrgyz Republic and Tajikistan external debt exceeded 100 per cent of GDP by late 2000 and debt service absorbed over half the budget revenue. In 2003, the ratio of net present value of external debt to exports and central government revenue was 223 per cent and 416 per cent, respectively, for Kyrgyz Republic and 142 per cent and 320 per cent, respectively, for Tajikistan. Georgia and Armenia have lower amounts of debt but their debt is still large (Table 6.2). This debt burden is the more problematic, given the large public investment needed in human and physical capital.

*Table 6.2* Growth in external debt 1992–1999 and debt service 2003 of four resource-poor countries

| Country/ group | Debt/GDP 1992 (%) | Debt/GDP 1999 (%) | NPVDebt/ exports (%) | NPV/Govt revenue (%) | Debt service/ exports (%) | Debt service/ govt. revenue (%) |
|---|---|---|---|---|---|---|
| Armenia | 5 | 46 | 97 | 179 | 8 | 20 |
| Georgia | 0 | 60 | 145 | 404 | 16 | 46 |
| Kyrgyzstan | 0 | 135 | 223 | 416 | 21 | 43 |
| Tajikistan | 0 | 109 | 142 | 320 | 11 | 27 |

*Source*: IMF 2001: 6–7, IMF 2004: 15–16.

*Note*: Debt/GDP ratios data for all CCA countries 2002: Armenia 49%; Azerbaijan 23%; Georgia 54%; Kazakhstan 72%; Kyrgyzstan 112%; Tajikistan 95%; Turkmenistan n.a.; Uzbekistan 58% (World Bank 2004).

*Explaining performance: initial conditions and policies*

Apart from civil conflicts and wars, what other factors played a role in these outcomes and what are the implications for future economic performance? At the conceptual level, it is easily argued that the economic performance of the resource-poor countries has been shaped by the initial conditions and policies followed after the FSU collapsed (de Melo *et al.* 2001; Falcetti *et al.* 2001). We distinguish between three types of initial conditions: structural, institutional and macroeconomic. Under these three broad categories, de Melo *et al.* (2001) identify eleven initial conditions, shown in Table 6.3 (which adds estimates of resource transfers from the center).

Turning to structural factors first, and apart from natural resources, there are at least six that we identify. These are location and infrastructure, initial GDP, trade dependence and terms of trade, transfers from the former Union, over-industrialization and urbanization. With the exception of Georgia, which has an opening to the Black Sea, the remaining resource-poor countries are land-locked and most of their transport infrastructure is oriented towards the FSU, especially in the Kyrgyz Republic and Tajikistan. With independence these countries became more insular and isolated with adverse implications for trade links. In addition, the four resource-poor countries are also small, with relatively small populations, so that the compression in GDP has further shrunk the capacity of their domestic markets to support viable scale-sensitive manufacturing.

The next three indices by and large determined income levels in the resource-poor countries. Trade dependence, which reflected flows of goods within one big country under central planning range around 24 to 31 per cent of GDP for the four countries. While terms of trade data are not available prior to the collapse of the FSU (and did not matter as long as the Union existed), planners ensured that inter-republican trade flows took place without reference to either relative scarcities of goods in the Union or world prices. The fact that some of the republics ran large trade deficits was reflected in transfers from the Union. These deficits were recorded in inter-republican trade balances and, to a large degree, were covered by Union transfers. These transfers were about 40 per cent of GDP in 1989–90 for Tajikistan and 20 per cent for Kyrgyz Republic.

Industrialization is another variable affecting economic performance. Central planning attached great importance to industrialization and large inter-republican trade flows and transfers from the center reflected this policy. However, industrialization that is not aligned with a country's resource base is a distortion that can be measured by the difference between the actual share of industry in GDP and the share predicted by Syrquin and Chenery (1989). As shown in Table 6.3 both Armenia and Georgia were over-industrialized while this is much less the case in the Kyrgyz Republic and not at all true for Tajikistan. In other words, central planning distorted the structure of the economies of Tajikistan and the Kyrgyz Republic less than that of Armenia

Table 6.3 Indices of initial conditions

| Country/group | PCGNP ($PPP) 1989 | Urbanization (% population 1990) | Years under central planning | Macro-economic distortion[1] | Over-industry (% GDP 1990) | Average GNP growth (1985–89%) | Trade dependence 1990 (%) | Presence of state institutions | Location |
|---|---|---|---|---|---|---|---|---|---|
| Resource-poor | | | | | | | | | |
| Armenia | 5,530 | 68 | 71 | 0.79 | 20 | 2.7 | 25.6 | 0 | 0 |
| Georgia | 5,590 | 56 | 70 | 0.84 | 8 | 2.4 | 24.8 | 0 | 0 |
| Kyrgyz Republic | 3,180 | 38 | 71 | 1.03 | 6 | 5.2 | 27.7 | 0 | 0 |
| Tajikistan | 3,010 | 32 | 71 | 1.01 | 0 | 1.9 | 31.0 | 0 | 0 |
| Resource-rich | | | | | | | | | |
| Azerbaijan | 4,620 | 54 | 70 | 1.00 | 8 | 0.8 | 29.8 | 0 | 0 |
| Kazakhstan | 5,130 | 67 | 71 | 1.07 | −4 | 4.3 | 20.8 | 0 | 0 |
| Turkmenistan | 4,230 | 45 | 71 | 1.27 | −1 | 5.0 | 33.0 | 0 | 0 |
| Uzbekistan | 2,740 | 41 | 71 | 1.15 | −4 | 3.9 | 25.5 | 0 | 0 |

Source: de Melo et al. 2001: 5–6 and 17.

or Georgia. Even so the importance of FSU defense industries in Armenia and Kyrgyz Republic exacerbated the collapse of manufacturing in those countries (Ofer and Pomfret 2004).

Initial institutional conditions are particularly important and they are proxied by state independence, development of state institutions and years under central planning. None of the resource-poor countries were independent nor at the center of federalized states like Russia before 1989. This implied the need to set up the institutional infrastructure for a democratic market-based economy, including parliaments, national banks, treasuries, customs, ministerial reform, and above all, redefinition of the role of the State. This is one of the defining differences between the CEE countries and the CIS with the exception of the Baltic states so given their lack of fiscal resources to restructure their public administrations, the development of public institutions was bound to be more difficult for the resource-poor countries. Finally, unlike the CEE countries and Baltic states, the CIS tended not to have a single generation with market experience, and the lack of familiarity with free market mechanisms may be more problematic for the poorer CIS countries because western firms and individuals in professions like accounting, auditing and the law are much more easily attracted to resource-rich countries like Azerbaijan and Kazakhstan than they are to resource-poor countries.

Having reviewed the initial conditions, we now examine policy reform. We rely on the EBRD's transition indicators to understand how far these countries have reformed themselves. As shown in Table 6.4, while there has been reasonable progress in price and trade liberalization, structural reform and institutional development lag. Even so, Kazakhstan is the only resource-rich country that reformed faster than the resource-poor countries as a group, while Azerbaijan, Turkmenistan and Uzbekistan are clearly behind. One explanation for this difference is that the resource-poor countries reformed in order to attract financing from the IFIs. Indeed, most of the IFI lending early in the transition replaced Russian transfers, albeit at smaller amounts because there was no 'Marshall' type of bilateral assistance. However, IFI support came in the form of loans and not grants, which even on concessional terms contributed to the debt problem. Moreover, a significant portion of the IFI debt appears to have financed consumption, which is understandable given the income compression, particularly during the early years of transition. The structure of external debt seems to confirm that view, because the IFIs hold about half the total debt. With hindsight, it might have been better to provide donor grants to mitigate revenue losses from GDP at the outset of reform and then link IFI loans to investment in reform (Hebling *et al.* 2004).

With regard to the implications of this analysis for the past and future development prospects of the resource-poor countries, de Melo *et al.* (2001) and Falcetti *et al.* (2001) conclude that both initial conditions and reform policy shaped economic performance in all transition countries. Falcetti *et al.*

Table 6.4 EBRD economic transition indicators 2003[1]

| Country/group | Privatization | Govt + firm restructure | Price liberalization | Trade liberalization | Competition policy | Financial reform | Infrastructure reform | Overall index |
|---|---|---|---|---|---|---|---|---|
| Mid-income | | | | | | | | |
| Central + E. Europe | 3.9 | 3.0 | 4.2 | 4.3 | 2.7 | 3.2 | 2.9 | 3.5 |
| Northern CIS + SEE | 3.8 | 1.9 | 3.8 | 3.5 | 2.3 | 2.3 | 2.2 | 2.8 |
| Russia | 3.5 | 2.3 | 4.0 | 3.3 | 2.3 | 2.3 | 2.3 | 2.8 |
| Lower income | | | | | | | | |
| East Asia[2] | 2.0 | 2.1 | 2.9 | 2.5 | 1.8 | 1.5 | n.a. | 2.1 |
| Caspian Basin | 3.1 | 1.9 | 3.6 | 4.2 | 1.8 | 2.0 | 1.8 | 2.5 |
| Resource-poor | 3.4 | 2.0 | 4.2 | 3.7 | 1.9 | 2.1 | 1.8 | 2.8 |
| Caspian | | | | | | | | |
| Armenia | 3.5 | 2.3 | 4.3 | 4.3 | 2.0 | 2.2 | 2.3 | 3.0 |
| Georgia | 3.7 | 2.0 | 4.3 | 4.3 | 2.0 | 2.0 | 2.3 | 2.9 |
| Kyrgyzstan | 3.5 | 2.0 | 4.3 | 4.3 | 2.0 | 2.3 | 1.3 | 2.8 |
| Tajikistan | 3.0 | 1.7 | 3.7 | 3.7 | 1.7 | 1.7 | 1.3 | 2.4 |
| Resource-rich | 2.7 | 1.8 | 3.4 | 2.5 | 1.7 | 1.9 | 1.7 | 2.2 |
| Caspian | | | | | | | | |
| Azerbaijan | 2.9 | 2.3 | 4.0 | 3.7 | 2.0 | 2.0 | 1.7 | 2.7 |
| Kazakhstan | 3.5 | 2.0 | 4.0 | 3.7 | 2.0 | 2.7 | 2.3 | 2.9 |
| Turkmenistan | 1.5 | 1.0 | 2.7 | 1.0 | 1.0 | 1.0 | 1.0 | 1.3 |
| Uzbekistan | 2.9 | 1.7 | 2.7 | 1.7 | 1.7 | 1.7 | 1.7 | 2.0 |

Source: EBRD 2003: 18, except East Asia from IMF 2000: 134.

Note:
1 The privatization and financial reform indices are collapsed from two readings into one, weighting all the original eight readings.
2 Data for 1999.

(2001) argue that the collapse of output through the mid-1990s and the relatively slow supply response to reform were largely determined by the initial conditions and, in the resource-poor countries, by the effects of civil strife. But which initial conditions are likely to persist in their effects on future development patterns? We provide some answers below before analyzing the set of idiosyncratic factors (domestic, regional and international), which may override some of the unfavorable initial conditions.

First, it is clear that the loss of transfers from the Union had a large and persistent impact on the Tajik and Kyrgyz economies. As noted earlier, these two countries abruptly lost 40 per cent and 20 per cent of their incomes and this fundamentally changed the structure of their economies, with industrial output falling sharply and agriculture and later services expanding significantly (Table 6.5). A second factor related to subsidies is the change in the terms of trade for these countries, which import almost all their energy. The move to international prices for energy imports has persistently impacted the structure of these economies. The loss of subsidies and the loss of traditional markets rendered many SOEs unprofitable, requiring deep restructuring, privatization or liquidation. This need is still not well understood in the resource-poor countries, so that many idle SOEs remain in the public sector. There is an understandable political economy dimension to this retention of SOEs, but large-scale privatization still lags in the four resource-poor countries and hampers private sector growth.

Second, two sets of institutional issues are becoming important for future development. The first is that these countries are the periphery that lost the center, in sharp contrast to the CEE countries and the Baltics. With no prospect of joining a larger economic and political entity like the EU, these countries drifted into independence with power structures that did not necessarily aim to improve citizen welfare. Expressed another way: the limited

*Table 6.5* Change in employment composition, by sector 1990–1999 (% total)

|  | Agriculture | Industry | Non-market services | Market services |
|---|---|---|---|---|
| Central + East Europe | 16 → 12 | 41 → 33 | 20 → 24 | 22 → 31 |
| Caspian Region | 34 → 45 | 28 → 16 | 25 → 20 | 14 → 19 |
| Mineral-rich | 37 → 36 | 25 → 18 | 23 → 20 | 14 → 23 |
| Azerbaijan | 45 → 29 | 22 → 12 | 18 → 20 | 15 → 26 |
| Kazakhstan | 22 → 25 | 31 → 18 | 25 → 17 | 17 → 38 |
| Turkmenistan | 42 → 49 | 21 → 19 | 23 → 19 | 13 → 13 |
| Uzbekistan | 40 → 39 | 25 → 21 | 24 → 24 | 12 → 14 |
| Resource-poor | 30 → 54 | 31 → 13 | 26 → 20 | 13 → 14 |
| Armenia | 18 → 43 | 42 → 19 | 27 → 24 | 12 → 13 |
| Georgia | 26 → 54 | 30 → 10 | 27 → 20 | 14 → 20 |
| Kyrgyzstan | 33 → 53 | 28 → 12 | 25 → 19 | 13 → 16 |
| Tajikistan | 43 → 65 | 22 → 10 | 23 → 18 | 11 → 7 |

*Source:* Estimated from Raiser *et al.* 2001.

prospects of sustained development have shifted the imperative of the natural resource endowment discussed in Chapter 2 away from wealth creation and towards rent-seeking at the expense of productive activity. Consequently, the inherited large cadre of poorly paid public servants is now a serious threat to growth because, as analyzed in more detail in Chapters 7 and 8, an increasingly predatory civil service is deterring private investment and locking in a growth-repressing vicious circle of public sector predation, low investment, low tax revenue and inadequate private sector job creation. We consider what can be done in the next section and analyze emerging constraints as well as options for improvement.

### Domestic political transition and the nature of the political state

As the CIEN model suggests (Chapter 2) political reform to more open and democratic systems has generally proceeded faster in the resource-poor countries than the resource-rich countries. The Kyrgyz Republic, Armenia and Georgia rank higher than their surrounding neighbors and Tajikistan tolerates more dissent than Uzbekistan and is not far beyond Kazakhstan (Table 4.10). While this is welcome, it may not yield an incentive structure that will support productive activity. The achievement of peace in Georgia, Armenia and Tajikistan necessitated the accommodation of the demands of various warring parties and these now represent formidable interest groups retarding reform and constraining the actions of the state and how its citizens perceive it. Such local conditions override the imperative afforded by resource paucity to create wealth: they limit the autonomy of the state and narrow its aims so that it does not function as a developmental political state.

In Tajikistan, for example, local governments block farm privatization, which is vital to poverty reduction in rural areas where 70 per cent of the poor live.[2] The government uses informal quotas on cotton production to force farmers to plant cotton from which rents are extracted. Raw cotton costs about US$1 per kilo in international markets while the official price to farmers ranges from 4 to 15 cents per kilo. Furthermore, the political balancing act of the government has delayed public administration reform (like restructuring ministries), both at the local and central levels. The reform would cut staff but it is not politically feasible. The result is a large public administration, including legions of inspectors in various ministries, domestic security personnel and ubiquitous police, which extracts rents from the private sector and drives businesses into the shadow economy.

Armenia has the best political system and is judged by Freedom House to be the most free of the resource-poor countries. Unfortunately, the defining element of post-Soviet Armenian politics has been the Nagorno-Karabakh conflict with Azerbaijan. Since then, political leaders from Karabakh received prominent government posts and the key objective has become protection of the interests of Armenians in Karabakh, perhaps at the expense of other Armenian citizens. Institutional reform has been neglected until recently and there have been a number of high-profile corruption cases. Although corruption in Armenia is significantly lower than in other CCA countries (Table 4.10), it is ubiquitous and pervades all levels of government, so that the investment climate is weakened and domestic investment could fall below the level required to sustain the rapid economic growth rates of recent years.

Georgia is perhaps the most unfortunate in terms of political transition and political stability. The unsettled conflicts in Abkhazia and South Ossetia prevented many policies from being implemented across the whole country and rendered security problematic. Although Shevardnadze's efforts to rebuild the government were impressive and appreciated by the international community, his power was weak and the government's capacity extremely limited. The patronage system was important for key government posts. Implementation of reforms and decrees often depended on negotiations among central, local and regional officials. As in Armenia, corruption was a serious problem, but much more arbitrary and systemic, with police, courts and customs all taking bribes openly. However, the abrupt regime change in late 2003 created an opportunity for marked improvement.

The Kyrgyz Republic is the most advanced in terms of economic and political reforms in Central Asia. However, the momentum of the early years of transition has faltered and the investment climate is difficult. Institutional reforms have lagged so that GDP growth slowed from 1998 and was negative in 2002. This performance is insufficient to reduce poverty so there is an urgent need to promote the private sector. There is no question that the Kyrgyz Republic is the most open political regime in Central Asia, and the announcement by President Akaev that he will retire from office by 2005 is a welcome development, which, however, could yet lead to virulent political competition among the elite.

To summarize, despite the incentive to generate wealth that a resource-poor endowment might be expected to confer, political and economic reforms have yet to produce an environment conducive to capital accumulation. Rather, the perceived pessimistic prospects for long-term development foster intense competition for power and the short-term gains from the rent-seeking opportunities that it unlocks, but this comes at the expense of badly needed reforms. The next section argues that improved prospects require action at the regional and international levels.

## External interventions for improved transition

### *Removal of regional constraints on reform*

A number of issues, almost totally regional in character, and ranging across water resources, power and transport, and lack of co-operation in these three areas hurt the resource-poor countries and undermine both their growth potential and their very existence as meaningful nation states. As discussed in Chapter 10, both Tajikistan and the Kyrgyz Republic have abundant water resources from the Syr Darya and Amu Darya, which are critical for growing cotton and other crops downstream in Kazakhstan, Uzbekistan and Turkmenistan. However, Tajikistan and the Kyrgyz Republic lack sufficient storage capacity so this important resource flows freely to their neighbors without much benefit to their own economies (Kennedy *et al.* 2004; Weinthal 2003). In addition, energy, particularly hydro-electricity, is in short supply in parts of Tajikistan and the Kyrgyz Republic. Yet, although dams could be built to resolve both problems, the agreement of Kazakhstan and Uzbekistan is needed to avoid a conflict and the indications are that this may not easily be secured.

Even if agreements could be secured, the financing required by the dams depends on securing export markets within the Central Asian region for part of the additional power. Tajikistan currently seeks more than $1 billion in funding for two dams (Sangtuda and Ragun) that were half-built during Soviet times, an amount that is the same size as Tajik GDP. Similarly, the Kyrgyz Republic seeks finance for the Kambarata dam, also half-built, whose completion requires another US$0.8 billion. These projects compete with each other and it is possible that neither will be completed. Their completion depends on securing export markets in Kazakhstan and Pakistan and possibly Afghanistan and Iran, which would be the first step in obtaining commercial funds. In other words, the exploitation of their comparative advantage by Tajikistan and the Kyrgyz Republic depends on regional factors largely beyond their control.

Trade and transport links present a second set of regional issues that are seriously hurting Tajikistan and the Kyrgyz Republic, as explained more fully in Chapter 9. Tajikistan depends almost fully on Uzbekistan for its rail transport and trade and in the absence of good political relations it experiences major problems. The Uzbek authorities now require visas from Tajik citizens, and visa and customs officials make it difficult to cross the border, often demanding bribes and harassing Tajiks. Elsewhere, Kyrgyz exports to Kazakhstan have more than halved since 1998 even though Kazakhstan registered strong economic growth during the 1998–2004 period, suggesting that there are serious informal trade restrictions. Numerous treaties and a customs union between the Caspian Basin countries and Russia have all failed to facilitate trade, to the detriment of Tajikistan and the Kyrgyz Republic. Yet the benefits of domestic reforms can only be fully realized if there are working trade and transport arrangements in the region.

In the Caucasus, both ongoing and dormant civil strife have negative impacts on trade. Although the official tariffs of the Caucasian countries are not high by international standards and they are falling and becoming more uniform, unofficial barriers to trade remain substantial. For example, Molnar and Ojala (2003: 13) report that truck drivers must pay $1,800–2,000 to travel with Ministry of Security guards through Georgia, en route from Armenia to the USSR, a similar amount to what would be paid at illicit roadblocks in the absence of the guard. Despite the region's high transport costs it exports goods with low value/weight ratios including energy (Azeri oil and gas), minerals (Armenian copper concentrate and molybdenum) and scrap metal (in all three countries as a consequence of dismantling obsolete FSU plants). The unofficial barriers to trade are most widespread and severe in Azerbaijan, more random in Georgia (which has now hired foreign customs officials) and least oppressive in Armenia, according to Polyakov (2001). But Armenia incurs substantially higher costs because it cannot officially ship goods across the borders of Turkey and Azerbaijan. The disruption of natural trade flows also imposes especially high energy costs on Armenia, yet all three South Caucasus countries as well as Turkey would benefit from the rationalization of energy supply that the normalization of regional relations would allow.

With rising per capita incomes, the potential gains from improved trade links increase, according to Polyakov (2001), and such gains are not only in high weight/value goods, but also in low weight/ value goods such as cement, building stone and tiles, where considerable efficiency gains would accrue from fuller use of surplus capacity. However, gains from the normalization of trade relations within the Caucasus would not be evenly shared, at least through the short and medium term. The gains would be of greatest benefit to Armenia and might initially divert transit traffic from Georgia, according to Molnar and Ojala (2003: 10). Polyakov (2001) agrees and projects that Armenia can double its exports, halve its trade deficit and boost its GDP by 30 per cent as a consequence of normalized trade links, whereas Azerbaijan could boost its exports by only 11 per cent and gain barely 5 per cent in GDP while reducing its trade deficit by one-quarter. As Chapter 9 shows, however, freer Caspian regional trade will not solve all the trade problems, but regional efforts to remove transport barriers are also required to reach what Chapter 9 concludes are the potentially more promising export markets among near neighboring countries like Russia, China, Iran and Turkey.

### Role of the international community in accelerating transition

The compression in output within the four resource-poor countries that followed the transition shock was both much deeper and ran for much longer than many economists expected. This is sometimes attributed to a combination of faltering commitment to reform and shocks, notably civil strife and the Russian financial crisis of 1998. However, this chapter has argued that adverse initial conditions played a much more important role in impeding reform than other explanations allow. In particular, a combined legacy of deficient national institutions and social capital that is characterized by bonding at family, regional and clan levels weakens the capacity to pursue reform designed to further the *national* interest. The absence of realistic aspirations to participate in a successful economic union like NAFTA or the EU has sapped faith in national development so competition emerges between groups to further the group interest by capturing rents. Such political motivations undermine regime security and also discourage co-operation between governments within the region, which as shown above impose sizeable economic costs and sap the potential benefits of reform.

Whatever the reason, the transition shock was associated with a sharp accumulation in external debt, which in the early 1990s largely reflected unpaid imports that in the case of Georgia, for example, were mainly from Turkmenistan but also from Russia. It may have been the case that the newly independent governments initially had some expectation that the debt would not need to be repaid, as had been the situation within the FSU. This was not to be, however, and subsequent growth in debt through the late 1990s was associated with lending by the IFIs and rising foreign aid (Table 6.6). Such lending was in support of measures to stabilize and restructure the economy and to enhance each country's debt service capacity by boosting growth in GDP, exports and government revenues. As a consequence, the share of multilateral debt typically rose to half the total external debt and although the increase in debt was anticipated and many program targets were met, under-performance in other aspects of reform combined with external shocks to push growth in debt service capacity below the levels targeted (IMF 2001). Table 6.2 traces the build-up in debt, which by the early 2000s had become especially difficult to service for Tajikistan but was most problematic of all for the fastest reformer, Kyrgyzstan.

The case of Kyrgyzstan is particularly instructive. Much of the later borrowing was channeled into public investment, which reached 9 per cent of GDP in 2000, in order to improve infrastructure. Yet even with a total investment rate of 19.4 per cent of GDP and a sharp improvement in the incremental capital output ratio (ICOR) from 5.8 to 3.9 during 1995–2002, the IMF (2001) still estimates that net capital stock declined. In addition to public investment the opening of a sizeable goldmine and improvements in agriculture also drove GDP growth, as inputs were more efficiently deployed and yielded strong gains in total factor productivity. However, the debt

*Table 6.6*　Aid receipts, CCA countries 1993–2000 (% GNI)

|  | *1993–96* | *1997–2000* | *1993–2000* | *GDP 2002 as % 1989* |
|---|---|---|---|---|
| Resource-rich | *1.10* | *1.71* | *1.40* | *87* |
| Azerbaijan | 3.04 | 3.40 | 3.22 | 64 |
| Kazakhstan | 0.31 | 0.96 | 0.64 | 86 |
| Turkmenistan | 0.63 | 0.69 | 0.66 | 91 |
| Uzbekistan | 0.40 | 1.78 | 1.09 | 106 |
| Resource-poor | *7.15* | *11.28* | *9.94* | *61* |
| Armenia | 9.86 | 10.01 | 9.94 | 78 |
| Georgia | 8.96 | 6.30 | 7.63 | 38 |
| Kyrgyzstan | 5.65 | 17.53 | 11.59 | 70 |
| Tajikistan | 4.14 | 11.29 | 7.72 | 57 |

*Source:* World Bank 2004, except column 1: EBRD 2002: 58.

service capacity of the reforming economy failed to keep pace with the growth in debt. One reason may be that infrastructure investments have a long-term payback, while the sharp rise in public expenditure may have crowded out private investment, an outcome not helped by the deterrent to FDI caused by regional geopolitical instability, not least the Afghan war. Moreover, the real effective exchange rate of the Kyrgyz Republic depreciated by two-fifths during 1996–2001, a factor working against debt service, yet the country was unable to offset this by taking full advantage of its growing competitive edge, partly because of the Russian financial crisis and partly because of official and unofficial trade barriers erected by its larger neighbors, notably Uzbekistan and Kazakhstan. Although GDP growth averaged a respectable 5 per cent per annum and the incidence of poverty fell to 55 per cent of the population, the disappointing growth in exports combined with a GDP growth rate that was 2–3 per cent lower than its potential to push debt service capacity below the level expected by the IFIs.

In contrast, Tajikistan used its borrowing to substitute for the loss of union transfers and directed the bulk of the loans into consumption aimed, understandably, at easing the social costs of the combined transition shock and civil war. Moreover, reform was delayed by civil strife and when it did finally commence it could not be pursued vigorously because of the need to mollify the protagonists in the civil war and also vested interests in local government, the remaining state farms and the energy SOEs. Although both private agriculture and more recently manufacturing exhibited strong growth potential, the country remains over-dependent on exports of aluminum, cotton and electricity for earning its foreign exchange. Moreover, Tajikistan is especially heavily dependent upon electricity generation, which does not recoup its costs (the energy sector as a whole has quasi-fiscal deficits of more than 10 per cent of GDP annually) and effectively subsidizes not only household consumers and small businesses but also the importers of its aluminum and hydro-electricity.

External shocks and faltering reform efforts also lie behind the build-up of debt in the two resource-poor countries in the Caucasus. Armenia channeled more multilateral assistance into consumption than expected, due to slower than planned disbursement of investment funds, while faltering reforms and the political crisis in 1999 deterred private investment. The subsequent rebound in vigorous export-led GDP growth, helped by a 20 per cent depreciation in the real exchange rate after December 1999, is helping to close the fiscal and current account gaps so that debt service will become even more manageable if the newly strengthened government maintains its renewed interest in reform. A similar change in government response, and subsequent debt service capacity, may occur in Georgia, under the new government that swept to power in 2003. However, in contrast to Armenia, this change takes place against a legacy of sluggish GDP growth, unusually low tax revenues and even less respect for civic institutions.

Chronic weaknesses in national institutions and the negative externalities from regional political frictions continue to hamper the transition in all four resource-poor countries. Yet with western assistance, they have all made progress both in stabilizing their economies and in restructuring them (perhaps least in Tajikistan and most in Armenia). The IFIs have drawn up strategies to strengthen debt service capacity and ensure the debt burden is sustainable through the medium term and long term (IMF 2002). Moreover, the conditionality associated with these strategies will reinforce the commitment to economic reform, which will rely strongly on providing efficiency incentives to farmers and small businesses, whose eventual success will help to rebuild social capital and strengthen political accountability. Without continued western support, however, including political support to broker peaceful solutions to regional conflicts in both the Caucasus and Central Asia, neither the prospect of rising welfare nor of improved debt service capability is likely to be sustained.

## Synthesis and conclusions

This chapter has argued that initial diagnoses of tardy reform as the cause of the disappointing transition trajectories of the resource-poor countries of the Caucasus and Central Asian region is too simple. It neglects the critical role of initial conditions. In addition to key factors such as remoteness from democratic market-driven economies, relatively high levels of macro-economic distortion arising from lengthy exposure to central planning and exceptionally sharp GDP compression, the resource-poor countries have also been hampered by the absence of national institutions, one important manifestation of which is an inheritance of social capital that works against the national welfare. It is perhaps this latter factor more than any other that overrides the incentive for national wealth creation that the resource-driven development models suggest should emanate from the absence of natural resource rents. Rather, it seems that even resource-poor countries can yield sufficient natural resource, geopolitical and contrived rents to tempt sub-groups at all levels within society to prosper by capturing a disproportionate share of the rent, but at the expense of national welfare. World Bank (2004) estimates of adjusted net saving suggest that the resource-poor countries were liquidating their wealth-generating assets, albeit at a much slower rate than the four resource-rich CCA countries (Table 10.4, final column).

Not only do small domestic markets, policy capture and the distortion of economic incentives by vested interests hamper transition reform, but fractured external relations compound these internal difficulties. For example, apart from expanding trade in agro-processed products and fruit and vegetables, Tajikistan and the Kyrgyz Republic need to use their abundant water resources more productively, which cannot be achieved without reaching agreements with Uzbekistan and Kazakhstan. Elsewhere, Armenia and Georgia need improved political relations with their immediate neighbors to take full advantage of their trade potential. The inability and/or the unwillingness of the larger neighbors in Central Asia, Kazakhstan and Uzbekistan, to factor in inter-temporal dimensions of trade and regional integration is one of the major bottlenecks for improving welfare in the region. Since, as Chapters 7–12 amply demonstrate, a decade of transition has done little to remedy these problems, we argue that the international community has an important role to play as well, ranging from donor assistance and debt relief to honest power broker in settling disputes. Such positive developments on the regional and international fronts will foster the emergence of stronger private sectors and new elites in the resource-poor countries, which are critical for developing the political competition and institutions that will support market-based democratic systems through the long-term.

## Notes

1   In 2001 the poverty headcount index for Armenia was 37 per cent (18 per cent in 1988) compared with 23 per cent (37 per cent) for Georgia, 55 per cent (59 per cent) for the Kyrgyz Republic and 56 per cent (59 per cent) in Tajikistan (IMF 2004: 9). This index may overstate actual poverty, however.
2   World Bank Poverty Assessment Report (2000) and Poverty Reduction Strategy of Tajikistan (2002).

## References

De Melo, M., Denizer, C., Gelb, A. and Tenev, S. (2001) Circumstance and choice: The role of initial conditions and policies in transition economies, *World Bank Economic Review* 15(1), 1–31.

EBRD (2002) *Transition Report 2002: Agriculture and Rural Transition*, London: European Bank for Reconstruction and Development.

EBRD (2003) *Transition Report 2003: Integration and Regional Cooperation*, London: European Bank for Reconstruction and Development.

Falcetti, E., Raiser, M. and Sanfey, P. (2001) Defying the odds: initial conditions, reforms and growth in the first decade, EBRD Working Paper 55, London: EBRD.

Fischer, S. and Sahay, R. (2000) The transition economies after ten years, IMF Working Paper 00/30, IMF, Washington DC.

Hebling, T., Mody, A. and Sahay, R. (2004) Debt accumulation in the CIS-7 countries: Bad luck, bad policies or bad advice? in: Shiells, C.R. and Sattar, S. (eds.) *The Low-Income Countries of the Commonwealth of Independent States: Progress and Challenges in Transition*, Washington DC: IMF and World Bank, 15–50.

IMF (2000) *World Economic Outlook: Focus on Transition Economies*, Washington DC: International Monetary Fund.

IMF (2001) *Armenia, Georgia, Kyrgyz Republic, Moldova and Tajikistan: External Debt and Fiscal Sustainability*, Washington DC: International Monetary Fund.

IMF (2002) *Poverty Reduction, Growth and Debt Sustainability in Low-Income CIS Countries Sustainability*, Washington DC: International Monetary Fund.

IMF (2004) *Recent Policies and Performance of the Low-Income CIS Countries: An Update of the CIS-7 Initiative*, Washington DC: International Monetary Fund.

Kennedy, D., Fankhauser, S. and Raiser, M. (2004) Low pressure, high tension: The energy-water nexus in the CIS-7 countries, in: Shiells, C.R. and Sattar, S. (eds.) *The*

*Low-Income Countries of the Commonwealth of Independent States*, Washington DC: IMF, 283–306.

Molnar, E. and Ojala, L. (2003) Transport and trade facilitation issues in the CIS-7, Kazakhstan and Turkmenistan, Paper prepared for the CIS-7 Conference, Lucerne, January 20–22.

Ofer, G. and Pomfret, R. (2004) *The Economic Prospects of the CIS: Sources of Long Term Growth*, Cheltenham: Edward Elgar.

Polyakov, E. (2001) Changing trade patterns with conflict resolution in the South Caucasus, World Bank Working Paper 2593, Washington DC: World Bank.

Raiser, M., Schaffer, M. and Schuchardt, J. (2001) Economic development, structural change and transition, Working Paper, Edinburgh: Department of Economics, Heriot-Watt University.

Syrquin, M. and Chenery, H.B. (1989) Patterns of development, 1950 to 1983, World Bank Discussion Paper 41, World Bank, Washington DC.

Weinthal, E. (2003) *State Making and Environmental Cooperation: Linking Domestic and International Politics in Central Asia*, Cambridge MA: MIT Press.

World Bank (2004) *World Development Indicators 2004*, Washington DC: World Bank.

# Part III

# Political economy constraints

# 7 Deficient social capital and its consequences for sustained reform

*Erica Johnson and Richard M. Auty*

## Introduction

Chapters 3–6 have demonstrated how differences in the natural resource endowment combined with other initial conditions (principally the length of exposure to central planning, proximity to the EU and the scale of GDP compression) to vary the pace of reform among the CCA countries. All eight CCA countries eventually achieved macroeconomic stabilization and seven of them subsequently experienced fairly rapid GDP growth, the exception being the 'gradual reformer' Uzbekistan. However, as is the case with many developing market economies that were distorted by maladroit policies during the 1960s and 1970s, reform in the CCA countries met with more success in stabilizing the economy than in competitively restructuring it. This outcome suggests that the current strong rates of economic growth in most CCA countries may not be sustainable. Rather, rapid growth has been driven either by FDI and/or high energy prices (Azerbaijan, Kazakhstan and Turkmenistan); geopolitical rent that flowed mainly into consumption rather than investment (Tajikistan and Kyrgyzstan) or external remittances (Armenia and Georgia). Investment has, at best, arrested the continued deterioration in infrastructure, as in Armenia but not yet elsewhere, whereas growth in non-hydrocarbon tradaeables like manufacturing and agriculture is driven more by the re-activation of existing ageing capacity rather than by investment in new facilities.

The disappointing progress in competitive restructuring of the economy is caused in part by the failure to create an enabling environment for new private sector firms, whether they are farms, small and medium enterprises (SMEs) or larger state enterprises awaiting privatization. This is reflected in the high fraction of GDP that is hidden in the gray economy to escape excessive taxation, government regulation and harassment by the civil service. The share of the gray economy is estimated to be as high as 50 per cent in the CCA countries (Aslund 2004). The lop-sided nature of the transition rebound and its fragility retard growth in employment and thereby slow poverty alleviation. It also hampers efforts to revive the transition-induced collapse in government revenue, to a share in GDP commensurate with social obligations such as paying civil service wages, health care and education, etc. The resulting gross inadequacy of public salaries leads to predation by civil servants, many of whom attempt to make up the wage deficiency to meet their day-to-day needs.

At a deeper level the unsatisfactory progress with economic restructuring reflects deficiencies in the three key sanctions against anti-social governance (political accountability, social capital and legal institutions). This chapter focuses upon how deficient social capital and defective institutions interact to impede economic restructuring. We define social capital as the trust and institutions that reduce transaction costs (Auty and Gelb 2001: 8–9) and, as such, help speed economic transition. The way in which inadequate political accountability constrains the economic and political reform required to sustain economic recovery is analyzed in the next chapter, Chapter 8.

This chapter is structured as follows: the next section (pages 116–118) summarizes the literature concerning the definition and measurement of social capital. The third section (pages 118–120) recaps the hypothesized interaction between rents, the development trajectory and social capital in the CIEN and STEX models and spells out its implications for the CCA countries. The subsequent sections elaborate on the impacts of social capital on economic restructuring. More specifically, the fourth section (pages 120–124) explores how severe GDP compression corroded an already flawed social capital endowment and created self-locking vicious circles of predation that inhibit competitive investment. The fifth section (pages 125–127) analyzes the impact of such corruption on institutions, the gray economy and investment. The penultimatic section (pages 127–129) examines the more extreme manifestations of deteriorating social capital such as growth in violent crime linked to narcotics and terrorism. The conclusion draws the policy implications for the political elites, as well as for ongoing reform.

## The nature of social capital and its measurement

A growing body of evidence suggests that social capital is critical to sustainable development and poverty reduction in developing countries (Knack and Keefer 1997; Dasgupta and Serageldin 1999; Paldam and Svendsen 2002; World Bank and IMF 2002; Djankov *et al.* 2003).[1] At the same time, however, standard textbooks on the economic transition neglect social capital (Paldam and Svendsen 2002: 2). The literature linking social capital and development that does exist has been largely produced within the disciplines of sociology and more recently political science (Schneider *et al.* 1997; Paldam and Svendsen 2002: 4). Economists have been more hesitant to employ the term, partly because of problems of definition and above all of measurement.[2]

Coleman (1988) is credited with introducing the concept of social capital, and his original definition envisioned a private and public good, benefiting individuals or a network of individuals within a confined group. As used by Coleman, social capital could develop, for example, among a group of diamond traders in New York City but would not extend outside of the closed group to the general society. A more popularized definition of the concept was developed by Putnam (1993), who viewed social capital as the positive feedback between individuals' sense of civic duty, their participation in social life and the efficiency of existing institutional arrangements for contract enforcement. In Putnam's view, moral obligations are reinforced in social networks, cheating is expensive and civic participation enhances formal rule compliance and improves the accountability of government.

While social capital was initially conceived of as having a positive effect on society, subsequent research revealed that social capital could also exhibit an important 'downside' (Portes and Landholt 1996). Thus two opposing propositions regarding the effects of social capital on economic growth have emerged – 'the "Putnam effects" (civic associations facilitating growth by increasing trust) and the "Olson effects" (associations stifling growth through rent-seeking)' (World Bank 2002: URL). The Olson effect reflects isolated and parochial communities, special interest groups or networks such as energy cartels, drug and crime groups, protection rackets, mafia, and even militia that can hinder economic and social development by corroding social capital (Grootaert 1998: 2; World Bank 2002: URL).[3]

Thus,

> a society with many trusting and trustworthy individuals develops 'virtuous circles' of cooperative action. By contrast, a society with many distrustful people orientated toward short-run payoffs ... generates 'vicious circles' of perpetual defection. Such an environment leads to a high level of corruption, favoritism, and (justifiable) cynicism about formal democratic laws and procedures (Hanson 2001: 137)

This balance between positive and negative social capital influences the quality of government, the level of corruption, the rate of economic growth and the likelihood of sustainable development. Unfortunately, the social capital of the CCA region is associated with rent-seeking, corruption, low trust and deficient institutions.

In democratic societies, researchers have measured social capital using proxies such as hours spent volunteering, membership in civic organizations, voting trends and trust in government (World Bank 2002: URL). The quality and the use of courts and legal systems (as compared to the use of clubs, networks and other informal mechanisms) to resolve disputes have also been proposed as measures of social capital (Collier 1998: 15).[4] In addition, surveys of the strength of civil liberties, property rights and the rule of law have been used (Knack and Keefer 1995; Lane and Torell 1996 cited in Knack 1999; Rodrik 1998).

In developing countries, scholars have employed proxies for social trust that include measures of income inequality, quality of schools and educational levels, ethnic composition of society,[5] telephone density, and urban density[6] (Narayan and Pritchett 1996, cited in Collier 2000; Knack and Keefer 1997; Alesina and La Ferrara 2000, cited in Raiser *et al.* 2001; and Bjornskov 2003). With regard to the FSU, Johnson *et al.* (1997) estimate rates of corruption in terms of the gap between GDP as measured by electricity use and officially reported GDP. The greater the degree to which the electricity measure of GDP exceeds the official figure, the larger the gray economy, the lower the trust in government institutions and the greater the presumed corruption. Since 1999, business surveys have begun to provide time series data on aspects of social capital (Hellman *et al.* 2003).

## Modeling the dynamics of social capital

This section sets out the implications of the rent-driven political economy models for social capital formation and then notes the degree to which the CCA countries conform.

### Social capital and PCGDP in the developing market economies

Urbanization appears to play a key role in social capital formation and to yield two contrasting forms of social capital, depending on the importance of rent in the development process. The competitive industrialization that is associated with the low-rent (resource-poor) CIEN model tends to expand bridging and linking social capital in the form of numerous diverse and autonomous civic associations, which confer voice on local communities. Moreover, low-rent countries accumulate their social capital faster than high-rent countries because they industrialize earlier, i.e. at a lower PCGDP (Woolcock *et al.* 2001; Auty 2004). Finally, the rate of social capital formation in the CIEN model appears to trace an S-shaped curve with rising PCGDP. This implies that it accumulates slowly at first before accelerating from a relatively low-income level as urbanization accelerates, before decelerating at high-income levels.

More specifically, at low-income levels transaction costs are high because many markets are missing due to the low density of *economic* activity and absence of the physical infrastructure that facilitates exchange.[7] In these circumstances, most transactions occur over short (i.e. local) distances (Woolcock and Narayan 2000). In such cases, bonding social capital dominates because it provides individuals with insurance against risk, although the community as a whole is not protected from unforeseen shocks. Bonding social capital relies strongly on kinship and direct personal links, which imposes obligations on successful individuals to share their good fortune with the group. However, this impedes development at low-income levels because it constrains saving and investment and can stifle non-conforming activity of an innovative and entrepreneurial nature (Stiglitz 1995).

The process of urbanization within a market economy allows individuals to reduce their dependence on kin and local groups by extending social links beyond a specific village or town through regional associations. Such *bridging* and *linking* social capital provides an alternative and more flexible means of risk reduction to bonding social capital. Moreover, the associated expanding spatial horizon also allows scale thresholds to be crossed to create viable markets and increase the division of labor, which has been identified as a key to sustained increases in productivity and welfare. Consequently, the earlier urbanization of resource-poor countries not only accumulates a less constraining social capital that confers voice on a proliferating group of civic associations, but also accelerates the emergence of an integrated settlement hierarchy (of villages nesting in the hinterlands of towns, which in turn nest in those of cities) that facilitates specialization and exchange.

In contrast, urbanization that is driven by a rent-driven patronage system under the STEX development trajectory renders individuals beholden to the state through a system of hierarchic social relations, which may be paternalistic (as in Saudi Arabia and Kaunda's Zambia, for example), with allegiance to a specific individual, or else controlled more impersonally through direct surveillance and repression (as in the USSR). In consequence, social capital formed under urbanization that is rent-fed lacks the autonomy and voice of the civic associations formed by competitive urbanization.

However, there is some evidence from the mature market economies that the rate of social capital formation decelerates and its quality may regress at higher income levels. This is because at higher income levels, institutions and pressure groups may become so powerful and specialized in their aim as to *raise* transaction costs by pursuing single-issue interests at the expense of the broader social interest, which is more diffuse (Killick 1995). These 'Olson effects' are particularly associated with countries that enjoy prolonged periods of stability like Britain in the mid-twentieth century (Olson 2000) or the Soviet republics prior to the late 1980s. Importantly for the present study, Raiser *et al.* (2001) correctly identify deficient social capital as a legacy of central planning that weakens a critical buttress against anti-social governance.

### Social capital in the FSU

Explanations for the level and quality of social capital in the transition countries suggest that it is inversely related to: a country's endowment of natural resources; geographic distance to the EU (Brussels); the number of years spent under central planning and the share of pre-shock exports to COMECON. It is positively linked to current democratic leadership, historic exposure to democracy, a Protestant religious tradition, political decentralization and openness to trade (Hanson 2001; Raiser *et al.* 2001; Treisman 2000). Many of these factors have been used to explain the more rapid and stable recovery of the CEE states compared with those of the FSU.

Some observers conclude that severe deficiencies in social capital existed during the Soviet era (Tsukatani 1998; Levin and Satarov 2000). They suggest that social capital deficiencies and the associated bureaucratic corruption (which we define as illicit acts by public employees abusing their official positions for personal gain) and crime were simply masked by policies of the command economy. Communism discouraged group associations other than the Party, thereby reinforcing narrow and secretive circles of trust, a form of bonding social capital, which sapped wider and pluralistic loyalties and proved an effective vehicle for rent-seeking when the system collapsed. However, other scholars consider that corroded social capital is a characteristic of the post-Soviet experience. For example, Treisman (2000) argues that social capital is positively correlated with per capita income so that it may regress substantially if per capita incomes fall precipitately, as they did in the 1990s through much of the CCA region (Table 6.1).

Although the pre-conditions that fed corruption were probably present in the Soviet Union by 1989, the corrosion of social capital appears to have been sharply exacerbated in direct proportion to the scale of post-Soviet GDP compression (and associated public sector revenue loss). The diminishing efficiency of the command economy throughout the 1970s and 1980s was associated with perverse incentives regarding work effort and rewards. The shock of the transition then delivered a splintering blow to the brittle Soviet institutions.

The level of economic development has recently been shown to be an important factor associated with levels of corruption and social capital (Treisman 2000). At the same time, however, using data from the World Values Survey, Raiser *et al.* (2001: 27) caution that there may be a spurious relationship between social capital and economic growth in transition economies because variations in per capita income and the quality of social capital may really be joint products of the same underlying causes. Nevertheless, GDP compression and declining PCGDP do appear to be linked to social capital corrosion in the CCA region. For example, the CAA states, especially the resource-poor ones, experienced the most severe GDP compression of all the transition countries as Table 7.1 shows with reference to changes in GDP and income gini coefficients.[8] If social capital accumulates with *rising* per capita income, then it may also be expected to deteriorate in the face of *declining* per capita income, especially if the decline is abrupt, sustained and threatens destitution, as it did in most of the CCA countries. The next three sections examine, respectively, the impact of GDP compression on social capital, the response of investors and the consequences for crime in the CCA countries.

## GDP compression and the corrosion of social capital

Treisman (2003: 20) finds that the strongest and most robust determinant of corruption and state capture in the transition states is the level of economic development.[9] The PCGDP of the CCA countries was already lagging behind that of the northern CIS and CEE countries and the growth collapse

*Table 7.1* Revenue, expenditure and fiscal compression, comparator transition economies 1992–1998

| Pre-condition group | Income inequality (gini 1996–99) | Government expenditure (% GDP) | | | Fiscal gap 1992 (% GDP) | Fiscal gap 1998 (% GDP) |
|---|---|---|---|---|---|---|
| | | 1992 | 1995 | 1998 | | |
| Mid-income | | | | | | |
| Central + E Europe | 0.31ₐ | 42.7 | 44.7 | 44.3 | −2.1 | −2.7 |
| Northern CIS + SEE | 0.37 | 50.5 | 41.0 | 37.1 | −5.0 | −3.1 |
| Russia | 0.49 | 57.9 | 39.6 | 39.5 | −6.1 | −8.0 |
| Low income | | | | | | |
| East Asia | 0.38 | 20.2 | 19.1 | 18.8 | −5.2 | −6.2 |
| Resource-poor Caspian | *0.49* | *50.1* | *35.3* | *24.4* | *−32.1* | *−5.8* |
| Armenia | 0.59 | 64.3 | 31.0 | 24.8 | −37.6 | −4.2 |
| Georgia | 0.43 | 55.7 | 17.6 | 21.5 | −45.5 | −5.1 |
| Kyrgyzstan | 0.47 | 31.4 | 34.0 | 28.1 | −14.7 | −10.0 |
| Tajikistan | 0.47 | 65.7 | 18.7 | 15.8 | −30.5 | −3.8 |
| Mineral-rich Caspian | *0.40*ᵦ | *45.9* | *29.4* | *26.2* | *−8.6* | *−3.9* |
| Azerbaijan | n.a. | 80.0 | 45.9 | 18.8 | −29.0 | −1.7 |
| Kazakhstan | 0.35 | 31.9 | 26.2 | 25.8 | −7.4 | −7.6 |
| Turkmenistan | 0.45 | 28.9 | 12.1 | 25.8 | 13.3 | −2.7 |
| Uzbekistan | n.a. | 42.8 | 32.0 | 34.5 | −11.3 | −3.4 |

*Source:* Tanzi and Tsibouris 2001: 246–247, except column 1: World Bank 2001: 140 and row 1 ADB 2000: 264.

*Notes*
a Excludes Slovak Republic.
b Excludes Azerbaijan and Uzbekistan.

associated with the initial stage of the transition amplified that gap. By rapidly replacing political control with functioning market institutions the CEE countries succeeded in developing the most effective social capital, the smallest unofficial economies, the healthiest public finances and also the highest political accountability (Johnson *et al.* 1997: 2). In the CCA countries, by contrast, the majority of the ruling elites are stalwarts of the old communist system who retained tighter control of the economy.[10] They benefit from maintaining a patronage network that is threatened by market reform and increased political accountability so they have often stalled or stopped anti-corruption activities, while some leaders have selectively applied anti-corruption penalties to attack their political opponents.

Whereas the initial compression in GDP averaged about one-fifth among the CEE countries and one-third among the northern members of the CIS, it averaged 44–66 per cent among the CCA countries (Table 6.1). Regions that experienced modest compression resumed GDP growth earlier and experienced less contraction in public sector revenues (Table 7.1), less corrosion of social capital and less corruption. The CCA countries as a group had inferior institutions to those of the other regional groups of transition economy, including East Asia. Yet, even the region with the least corroded social capital, the CEE countries, lagged in terms of 'civil infrastructure' (rule of law and government effectiveness) compared with non-socialist countries at a similar level of income by one standard deviation, equivalent to dropping forty places among the 172 countries observed (Wyatt 2003: 236). The CCA countries fared even worse.

Treisman (2003: 24) suggests that the post-communist countries are corrupt primarily because they are poor, and the poorest among them are the most corrupt. Table 7.2 confirms that within the CCA countries, the greatest economic compression and contraction in social expenditure was associated with the worst rates of corruption and state capture. In part this may also be due to a decrease in the level of monitoring due to the contraction of resources allocated to bureaucracies in times of economic crisis (Bjornskov 2003: 7). Certainly, Tajikistan emerges with the highest GDP compression, among the lowest per capita GDP, the weakest institutions and high rates of corruption (Table 7.2). The much steeper contraction of government revenue in the resource-poor countries (Table 7.1) occurred *despite* access to geopolitical rents of around 10 per cent or more of GDP annually (Table 6.4). By the end of the 1990s the economic recovery was already stronger in the resource-rich CCA countries, excluding Uzbekistan, and from a less depressed GDP nadir, than in the resource-poor ones. Income inequality was less extreme in the resource-rich countries, almost certainly because they experienced a more limited compression of GDP.

*Table 7.2* Corruption indices, by country

| Country group | Index of graft 2001 | Black economy 1995 (% GDP)$_a$ | State intervention 2002 [1999] (% frequency) | Bribe tax 2002 [1999] (% sales) |
|---|---|---|---|---|
| Mineral-rich Caspian | −0.92 | 34.0 | 25.8 [43.9] | 2.1 [4.3] |
| Azerbaijan | −1.05 | 61.0 | 27.5 [59.5] | 2.7 [3.7] |
| Kazakhstan | −0.83 | 34.0 | 29.7 [26.1] | 2.1 [1.9] |
| Turkmenistan | −1.12 | n.a. | n.a. [n.a.] | n.a. [n.a] |
| Uzbekistan | −0.66 | 7.0 | 20.2 [46.2] | 1.5 [2.5] |
| Resource-poor Caspian | −0.86 | 63.0 | 32.7 [35.1] | 2.5 [6.8] |
| Armenia | −0.80 | n.a. | 14.3 [40.3] | 0.9 [4.2] |
| Georgia | −0.69 | 63.0 | 37.8 [36.8] | 2.7 [3.5] |
| Kyrgyzstan | −0.85 | n.a. | 43.7 [28.2] | 3.7 [2.4] |
| Tajikistan | −1.08 | n.a. | 35.1 [n.a.] | 2.6 [n.a.] |
| Memo Item | | | | |
| C. Europe + Baltic | 0.40 | 23.2 | 17.8 [23.2] | 0.9 [3.3] |

*Source:* World Bank 2002 and EBRD 1999: 28; except a = Johnson *et al.* 1997.

Both higher incomes and lower income inequality in the resource-rich CCA countries might be expected to reduce the corrosion of social capital, so the fact that corruption levels were similar to the resource-poor countries (Table 7.2) suggests the resource curse may be at work in countering the benign effect of more modest GDP contraction on corruption. Transparency International's (2002) Corruption Perceptions Index ranks oil-rich Azerbaijan and Kazakhstan among the world's most corrupt states. By contrast, Turkmenistan, which experienced a less intense contraction and has a significantly higher PCGDP measured in purchasing power parity terms, appears to be the regional state most affected by state capture.

A particularly worrying feature of the degraded social capital in the CCA region is its potential to generate self-reinforcing negative circles when incomes decline. This process is summarized in Figure 7.1, which shows how two interlocking vicious circles perpetuate the system. Among the lower tiers of government, the collapse of public revenues drove rates of remuneration in the over-staffed public sector to levels that obliged public employees to seek ways to make up the five-fold or more extra income they required to meet their basic needs. Underpaid public officials abuse the state monopoly in the provision of key services to levy illegal imposts on the private sector. The payment of these imposts diverts public sector effort into rent-seeking behavior, away from both the efficient provision of public services by government employees and from efforts to improve efficiency by the private firms they harass. This raises the cost of production and depresses investment while also encouraging firms to seek exemptions from legitimate taxation in order to offset the costs imposed by rent-seeking (the Government Revenue circuit in Figure 7.1). This reduces the flow of legitimate revenue into the public sector and, when combined with the retarded private sector employment

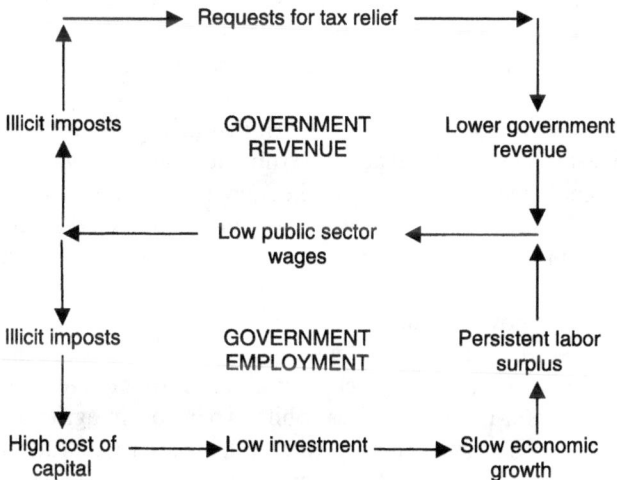

*Figure 7.1* Vicious circles of rent-seeking behavior.

creation arising from low investment, leaves workers trapped in low-paid public sector jobs (the Government Employment circuit in Figure 7.1). In this way the corruption of the public sector becomes self-perpetuating by repressing the economy and compressing government revenue.

At higher tiers of government, officials can capture sizeable rents, which may be contrived rents (created by abuse of government monopoly), natural resource rents (especially in the case of point source resources such as minerals) or geopolitical rents (such as international aid). All three rents offer substantial enrichment to officials capable of siphoning them away through, for example, the corrupt management of state-owned enterprises (Aslund 2000). Aspirants to senior positions make payments many times the size of the official annual salary in order to secure a post that taps rent-seeking opportunities (Economist 1998). At best such corruption diverts public expenditure away from more desirable outlets (such as health and education) and into capital-intensive white elephant projects where construction work provides lucrative scope to pad costs and levy bribes from contractors. At worst, such funds are entirely lost to the domestic economy through capital flight.

Corruption has adversely affected the restructuring of the CCA economies. Table 6.5 summarizes changes in employment creation within the transition economies and the degree of dependence on public sector employment. It identifies very different patterns of employment creation, with far more competitive jobs created in the CEE countries than in the CCA region. In particular, the CEE countries experienced a shift of labor out of the tradeable sectors, mainly from industry (whose share of employment fell by 'only' one-fifth) but also out of agriculture, and into services, mainly into market services. In contrast, the CCA countries experienced a much bigger contraction (by two-fifths) in manufacturing employment together with a one-fifth decline in employment in government services. The sector that attracted the most workers is agriculture, however, rather than market services, and much of that agriculture is of a subsistence nature and outside the formal economy.

Within the CCA region, the mineral-rich countries as a group experienced a more modest fall in industrial and government service employment together with a very small decline in agricultural employment (Table 6.5). Their losses were offset by a rise in market services that almost doubled their employment share. This outcome is most pronounced for oil-rich Azerbaijan and Kazakhstan, and is consistent with Dutch disease effects, notably in Kazakhstan, where the government unwisely subsidizes the non-mineral tradeable sectors (Chapter 4). The absence of a booming mineral sector in the resource-poor countries caused employment contraction to be even more severe in industry and non-market services, while expansion in agriculture, mostly subsistence, was correspondingly greater. This pattern reflects the limited creation of employment within the formal economy, which is examined next.

## Bureaucratic corruption and the gray economy

There is cross-country evidence that corruption represses economic growth. Taking a corruption index based on country risk studies, which ranges from 0 most corrupt to 10 least corrupt, Mauro (1995) reports that a movement of two points up the scale would increase investment by 4 per cent and the annual per capita GDP growth rate by 0.5 per cent. Corruption harms economic growth by discouraging investment, skewing public investment away from a welfare-maximizing trajectory (ibid.) and diverting effort into wealth transfer at the expense of wealth creation. Bribery typically requires an initial payment and thereafter calls for a percentage of the returns, so that corruption functions as a form of illicit tax, lowering the real rate of return on projects and thereby reducing the level of investment. Firms may find that in addition to formal taxes, they are burdened by illicit taxes levied by both prominent officials and under-paid minor bureaucrats. In addition, where the state fails to guarantee law and order, the costs of doing business may be further raised by the need to enforce contracts through recourse to the 'private' sector in the form of the mafia.

Mauro (1997) notes that the provision of public goods provides major opportunities for rent-seeking and corruption that, in turn, repress economic activity. Corruption can have adverse budgetary consequences where it leads to tax evasion or raises the cost of public expenditure in relation to what it would be if it were rent-free. In addition, by inflating public investment contracts and also directing such contracts to firms without effective competitive bidding, the efficiency of public investment is likely to be reduced.

Moreover, public investment may be skewed away from a social welfare maximizing trajectory if officials prosper by diverting funds into large capital-intensive investments that are prone to cost overruns (Murphy 1983). Mauro (1997) finds that outlays on education, welfare payments and social insurance tend to decline with increasing corruption.

Bureaucratic corruption typically manifests itself when politicians exercise control rights over business, including exercising regulatory powers over privatized and private firms, regulations and restriction of entry, control over the use of land and real estate that private businesses occupy, the determination and collection of taxes on businesses, the right to inspect firms and close them if regulations are violated, control over international trade and foreign exchange transactions, and even the power to set prices (Johnson *et al.* 1997: 2). Bureaucratic corruption creates an interest in imposing burdensome procedures in obtaining licenses and permits, in order to increase bribes (Knack 1999: 24).

Grease payments or bribes that enable acquisition of licenses, smooth customs procedures, win public procurement projects or gain access to provision of government services are very common in the region. In addition, citizens of these regional countries pay bribes for officials to overlook minor or major infractions. Moreover, corruption by police, particularly traffic police, and in the health care services has been estimated to account for half of the bribes in transition countries (World Bank 2000: 9). Bribes to the educational system, particularly higher education, are also very common, and, there are cases of individuals paying bribes to gain access to their pension payments.[11]

As greater and greater segments of the society are forced to interact with corrupt government officials and pay bribes, social capital further declines and the gray economy grows. The higher is the share of the unofficial economy, the lower are the official tax collections and hence the supply of public goods to the official sector also declines (Johnson *et al.* 1997: 7). As the businesses and citizens of these societies seek to escape bureaucratic predation by entering the unofficial sector, they receive fewer and lower-quality public services. In addition, wages (and worker productivity) are also lower than would be expected in a normal formal sector. In the states of the region with a relatively large unofficial economy and low tax revenues, firms operating officially recognize that they are better off in the unofficial sector and move. Their move has a deleterious effect on the budget and the provision of public goods in the official sector, which causes more firms to switch to the unofficial economy. This vicious cycle leads to the extreme equilibrium where the whole economy is unofficial (ibid.: 9).

State capture (whereby firms, groups or individuals influence laws, regulations, decrees and government policy to their own advantage through illicit payments to public officials) and administrative corruption (the intentional abuse of government power by public officials to benefit state or non-state actors) are both prevalent. State capture, however, is a particular problem in the regional states that are richly endowed with natural resources and those states well positioned on transit routes such as Georgia, because economic power and natural resource wealth are concentrated in a few key sectors (World Bank 2000: 28). Although resource-rich countries are more prone to state capture and corruption, and Azerbaijan has high levels of both, Treisman (2003: 9–10) describes the Central Asian republics and Georgia and Armenia as having low capture but a high bribe burden.

In this environment, investment in long-term bricks and mortar is discouraged and business transactions are pushed into the gray economy, where the informal entrepreneurs do not pay taxes but often are bullied by protection rackets. Ironically, studies show that households earning income from the unofficial economy are more likely to pay bribes (be subject to corruption) than households that do not earn income from unofficial economy (World Bank 2000: 21). In Georgia, for example, where state capture and administrative corruption are both high, 30 per cent of households claim to pay bribes (ibid.: 21). Nevertheless, households operating in the unofficial economy tend to be slightly more affluent than their legitimate counterparts.

Underdeveloped public administrations and low levels of development of civil society both weaken the mechanisms by which to break from corruption and increase government accountability and social capital. Nevertheless, the final two columns in Table 7.2 suggest some amelioration of corruption was perceived to have occurred in the CCA region during the period 1999–2002. Paradoxically, rapidly reforming Kyrgyzstan regressed, but this was during a time of decreasing trading opportunities due to obstruction by neighboring states. Moreover, that backsliding appears to have reversed since 2002 as, with the exception of Uzbekistan, trade with neighboring states has dramatically accelerated and incomes have correspondingly risen (Aslund 2004). Even so, corruption at all levels has exacerbated the dire circumstances of the impoverished populations and encouraged more radical segments in those societies, impatient with declining economic conditions, to seek extreme remedies.

## The proliferation of violent responses to declining social capital

A growth collapse such as followed the demise of the Soviet Union is an important pre-requisite for civil strife because it creates high unemployment, notably among young males who are more likely than others in society to resort to violence to improve their lot. Manifestations of this outcome in the CCA region include increased drug trafficking, arms smuggling and terrorist activity. The value of the global trade in illicit drugs is estimated by the United Nations at $400 billion, equivalent to one-twelfth of world trade. Gross profit margins of up to 300 per cent insulate traffickers from seizures, believed to comprise over one-third of cocaine and one-tenth for heroin (Financial Times 1997), and also from fluctuating crop prices and courier charges (Economist 2000). Poppy cultivation in the Central Asia is thus exponentially more profitable than the production of foodstuffs and also requires far less water from Central Asia's limited supply than does food production. This is, therefore, one activity in which the penalty of the CCA region's remoteness (Raballand 2002) is all too easily surmounted: throughout the region drug smuggling and dealing provides funds for illegal military and political purposes, notably to purchase arms and support extremist movements.

The region's porous borders and weak government control have made the CCA region one of the main routes for transporting opium from Afghanistan through Russia and into Europe.[12] While poppy cultivation in Afghanistan was estimated to produce close to 75 per cent of the global heroin supply, there have also been increasing reports of farmers in Central Asia growing opium. In fact, the United Nations Drug Control Program reported that smugglers in Central Asia and the South Caucasus control 50 per cent of Afghanistan's heroin supplies (cited in Kattoulas 2002). Working as a courier or a smuggler is a lucrative job for desperate individuals trying to eke out a living in the CCA countries. In addition to shipping narcotics to western markets, some evidence of drug rings taking root in Russia have been found, and estimates say that at least one-third of earnings are sent back home. These remittances are suspected of funding terrorist partners at home (Kattoulas 2002). Moreover, the Council of Foreign and Defense Policy warned in 2001 that in Tajikistan drugs were now the 'chief source of funding for Islamic armed opposition' (ibid.).

Tajikistan is a particularly favorable route for shipping narcotics because of the extreme destruction of the social fabric, the fall in living standards, and the collapse of law enforcement institutions. Tajik officials estimate some 200 tons of various narcotics traverse the country annually, equivalent to around 40 per cent of Russian consumption, and of which barely 1 per cent is apprehended. More recently, Turkmenistan began producing drugs in the irrigated areas of the Karakum Desert, presumably sanctioned by the very highest authority. Still further west Azerbaijan acts as a conduit for drugs arriving from Iran as well as from Afghanistan. Meanwhile, Olcott (2002: 43) reports that a sizeable fraction of the Kyrgyz population may be involved in the production, refining and transport of drugs with a street value of $14 billion in 1999, while the total value of the Afghan opium poppy crop at that time was $183 million at the farm gate but as much as $100 billion in final sales, much of which was substituted when the Taliban regime collapsed.

Widespread corruption allows narcotics trafficking to flourish. In many cases the local elite tax narcotics production and transit and are therefore not likely to help curb drug production in the region unless there are greater international incentives (Cornell and Specter 2001; Cottrell 2002). Indeed political leaders sometimes use the war on drugs as an opportunity to crack down on political opposition. Allegations of drug trafficking at border crossings are also a way to not only interdict drugs but also to extract bribes, and strip searches at borders have become so prevalent that many women now 'avoid cross-border travel whenever possible' (Lubin *et al.* 2002: 18). According to Lubin, 'the situation has contributed to a further destruction of the formerly strong social ties that united relatives living in different republics and now in neighboring CIS countries.' This situation implies corrosion of social capital not only within national boundaries but also a decline of social trust among the states of the region.

A not unexpected side effect of the transit of drugs through the region is the increase in the number of drug users. Drug addiction, which was only a minor problem in the 1980s, is now rampant in the region, as poor social and economic conditions cause many to escape into drugs (Special Report 2002). As social services and health care deteriorate and poverty increases these concerns loom ever larger on the horizon for these countries and severely debilitate the accumulation of social capital throughout the region, with serious implications for the rest of the world. The drug trade is having an adverse effect on social capital within the region, as well as upon family life and traditional communities. Yet despite the negative social costs, many still see drug trafficking and production as one of few ways to earn money (Lubin *et al.* 2002: 19).

Finally, it is widely believed that nuclear fissile material is being stolen from official sites in countries like Uzbekistan, Turkmenistan and Azerbaijan and loaded into trucks that smuggle it past border controls that lack the equipment required to check for its presence (Lubin 1999: 216). The principal destination for such material is believed to be Iran, although that country allows International Energy Agency inspections of its nuclear facilities as a participant in the Nuclear Non-Proliferation Treaty. However, there is increasing concern that non-state agents may have been able to purchase such material for use in terrorist outrages.

## Conclusions: solutions to social capital decline in the region

In contrast to the CEE countries, social capital within the CCA countries exhibits strong Olson (negative) effects. These effects reflect weak EU influence in the CCA region but above all massive GDP compression and associated decline in per capita incomes. The resource-poor countries were especially adversely affected by GDP compression (and civil strife), which along with their lower mean PCGDP may explain levels of corruption on a par with the mainly wealthier resource-rich CCA countries. Those who remained in public sector employment and/or dependent on state pensions experienced extreme income compression. Many civil servants sought to supplement their incomes by abusing the state's monopoly of public service provision. In more extreme cases, people resorted to extracting rents by violence through criminal activity, narcotics and other smuggling and terrorism.

These conditions retarded economic restructuring because new investment and business start-ups were either deterred or else driven into the gray economy, where net illicit imposts may be less, but efficiency is lower due to limited access to services so that labor productivity is low and job creation slower. Many people responded by retreating into subsistence farming or by seeking work abroad. The resulting negative socio-economic impacts are self-sustaining because limited investment in competitive economic activity produces insufficient jobs to pull people out of the under-funded state sector. It also depresses tax revenues so public sector wages cannot be raised to adequate levels. In this way corruption becomes locked into the system.

A sustained improvement in social capital will be difficult to achieve. Treisman (2000) finds that the past exerts as much, if not more, influence on present levels of social capital as current policy. Moreover, in order to have an effect in decreasing corruption, democracy has to be long-lived while trade liberalization must be extensive. Although corruption hampers economic growth, countries can grow their way out of it, according to Treisman (2000) because economic growth spurs competition that reduces rent-seeking opportunities. Raiser et al. (2001) report that NGOs can help build social capital, but their operation depends on government permission. For this and other reasons, the role of the government is critical to completing economic restructuring. The dynamics of the political state in the CCA region are therefore discussed in Chapter 8.

## Notes

1 Social capital is also an important theme of research in developed states. Analyzing and interpreting the levels of social capital within established democracies has been the source of recent scholarly debate. For two views on the decline of social engagement in the United States, see Putnam (1995 and 2001) and Bennett (1999).

2 See for example, Kenneth J. Arrow (2000), 'Observations on Social Capital,' in Dasgupta and Serageldin (2000).

3 A causal link between social capital and corruption still has not been clearly identified, but most studies agree that the higher the trust in a society, the lower the corruption and that economic development is a strong explanation for both (Uslaner 2001; Bjornskov and Paldam 2002; and Bjornskov 2003).

4 Trust in courts, and the legal system overall, has also been used to explain the prevalence of the unofficial economy in transitional countries. In comparing Russia and Ukraine with Poland, the Slovak Republic, and Romania, Johnson *et al.* (1999) find that less faith in the court system affects the size of the unofficial economy, as does higher tax rates, worse bureaucratic corruption and greater incidence of mafia protection.

5 Interestingly, while ethnicity is regularly used as a measure of social cohesion, Collier's tests indicate that it may not be adequate. While Collier finds that ethnicity is negatively correlated with trust, the relationship is not statistically significant (Collier 1998: 13). In fact, 'contrary to expectations, ethnic diversity reduces the risk of civil conflict because it is harder to form collective identity and collective action in a heterogeneous society' (ibid.: 22).

6 Collier finds that high and low urban density both have high correlation with high levels of social trust (ibid.: 17).

7 Rural India in the 1960s provides examples of market failure. The basic unit of socio-economic organization, the village, was too small to support competitive banking, crop markets and an all-weather road (Johnson 1970). In the absence of these facilities, little progress could be made in specializing in high-productivity crops, which is the required response where land is becoming scarce and labor relatively abundant. Meanwhile, real interest rates might reach triple figures (Johnson 1970) and a location more than 4 km from an all-weather road render transport costs too high to allow villages to adopt green revolution technologies (Owen 1967).

8 The one anomaly is Uzbekistan, which is following the staple trap model (Chapter 3) and so will eventually experience a growth collapse without policy reform. The model suggests that Uzbekistan's gradual reform merely postpones the demise rather than avoids it.

9 While arguing that there is nothing particularly post-communist about the levels of corruption in the transitioning states, Treisman also acknowledges that the reverse relationship may also true. 'It may be that corruption or state capture exacerbated the economic crisis rather than the crisis inducing corruption or capture' (Treisman 2003: 20).

10 While the president of Kyrgyzstan comes from an academic background, the bulk of his career was spent serving as a functionary in the high levels of the Soviet Academy of Sciences.

11 There are those who argue that bribe payment does not necessarily decrease the efficiency of bureaucracy and may, in fact, even improve services beyond the level attained by employees paid only a regular salary (Rose-Ackerman 1978: 6–7). It seems, however, that repeated exposure to graft reduces trust, narrows the circles of public interaction, diminishes social capital and, in the long term, creates inefficiencies within a society.

12 CCA borders are still highly porous and the regional governments do not have the

resources to enforce their territories. In response to such uncertainty, Uzbekistan elected to mine its borders as a means of enforcing national boundaries, in addition to stricter controls and erecting fences. Tajikistan has 20,000 Russian troops and border guards to patrol its boundary with Afghanistan.

# References

Abed, G.T. and Gupta, S. (eds.) (2002) *Governance, Corruption, and Economic Performance*, Washington DC: International Monetary Fund.

Aslund, A. (2000) Why has Russia's economic transformation been so arduous?, in: Pleskovic, B. and Stiglitz, J.E. (eds.) *Annual World Bank Conference on Development Economics 1999*, Washington DC: World Bank DC, 399–424.

Aslund, A. (2004) *The Kyrgyz Republic: Reinforce Economic Growth through Lower Taxes and Better Governance*, Washington DC: Carnegie Endowment for International Peace.

Auty, R.M. (2004) Natural resources and Civil strife: A two-stage process, *Geopolitics* 9(1), 29–49.

Auty, R.M. and Gelb, A.H. (2001) Political economy of resource abundant states, in: Auty, R.M. (ed.) *Resource Abundance and Economic Development*, Oxford: Oxford University Press, 126–144.

Bennett, W.L. (1999) The uncivic culture: Communication, identity, and the rise of lifestyle politics, American Political Science Association Net, September, http://www.apsanet.org/PS/dec98/bennett.cfm.

Bjornskov, C. (2003) Corruption + Social Capital, http://www.asb.dk/nat/workshop/2003/CHBJ2001.PDF

Bjornskov, C. and Paldam, M. (2002) Corruption trends and social capital, Paper submitted to the International Workshop on Corruption, Goettingen, November.

Coleman, J.S. (1988) Social capital in the creation of human capital, *American Journal of Sociology* 94, Supplement, S94–S120.

Collier, P. (1998) Social capital and poverty, Social Capital Initiative Working Paper 4, December, http://www.inform.umd.edu/EdRes/Colleges/BSOS/Depts/IRIS/IRIS/docs/SCI-WPS–04.pdf.

Collier, P. (2000) Doing well out of war: An economic perspective, in: Berdal, M. and Malone, D.M. (eds.) *Greed and Grievance: Economic Agendas in Civil War*, London: Lynne Rienner, 91–111.

Cornell, S. and Specter, R. (2001) Central Asia: More than Islamic extremists, *The Washington Quarterly* 25(1).

Cottrell, R. (2002) Asian entanglement, *Financial Times*, April 16, http://news.ft.com/.

Dasgupta, P. and Serageldin, I. (eds.) (1999) *Social Capital: A Multifaceted Perspective*, Washington DC: World Bank.

Djankov, S., Glaeser, E., La Porta, R., Lopez-de-Silanes, F. and Shleifer, A. (2003) The new comparative economics, *Journal of Comparative Economics* 31, 595–619.

EBRD (1999) *Transition Report 1999: Ten Years of Transition*, London: European Bank for Reconstruction and Development.

Economist (1998) Central Asia Survey, *The Economist*, February 7.

Economist (2000) The Andrea coca wars, *The Economist*, March 4, 25–27.

Financial Times (1997) Illicit drugs trade is put at $400 billion, *Financial Times*, June 26.

Grootaert, C. (1998), Social capital: The missing link? Social Capital Initiative Working Paper 3, http://www.inform.umd.edu/EdRes/Colleges/BSOS/Depts/IRIS/IRIS/docs/SCI-WPS-03.pdf.

Hanson, S.E. (2001) Defining democratic consolidation, in: Anderson, R.D. Fish, S., Hanson, E. and Roeder, P.G. *Communism and the Theory of Democracy*, Princeton: Princeton University Press.

Hellman, J.S., Jones, G. and Kaufmann, D. (2003) Seize the state, seize the day: State capture and influence in transition economies, *Journal of Comparative Economics* 31, 751–773.

Johnson, E.A.J. (1970) *The Organisation and Use of Space in the Developing Countries*, Cambridge MA: Harvard University Press.

Johnson, S., Kaufman, D., McMillan, J. and Woodruff, C. (1999) Why do firms hide? Bribes and unofficial activity after Communism, EBRD Working Paper 42.

Johnson, S., Kaufman, D. and Shleifer, A. (1997) The unofficial economy in transition, *Brookings Papers on Economic Activity*, Washington DC: Brookings.

Kattoulas, V. (2002) Russian Far East crime central, *Far Eastern Economic Review*, May 30.

Killick, T. (1995) *The Flexible Economy*, London: Routledge.

Knack, S. (1999) Social capital, growth, and poverty: A survey of cross-country evidence, Social Capital Initiative Working Paper 7, http://www.inform.umd.edu/EdRes /Colleges/BSOS/Depts/IRIS/IRIS/docs/SCI-WPS-07.pdf.

Knack, S. and Keefer, P. (1997) Does social capital have an economic pay-off? A cross-country investigation, *Quarterly Journal of Economics* 112, 1250–1288.

Levin, M. and Satarov, G. (2000) Corruption and institutions in Russia, *European Journal of Political Economy* 16, 113–132.

Lubin, N. (1999) New threats in Central Asia and the Caucasus: Energy: A source of wealth or instability?, in: Menon, R., Fedorov, Y.E. and Nodia, G. (eds.) *Russia, the Caucasus and Central Asia: The Twenty-first Century Security Environment*, Vol. 2, London: M.E. Sharpe, 205–225.

Mauro, P. (1997) Why worry about corruption? *Economic Issues* 6, IMF, Washington DC.

Murphy, K.J. (1983) *Megaprojects in the Third World: An Analysis of Transnational Partnerships*, Boulder CO: Westview Press.

Office of the Coordinator for Counter-terrorism (2002) Patterns of global terrorism, *US Department of State Eurasia Overview*, www.state.gove/s/ct/rls/pgtrpt/2001/html/10239.htm

Olson, M. (2000) Dictatorship, democracy and development, in: Olson, M. and Kahkonen, S. (eds.) *A Not-so-Dismal Science: A Broader View of Economies and Societies*, Oxford: Oxford University Press, 119–137.

Olcott, M. (2002) Central Asia, in: Ellings, R.J. and Friedberg, A.L. (eds.) *Strategic Asia 2002–03: Asian Aftershocks*, Seattle: The National Bureau of Asian Research.

Olcott, M.B. (2002) *Kazakhstan: Unfulfilled Promise*, Washington DC: Carnegie Endowment for International Peace.

Owen, W. (1967) *Distance and Development*, Washington DC: Brookings Institution.

Paldam, M. and Svendsen, G.T. (2002) Missing social capital and transition in Eastern Europe, *Journal for Instititional Innovation, Development, and Transition* 5, 21–34.

Portes, A. and Landolt, P. (1996) Unsolved mysteries: The Tocqueville files II, *The American Prospect* 7, 18–22.

Putnam, R.D. (1993) *Making Democracy Work: Civic Traditions in Modern Italy*, Princeton: Princeton University Press.

Putnam, R.D. (1995) Tuning in, tuning out: The strange disappearance of social capital in America, *PS: Political Science and Politics* 28, 664–683.

Putnam, R.D. (2001) *Bowling Alone: The Collapse and Revival of American Community*, New York: Touchstone Books.

Raballand, G. (2002) The determinants of the negative impact of land-lockedness on trade: An empirical investigation through the Central Asian case, Working Paper, Paris: ROSES, Sorbonne University.

Raiser, M., Haerpfer, C., Nowotny, T. and Wallace, C. (2001) Social capital in transition: a first look at the evidence, EBRD Working Paper 61, February.

Rose-Ackerman, S. (1978) *Corruption: A Study in Political Economy*, New York: Academic Press.

Schneider, M., Teske, P., Marschall, M., Mintrom, M. and Roch, C. (1997) Institutional arrangements and the creation of social capital: The effect of public school choice, *American Political Science Review* 91(1).

Shkolnikov, V. (2002) Democratization assistance in the Caspian Region, *Caspian Studies Program Policy Brief* 7 (May).

Special Report (2002) The drug trade in Central Asia, *Asia Today*, April 10, www.asiasource.org/news/at_mp_02.cfm?newsid=72136.

Stiglitz, J.E. (1995) Social absorption capability and innovation, in: Koo, B.H. and Perkins, D.H. (eds.) *Social Capability and Long-Term Economic Growth*, Basingstoke: Macmillan, 48–81.

Tanzi, V. and Tsibouris, G. (2001) Transition and the changing role of government, in: Havrylyshyn, O. and Nsouli, S.M. (eds.) *A Decade of Transition: Achievements and Challenges*, Washington DC: IMF.

Transparency International (2002) Corruption Perception Index, www.transparency.org/cpi/2002/cpi2002.en.html

Treisman, D. (2000) The causes of corruption: A cross-national study, *Journal of Public Economics* 76(3), 399–458.

Treisman, D. (2003) Postcommunist corruption, in: Fidrmuc, J. and Campos, N. (eds.) *Political Economy of Transition and Development: Institutions, Politics and Policies*, Berlin: Kluver, 201–226.

Tsukatani, T. (1998) The Aral Sea and socio-economic development, in: Kobori, I. and Glantz, M.H. (eds.) *Central Eurasian Water Crisis: Caspian, Aral and Dead Seas*, Tokyo: United Nations University, 53–74.

Uslaner, E. (2001) Trust and corruption, Paper presented to Conference on Political Scandals, Past and Present, University of Salford.

Woolcock, M. and Narayan, D. (2000) Social capital: implications for development theory, research and policy, *World Bank Research Observer* 15(2), 225–249.

Woolcock, M., Isham, J. and Pritchett, L. (2001) Social capital and natural resources, in: Auty, R.M. (ed.) *Resource Abundance and Economic Development*, Oxford: Oxford University Press, 76–92.

World Bank (2000) Anticorruption in transition: A contribution to the policy debate, Washington DC: World Bank, http://lnweb18.worldbank.org/eca/eca.nsf/Attachments/Anticorruption+in+Transition:+A+Contribution+to+the+Policy+Debate/$File/Anticorruption+in+Transition.pdf.

World Bank (2001) Making transition work for everyone: Poverty and inequality in Europe and Central Asia, Washington DC: World Bank, Chapter 4, lnweb18. worldbank.org/eca/eca.nsf/Attachments/ ECAPOV+Chapter+4/$File/chapter4.pdf.

World Bank (2002) Social capital for development, PovertyNet, October 10, www. worldbank.org/poverty/scapital.whatsc.htm.

World Bank and IMF (2002) Poverty reduction, growth, and debt sustainability in low-income CIS countries, Working Paper, February 4.

Wyatt, G. (2003) Corruption, productivity and socialism, *Kyklos* 56(2), 233–244.

# 8 Incentives to reform in the Caucasus and Central Asian political states

*Richard M. Auty and Indra de Soysa*

## Introduction

The previous chapter identified the dependent form of social capital that was inherited from the Soviet Union as a primary obstacle to both economic restructuring and the emergence of pluralistic political systems in the CCA countries. This chapter examines why and how the political states in the region have perpetuated this state of affairs. It also evaluates the prospects of the ruling elites re-aligning their interests with those of society at large.

More specifically, the chapter identifies a continuum of political states within the CCA region, ranging from an autocracy to a diffusing oligarchy, as the product of the rent-driven patronage systems by which the ex-communist elite maintained power after independence. Seven of the eight countries in the CCA region were benefiting from a vigorous economic rebound that emerged in the late 1990s, but such growth is not sustainable over the long-term without further market reform. This chapter argues that growth collapses threaten the dynastic aspirations of the CCA elites, requiring them to constrain their damaging rent extraction and distribution in order to sustain wealth creation. But this will entail political as well as economic reforms, according to the CIEN and STEX models.

The CIEN and STEX models (see Chapter 2) underpin the basic thesis so we briefly recap them here. They paint contrasting paths for the evolution of the political economy of rent-poor and rent-rich countries. The CIEN model suggests that all else being equal the absence of rents motivates the state to create wealth by promoting sustained rapid PCGDP growth, which strengthens the three key sanctions against anti-social governance. This drives incremental political change toward a democracy that is consensual via a benevolent autocracy and a diffusing oligarchy.

In contrast, the STEX model suggests that the pre-occupation of resource-rich states with the extraction of rent, which they invariably deploy in a manner that distorts the economy and leads to a growth collapse, erodes sanctions against anti-social governance. However, a growth collapse discredits the regime in power and creates scope for abrupt political change, which may cause democratization where external conditions are favorable.

Such exogenous democratization is therefore abrupt, but it is also unstable and subject to regression because strong income inequality (an outcome of rent-fed growth) polarizes the democracy and therefore generates redistributive conflicts. The political economy models therefore imply that political regimes neglect wealth creation at their peril. They also suggest that resource-poor countries face superior long-term prospects for both their political and economic evolution because they have less scope to neglect wealth creation than their resource-rich counterparts.

Chapters 3–6 have identified points of congruence with the models and also points of departure from them. Chapter 7 has confirmed the critical role played by the legacy of social capital in explaining the departures, especially among the resource-poor CCA countries. Following the collapse of central planning, the political states of the CCA region initially adopted systems of government with centralized elected presidencies, accountable to elected parliaments and subject to inherited Soviet law. However, weaker levels of social cohesion in the CCA countries compared with the CEE countries (EBRD 1999: 108) diminished the political challenge to the CCA elites, who were able to focus on adjusting the balance of power among themselves between central government and the regions, mainly the oblasts (Jones Luong 2002). Although intra-elite challenges did emerge, and they led to civil strife in Georgia and Tajikistan, for the most part the elite espoused patronage systems that perpetuated the dependent social capital of the Soviet era. The elites draw upon natural resource rent (which has been exceptionally large in the resource-rich countries), as well as contrived rent and geopolitical rent to replace the lost subventions from the Soviet Union.

The overwhelming priority of the post-Soviet elite was the welfare of family and associates. Few of them viewed democracy as inherently either necessary or desirable, provided this dependent bonding social capital was sustained. Moreover, whereas economic reform was initially useful to the elite because it allowed them to capture assets from the state, ongoing reform increased competition and economic growth, which reduce contrived and geopolitical rents, respectively (Aslund 2000). In this context, the strains of nation building and latent threats of conflict from ethnic and Islamist groups came to provide useful pretexts to postpone reform and concentrate power on the center throughout the CCA region. This accretion of power was accomplished by rigging presidential and parliamentary elections, changing the constitution to lengthen the presidential term and/or heighten presidential powers, repressing political opponents and limiting free speech and the judicial process.

Table 8.1 (last line) confirms that in contrast to a CEE country like Hungary, the growth collapse that accompanied the demise of the Soviet Union did not bring incremental change toward democracy in the CCA region. Rather, political freedom and civil liberties were repressed from an early stage, and, if anything, regressed even in the resource-poor countries, albeit distinctly less so in Armenia and Georgia. This regression in the

*Table 8.1* Political freedom indices: Caucasus, Central Asia and comparators 1991–2001

| Country/group | 1992 | 1993 | 1994 | 1995 | 1996 | 1997 | 1998 | 1999 | 2000 | 2001 | 2002 |
|---|---|---|---|---|---|---|---|---|---|---|---|
| Mineral-rich CCA | 6,5 | 6,6 | 7,6 | 7,6 | 7,6 | 7,6 | 7,6 | 7,6 | 7,6 | 7,6 | 7,6 |
| Azerbaijan | 5,5 | 5,5 | 6,6 | 6,6 | 6,6 | 6,5 | 6,4 | 6,4 | 6,4 | 6,5 | 6,5 |
| Kazakhstan | 5,4 | 5,5 | 6,4 | 6,5 | 6,5 | 6,5 | 6,5 | 6,5 | 6,5 | 6,5 | 6,5 |
| Turkmenistan | 6,5 | 7,6 | 7,7 | 7,7 | 7,7 | 7,7 | 7,7 | 7,7 | 7,7 | 7,7 | 7,7 |
| Uzbekistan | 6,5 | 6,6 | 7,7 | 7,7 | 7,6 | 7,6 | 7,6 | 7,6 | 7,6 | 7,6 | 7,6 |
| Resource-poor CCA | 5,4 | 5,4 | 5,5 | 5,5 | 5,5 | 5,5 | 5,5 | 5,5 | 5,5 | 5,5 | 5,5 |
| Armenia | 5,5 | 4,3 | 3,4 | 3,4 | 4,4 | 5,4 | 5,4 | 4,4 | 4,4 | 4,4 | 4,4 |
| Georgia | 6,5 | 4,5 | 5,5 | 5,5 | 4,5 | 4,4 | 3,4 | 3,4 | 3,4 | 4,4 | 4,4 |
| Kyrgyzstan | 5,4 | 4,2 | 5,3 | 4,3 | 4,4 | 4,4 | 4,4 | 5,5 | 5,5 | 6,5 | 6,5 |
| Tajikistan | 3,3 | 6,6 | 7,7 | 7,7 | 7,7 | 7,7 | 6,6 | 6,6 | 6,6 | 6,6 | 6,6 |
| Comparators | | | | | | | | | | | |
| Angola | 5,4 | 6,6 | 7,7 | 7,7 | 6,6 | 6,6 | 6,6 | 6,6 | 6,6 | 6,6 | 6,6 |
| Sri Lanka | 4,5 | 4,5 | 4,5 | 4,5 | 4,5 | 4,5 | 3,5 | 3,4 | 3,4 | 3,4 | 3,4 |
| Trinidad + Tobago | 1,1 | 1,1 | 1,1 | 1,2 | 1,2 | 1,2 | 1,2 | 1,2 | 1,2 | 1,2 | 2,2 |
| Hungary | 2,2 | 2,2 | 1,2 | 1,2 | 1,2 | 1,2 | 1,2 | 1,2 | 1,2 | 1,2 | 1,2 |

*Source:* Freedom House 2004.

*Note:* Democracy among the states of the CCA region, with higher values representing less democracy based on Freedom House coding of political rights. The code measures political liberty and civil rights on a scale of 1–7, with lower numbers representing more freedom. Values between 1 and 2.5 are coded as 'free', between 2.5 and 5.5 as 'partly free' and 5.5 and 7 as 'not free'.

resource-poor countries reflects the impact of initial conditions other than the resource rents (see Chapter 2). In particular, Chapters 6 and 7 show that the exceptional severity of GDP compression in the resource-poor countries, aggravated by civil strife, further eroded the weak social capital and governance inherited from the USSR to levels that have more in common with the resource-rich FSU countries than with the CEE countries. Expressed another way: the negative impact on sanctions against anti-social governance of the exceptionally sharp contraction in PCGDP in the resource-poor countries offset the potential pro-democratization effects arising both from low natural resource rent as well as the enhanced dependence on the IFIs that inevitably accompanied it (Table 6.6).

Nevertheless, Table 8.1 does identify differences in levels of freedom and civil liberties among the CCA region's political regimes. The most repressive regimes are the predatory autocracies of Uzbekistan and Turkmenistan, which as Chapter 3 argues, were least susceptible to IFI influence because their access to sizeable natural resource rents required little DFI. Political conditions have been marginally freer in oil-rich Azerbaijan and Kazakhstan, which are classified as concentrated oligarchies, where presidential families and an estimated one to two thousand other families with strong business and regional links have cohered to dominate the patronage system. Among the four resource-poor countries, even Kyrgyzstan, which has interacted most with the IFIs, has functioned as a concentrated oligarchy, as has Tajikistan, although both are fractured because their elites are less cohesive than those in the oil-rich countries. Finally, Armenia and Georgia may be transforming into diffusing oligarchies because their elites have struggled to prevent upwardly mobile groups from eroding their patronage.

This chapter explores the dynamics of each of these four sets of political states in order to explain the incentives it has faced and how it has responded, and also to evaluate the prospects for welfare-enhancing change in the incentives. It is structured as follows. The next section, (pages 138–141), examines the autocracies and argues that pressure for radical change has accumulated gradually in Uzbekistan, while Turkmenistan may soon abruptly face similar pressure. The third section (pages 142–143) explains the marked swings in the political stances of the oil-rich elites, and identifies recent optimistic trends. The fourth section (pages 144–145) evaluates the dynamics of the fractured oligarchies of Tajikistan and Kyrgyzstan and examines the likelihood of the rifts pushing them towards diffusing oligarchies. The fifth section (pages 146–148) analyzes the momentum of the two diffusing oligarchies in the south-west Caucasus. The final section (pages 148–150) summarizes the policy implications.

## Predatory autocracies in Turkmenistan and Uzbekistan

Turkmenistan and Uzbekistan remain predatory authoritarian political states, which have used their sizeable natural resource rents to maintain substantial state control of the economy. Political repression is at its most extreme and institutions are weakest in Turkmenistan where the president, Niyazov has used the rents from natural gas to build a cult of personality (Lubin 2000). The president retains the right to enact laws and has the power to appoint within the judiciary and the executive, and to dissolve the parliament. Opposition parties are considered 'unnecessary' and what little open dissent that does surface is quickly quashed. The Turkmenistan government is reported to have advised the IMF that it requires no assistance provided the IMF revives neighboring economies so that their demand for natural gas increases along with their capacity to pay for it in cash rather than by bartering shoddy goods. As described in Chapter 3, the government has sought to avoid social dislocation by subsidizing water, gas and electricity for households and enterprises.

Such a regime is brittle and could abruptly implode with the demise of its leader (Collins 2004). The president underwent open-heart surgery in 1998 and narrowly escaped assassination in November 2002. Yet Niyazov has no chosen successor, so his death could herald change for the better or for the worse. But regardless of who is in power, Turkmenistan's leadership will need to radically change the policy of 'neutral disengagement' from the international community that the gas rents have hitherto rendered feasible because such a policy is based upon a sustained expansion of gas production and of the gas transportation network, which is not, to date, occurring (Repkine 2004: 156–62). Turkmenistan is therefore heavily dependent on market access through the Gazprom network. But, because Gazprom is a direct competitor, it squeezes the export rents well below world prices (see Chapter 5). Yet access to alternative markets in Western Europe requires financing a commercially unattractive pipeline under the Caspian Sea, while efforts to expand exports to South Asia via Iran have stalled. Agriculture provides the Niyazov regime with its other main source of rent, but resources are wastefully used in an over-ambitious expansion of capacity (Chapter 5) while the existing distribution system is being liquidated (Chapter 9). It is difficult to escape the conclusion that, regardless of who rules, the current high level of economic autarky and central control is not sustainable.

The Uzbek president rapidly concentrated power on the center, bypassing all but a few oblast rivals to reach directly to the local government. His government also quickly diminished the role of the IFIs (Jones Luong 2002) by reversing an early start on trade reform and opting for a multiple exchange rate system to increase scope for rent extraction. The central government came to depend heavily on agricultural rent for its revenue, so in marked contrast to China (see Lau *et al.* 2000), agriculture has undergone minimal reform (Table 8.2). Moreover, as in Turkmenistan, agricultural assets are being liquidated (see Chapter 9) because, in addition to any rent, part of the farmer's return is also being extracted by the state. As a result, agriculture cannot play its natural role as the dynamic market sector within Uzbekistan's faltering 'gradual' reform strategy.

*Table 8.2* Indices of agricultural reform, CCA countries

| Country/group | Price + market | Land reform | Agro- processing | Rural finance | Institutions | Total score | % Individual owned land |
|---|---|---|---|---|---|---|---|
| Mineral-rich | 5 | 5 | 5 | 4 | 4 | 4.6 | 13 (1997) |
| Azerbaijan | 8 | 8 | 6 | 6 | 5 | 6.6 | 5 (1995) |
| Kazakhstan | 6 | 5 | 7 | 6 | 5 | 5.8 | 24 (1998) |
| Turkmenistan | 2 | 3 | 2 | 1 | 3 | 2.0 | 8 (1998) |
| Uzbekistan | 4 | 4 | 4 | 2 | 3 | 4.4 | 14 (1998) |
| Resource-poor | 8 | 7 | 6 | 6 | 5 | 6.4 | 45 (1998) |
| Armenia | 8 | 8 | 8 | 7 | 6 | 7.4 | 90 (1998) |
| Georgia | 9 | 7 | 5 | 7 | 5 | 6.6 | 44 (1998) |
| Kyrgyzstan | 7 | 7 | 6 | 6 | 5 | 6.2 | 37 (1998) |
| Tajikistan | 6 | 6 | 5 | 3 | 4 | 4.8 | 9 (1998) |

*Source:* EBRD 2002: 78. Rated on a scale of 1–10, with 10 indicating completed reform.

However, gradual reform has allowed the Uzbek government to main-tain its revenue above 30 per cent of GDP (Pomfret and Anderson 1997) and sustain ambitious social provision, which together with popular appreciation of the government's prevention of civil strife has raised toler-ance by the majority of autocratic governance. The erstwhile low level of geopolitical rent (Table 6.6) rose in return for swift support for US inter-vention in Afghanistan. This move brought increased repression (Walker 2003), and the president recently 'won' a further seven years in office with 91 per cent of the vote (Aslund 2003). However, in the summer of 2004, the US government cancelled money intended for the Uzbek government because of lack of reform (although military funds continue to flow) and several IFIs came under pressure to reconsider project-funding through the Uzbek state.

Yet the incentive for reform in Uzbekistan intensifies as infrastructure decays, rent loses buoyancy, economic growth lags far behind regional rivals and the debt burden remains excessive. The squeeze on revenue arising from a weak economy also intensifies the center–region political contest. Local gov-ernment officials withhold revenues from the center in response to the simul-taneous increase in central government claims on dwindling cotton revenues (which were previously evenly shared between central and regional govern-ments), and the imposition of unfunded mandates to provide social services (Jones Luong 2003: 22). Nor are local leaders brought to heel by the increased frequency with which the central government replaces lower-tier government leaders. In fact, the frequent rotation of local and regional lead-ers encourages the officials concerned to maximize their rent extraction while they can. This impairs the required build-up of trust and social capital at local government levels.

The squeeze on local officials between higher tiers of government on the one hand and the population on the other encourages them to reduce the amount of cotton and wheat that they surrender to higher tiers; to illegally appropriate collective farmland and assets for lease to private farmers; and also to levy road fines, market duties and demands for unpaid labor on local people. This represses incentives not only for farmers and exporters, but also for SMEs. Uzbek SMEs have been particularly squeezed in order to extract resources to the benefit of local state-owned farms and state-owned enterprises (SOEs). The state is the full or majority shareholder in half of all SMEs, which account for most employment in the sector (ibid.: 16). This increases the control of officials over rent extraction but at the cost of discouraging SME formation and expansion. SMEs are better off remaining small (and individually owned) so that their low profile reduces the risk of attracting predatory government attention.

It seems clear that the system of rent extraction and deployment, which sustains Uzbekistan's concentrated oligarchy, is increasingly counter-productive. At the local level, the incentives send contradictory signals to economic agents because they are complex and opaque. Both economic agents and predatory government officials have difficulty working out the implications of reform for their own welfare, as Krueger (1991) reports to have been the case under predatory governments in many countries of sub-Saharan Africa during the 1960s and 1970s. Not only are rents being extracted from agriculture at the expense of liquidating the productive assets but also, consistent with the STEX model's emergent staple trap, a large fraction of the rent that is invested has gone into protected industry that has no incentive to compete and uses the rent inefficiently. The economy-wide incremental capital/output ratio of Uzbekistan is twice that of comparator countries in East Asia (Repkine 2004: 193), and possibly higher if government GDP growth data are overstated. This indicates a very low level of investment efficiency, so it is little wonder that economic growth has faltered. Uzbek rent extraction is neither efficient nor sustainable, so that it is in the interest of Karimov and the elite, central and local alike, to improve efficiency by raising the productivity with which agricultural, and other, resources are used.

The rate at which the economic and therefore political strength of Uzbekistan is being eroded relative to Kazakhstan suggests that national sentiment driven by fears over defense capability could provide the catalyst for economic and institutional reform. If not, the STEX model suggests that a growth collapse will do so. But the inefficient Uzbek system of rent extraction and distribution also provides scope for a powerful oblast leader to recognize the declining sustainability of the system and to respond by pioneering the reform of agricultural incentives. Such a move might shift Uzbekistan's autocracy toward a fractured concentrated oligarchy, or even toward a diffusing oligarchy. Similarly, Turkmenistan will abruptly face the dilemma of economic reform or growth collapse if, as seems increasingly likely, the expanding gas rents upon which government patronage depends should abruptly halt.

## Concentrated oligarchies in Azerbaijan and Kazakhstan

The concentrated oligarchies of Azerbaijan and Kazakhstan remain somewhat less repressive than the Turkmen and Uzbek autocracies, but their presidents became increasingly authoritarian during the 1990s (Table 8.1). There
are, however, interesting differences between the regimes, notably the greater
strength of civil society in Azerbaijan (not recognized by Freedom House,
however) and the transfer of power to a new generation in that country. This
might make Azerbaijan a bellwether for change in Kazakhstan, whose expanding middle class may be expected to push for reform when Nazarbaev retires.

In Azerbaijan the 1995 constitution rendered the country's three high
courts (Constitutional, Supreme and Economic) subservient to the president,
and parliament's power to scrutinize the budget and impeach the president
became nominal when the president's supporters 'won' all but eight of the
125 seats. In the absence of an impartial judiciary and civil service, ministries
form lines of patronage whose ability to deliver rewards (such as tax relief,
relaxed regulation, preferential contracts and access to SOEs) depends upon
proximity to the Aleyev family, its 'tribe' from Nakhichevan and cronies from
the Soviet era (Hoffman 2000). Examples of rapacious rent-seeking include
the Minister of Health and the chairman of the state shipping corporation,
who were appointed in return for helping the senior Aleyav to power. In 2003,
the president's son succeeded him after 'winning' more than 80 per cent of
the votes cast in the election, although it is likely that his actual margin of
victory was much more slender.

Chapter 3 has demonstrated that much of the rent generated by Azeri
oil leaked on to domestic markets as subsidies for households and firms.
However, the $1.5 billion of oil exported during 1996–2000 may have con-
tributed several $100 millions to presidential assets, which are augmented by
cuts on business deals ranging from construction through trade. Uncoordin-
ated rent-seeking at all levels of government has deterred private investment
in long-term wealth creation and it pushed the gray economy to an estimated
61 per cent of official GDP by 1995 (Johnson *et al.* 1997), exacerbating
the unbalanced growth of the oil-driven economy. In 1999, the sudden fall in
oil prices and anti-government riots in several regions, including the president's regional base, combined to deliver a political shock. The ageing president began to constrain rent-seeking by his son's rivals for the succession and
re-activated economic reform including setting up an internationally audited
oil fund (which still remains open to presidential abuse) and accelerating
privatization. In 2003, the incoming president declined to re-appoint some
rent-seeking ministers and immediately commissioned action plans for
improved economic management. The new Azeri regime's incentive to reform
may be strengthened by the overthrow in November 2003 of a corrupt regime
by civic associations in neighboring Georgia, but vested interests are sure
to test its resolve. It is therefore premature to conclude that Azerbaijan is
moving towards a diffusing oligarchy, but it may do so.

In Kazakhstan, the government sidelined parliament from 1995. In 1999, with major FDI committed, the president banned his main opponent from elections and 'won' with more than 80 per cent of the vote. More than half the MPs would have lost without manipulation of the vote (Financial Times 2000). Yet the Kazakh parliament retains greater capacity to scrutinize public spending than in Azerbaijan. Civil society is weaker, however: leading dissenters are first ignored, then harassed by the state bureaucracy and finally bought off (and effectively muzzled) with a 'position' within the government. In contrast to Azerbaijan, ministries in Kazakhstan appear to have been less of a conduit for rent-seeking by the elite than monopolistic businesses. The Kazakh elite favored early reform in order to capture potentially lucrative monopolies and then lost interest in further reform because expanding competition would end the business monopolies. President Nazarbaev may have amassed assets in excess of $1 billion.

However, even if the central government wanted to accelerate reform, the fact that reform must be implemented at the regional and local level means that it may not be carried out. Taxation, regulation and much expenditure are administered at the regional level, and executed by officials who have stronger obligations to, and dependence upon, the regional leadership rather than the national leadership. One consequence is the ad hoc character of the state sector: the tax effort (rates of achievement of tax targets) and levels of expenditure in different fiscal categories all vary widely, not only between oblasts but also from year to year within individual oblasts (Jones Luong forthcoming). Both revenue extraction and public expenditure are therefore capricious, which saps investor confidence as well as the coherence of central government economic policy. For instance, regional leaders frequently oppose privatization of local SOEs, turning a blind eye toward 'their' SOEs that cannot meet their obligations to government agencies and input suppliers. This creates fiscal imbalances that oblast and local government leaders balance at the expense of other economic agents, often in the private sector. Local governments target SMEs to balance their finances, whereas regional governments raid FDI, an especially lucrative option where the natural resource endowment attracts much inward investment. Kazakh federalism is clearly not particularly 'market-supporting'.

Yet a pressure point has emerged that may re-start reform and reverse the authoritarian drift. This arises from disclosures regarding offshore accounts that strengthen the desire of an emerging middle class to boost political accountability of Nazarbaev's oligarchy (Aslund 2003). The trial in the United States of key intermediaries believed to have brokered bribes from international oil companies to senior Kazakh officials already constrains the ability of the president to travel overseas and may lie behind measures floated in mid-2004 to increase the transparency of parliamentary and presidential elections.

## Fractured oligarchies in Tajikistan and Kyrgyzstan

Despite increasing inflows of geopolitical rents (Table 6.6), and the pro-reform conditions attached to them, resource-poor Kyrgyzstan and Tajikistan remain relatively authoritarian states (Table 8.1). Weak central governments in each country have, however, been unable to implement many of the economic reforms that they espoused under the prompting of western donors (once civil strife ceased in the case of Tajikistan). Yet, strife-free Kyrgyzstan initially made rapid progress in sanctioning both economic and political reform.

Mikhalev and Heinrich (1999) provide some insight into the social restructuring in Kyrgyzstan during the transition. The reforms consolidated the power of the former Soviet elite together with younger groups of urban-based entrepreneurs in banking and trading, who comprised no more than 5 per cent of total households. The 'upper' middle class is perhaps one-tenth of all households, while the middle class contracted to barely one-third of the population due to a sharp fall in the income of state-employed professionals. Real wages fell by two-thirds and pushed the poverty rate above 50 per cent of the population, mostly in rural areas, especially the south. In this context of a shrinking middle class, the momentum towards a consensual democracy slowed through the late 1990s and the government became more authoritarian, ostensibly in response to the threat from Islamic militants and pressure from Uzbekistan (Walker 2003).

Behind the authoritarian drift lay a power struggle, first between the northern and southern clans in which the former backed Akaev for president and then, between the president and the northern elite. In fact, Jones Luong (2002) argues that the perceived initial weakness of Akaev rather than any strong belief in democracy may have strengthened pro-democracy reforms in the mid-1990s. In contrast, Collins (2004) suggests that Akaev initially favored democracy over clan loyalties. Thereafter, however, he increasingly favored his relatives' clans, causing outsider clans to make up for lost central influence by strengthening their own patronage networks, further diluting the coherence of central policy. Consequently, as elsewhere in the region, local officials stymie implementation of reform by squeezing SMEs to extract revenue to sustain SOEs, which often remain dependent on sizeable public subsidies. In addition, many *privatized* firms continue to rely on subsidies because the owners are mainly managers and workers, who continue to operate with little change in efficiency. New enterprises therefore require access to personal networks and clan connections in order to survive, so rent-seeking and monopolistic practices flourish along with the underground economy. Corruption actually intensified in Kyrgyzstan during 1999–2002, whereas it fell in most other CCA countries (Table 7.2). However, the data in Table 7.2 reflect a period of acute trade repression by neighboring states, which Aslund (2004) reports has subsequently eased, improving the economic growth rate. This recent economic improvement, along with President Akaev's decision not to seek re-election in 2005, revives the possibility that Kyrgyzstan may be returning to the CIEN political economy trajectory.

The unusually severe civil strife in Tajikistan arose from the fact that, unlike other Central Asian states, new elites emerged to challenge the dominance of the established (northern) elite. Collins (2004) argues the factions were clan-based. The northern group misjudged the resulting negotiations and offered too few concessions, triggering violence (Jones Luong 2002). Eventually, Russian backing for Rakhmanov brought an end to the conflict. Conditions began to improve in 1997 when peace was agreed with the Islam-led United Tajik Opposition (UTO). These moves further reduced the initial political dominance of the northern city of Leninabad over the majority south and led to an election to the Lower House in February 2000. Although the election did not meet basic standards of fairness, power was somewhat diffused because the ruling party took less than three-fifths of the seats while Islamic groups and communists took one-quarter and one-eighth of the seats, respectively. Unfortunately, Tajikistan's neighbors were unsettled by the democratic drift and by the legitimization of Islamic parties, some of whose sympathizers backed Tajikistan-based insurgency campaigns into Uzbekistan and Kyrgyzstan. Moreover, Rakhmanov appears to have pushed his clan's interests at the expense of others, despite the peace accord, thereby keeping clan tensions simmering and losing control over much rent-seeking activity.

However, the peace settlement increased the inflow of foreign aid and direct investment into Tajikistan, while catch-up economic reform and rapid GDP growth gave the Tajik government a respite. Yet many of the reforms cannot be put into practice (see Chapter 6) because the peace accord entails political balancing acts that compromise economic reform and sap macro policy coherence. As elsewhere in Central Asia, regional and local officials neutralize the potential gains from agricultural liberalization (Table 8.2) by imposing their own crop quota systems, withholding inputs to non-acquiescing farmers and allocating land to favored groups. Moreover, the scale of plundering by local government officials more than halved the number of SMEs during 1996–2000: many SME owners found it expedient to operate as individually owned firms. Even where the central government does control assets, privatization of large SOEs lags, notably the aluminum smelter, power generation and other heavy industry. This is because these large SOEs are important sources of revenue and patronage for the central administration, and they are also easier to control because they are located near the capital city, Dushanbe (Jones Luong 2003). In summary, inadequate central control and local patronage networks water down IFI-backed reforms. In contrast to Kyrgyzstan, the fractured oligarchy of Tajikistan risks disintegration rather than dissolution. This might be avoided if sustained IFI assistance can demonstrate the gains from wealth creation in at least one of the competing fiefdoms.

## Diffusing oligarchies in Armenia and Georgia?

The EBRD (1999: 108) index of social cohesion within the FSU countries in the early 1990s identifies Armenia and Georgia as distinctly different from the other CCA countries. The index measures social cohesion in terms of the share of seats won by the communist party and the largest non-communist party in the first transition election. Social cohesion is higher the higher the share of seats won by the non-communist party and the lower the share won by the successor communist party. On this measure, social cohesion at the outset of the transition among the four principal groups of countries in transition to a market economy (Table 2.4) was highest in the CEE countries and lowest in the CCA countries. The five Central Asian countries cluster at one extreme of the spectrum, with the communist party virtually unchallenged in the first transition election. Most CEE countries are at the other extreme, with high shares of seats won by the non-communist party. Armenia and Georgia have more affinity with the CEE group: both experienced strong early challenges to communist leadership and both harbor aspirations of links to the EU, which, along with the absence of resource rents and concomitant access to geopolitical rent, render them more amenable to IFI pressure for economic and political reform.

Yet neither Georgia nor Armenia met their early promise for economic and political reform. Under central planning the Georgian economy prospered by selling prized goods at a premium (often illegally) within the Soviet Union, but those goods were uncompetitive in world markets. The interaction of ethnic feuding, pervasive criminal gangs and state corruption caused one-third of Georgian territory to slip from central control in the early 1990s, often with Russian connivance. Russia intervened in support of secessionist groups, partly because it held Georgians responsible for abetting rebels in the southern fringe of the Russian Federation (Lieven 2001). There is contempt for the law and individuals seek either to accumulate enough money to be powerful enough to deal with this environment or to gain the patronage of someone who is. Such patrons included the president's family and cronies, mafia and high officials such as the minister of transport. Rackets involving the smuggling of duty-rich items such as cigarettes and petroleum helped depress the share of government revenue in GDP to the lowest in the region (Table 8.3), squeezing public sector wages and strengthening the incentive for civil servants to resort to petty corruption.

Western assistance failed to stem the political and economic deterioration in Georgia and efforts by the government to build bridges to the West by, for example, seeking NATO membership proved disappointing. Nevertheless, two hopeful recent developments are the construction of the Ceyhan–Baku pipeline through Georgian territory, which heightens western interest in the country's progress, and the peaceful overthrow of the president in November 2003. The latter followed a grossly fraudulent election in which the president claimed more than 80 per cent of the vote whereas a figure one-tenth that

*Table 8.3* General government revenue, selected years 1993–2001 (% GDP)

|  | *1993* | *1997* | *2001* |
|---|---|---|---|
| Resource-poor | *22.1* | *17.9* | *17.3* |
| Armenia | 28.9 | 19.7 | 16.5 |
| Georgia | 12.4 | 14.3 | 15.3ₐ |
| Kyrgyzstan | 24.7 | 23.9 | 22.2 |
| Tajikistan | n.a. | 13.7 | 15.2 |
| Resource-rich | *28.1* | *22.0* | *25.2* |
| Azerbaijan | 33.5 | 19.1 | 22.1 |
| Kazakhstan | 21.1 | 13.5 | 21.3 |
| Turkmenistan | 22.6 | 25.4 | 25.2 |
| Uzbekistan | 35.3 | 30.1 | 32.0 |

*Source:* Cottarelli and Doyle 2001: 38; EBRD 2002: 62.

size seems more accurate. A younger generation of business leaders and technocrats combined to invade the parliament and peaceably remove the incumbent. The leader of the grass roots movement secured a substantial mandate
for reform from reasonably fair elections in spring 2004. The new president
moved swiftly to reincorporate one of the three secessionist enclaves under
central government control and also received pledges of $1 billion in external
funds to support sustained reform. The success of the new regime may have a
potentially profound demonstration effect for the neighboring regimes in
Armenia and Azerbaijan.

Early in the transition, the government of Armenia was warned by the IFIs
that the pursuit of military objectives against Azerbaijan would be at the cost
of failure to realize the country's substantial economic potential (personal
communication, A. Gelb 2003). The warning was set aside and the country's
long-term prospects continue to be blighted by the unstable outcome of that
now 'dormant' conflict. Armenia relies strongly on a powerful US lobby and
Russian military support to shore up its fragile borders (see Chapters 6 and
11). As with Kyrgyzstan, severe restrictions on trade arising from the block-
ade by Azerbaijan and Turkey along with extortionist bribes to secure transit
through Georgia sharply constrain domestic investment opportunities.

Yet Armenia's parliament retains more power than elsewhere within the
CCA region and its relatively good record on civil rights led to its acceptance
into the Council of Europe. Political progress did halt, however, when several
prominent parliamentarians were murdered after elections in 1999, but the
momentum has since recovered. The parliament voted in 2001 to reduce taxes
on business in an attempt to shrink the unofficial economy and stimulate
investment and job creation. But elections in 2003 were rigged, with the
'winner' receiving an unearned extra 10 per cent of the vote, sufficient to
confer a majority, causing a dispute that opposition parties failed to exploit
fully. Yet corruption has been controlled more tightly than in Georgia and
privatization of key infrastructure has proceeded fast enough to halt its

*Table 8.4* Privatization: private share of GDP 2000 and government receipts (% GDP)

|  | Private output share 2002 | Cumulative receipts 1994 | Cumulative receipts 2002 |
|---|---|---|---|
| Resource-poor | *63* | *4.9* | *10.3* |
| Armenia | 70 | 3.4 | 9.7 |
| Georgia | 65 | 14.6 | 23.1 |
| Kyrgyzstan | 65 | 0.6 | 2.7 |
| Tajikistan | 50 | 1.1 | 5.6 |
| Resource-rich | *50* | *1.0* | *5.7* |
| Azerbaijan | 65 | 0.0 | 2.4 |
| Kazakhstan | 65 | 3.0 | 16.6 |
| Turkmenistan | 25 | 0.1 | 0.6 |
| Uzbekistan | 46 | 0.7 | 3.0 |

*Source:* EBRD 2002: 114–217.

deterioration (Table 8.4). Rapid economic growth recently reached 10 per cent annually, although unemployment stands at 27 per cent, even though one-quarter of the population has emigrated to find work. Some 37 per cent of the population remains in poverty and remittances account for one-fifth of income and have played a key role in driving the recent high rate of GDP growth. This, together with the demonstration effect from Georgia of what emerging business and civil service technocrats can achieve politically may combine with the country's EU aspirations and external dependence to constrain the incumbent president and sustain Armenia's convergence towards the CIEN trajectory.

## Conclusions: some policy implications of CCA regional political dynamics

The CCA countries, especially the resource-abundant-ones faced the least propitious initial conditions for reform among the four principal geographical groups of transition economies. Yet the incentive to reform conferred by limited rents on political states in the four resource-poor countries, which included a high reliance on IFI assistance (with its pro-reform conditionality), was more than offset by the erosion of an already weak dependent social capital by a combination of civil strife (in three of the resource-poor countries) and massive contraction in PCGDP. Although the resource-poor countries did pursue economic reform faster than their resource-rich counterparts and on average tended to tolerate greater political freedom, early moves towards democracy regressed and the political norm in the CCA region has drifted toward autocratic regimes.

One result of this outcome is a disjuncture between the outward-looking and long-term national economic and political reform strategy favored by the IFIs and the inward-looking patronage-dispensing agenda of central, regional and local governments alike. The CCA region's largely unchallenged elites maintained their power through patronage networks that advantaged family and associates. This retention of bonding social capital by the region's leaders puts kinship and in-group obligations far above considerations of national social welfare. The elites were able to compensate for the loss of Soviet subventions by extracting natural resource, geopolitical and contrived rents. Indeed, initial support for economic reform reflected opportunities to capture state assets cheaply with which to garner rents from still imperfect markets. Ongoing reform held less appeal because rising competition shrinks rent-seeking activity.

Even if the central government wished to accelerate economic reform, it would have difficulty executing it on the ground. The same bonding social capital that motivates elites to cohere at the national level also sustains patronage networks at lower tiers of government. These networks yield conflicting results that are not always clear to those maintaining them, but to the extent that they impair new business formation and long-term investment, they jeopardize the recent economic rebound and are not sustainable. These conditions carry a high propensity for resources freed by reform for more efficient uses to be squandered and for reform to stall entirely. Although the anti-reform drift has accompanied the spell of rapid GDP growth arising from the transition rebound, Chapters 4–6 suggest this economic performance is not sustainable so that regimes will need to promote wealth creation to avoid growth collapses that would threaten their dynasties. The CIEN model indicates that if economic reform occurs, rising incomes will nurture political moves toward democratization.

All four types of political regime in the CCA region need to create wealth in order to sustain GDP growth. Consequently, the long-term dynastic ambitions of the elites will require them to realign their interests more closely with those of society at large to create wealth. Uzbekistan is under the most pressure to implement reforms to improve economic efficiency because its lackluster economic performance is causing its economic and political clout to fall increasingly far behind that of its regional rival, Kazakhstan. In addition, the STEX model suggests it faces the real and imminent prospect of experiencing a growth collapse. Turkmenistan could follow suit if its development strategy continues to rely almost exclusively on expanding exports of natural gas, should energy prices collapse or emerging transport bottlenecks choke off growth opportunities.

Oil-rich Azerbaijan and Kazakhstan face the least immediate pressure to reform as long as there is not an energy price collapse through the short and medium term, but there is some evidence that the leaders in both countries are aware that they can most assuredly bolster their long-term positions by prudently managing the oil boom to promote a more developmental regime.

Among the resource-poor countries, first Armenia, and then Georgia, moved further along the transition to a diffusing oligarchy, and the interaction between them may combine with stronger western influence to sustain this movement. In contrast, Kyrgyzstan and Tajikistan lag, and Tajikistan could fragment without carefully targeted external assistance, including help from regional neighbors. Part V assesses what form such external assistance might take, but first, Part IV examines how the political economies of the CCA countries have limited mutually beneficial regional co-operation with reference to trade, environmental issues and military security.

## References

Aslund, A. (2000) Why has Russia's economic transformation been so arduous? in: Pleskovic, B. and Stiglitz, J.E. (eds.) *Annual World Bank Conference on Development Economics 1999*, Washington DC: World Bank, 399–424.

Aslund, A. (2003) Sizing up the Central Asian economies, *Journal of International Affairs* 56(2), 75–87.

Aslund, A. (2004) *The Kyrgyz Republic: Reinforce Economic Growth through Lower Taxes and Better Governance*, Washington DC: Carnegie Endowment for International Peace.

Collins, K. (2004) The logic of clan politics: Evidence from the Central Asian trajectories, *World Politics* 56, 224–261.

Cotarelli, C. and Doyle, P. (2001) Disinflation in transition 1993–97, in: Havrylyshyn, O. and Nsouli, S.M. (eds.) *A Decade of Transition: Achievements and Challenges*, Washington DC: IMF, 12–82.

EBRD (1999) *Transition Report 1999: Ten Years of Transition*, London: European Bank for Reconstruction and Development.

EBRD (2002) *Transition Report 2002: Agriculture and Rural Transition*, London: European Bank for Reconstruction and Development.

Financial Times (2000) Kazakhstan: A survey, *Financial Times* December 11.

Freedom House (2004) *Freedom in the World Ratings 1973–2002*, London: Freedom House.

Hoffman, D. (2000) Azerbaijan: The politicization of oil, in: Ebel, R. and Menon, R. (eds.) *Energy and Conflict in Central Asia and the Caucasus*, Lanham MD: Rowman and Littlefield, 55–77.

Johnson, S., Kaufman, D. and Shleifer, A. (1997) The unofficial economy in transition, *Brookings Papers on Economic Activity* 2, 159–239.

Jones Luong, P. (2002) *Institutional Change and Political Continuity in Post-Soviet Central Asia: Power, Perceptions and Pacts*, Cambridge: Cambridge University Press.

Jones Luong, P. (2003) Political obstacles to economic reform in Uzbekistan, Kyrgyzstan and Tajikistan: Strategies to move ahead, Department of Political Science Working Paper, Yale University.

Jones Luong, P. (Forthcoming) Economic 'decentralization' in Kazakhstan: Causes and consequences, in: Jones Luong, P. (ed.) *The Transformation of Central Asia: State-Societal Relations from Soviet Rule to Independence*, Ithaca NY: Cornell University Press.

Krueger, A.O., Schiff, M. and Valdes, A. (1991) *Political Economy of Agricultural Pricing Policies*, Baltimore MD: Johns Hopkins University Press.

Lau, L.J., Qian, Y. and Roland, G. (2000) Reform without losers: An interpretation of China's dual-track approach to transition, *Journal of Political Economy* 108, 120–143.

Lieven, A. (2001) Georgia: A failing state? *Eurasianet* January 30.

Lubin, N. (2000) Turkmenistan's energy: A source of wealth or instability?, in: Ebel, R. and Menon, R. (eds.) *Energy and Conflict in Central Asia and the Caucasus*, Lanham MD: Rowman and Littlefield, 107–121.

Mikhalev, V. and Heinrich, G. (1999) Kyrgyzstan: A case study in social stratification, UNU/WIDER Working Paper 164, Helsinki: UNU/WIDER.

Pomfret, R. and Anderson, K.H. (1997) Uzbekistan: Welfare impact of slow transition, WIDER Working Paper 135, UNU/ WIDER, Helsinki.

Repkine, A. (2004) Turkmenistan: Economic autarky and recent growth performance, in: Ofer, G. and Pomfret, R. (eds.) *The Economic Prospects of the CIS*, Cheltenham: Edward Elgar, 154–176.

Walker, E.W. (2003) Islam, Islamism and political order in Central Asia, *Journal of International Affairs* 56(2), 21–41.

# Part IV

# Synergies of resource-rich and resource-poor CCA countries

# 9 The importance of good neighbors

## Regional trade in Central Asia

*Clemens Grafe,\* Martin Raiser and Toshiaki Sakatsume\*\**

## Introduction

With the increased geo-political attention given to Central Asia in the aftermath of 9/11, the question of these economies' future economic prospects has also received rising interest. The economies of the five Central Asian countries depend heavily on their primary sectors. Their integration into the world economy has remained incomplete and geared mainly towards the exploitation of their natural resource endowments. Both economic diversification and better outlets for the region's natural resources remain key challenges. While the topic of improved transport infrastructure for natural resources out of the region has been widely discussed in the literature, less attention has been given to the regional aspects of integration. Also, we concentrate on Central Asia rather than the Caucasus.[1] Market access for manufactured products from Central Asia is naturally hampered by high transportation costs linked to the region's relative geographical isolation. Given this constraint several observers have pointed towards increased regional cooperation and enhanced regional trade as central elements of a future sustainable development strategy.

We take stock of recent trends in the geographical and product composition of foreign trade in the five Central Asian countries.[2] The main aim is to explore the scope for regional trade to provide a significant contribution to the region's future development prospects and assess the extent to which protectionist policies currently prevent the benefits from regional trade from being fully realized.[3] We offer two main conclusions that may not have received enough attention in the discussion so far.

First, the scope for regional trade among just the five Central Asian countries is rather limited. This might be the ultimate reason why political initiatives in the past to integrate just this smaller region have never been followed up. However potential benefits from integration rise sharply once the concept of the 'region' is widened to include large regional neighbors – essentially China, Iran, Turkey, Russia and ultimately the Indian subcontinent. It is the liberalization of trade relations in this wider region that should lie at the heart of a strategy of increased integration into the world economy for the countries of Central Asia. However, present policies in Central Asia directly limit market access to this wider regional market by artificially increasing already high transit costs. Better transit, not only increased intra-regional trade, would be a central benefit of more open policies.

Second, the impact of current protectionist policies differs significantly across the five Central Asian countries and also across types of firms. The smaller countries, the Kyrgyz Republic and Tajikistan in particular, and medium-sized firms in all countries would be the main beneficiaries of more open trade relations among the countries of Central Asia. However, the smaller countries and the small and medium enterprises are not politically powerful enough to overcome the resistance of larger countries and vested interests of larger industrial firms. This is why the international community has an important role to play to facilitate better regional cooperation. It could do so by investing in projects that would benefit market access for all parties concerned on condition that the larger countries lower the artificial barriers that lock out producers from smaller countries from their own markets as well as the markets of the wider region.

It should be noted in any discussion of regional cooperation that the aims and interests of the different parties concerned are at least in part shaped by broader geo-political developments. We believe that the potentially large benefits for Central Asia would be enough of an incentive for their governments to actively support initiatives to integrate the wider region. However, as Chapter 8 has argued the broader *political* landscape of Central Asia is a potential major stumbling block. Although the region is geographically isolated it is of great strategic interest to the world's major powers. Iran has been included in the axis of evil by the United States. Russia continues to see Central Asia as its sphere of influence. China is concerned about pan-Turkic aspirations of the ethnically Turkic population in its western provinces and this shapes its security interests in Central Asia. The danger is that should any of these larger geo-political interests enter into conflict with one another, the Central Asian countries could be forced to choose sides. This chapter will largely abstract from such wider considerations, but we will return to them in the conclusion and they are also addressed in Chapters 12–14.

The remainder of this chapter proceeds as follows. The next section (pages 157–162) reviews recent trends in the geographical composition of trade from, and within, Central Asia. It examines the scope for regional trade by comparing Central Asia to other regional trading blocks around the world. It shows how the dependence on intra-regional trade differs among the five countries. It also points out how, by redefining the 'region' to include major regional neighbors, the scope for regional trade changes very significantly. The third section (pages 162–165) turns to the commodity composition of trade and charts the growing resource dependence of all five Central Asian countries over the past decade. The bilateral trade patterns among the Central Asian countries differ significantly: Kazakhstan, the Kyrgyz Republic and Tajikistan show a more diversified trade pattern within the region, with more reliance on exports of agricultural products and manufactures, whereas Turkmenistan and Uzbekistan export predominantly natural resources to the other Central Asian countries. The fourth section (pages 165–172) examines the evolution of trade policies over the past decade and lists some of the main obstacles to intra-regional trade in addition to transit from the region. The chapter concludes with some policy recommendations both for governments in the region and for the international community.

## All roads to Brussels? Changes in the geographical composition of trade

Already in Soviet times, the countries of Central Asia served to a large extent as a raw material depot for the industries of other Soviet republics (see Chapter 3), although communist industrial policy had led to the establishment of some local processing facilities and other manufacturing industries, particularly in Kazakhstan. Since the start of transition, the – clearly excessive – degree of concentration on trade within the former Soviet republics has greatly diminished. At the same time, the dependence on commodity exports has further increased, as new mineral deposits have been developed and many of the older industries proved unable to withstand market forces.

Figure 9.1 summarizes the changes in the geographical trade patterns for the five countries of Central Asia between 1995 and 2001. The figure shows that on average exports within the region have declined from around 13 per cent of total exports in 1995 to 6 per cent in 2001. This decrease is partially explained by the increase in exports of natural resources, which tend to be shipped outside the region. Nonetheless, even in value terms (US$) exports to the region declined between 1995 and 2001, although the decline was concentrated in Kazakhstan, Tajikistan and Uzbekistan. If we add Russia and the remainder of the CIS, exports to former Soviet republics declined from over half of the total in 1995 to around one quarter in 2001. Interestingly, the main shift has not been to Europe (which was already the largest export destination in 1995), but rather to other market economies (including the USA, East Asia, and trade entrepots such as the Caribbean) and to regional non-CIS neighbors, such as China, Iran and Turkey. Figure 9.1 also reveals a broadly similar but much less accentuated pattern for imports from Central Asia.

It is instructive to look at these trends at the country level. Table 9.1 shows the geographical composition of trade by country. The differences are very striking. In Kazakhstan, exports to other Central Asian countries accounted for just 3 per cent of the total in 2001 (down from 6 per cent in 1995), while in the Kyrgyz Republic this figure was as high as 30 per cent (down from 47 per cent in 1995). Similarly, Kazakhstan receives only around 3 per cent of its imports from other Central Asian countries, while Tajikistan receives close to half of all imports from the region. Uzbekistan takes a middle position, while Turkmenistan does not appear to be highly integrated with the rest of Central

## Imports

## Exports

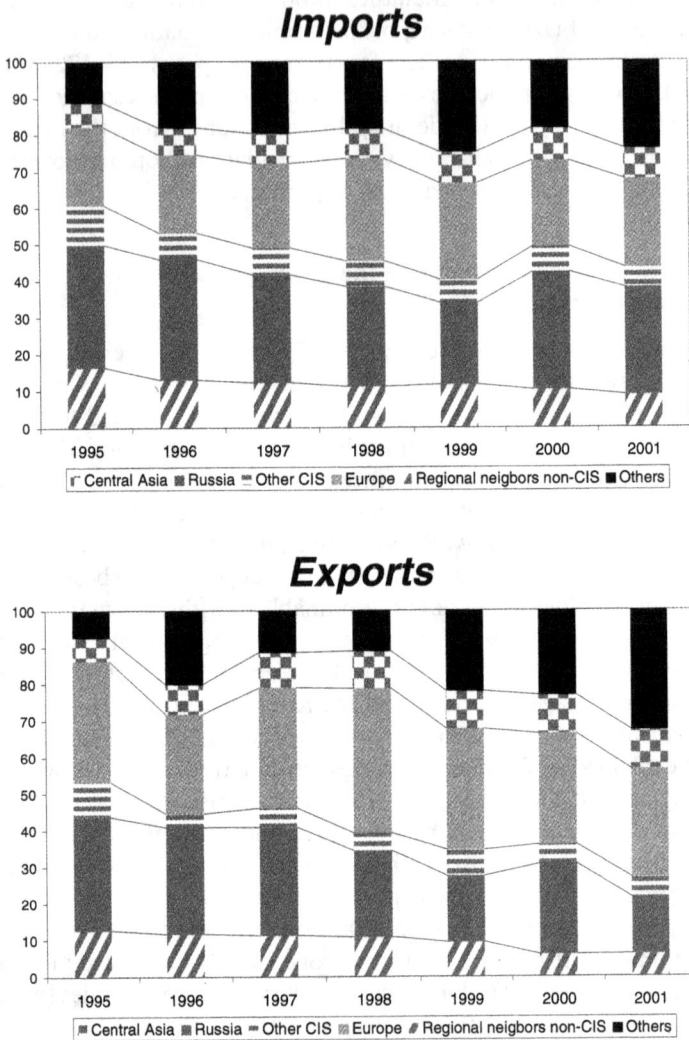

*Figure 9.1* Direction of trade (simple average of five Central Asian countries).

*Source:* IMF Direction of Trade (2002).

Asia. The asymmetry in dependence on regional trade creates a problem for discussions on regional cooperation, because incentives to cooperate are clearly unequal.[4]

The picture of dependence on regional trade changes considerably if we widen the concept of the 'region' to include Russia to the north, Iran and Turkey to the west and China to the east. Russia is a major trading partner for all five Central Asia republics and particularly for Kazakhstan, a reflection of the Soviet legacy but also of geographical proximity. China accounts

*Table 9.1* Direction of trade by country

| Kazakhstan | Exports | | Imports | |
|---|---|---|---|---|
| | 1995 | 2001 | 1995 | 2001 |
| Total CIS | 54.6 | 22.6 | 69.7 | 50.2 |
| Regional neighbors in CIS | 6.0 | 3.1 | 14.6 | 2.8 |
| Russia | 44.8 | 16.6 | 49.9 | 45.9 |
| Other CIS | 3.8 | 3.0 | 5.3 | 1.5 |
| Total non-CIS | 45.4 | 77.4 | 30.3 | 49.8 |
| Europe | 30.9 | 31.7 | 18.2 | 30.5 |
| Regional neighbors non-CIS | 7.9 | 11.5 | 4.5 | 8.3 |

| Kyrgyz Republic | Exports | | Imports | |
|---|---|---|---|---|
| | 1995 | 2001 | 1995 | 2001 |
| Total CIS | 73.3 | 48.4 | 68.6 | 53.3 |
| Regional neighbors in CIS | 46.8 | 30.4 | 37.5 | 33.5 |
| Russia | 23.6 | 15.3 | 26.8 | 17.4 |
| Other CIS | 2.9 | 2.6 | 4.3 | 2.4 |
| Total non-CIS | 26.7 | 51.6 | 31.4 | 46.7 |
| Europe | 20.3 | 38.6 | 1.8 | 15.3 |
| Regional neighbors non-CIS | 5.4 | 10.2 | 8.9 | 17.6 |

| Tajikistan | Exports | | Imports | |
|---|---|---|---|---|
| | 1995 | 2001 | 1995 | 2001 |
| Total CIS | 33.5 | 32.4 | 58.9 | 78.2 |
| Regional neighbors in CIS | 19.2 | 15.7 | 41.7 | 44.8 |
| Russia | 12.7 | 16.1 | 16.8 | 18.8 |
| Other CIS | 1.6 | 0.7 | 0.4 | 14.6 |
| Total non-CIS | 66.5 | 67.6 | 41.1 | 21.8 |
| Europe | 59.5 | 49.0 | 35.2 | 9.7 |
| Regional neighbors non-CIS | 2.0 | 16.1 | 0.6 | 2.8 |

| Turkmenistan | Exports | | Imports | |
|---|---|---|---|---|
| | 1995 | 2001 | 1995 | 2001 |
| Total CIS | 49.3 | 37.8 | 54.5 | 32.5 |
| Regional neighbors in CIS | 8.5 | 7.4 | 4.8 | 4.7 |
| Russia | 3.6 | 3.0 | 7.0 | 9.7 |
| Other CIS | 37.3 | 27.5 | 42.7 | 18.2 |
| Total non-CIS | 50.7 | 62.2 | 45.5 | 67.5 |
| Europe | 33.9 | 24.9 | 20.8 | 18.9 |
| Regional neighbors non-CIS | 8.9 | 26.0 | 15.0 | 15.7 |

| Uzbekistan | Exports | | Imports | |
|---|---|---|---|---|
| | 1995 | 2001 | 1995 | 2001 |
| Total CIS | 55.3 | 33.4 | 51.7 | 27.6 |
| Regional neighbors in CIS | 20.8 | 10.2 | 14.3 | 10.6 |
| Russia | 29.7 | 16.7 | 29.9 | 12.0 |
| Other CIS | 4.9 | 6.5 | 7.5 | 4.9 |
| Total non-CIS | 44.7 | 66.6 | 48.3 | 72.4 |
| Europe | 31.3 | 19.4 | 24.6 | 19.8 |
| Regional neighbors non-CIS | 3.1 | 1.3 | 6.7 | 4.6 |

*Source:* IMF Direction of Trade 2002.

for around 7 and 9 per cent of the total trade of Kazakhstan and Kyrgyz Republic, respectively; Iran in 2001 took around 20 per cent of Turkmen exports and accounted for 5 per cent of imports, while Turkey plays an important role in the exports of Tajikistan and in imports into Turkmenistan. While the dependence on regional trade is the lowest for Kazakhstan for the narrowly defined region, the dependence on regional trade in the wider sense is among the highest at close to 40 per cent of the total. It is the smallest for Uzbekistan with just 13 per cent of trade conducted with the wider region. Moreover, exports from Central Asia to the region in this wider sense have actually increased by around 20 per cent since 1995 and maintained a more or less constant share in total exports. Regional cooperation on trade and transit issues is thus likely to be more effective if it includes at least Russia and possibly the non-CIS regional neighbors, as this would not only make it more attractive for Kazakhstan but also provide additional benefits to the other Central Asian economies. This, of course, also makes it more difficult, as the large regional neighbors, as well as the USA as a key player in the region, do not always have congruent interests.

Is regional trade dependence in Central Asia large or small? In other words, is there scope for increased trade with other countries in the region? We examine this issue in two ways. First, we look at other regional trading blocks around the world to examine the scope for regional trade. As Figure 9.2 reveals, trade within Central Asia is at the lower end of trade in other regional trading blocks. However this finding may be spurious. The figure also shows that trade within regional blocks tends to increase dramatically if

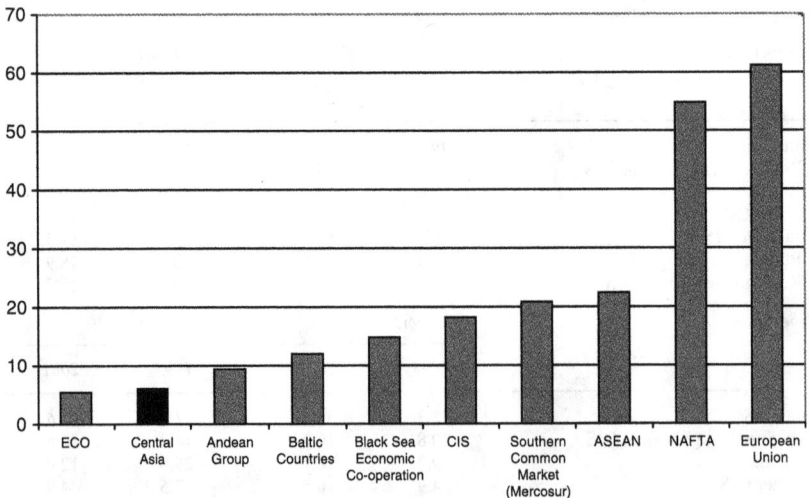

*Figure 9.2* Intra-regional trade of trade blocs as percentage of total exports of each trade bloc (per cent in 2001).

*Source:* UNCTAD and authors' calculations.

these blocks include one or several large and relatively wealthy economies. Intra-regional trade in the EU accounts for over 60 per cent of total exports; within NAFTA this ratio is 58 per cent. Even within ASEAN and Mercosur, regional exports make up more than 20 per cent of total exports. The largest shares of intra-regional trade among regions of small economies are in the Baltic and in the Black Sea Economic Cooperation Area, at 12 and 14 per cent respectively. Taking the latter as a benchmark, there is scope for expansion of intra-regional trade within Central Asia but it is not large. When we add Russia, China, Iran and Turkey as major regional neighbors, even at current levels trade with regional neighbors in Central Asia is relatively high. However this comparison ignores the key geographical characteristic of Central Asian countries, being sandwiched in between some of the largest countries of this world.

The second way to check whether regional trade is high or low and whether it would likely expand under more open trade policies is to create a benchmark from global trade patterns. The established model in the economic literature to predict the level of trade between two countries is the so-called gravity model. This model relates the geographical composition of trade to the relative size of a country's trading partners and to their geographical distance from the home country (Deardorff 1995). Kazakhstan trades a lot with Russia, because it is a relatively large economy and also very close; the Kyrgyz Republic trades a lot with Kazakhstan for the same reasons. A variety of gravity models have been estimated for a worldwide sample of countries and benchmarks derived for the region (EBRD 1999; Fidrmuc and Fidrmuc 2000). The estimations in these two studies confirm that there was an excessive degree of trade concentration within the former Soviet Union, and that this had not disappeared by the late 1990s. The latter study for instance showed that trade flows among the former Soviet republics in 1998 were still around 30 times the predicted 'normal' levels, given these economies' GDP and distances from one another. The Transition Report in turn showed that exports from Central Asia to Europe and to non-transition economies in general were between one-quarter and one-half of the predicted level. This suggests that there appears to be scope to increase trade with non-CIS neighbors, while trade with Russia is unlikely to recover to levels seen in the early 1990s.

However, Djankov and Freund (2000) and Rabelland (2003) qualify these results in two important ways. The first of the two studies showed that there has been an increase in 'home bias' in trade between nine Russian regions and 14 former Soviet republics between 1994 and 1996. During Soviet times Russian regions were trading as much with Central Asian republics as with each other if one controls for distance and size of the regional economy. In contrast, following the break-up of the Soviet Union, trade within Russia has been around 60 per cent higher than trade between Russian regions and former Soviet republics. Apart from Georgia and Moldova, two countries which have clashed politically with Russia, namely Uzbekistan and the Kyrgyz Republic, have seen the sharpest fall of trade with Russia among the 14 republics. The size of the home bias across the 14 former Soviet republics appears to be related to the level of tariff protection in place against bilateral trade with Russia. While not inconsistent with a general picture of gradual disintegration with Russia, these results point to the role of trade policy in determining intra-regional trade flows. Noting that Uzbekistan appears to be the least integrated with the wider region, it is possible to conjecture that this relative regional isolation is at least in part due to the protectionist policies adopted by Uzbekistan in recent years (see next section). The case of Kyrgyzstan is less obvious, which despite its relatively liberal trade regime has seen the third-largest degree of disintegration with Russia among the 14 former Soviet republics.

Rabelland (2003) further shows that Central Asia's geographical position as one of the largest landlocked regions in the world significantly affects its access to world markets. The study found that additional border crossings in trade between a home country and the country of final destination could be as big an impediment to trade as pure geographical distance. The Central Asian economies may not be as integrated with the rest of the world not only because of the legacy of excessive integration with the other former Soviet republics, but also because unusually high transport costs impede access to other markets. As we will show below, at least some of these costs are man-made and relate to transit obstacles faced by exporters from Central Asia and importers into the region. Improved regional cooperation might not necessarily lead to increased intra-regional trade, but might be critical for improved market access to the rest of the world. This argument further emphasizes the need to include Russia in particular in discussions on regional cooperation in trade and transit matters, since it accounts for the bulk of transit trade from the region.[5]

## Hooked on commodities: the product composition of trade

The risks and potential benefits of commodity dependence in economic development have been a topic of debate for several decades. In the 1960s, Raul Prebisch among others argued that commodity exporters faced secular declines in their terms of trade, largely because of low-income elasticities of demand for commodities. This view was later disputed on the basis of little evidence since the 1950s of any trend in relative prices of commodities. Recent contributions have stressed the volatility of commodity prices and the costs of insuring against or managing such volatility. Moreover, the political economy of resource dependence often favors a distorted pattern of development. Thereby resource rents are consumed by a bloated public sector rather than invested and this reduces the competitiveness of the non-resource sector and increases the economy's vulnerability to price shocks (see e.g. Auty and Mikesell 1998; Auty 2001 for a discussion and review of the literature).

In the context of Central Asia, Chapter 3 has highlighted in particular the tendency for resource-rich countries to reform less than resource-poor countries. The relatively slower progress in economic reform in Central Asia compared to other regions in Eastern Europe and the former Soviet Union reduced the attractiveness of the non-resource sector for investment, thereby perpetuating resource dependence. Although Azerbaijan and Kazakhstan in particular have recently adopted a set of macroeconomic policies (including the creation of a stabilization fund) that should help them to cushion commodity price volatility in the future, the quality of the business climate remains below that achieved in much of Eastern Europe. The foundations for economic diversification thus need to be strengthened through more structural reforms.

The above argument has a direct application in the context of foreign trade. As Auty (2001) demonstrates, protectionist trade policies have often exacerbated commodity dependence in developing countries. This is because such policies are an implicit tax on exports by raising the costs of imported inputs and non-tradables, and by reducing the scope for productivity increases through modern technology embodied in imported goods and services. Despite the original intention to support diversification through protecting and subsidizing domestic industry, protectionist trade policies usually achieve exactly the opposite. If rich resource endowments reduce incentives to reform, then the lack of reform further exacerbates resource dependence and a country may be locked in a staple trap.

With the possible exception of Kazakhstan, which had a relatively well-diversified trade structure during Soviet times, the countries of Central Asia were always highly dependent on commodity exports. As Table 9.2 demonstrates commodity dependence has remained very high, with the three largest commodities accounting for as much as two-thirds of total exports in 2000. This compares to around 50 per cent in Russia and as little 15 per cent for a country like Poland. The concentration of trade measured by the Hirschmann index (ranging from 0 for perfectly diversified trade to 1 for a country exporting just one single product) is extraordinarily high at 0.4–0.5, compared to 0.3 in Russia, 0.25 in Moldova, 0.15 in the Baltics and 0.07 in Poland. Moreover, the concentration index more than doubled between 1996 and 2000 in Kazakhstan and the Kyrgyz Republic. This information suggests that, if anything, commodity dependence has increased in Central Asia over the past decade.

Probably the main reason for persistent or even increasing commodity dependence in foreign trade is the disintegration of the Soviet Union. Even peripheral republics like those in Central Asia were hosts for some large, state-led industrialization projects. The scale of these projects was geared toward supply for the entire Soviet Union and often the whole CMEA, affording some degree of trade in processed and manufactured goods. With the breakdown of the Soviet Union, these large industrial dinosaurs went into crisis and non-commodity based trade collapsed. This has been

*Table 9.2* Concentration of trade in Central Asia 2000

|  | Share of three largest products in total exports (%)[1] | Concentration Index[2] | Main export items |
|---|---|---|---|
| Kazakhstan | 71.1 | 0.476 | • Petrol<br>• Copper<br>• Iron |
| Kyrgyz Republic (1999) | 61.2 | 0.398 | • Gold<br>• Electricity<br>• Tobacco |
| Tajikistan | 79.0 | 0.541 | • Aluminum<br>• Electricity<br>• Cotton |
| Turkmenistan | 79.8 | 0.524 | • Natural gas<br>• Petrol<br>• Cotton |
| Uzbekistan[3] | 67.0 | 0.439 | • Cotton<br>• Mineral fuels<br>• Precious stones |
| Russia | 51.5 | 0.285 | • Petrol<br>• Natural gas<br>• Aluminum |

*Sources:* ITC Database International Trade Statistics.

*Notes*
1. Calculated by three-digit SITC.
2. Hirschmann index.
3. based on two-digit HS commodity category.

particularly true for those enterprises that used to be part of the Soviet military complex.

Yet, increasing trade barriers against regional neighbors and protectionist policies targeted primarily at manufactures may also have contributed to rising commodity dependence. Table 9.3 looks at the commodity composition of intra-regional trade. Trade flows are divided into three main categories: agriculture, natural resources and other (including all manufactured products). The evidence, although clearly very limited,[6] still reveals some striking patterns. Intra-regional exports from Kazakhstan and the Kyrgyz Republic are relatively well diversified, with agricultural products and other goods at least as important as natural resources. By contrast, Turkmenistan and Uzbekistan export almost exclusively natural resources to other Central Asian countries.[7] Another way to state this is to consider intra-regional trade flows net of the annual bilateral energy barter arrangements between upstream and downstream countries regarding the allocation of water quotas for the Syr Darya and Amu Darya rivers (see Kennedy 2003). The data in Table 9.3 suggest that net of such barter trade, intra-regional trade of

*Table 9.3* Bilateral trade by product category among the Central Asian countries 2000 (in US$ million)

| From / To | Kazakhstan | Kyrgyzstan | Tajikistan | Turkmenistan | Uzbekistan |
|---|---|---|---|---|---|
| Kazakhstan | – | 32 | 6 | 5 | 73 |
| Agriculture | | 8 | 0.5 | 0.5 | 2 |
| Oil and gas | | 12 | 1 | 4 | 57 |
| Others | | 12 | 4.5 | 0.5 | 14 |
| Kyrgyz Republic | 58 | – | 3 | 23 | n.a. |
| A | 19 | | 0 | 0 | n.a. |
| 0 | 23 | | 1.5 | 23 | n.a. |
| 0 | 16 | | 1.5 | 0 | n.a. |
| Tajikistan | 52 | 8 | – | 29 | 185 |
| A | 41 | 0.5 | | 0 | 5 |
| 0 | 8 | 5 | | 29 | 160 |
| 0 | 3 | 2.5 | | 0 | 20 |
| Turkmenistan | 7 | 5 | 5 | – | 35 |
| A | 1 | 0.5 | 0 | | 3 |
| 0 | 0 | 0 | 0 | | 0 |
| 0 | 6 | 4.5 | 5 | | 32 |
| Uzbekistan | 139 | n.a. | 98 | 6 | – |
| A | 72 | n.a. | 0 | 0 | |
| 0 | 0 | n.a. | 90 | 2 | |
| 0 | 67 | n.a. | 8 | 4 | |

*Source:* ITC TradeMap Database.

Turkmenistan and Uzbekistan is virtually zero. This is clearly a result of the protectionist policies that both countries have followed since the mid-1990s.

## Building a fence on top of a wall: trade policies and transport costs in Central Asia

The discussion has alluded at various points to man-made and natural obstacles to trade in Central Asia. This section will consider both in more detail.

Trade liberalization was part of the package of market reforms introduced early in the transition process in most countries in the region. Figure 9.3 shows the pattern of trade liberalization in Central Asia over the past decade and a half and compares it to the pattern in the front-runners to EU accession. The Kyrgyz Republic was the quickest to embrace relatively open trade and exchange rate policies and by 1995 had reached the same level of trade liberalization (as measured by the EBRD transition indicators) as the central and east European countries, including the Baltic states (CEE). Kazakhstan reached that level in 1996, but backtracked somewhat on its commitment

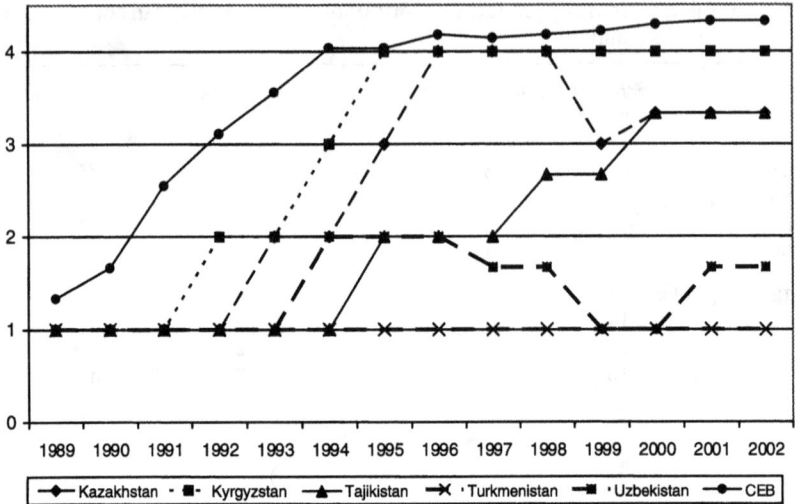

*Figure 9.3* Development of trade liberalization (EBRD transition indicators on trade and foreign exchange system).

*Source:* EBRD (2003).

to open markets after the Russian crisis. Tajikistan has been making recent progress, whereas in Uzbekistan trade and exchange rate liberalization have remained incomplete and inconsistent since the country's independence. In Turkmenistan progress has remained very limited indeed. The divergence that has opened up between the five countries in the region in terms of liberalization is much larger than elsewhere and in itself represents a serious obstacle to intra-regional trade and transit. To give just one example, the Kyrgyz Republic's WTO membership, achieved in 1998, has brought few benefits to the country, as its neighbors have increased trade barriers against Kyrgyz exports for fear that the Kyrgyz Republic might be used as 'Trojan horse' to enter the regional market by other WTO members.[8]

Tariff barriers do not contribute in a major way to man-made trade obstacles, with the exception of Uzbekistan. Average tariff rates ranged between 5 per cent in the Kyrgyz Republic and 18 per cent in Uzbekistan (not including an additional 20 per cent customs charge introduced in August 2002) compared to around 10 per cent in East Asia and Latin America (Figure 9.4). Instead, non-tariff barriers appear to be the biggest obstacles to trade. These include inefficient customs, cumbersome licensing procedures, labeling laws, and multiple obstacles to the efficient and competitive operation of freight handling and transport services. In Uzbekistan and Turkmenistan these are exacerbated by multiple exchange rate systems that limit import through restricted access to hard currency and act in many cases as implicit taxation for exports.[9]

There is little systematic evidence on these non-tariff barriers. The Business

Environment and Enterprise Performance Survey (BEEPS) offers some comparative evidence for 26 transition economies on the costs facing enterprises in Central Asia in relation to customs. This evidence suggests that since 1999, when the first round of the BEEPS was conducted, customs have improved significantly across the region (Table 9.4). Indeed, levels of delay at entry and exit in Kazakhstan and the Kyrgyz Republic are now down to levels observed in CEE, whilst slightly higher but still much improved in Tajikistan and Uzbekistan. Unofficial payments for customs clearance also seem to be

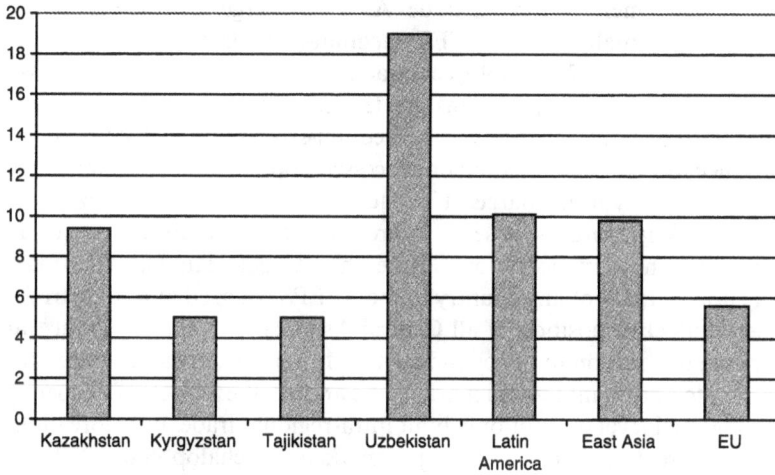

*Figure 9.4* Average tariff rates.

*Source:* World Bank and EBRD.

*Table 9.4* Average days to clear customs and frequency of unofficial payments

|  | Year | Average days to clear customs (inbound) | Average days to clear customs (outbound) | Unofficial payments/gifts paid to clear customs[1] |
|---|---|---|---|---|
| Kazakhstan | 1999 | 7.9 | 7.9 | 1.4 |
|  | 2002 | 3.4 | 3.4 | 1.8 |
| Kyrgyz Republic | 1999 | 6.4 | 6.4 | 1.1 |
|  | 2002 | 3.6 | 3.6 | 2.1 |
| Tajikistan | 1999 | N/A | N/A | N/A |
|  | 2002 | 9.9 | 9.9 | 2.4 |
| Uzbekistan | 1999 | 11.0 | 11.0 | 1.2 |
|  | 2002 | 3.7 | 3.7 | 1.6 |
| Central Europe and | 1996 | 2.9 | 2.9 | 1.3 |
| Baltic States | 2002 | 2.4 | 2.4 | 1.8 |

*Sources:* BEEPS (1999, 2002).

*Notes:* 1: Never, 2: Seldom, 3: Sometimes, 4: Frequently, 5: Usually, 6: Always.

in line with levels in CEE, although there is evidence that the incidence of corruption in the customs service has increased across the region.

The evidence in Table 9.4 should, however, be interpreted with significant caution. Only enterprises directly involved in foreign trade were asked to reply on time delays and unofficial payments faced at customs. Figure 9.5 shows that the proportion of firms actively involved in foreign trade is considerably smaller in Central Asia than in CEE, reducing the reliability of the responses on customs. Figure 9.5 also shows that there are striking differences both across countries in Central Asia and across types of firms in terms of their involvement in foreign trade. As a rule, large firms are more likely to trade than small firms. In CEE medium-sized firms (defined as firms with between 50 and 250 employees) trade almost as much as large firms. In Central Asia, medium-sized firms are less than half as likely to engage in foreign trade as large firms. It is these medium-sized firms that are most likely to produce locally manufactured or processed goods, whereas resource-based enterprises are typically large. The fact that so few medium-sized firms in Central Asia trade is at least indirect evidence of the costs they face in engaging in such operations. Note that Uzbekistan has the smallest proportion of firms of any country in the BEEPS engaged in foreign trade.

The landlocked position of all Central Asian countries means that transport costs, in addition to policy-induced trade barriers, are a key impediment to their integration into world markets. As argued above, lack of cooperation at the regional level can not only limit intra-regional trade, but more importantly increase transit costs to major markets. Michalopoulos (2003) and Molnar and Ojala (2003) provide excellent overviews of some of these issues,

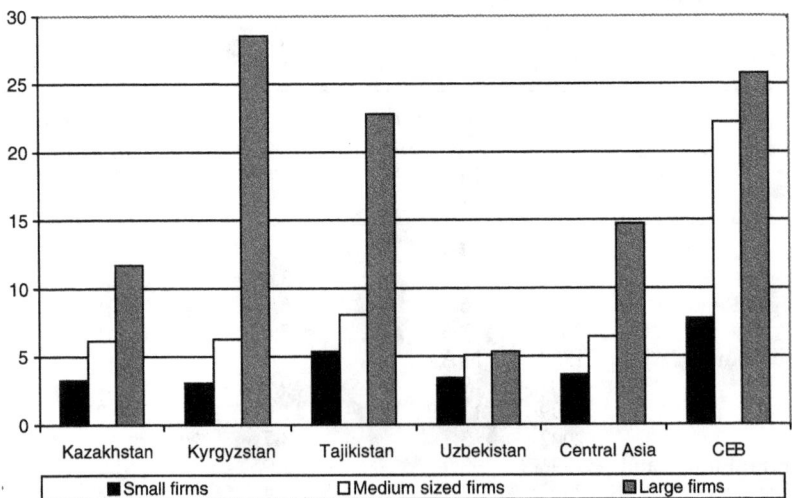

*Figure 9.5* Percent of firms that export by size of enterprises.

*Source:* BEEPS (2002).

and we can limit the discussion to just a few salient facts. Transport costs in landlocked countries are typically around three times higher than in developed countries. Transport can add around 15–25 per cent to the cost of goods supplied to and from Central Asia, causing a potentially severe competitive disadvantage. Note, however, that in some of the poorest states in Central Africa this ratio can go up to 50 per cent.[10]

The most serious impediments to transport and transit would appear to concern road rather than rail transportation. The railways in CIS countries operate on similar gauges and seem to be cooperating reasonably well. However, the railways are often in a monopoly position, and the lack of competition from private freight forwarding companies does imply higher costs than necessary for rail transportation. Transport by road faces significant official and unofficial charges. Transit fees for trucks in Central Asia are not particularly high by European standards, but have to be borne by single shippers, who often return empty from their journey. Also, the value of the goods transported is typically less on a weight basis than in developed countries, increasing the burden of transit fees on shippers. Unofficial payments can be very onerous: Kyrgyz shippers quote a total of US$ 1,500 in unofficial payments in transit through Kazakhstan to the Russian market. In addition to monetary costs, there are costs of delays associated with inspections at the border and various points throughout the country. For instance, concerns over abuse of the TIR Convention result in unnecessary inspections of TIR marked cargo in transit, and thus impose additional delays and higher costs for shippers from the region.

In addition to obstacles to formal trade, there are numerous barriers to informal or shuttle trade, which is a main source of income for many of the poorest people in Central Asia. Security concerns have led to the adoption of visa regimes, greatly hampering the movement of people across borders (or at least across official borders). Some 'green' border crossings have been mined, leading to repeated accidents. Uzbekistan has been particularly restrictive in this regard and in 2002 adopted several additional measures against shuttle traders, culminating in the outright closure of the Kazakh and Kyrgyz borders in late 2002 and early 2003. The Tajik border has also been repeatedly closed to individuals and remains a source of friction.

How can we measure the impact of these various impediments to trade and transit from Central Asia? One simple gauge, often used as a summary indicator in the literature, is the ratio of trade to GDP. Controlling for both income levels and size of the population[11] the ratio of trade to GDP in Central Asia is not particularly low. It ranges from around 60 per cent in the Kyrgyz Republic to over 140 per cent in Tajikistan. For comparison, trade ratios average around 60–80 per cent in the CEE and south and east European countries. However, these trade ratios are not a good guide to either the degree of openness or the potential welfare costs of trade and transit obstacles. Exchange rate distortions in Turkmenistan and Uzbekistan affect the measurement of US dollar GDP. Generous endowments with natural resources that can be easily sold at world market prices increase the ratio of trade to GDP.

We propose an alternative way of assessing the welfare costs of the lack of intra-regional cooperation and integration. It is based on the idea that in a world of frictionless trade and transport, prices across regional markets in Central Asia should be equalized or at least move closely in line with each other.[12] The higher the transport costs, the more prices will vary with the geographical distance of cities to each other. And the higher the policy-induced impediments to trade, the more prices are likely to diverge between locations in two different countries. We collected data for consumer price inflation of different groups of goods by region in Kazakhstan, Kyrgyz Republic and Uzbekistan. This allows us to construct relative price indices for different types of goods and different locations across Central Asia. If trade were frictionless and the non-tradable share of the costs were negligible, these indices should be constant in time. In the absence of a large share of non-tradable costs, the standard deviation of these time series should give us some idea of impediments to trade between regions in Central Asia. The degree to which prices of similar goods move together should be related to how far two regions are apart from each other if transport costs are import-ant. Similarly if tariff and non-tariff barrier hamper trade flows significantly, prices of the same goods should be correlated much less across countries than inside countries, even after we control for distance.

We correlate the standard deviation of the relative price indices with travel distances by road between different locations both within countries and across borders. Table 9.5 presents the correlation of food and non-food prices relative to those in the regions around the three capitals with the distance of the regions from the three capitals. Inside countries the correlation is clearly positive, in particular for Kyrgyzstan. This suggests that at least inside countries distance (a measure for transport cost) is an important determinant of relative price movements. Across borders the pattern is much less regular. Controlled for distance, prices around Bishkek (Chui region) are positively correlated with prices in the regions around Almaty and Tashkent (with the exception of food prices in Tashkent), which suggests that Kyrgyzstan has

*Table 9.5* Correlation of regional price levels for food, non-food and services with the distance from the three capitals.

|         |          | *Kazakhstan* | *Kyrgyzstan* | *Uzbekistan* |
|---------|----------|------------|------------|------------|
| Almaty  | food     | 0.39       | 0.82       | 0.16       |
|         | non-food | 0.29       | 0.39       | −0.09      |
| Chui    | food     | 0.02       | 0.87       | 0.16       |
|         | non-food | −0.01      | 0.82       | −0.08      |
| Tashkent| food     | 0.24       | −0.08      | 0.29       |
|         | non-food | 0.00       | 0.25       | 0.23       |

relatively low barriers for imports from its neighbors. The same cannot be said for prices in the regions around Almaty and Tashkent. Thus while distance is an important determinant of co-movements of prices of similar goods inside Kazakhstan and Uzbekistan, this regularity seems to disappear for co-movements with prices in neighboring countries. This suggests that the border effects dwarf the impact that physical transport costs have on market integration.

In theory the border effect consists of at least four components: tariff barriers, non-tariff barriers, exchange rate volatility that is not fully transmitted into prices and trend movements of the real exchange rate. Distinguishing these effects from the correlations is rather difficult. However, given that tariffs are relatively low and have remained fairly constant for much of the period, they are unlikely to explain the large movements in relative prices. Unfortunately the underlying prices are likely to have a sizeable non-tradable cost element. Thus, relative prices of similar goods might change over time because of trend changes, for instance of relative wages.

However, the relative prices of food, non-food and services prices in Kyrgyzstan and Kazakhstan do not appear to display any trend (Figure 9.6), suggesting that the relative price of non-tradables has not displayed any trend change and the price of non-tradables is unlikely to explain the border effect. The same cannot be said for Uzbekistan. Prices in Uzbekistan have decreased compared to Kazakhstan during the five years under investigation (Figure 9.7). In fact this trend movement dwarfs any other price movement over the period. Thus, it is no surprise that there is no systematic correlation of the standard deviation of regional prices with the distance between regions

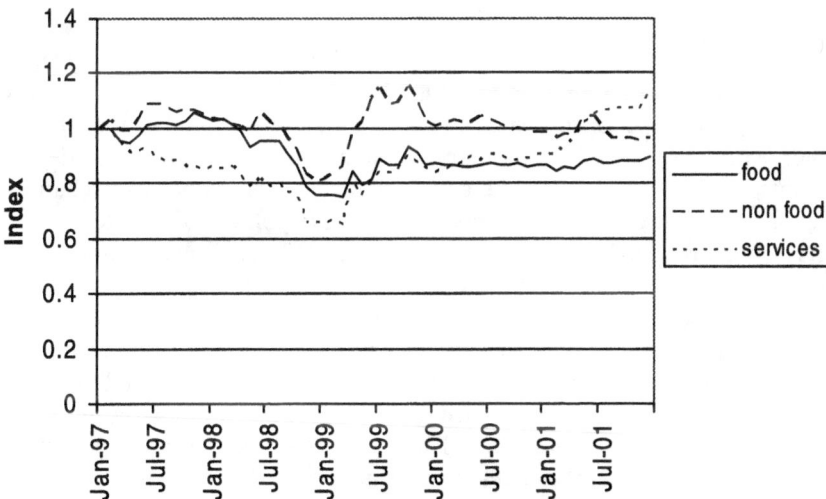

*Figure 9.6* Prices in Kyrgyzstan relative to Kazakhstan (Jan 1997 = 1).

*Source:* Offices of National Statistics in Kazakhstan and Kyrgyzstan.

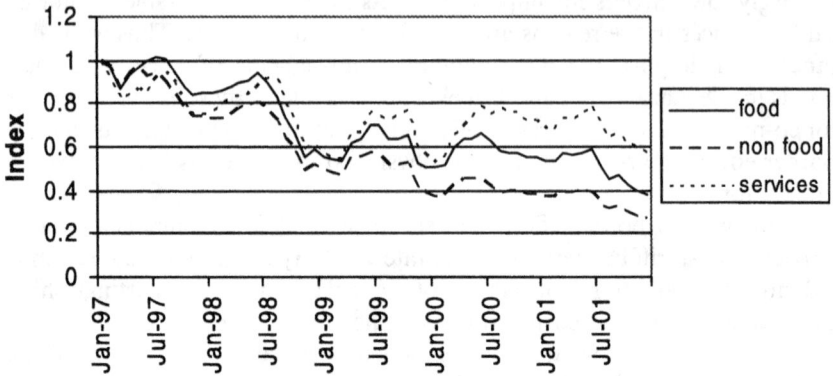

*Figure 9.7* Prices in Uzbekistan relative to Kazakhstan.

*Source:* Offices of National Statistics of Kazakhstan and Uzbekistan.

inside and outside Uzbekistan. According to the official price data, prices for non-food items in Uzbekistan have fallen by about 60 per cent compared to Kyrgyzstan and Kazakhstan since 1997.[13] Since many non-food items are normally easily tradable, this large change in relative prices gives some indication of the trade barriers that Uzbekistan has created. Goods can be priced at least 30 per cent higher or lower than in neighboring countries without arbitrageurs being able to even these price difference out. These results are a first indication of the relative size of impediments to trade between countries. We intend to pursue this line of research further in future work.

## Conclusions and policy recommendations

The attention recently placed by the international community on increased regional cooperation in Central Asia is justified. However, expectations regarding the scope for the expansion of regional trade should be moderated. The Central Asian market is not large enough to support a significant degree of intra-regional specialization and exchange.[14] This conclusion changes significantly, however, once the concept of the region is widened to include larger regional neighbors such as Russia and China. Transit rather than simply trade is the key issue for regional cooperation in Central Asia.

There is significant evidence pointing to the negative effects of restrictive trade policies in the region, in particular in Uzbekistan and Turkmenistan. First and foremost, trade restrictions are hurting these countries directly by reducing the competitiveness of their goods abroad and limiting the inflow of new technologies and investment. This can be seen clearly in the persistent dependence on natural resources as the main export item in all five countries, and the almost complete absence of non-resource based trade with the rest of Central Asia in the case of Uzbekistan and Turkmenistan. Second, trade and transit restrictions are hurting medium-sized companies in particular, which are far less active in foreign trade in Central Asia than in the front-runners among the transition economies, thus hampering the development of the most dynamic segment of the enterprise sector. Third, trade and transit restrictions are also hurting neighboring countries, limiting their export opportunities and increasing the cost of their imports. Weaker neighbors in turn reduce a country's own economic prospects. Fourth, there is suggestive evidence from data on prices that the welfare costs of current policies could be very high. For all of these reasons, trade liberalization should be pushed to the top of the policy agenda in Central Asia.

The potential benefits from increased regional cooperation are unequally distributed. Kazakhstan has little to gain as long as Russia is not involved, Turkmenistan remains largely isolated from the rest of Central Asia. The biggest potential gains from more regional cooperation within Central Asia would be derived by the Kyrgyz Republic and Tajikistan. Uzbekistan would also be likely to benefit, as experience from other regional trade blocks suggests that it is the largest countries that benefit most, because they can most easily exploit economies of scale and attendant pecuniary and non-pecuniary locational externalities (Auty 2003).

The implications of the asymmetry in the likely benefits from regional cooperation are that regional initiatives need the support from the international community to be effective. In particular, the following five points could be considered. First, the international community can contribute to the considerable investment needs to modernize the region's transport infrastructure. Such support could be made conditional on harmonization of regional transit regimes, with respect to transit fees for road transport, access rules for rail transport and the liberalization of the freight forwarding market. Indeed, existing project conditionality already incorporates some of these elements, but so far largely on a country-by-country basis. The international community should also press governments and transport operators in the region (including in Russia) to observe and implement the TIR Convention in order to avoid unnecessary costs and delays on road transit.

Second, competitive WTO accession should be discouraged. The countries of Central Asia would gain little by acceding to the WTO without their neighbors (and indeed without Russia), as the Kyrgyz experience demonstrates. The international community should therefore encourage joint accession and use the collective dynamics to press on the laggards. With Russia and Kazakhstan joining, for instance, Uzbekistan would have little recourse against anti-dumping action or other measures by both countries if it were not also a member, whilst facing increased competitive pressures.

Third, trading arrangements within Central Asia should, however, not be left hostage to the WTO accession process, particularly if coordination with Russia is required. Free trade within the CIS could be and should be established earlier, along the lines of the proposals in place for the Eurasian Economic Community. This would require rules of origin and appropriate technical tools to be available to customs offices – something the IFIs might be able to support. While theory suggests that customs unions are less efficient than simple free trade arrangements, in the present environment a CIS free trade area is unlikely to be implemented unless Russia's external tariff is safeguarded. Given that this tariff is already fairly high, it should be sufficient to satisfy the desire for some temporary trade protection by countries such as Uzbekistan.

Fourth, a solution also needs to be found to the issue of cross-border movements of people and migrant labor. Shuttle trade is a key source of income particularly for the poor in all Central Asian countries. Although there is little statistical information on the role of shuttle trade, and this chapter has therefore not presented any evidence on the phenomenon, the evident deterioration of living standards in Uzbekistan as a result of recent measures against shuttle traders bears witness to its importance. Visa requirements for travel within Central Asia and the CIS, whilst motivated out of concerns over security, are a major impediment to welfare-enhancing trade and temporary worker migration. A coordinated solution among the Central Asian countries is necessary to address this issue, and the international community could help with technical advice and direct support to border guards for security purposes.

Finally, we need to return to the caveat made about the role of the broader geo-strategic interests of Central Asia's main neighbors in moving towards more regional cooperation. The proposals made in this chapter rely to a significant extent on the cooperation and commonality of interests among these major regional partners (Afghanistan is just a gruesome reminder of what can happen when this is not the case). We would argue that Russia should be convinced that it should provide better market access and transit to the region out of its own strategic interest in Central Asia and also because it would be greatly affected by future political instability, were economic development to falter. A 'Russia'-centric view, embedded in Russia's own growing integration into the world economy through WTO accession, should not cause too much concern with the USA and the West more generally. China's interests similarly would be best served by a stable Central Asia. For Turkmenistan and Tajikistan, a thaw in the ice between the USA and Iran would provide significant new opportunities. At the moment, a key obstacle to more regional cooperation is Uzbekistan. The USA has particular leverage in this country and could try to use it – together with Uzbekistan's neighbors – to lobby for more openness. The agenda facing the region is complex. The multitude of external interests makes it more complex still. Analysts should be realistic in their expectations. But what this chapter has done is to start showing what is at stake for the countries of the region. It is hoped that this provides a motivation to make progress.

# Notes

* Clemens Grafe is at Birkbeck College, London.
** Martin Raiser and Toshiaki Sakatsume are with the Office of the Chief Economist, EBRD. The views expressed in this chapter are those of the authors and do not reflect the official position of the EBRD.
1 Polyakov (2001) has looked at similar questions for the Caucasus.
2 Michalopoulos (2003) offers a similar overview and shares several of our conclusions. The present chapter adds information available from the Business Environment and Enterprise Performance Survey (BEEPS) 2002, as well as a broader range of secondary sources.
3 Regional cooperation is important not just to improve market access for enterprises in Central Asia. Another critical task for regional cooperation is to find cooperative multilateral solutions to the region's looming environmental and resource management issues. In particular, regional cooperation is vital if an improved system of regional water management and energy trade is to be created. See Kennedy 2003.
4 Obviously the incentives for integration depend on potential trade and not existing trade. However, at least in the short run, existing trade is a reasonable indicator for potential trade.
5 There is of course a flipside to the argument about high transit and transport costs. Whilst impeding market access for exporters, they also shelter domestic producers from import competition. The Central Asian market as a whole is sufficiently large to attract investment geared at production for the home market and this could be an important asset for the region. However, because intra-regional trade among the Central Asian countries is impeded by various policy induced barriers, the attractiveness of the local market is reduced. Instead of turning an overall constraint into a local advantage, the governments in the region are simply making matters worse.
6 Trade flows are poorly recorded in Central Asia, leaving out most shuttle trade, which accounts for the bulk of trade in light manufactured goods (textiles, electronics etc.). Moreover, reporting to the UN, on which the analysis in this chapter is based, is not complete, leaving several gaps and forcing researchers to often rely on mirror statistics from trading partners to capture a country's trade.
7 Mineral fuels and oil products are the largest export item from Turkmenistan and Uzbekistan to all regional neighbours, except for exports from Uzbekistan to Turkmenistan (fertilizers). While mineral fuels and oil products feature importantly in the remainder of the region, they are much less dominant.
8 The experience of the Kyrgyz Republic is one instance of the role of outside interests. The Kyrgyz Republic needed the support of the IFIs and of western countries, given the loss of subsidies from Moscow. The resulting leverage of the 'West' was a key factor in pushing for early WTO accession.
9 Exporters have to surrender at least parts of their hard currency proceeds to the state at artificially appreciated exchange rates.
10 A piece in the *Economist* (2002) on land transport in Cameroon exemplified some of the typical constraints faced by transporters in developing countries.
11 Trade is higher in richer countries, but smaller in larger economies, which have more scope for diversified domestic production.
12 Engel and Roberts (1994) used this approach to estimate the impact of a national border of price co-movements between US and Canada. In their example, the impact of the border was not due to restrictive trade practices, but instead attributable to either neo-Keynesian sticky price phenomena or imperfectly integrated labor markets.
13 Uzbek prices are evaluated in US dollars at the black market exchange rate. While

this rate was significantly depreciated in 1997 it differed relatively little from the official exchange rate at the end of 2001.
14 This might change if Kazakhstan continues to outgrow its neighbours by a large margin and significant wage differentials open up across borders. However, these might lead at least initially to increased migration rather than to increased specialization across borders. In fact Kazakhstan is already attracting significant numbers of migrants from Uzbekistan and Kyrgyzstan.

## References

Auty, R.M. (2001) *Resource Abundance and Economic Development*, Oxford: Oxford University Press.

Auty, R.M. (2003) Gains from regional economic cooperation in the Caspian Basin Region: Lower transport costs, larger markets, increased competition and faster GDP growth, Working Paper 0303, Lancaster University: Department of Geography.

Auty, R.M. and Mikesell, R.F. (1998) *Sustainable Development in Mineral Economies*, Oxford: Clarendon Press.

Deardorff, A.V. (1995) Determinants of bilateral trade: Does gravity work in a neo-classical world? NBER Working Paper 5377, Cambridge MA: National Bureau of Economic Research.

Djankov, S. and Freund, C. (2000) Disintegration, CEPR Discussion Paper 2545, London: Centre for Economic and Policy Research.

EBRD (1999) *Transition Report 1999*, London: European Bank for Reconstruction and Development.

EBRD (2003) *Transition Report 2003*, London: European Bank for Reconstruction and Development.

Economist (2002) The road to hell is unpaved, *The Economist*, December 21.

Engel, C. and Roberts, J.H. (1994), How wide is the border? NBER Working Paper 4829, Cambridge MA: National Bureau of Economic Research.

Fankhauser, S., Kennedy, D. and Raiser, M. (Forthcoming) EBRD Working Paper London: European Bank for Reconstruction and Development.

Fidrmuc, J. and Fidrmuc, J. (2000), Disintegration and Trade, CEPR Discussion Paper 2641, London: Centre for Economic and Policy Research.

IMF (2002) *Direction of Trade*, Washington DC: IMF.

Kennedy, D. (2003) Regulatory reform and market development in power sectors of transition economies: The case of Kazakhstan, *EBRD Working Paper* 53, London: European Bank for Reconstruction and Development.

Michalopoulos, C. (2003), The integration of low-income CIS members in the world trading system, mimeo, World Bank, Washington DC.

Molnar, E. and Ojala, L. (2003) *Transport and Trade Facilitation Issues in the CIS 7, Kazakhstan and Turkmenistan*, Washington DC: World Bank.

Polyakov, E. (2001) Changing trade patterns with conflict resolution in the South Caucasus, Policy Research Working Paper 2593, Washington DC: World Bank.

Prebisch, R. (1963) *Towards a Dynamic Policy for Latin America*, New York: United Nations.

Rabelland, G. (2003) Determinants of the negative impact of being landlocked on trade: An empirical investigation through the Central Asian case, *Comparative Economic Studies* 45(4), 520–536.

# 10 Environmental problems and solutions in the Caspian and Aral Basins

*Anil Markandya and Richard M. Auty*

## Introduction

Managing environmental problems at the national level is relatively easy: ideally governments make users pay the social costs of the use of the resource by some means or other. Measures can include economic instruments, such as charges, or direct controls, such as limited access to the resource (Markandya *et al.* 2002). But even if governments cannot make users pay, they have recourse to other command and control policies that regulate the use of resources. In the case of international resources, like the Caspian Sea or the Aral Basin waters, the problem is more difficult. There is no authority that can impose a solution.[1] Hence a solution has to be agreed.

The literature is divided between those who argue that a successful agreement has to be based mainly on mutual self-interest (each party will only join if it sees itself as better off in the immediate future as a result) and those who argue that cooperation can occur even when it is not in the narrow interest of each party, but when each party can see that it is in its long-term interest to cooperate. Of course the latter does not mean that under the agreement any one party is worse off than it would be without the agreement. But it does mean that, when evaluating an agreement, each party will not renege if it is in its short-term interests to do so.[2]

This debate is not resolved and there is probably some element of truth in both positions. In the case of the Caspian Basin, the cooperative solution was relevant before the break-up of the former Soviet Union. For example, at that time two countries, the USSR and Iran, managed the Caspian Sea. Each had good reason to cooperate and did so in the broader interests of sustainable use of the resource. In the Aral Basin, a national solution applied to the sea, which was internal to the Soviet Union and water was distributed by Moscow. After the break-up of the USSR, however, the situation changed. The cooperative model became less compelling for the Caspian Basin, partly because the parties have no established relationship in this area and partly because they are unable to control their citizens, some of whose livelihoods came under serious threat after the dissolution, and some of whom are able to act outside the law with impunity, often making considerable profits from

doing so. For the Aral Sea, a new situation was created by the international-
ization of the basin.

This chapter first examines the Caspian Sea as an example of a common
resource, which poses the problem that because it is 'owned' by every one, it is
owned by no one and each party has an incentive to over-use the resource
(Hardin 1968). It outlines the major environmental problems in the next
section (pages 178–184) and then evaluates progress with solutions on pages
184–188. The final section (pages 188–194) then repeats the process for the
Aral Basin, where environmental damage is more acute.

## The principal environmental problems of the Caspian Basin

### Overview of Caspian Basin environmental problems

The Caspian Sea is the world's largest inland body of water, encompassing
some 44 per cent of the volume of all inland lakes and seas. The biodiversity
of the Caspian aquatic environment is derived from the long history of the
existence of the sea and its isolation, allowing ample conditions for speci-
ation. The number of endemic aquatic taxa, over 400, is impressive. There are
115 species of fish, of which a number are anadromous and migrate from the
Caspian up the rivers to spawn. The best-known of these is the sturgeon (the
sea contains over 80 per cent of the world's stock), which has provided a
valuable economic resource for over a century. In addition, many species of
birds visit the extensive deltas, shallows and other wetlands, their numbers
swelling enormously during the migration seasons. Terrestrial flora and
fauna are also quite diverse, and include several thousand flowering plants,
with a rate of endemicity locally reaching 20 per cent. These resources hold
tremendous potential for eco-tourism.

The current population around the Caspian is estimated at 5 million, with
the main urban centers concentrated on the western and southern shores.
Baku is the largest city on the Caspian coast, with a population of 1.7 million. The balance of the population resides in cities or towns ranging in size
from 20,000 to 670,000, plus about 1,000,000 rural inhabitants. The principal
economic activities in the Caspian Basin are fisheries, agriculture, petroleum
production and related downstream industries.

The Caspian governments have repeatedly identified sea level rise as the
leading environmental problem facing them. While this may be most urgent
in terms of alleviating human suffering, protecting valuable infrastructure
and preventing pollution incidents are also important. The Caspian is noted
for its fluctuations in water level. The lowest level for the last five hundred
years was reached in 1977 (−29 m below sea level). It is presently rising at a
rate of up to 20 cm per year, so it is a fair assumption that the level could
continue to rise from the current level (−26 m) until it reaches at least the 1900
level (−25 m), presenting the littoral states with many urgent investment
needs. Since 1977, water levels have risen 2.5 m, inundating residential areas,

transport, telecommunications and energy infrastructure, chemical and petrochemical industries, croplands and hatcheries. Thousands of residents have been evacuated from flooded homes, and up to 100,000 people in coastal cities and towns in Azerbaijan alone have been affected.

The ecological integrity of the Caspian is also under threat from pollution by particulate organic matter and excess inorganic nutrients (eutrophication) and by various toxic materials. In this regard the Volga is the most important source of this pollution: it drains the sewage of half the population of Russia, and of most of its heavy industry. Much of the Volga pollution is broken down *en route*, or deposited on the bottoms of the Volga reservoirs, but sufficient still reaches the Caspian to cause major imbalances, especially in the shallow north basin, which has limited absorption capacity. Spills have been generated by onshore and offshore oilfields, refineries and petrochemical plants, especially in Baku Bay. The large expanding Kashagan oilfield at the mouth of the Ural River in Kazakhstan[3] risks damage to the shallow sea and to the beluga sturgeon fisheries for which the Ural delta is one of the last breeding grounds. In addition, there are risks of earthquakes if the oil, which is found at high pressure, is removed, while stockpiles of sulfur are growing as by-products of oil and gas extraction. The sulfur is controversial, with the oil companies playing down the environmental and health risks because it can be sold to the chemical industry or re-injected into the oilfield or stored in safe underground bunkers. Unfortunately the market for sulfur is oversupplied and the re-injection and storage options both need time.[4] Oil production also generates shipping, which along with fishing vessels and others adds to the pollution threat.

There are also radioactive solid and liquid waste deposits near the Gurevskaya nuclear power plant in Kazakhstan, which is at long-term risk of flooding, while some waste that has been dumped in depressions over karstic formations may be leaking radioactivity. Other waste products from human activities (heavy industry, agriculture, weapons development, power generation, etc.) have already reached levels that make fish consumption hazardous in some areas. Massive bird and seal kills have also been reported, although the causes are not known for certain. The main ecological drivers appear to be organochlorines (especially DDT and its by-products) and heavy metals, especially off Baku (PADECO 2002).

### The sturgeon fishery

In recent times, there has been a drastic decline in the sturgeon catch. Landings decreased from around 30,000 tonnes in 1985 to 13,300 tonnes in 1990, down to 2,100 tonnes in 1994 and even less, around 1,000 tonnes, in the last few years. A quota system that was introduced together with a ban on pelagic fishing does not seem to have had the desired effect. Consequently, the Caspian sturgeon fisheries are thought to be in danger of being completely depleted within the next few years, so that urgent action is required to preserve this valuable resource. Over the last century the market value of caviar has provided a significant source of income and even after major falls in production, the worldwide street value of the caviar is still estimated at $3 billion.

The three main causes of decline are over-fishing, loss of spawning grounds, and water pollution and oil spills. With the collapse of the Soviet Union, the strong regulatory system that had existed since World War II also collapsed. Practices that had been banned under the regulatory system, such as fishing in the open sea, rather than in the rivers, started to be used by some states. Now only Iran, whose fisheries are tightly controlled, has the resources to implement effective management. Several states have regulations, but enforcement is limited due to lack of funding. As a result, the illegal catch in the Caspian and the Volga River is estimated at six to ten times the legal catch. The 1998 US Fish and Wildlife Survey estimated that 50 per cent of worldwide trade in caviar is illegal. For example, 1996 Turkish statistics record 121 tonnes of caviar exports, whereas Turkey does not have the means to produce anything like this amount of caviar. It is likely that these exports originated from illegal catches from the Caspian. Illegal trade has been reduced through trade restrictions, but given that one fish can still provide the equivalent of one month's salary, the incentive to catch sturgeon illegally is huge. It is thought that poachers catch almost all the sturgeons that attempt to reach the remaining spawning grounds, using illegal fishing gear like nets that do not allow a proportion of fish to escape.

The effects of poaching and illegal trade are not limited to the depletion of sturgeon stocks. They also result in a reduction of the quality, reputation and therefore price of internationally traded caviar. There is a mixing of caviar from different species, lack of washing, adding of the wrong amount of salt and mislabeling. This leads to a lower-quality product, a deterioration of the image of 'Russian Caviar', and a resulting drop in price. As an illustration of this, between 1990 and 1993, when control of the Caspian's sturgeon fisheries was effectively lost, the volume of caviar traded internationally *increased* by 30 per cent, but the value of the trade *decreased* by 5 per cent.

The availability of spawning grounds is crucial to the natural reproduction of sturgeon species. A shortage is thought to arise from the construction of numerous dams along the Volga River, and to a lesser extent, the Kura River. These dams have effectively barred the fish from their main spawning grounds, reducing such areas to a small fraction of their original size. In addition, the development of industrial complexes on the river banks with their subsequent discharges, coupled with non-point source run-off from intensive agriculture, has led to the pollution of the remaining waterways. In recognition that the Volga dams had reduced the spawning areas available for sturgeon, a system of hatchery production was developed, which functioned successfully until the current rise in water levels flooded a number of hatcheries. Presently the Ural is the last free-flowing river feeding into the Caspian, with only the upper part having been dammed, and it is the only one in which sturgeon still reproduce naturally. However, very little reproduction is taking place there; it is thought that the spawning population has been destroyed by a combination of poaching and pollution (Speer *et al.* 2000).

The third major problem facing the reproduction and quality of sturgeon stocks is the decline in recent decades of the water quality of the Caspian Sea. A key factor here is the fact that 10 million people live close to the Caspian, with 60 million more living in the Volga watershed. Although much of the coastline of Kazakhstan and Turkmenistan is undeveloped, sewers and industry, in particular the oil and mining industries, pollute the southern end of the sea. The majority is accounted for by sewage and waste from industry. The World Bank estimates that one million cubic meters of untreated industrial wastewater empty into Caspian annually. One problem area is the petrochemical complex in the Azeri city of Sumgayit, which emits hundreds of thousands of tons of toxic wastes each year to both air and water, resulting in a 'virtual dead zone around that city and Baku' (US Energy Information Administration 2000).

Pollution has had a severe effect on human health and both water and land quality. In Kazakhstan, people in the Caspian region are four times more likely to suffer from health conditions such as blood disease and tuberculosis than the average Kazakh. This is thought to be mainly due to oil-contaminated drinking water. In Baku, reproductive problems such as increased miscarriages and stillbirths have been observed. Fish populations, including sturgeon, have been badly affected by pollution. Since the late 1970s fish have suffered from hepatotoxic hypoxia, or muscle blistering. Pollution also affects the reproductive potential of sturgeon, although the precise nature of the effect is not currently known.

As noted, one possible technical solution is replacement of natural reproduction by aquaculture, including hatcheries. While natural reproduction is the most desirable outcome, a significant level of this is some way off, and in the meantime alternative means are required to prevent the disappearance of sturgeon species. Aquaculture can be used to control the entire life cycle of the sturgeon, or only part of it, for instance by using hatcheries to breed sturgeon artificially and release young fish in order to replenish stocks. The Soviet Union began programs for artificial reproduction in the 1950s, in the Volga and Kura Rivers and in recent years these hatcheries have provided an essential function in maintaining recruitment to sturgeon stocks. The condition of these hatcheries, however, is critical; without modernization and repairs they are likely to close. There are fears that with the sturgeon's natural environment worsening, the provision of hatcheries does not guarantee the preservation of the species (Williot 1998). An alternative is to breed and exploit sturgeon in captivity, while allowing the regeneration of natural stocks in the wild. This has achieved some success in Russia since 1994, when the BIOS research center for commodity sturgeon rearing was established in Astrakhan.

The issue of concern is that almost all these technical measures generate benefits across national boundaries. This means that any one country, looking narrowly at its own benefits and costs, will not undertake as much action as would be globally desirable. If all countries do that, the level of action will be well below the optimal. The only way out of this impasse is international cooperation, with each country committing to actions that are in the regional interest. Analysis has shown (Aguero and Zuleta 1994) that, with trans-boundary fish stocks, cooperation will always produce a better outcome in terms of the total benefit of the fishery than non-cooperation.

Turning to managerial solutions, the economics literature shows that where one party undertakes an activity that results in costs or benefits to another party, the first party is unlikely to account for these external effects, and will therefore not carry out the activity to the socially efficient extent. This difficulty applies to several aspects of the management of the Caspian Sea's sturgeon stocks. If individual nations regulate their fisheries to maximize the returns from their fish stocks, and do not account for the fact that they share fish resources with other nations, the management of the fish stocks is likely to be inefficient, and aggregate effort will be greater than the efficient level. Some form of international agreement on action is essential for success in this area.

There are various policy options for this agreement, the most attractive of which remains the one that restricts total allowable catch (TAC) to the sustainable and efficient level, while minimizing the costs of landing this catch. A TAC quota for each country, with additional restrictions on size, fishing location and season, is thought to be the best method of achieving conservation aims and increasing the rents from trans-boundary fisheries. Allowing these quotas to be tradable would increase efficiency. There are other actions which can also contribute to the solution and which also need some international agreement. One is for each country to invest in hatcheries. It can easily be shown that if each country invests in hatcheries to the extent that it is only compensated by an increased catch in its own territorial waters the level of investment will be sub-optimal. Any such investment benefits other parties as well and they should make some contribution to the country that provides the increased stock. Models for working out how much each should pay exist, but trust and verification possibilities are needed to reach an agreed solution.

Implementing a joint management of the stocks by all of the littoral states requires: 1. identifying the sustainable catch level, 2. finding the most cost-effective way of limiting total catch to a sustainable level, 3. dividing this total catch among the littoral states in a way that is perceived to be fair, and 4. compensating countries that make investment that benefit all parties. This is likely to involve rewarding states, by increased share of the total quota, for their contributions to stock reproduction by investment in hatcheries and the maintenance of spawning grounds, and possibly for reductions in pollution.

Any action, even if agreed at the regional level, is likely to fail, however, given the extreme poverty of many people in some of these countries, especially the FSU. The ability to police the actions of small fishermen is simply not there, and a commonality of interest between the 'police' and the local communities results in many a blind eye being turned. The only way to address this is to ensure that any program limiting catches is accompanied by a complementary program of coastal community development, which offers credible alternatives to the individuals who are currently making a living from banned and gray activities related to the sturgeon. This is something where the international community can help and indeed some of the actions discussed in the next section are based on that. But the Caspian program is only a start and much more can be done, with relatively small outlays resulting in significant environmental and social benefits.

### Oil spills

An analysis carried out by the World Bank has shown that the risks of oil spills are highest from the abandoned Kazakh flooded oilfields in the vicinity of the Tengiz field in the North Caspian. The crude oil there is very heavy and waxy and any spill could affect an area as large as 100 square kilometers. Once a spill occurred it would cause also great damage to the caviar exports from the region as well as tourism. The second most risky area from an ecological point of view is the Kashagan field. The potential consequences of a spill here would include damages to the abundance of marine mammals and habitats for 33 million migrating birds, as well as choking off local fishing and tourism. Other activities where the risks from oil spills are significant include the barging of oil (especially from Aktau to Baku), the Gunashli oilfield in Azerbaijan and the new Russian LukOil field.

The World Bank study concluded that environmental damages from an oil spill in the region are around $2,600 per ton of oil spilled, and would occur over a period of 6–10 years. These refer only to losses of tourism and fisheries and other third party damage claims, and exclude losses from taxation to the government as well as the losses from delays in the operations at the oilfield. Moreover they exclude losses associated with the environmental damages *per se*, i.e. the losses referred to as 'non-use values' measured in terms of the willingness of individuals who do not visit the area to pay for its conservation. In addition to the damage costs there are clean-up costs of around $1,000 per ton spilled. Typical spills, if they occurred would be of the order of 10,000 to 30,000 tons, implying environmental damages in the range of $26 million to $78 million and clean-up costs of $10–30 million. Most importantly the environmental losses would be borne by those least able to cope with them – those engaged in tourism and fisheries.

This problem can be tackled through a number of measures that include the development of coordinated safety and loss prevention programs by operators of fields; adoption of state of the art preventive measures, replacement of obsolete Soviet era platforms; spending $10–20 million to cap wells in sensitive areas; assigning clear responsibility for oil spills, particularly for the abandoned, flooded wells near Tengiz, which were owned by defunct FSU oil and gas firms; establishing stockpiles of equipment to fight spills (at a likely capital cost of $30 million) and extending insurance coverage for spills to exploration, production and pipelines so that compensation claims can be met.

By and large these measures are not costly for oil companies in this area. The costs are estimated at around $30 million a year, excluding the costs of increased insurance cover. This is less than 0.3 per cent of annual industry revenue.[5] It would reduce damages from spills by around 50 per cent and substantially lower the probability of a spill. One stumbling block is the fact that some risks come from past operations. It is imperative for the littoral states to ensure that these risks are minimized and appropriate actions taken as soon as possible. The Caspian Environment Program is an important vehicle for ensuring that all these actions are indeed taken.

## Cooperative policies: the Caspian Environment Program (CEP)

If the package of actions identified (strict quotas possibly operated under a tradeable system) plus development programs to assist communities to find alternative, more suitable livelihoods are to work, cooperation among the littoral states and support from the wider international community will be required. For the former it would be ideal if a legal agreement could be signed by all states, but this is difficult. In the meantime, while a Framework Convention for the Protection of the Marine Environment of the Caspian Sea is being developed under the auspices of UNEP, a major interim forum for cooperation, the Caspian Environment Program (CEP) has been launched. The overall goal of the CEP is to 'promote the sustainable development and management of the Caspian environment'. The program draws extensively on lessons learned from other regional seas programs, such as the Baltic and Black Sea Programs, and the Mediterranean Environmental Technical Assistance Program. These more mature programs have demonstrated that regional environmental cooperation can provide an effective forum for relevant agreements or conventions among parties (see Box 10.1 below). The rationale behind such a program is the recognition that, left to themselves, the littoral countries would probably not forge a consensus on what actions to take and would most likely not implement the actions they may agree upon. There are two main reasons for this. First, the newly formed states have very few resources to devote to environmental protection, which is, generally, long-term in its impacts. Not spending something today on protection does not immediately compromise the functioning of the economic systems in these countries. In this respect external resources are vital to the success of any cooperation and CEP is a vehicle for these to be made available to the region. Second, there is need to establish trust between the member states and that is a slow process, which best proceeds through smaller confidence-building measures, such as joint programs of training, monitoring, research

**Box 10.1**  Lessons learned from other regional seas programs

Other sea programs that are relevant to the Caspian include the Mediterranean Environmental Technical Assistance Programme (METAP) and the Black Sea Environment Program (BSEP), the Danube Basin Program and the Baltic Sea Programme. The process of developing Strategic Action Programs (SAPs) under the Danube Basin Program and the BSEP provides insights and experience in the process of national/ regional/international team cooperation dealing with multi-country environmental programs. The Baltic Sea Environment Programme provides a successful model for cooperation between international organizations and countries around a common environmental objective, and offers useful lessons on the use of environmental data to drive policy decisions for investments and institutional change. The following lessons have been learned from the regional seas programs:

- The government of each littoral state must be engaged at a senior level, and relevant Ministries in addition to Environment must be included in the policy decisions, including Foreign Relations, Fisheries, Industry, Privatization, Energy, Agriculture and Education.
- Ensure that effective measures are selected for implementation, that assistance matches needs and does not exceed the absorptive capacity of countries, and that both countries' and donors' expectations for the program are realistic in terms of achievable timeframes and outcomes.
- Require country contributions to the program to help ensure that authentic national and regional views are integral to the development and implementation of program activities, and that each state has a real stake in the success of the program. Country commitment to the goals of the program can be measured by willingness to finance high-priority investments from national budgets or loans.
- Recognize that longer-term analytical studies should be accompanied by shorter-term, immediate impact activities such as demonstration projects and projects identified and prepared through a priority investment portfolio process.
- Blend international and local expertise in preparation of pre-feasibility studies, training and technical assistance tasks so as to benefit from both perspectives.
- Link ongoing national environmental programs and strategic planning efforts (e.g. National Environmental Action Plans (NEAPs)) with regional programs to ensure effective coordination of programs and mutual benefit through shared information and human resources.

*continued*

- Recognize the critical role that stakeholders in the private sector and civil society can play, and create opportunities for such key stakeholders to work together.
- Appreciate that the process of interaction within the program – for example, to prepare a regional Strategic Action Program, to identify projects for investment, to manage implementation of tasks – can make a valuable contribution to establishing the working relationships and policy steps needed to solve environmental problems.
- Bear in mind that national or regional action plans should focus on activities that are financially and institutionally feasible for the countries concerned in the foreseeable future, rather than aiming at specific target levels of pollution reduction.

and the implementation of pilot projects where benefits are shared. Both these problems require some external agency to be involved in the process and this is a second role for the CEP.

Having noted the importance of an external agency in the cooperation it is critical that it not pre-empt the role of the member states. It is they who have to implement the projects and they who should be centrally involved in identifying the programs that should be funded. Following on from that, the states should also have an important financial stake in the success of the programs. Unless this is the case the CEP will be leading a supply-driven agenda that will fail in its objectives.

### Challenges in implementing a regional Caspian program

The first challenge is the problem of management. Statutory, administrative and procedural capabilities for environmental administration and management are weak in many countries in the Caspian region. Some are in the process of updating their laws for environmental management, and effective implementation is sporadic. Administrative structures tend to be biased towards inspection and enforcement, rather than education, information and compliance. CEP measures to address environmental policy and management needs provide assistance in the following three areas: institutional development and capacity building (including legal and regulatory issues); integrated coastal zone management (including sea level fluctuation) and development of a Framework Convention for the Protection of the Marine Environment of the Caspian Sea.

The CEP (2002) embraces three categories of activities:

- Caspian regional projects, such as the Bio-resources Network that involve two or more Caspian countries;
- Associated national projects, that are ongoing or planned activities

specific to one country that contribute to improved environmental management of the Caspian on a national basis;
- Associated regional projects or programs, which provide support to Caspian regional or national tasks. Examples include interstate (regional) programs supported by EU/Tacis (Tacis 1998) in the CIS countries on National Environmental Action Plan (NEAP) development, public awareness, and widening the EAP process to facilitate project preparation.

The second challenge is institutional development and capacity building. Effective regional cooperation will require effectively applied and harmonized national legislation, standards and environmental regulations, based on agreed common environmental standards, a regional chemical and oil pollution incident preparedness plan and a Caspian Regional Strategic Action Program (SAP).

Various partnerships are critical to the cooperative process in the Caspian. Three types of partnerships are needed to help the region meet its environmental and sustainable development challenges: first, partnership at the national and local levels among different government agencies, and between government, the community and polluting enterprises; second, partnership at the regional level between the Caspian countries; and third, partnership at the international level between the international finance community, the Caspian countries, bilateral assistance programs and international companies that have a great interest in the region. The CEP is a mechanism through which each of these partnerships can work for the region.

The littoral states need to develop a partnership because most actions will have to be coordinated between them and there has to be some conviction on the part of each that the others will honor their part of any agreement. As noted earlier, this is a slow process but one that has to progress so that, eventually, the external agencies disassociate themselves from the process and leave it to the countries to manage any cooperative program.

International partners are also needed because the Caspian is a resource that has attracted significant global concern so there is a need for wide consultations with international partners on the contents of a strategic approach to address the region's environmental problems. This process has already begun, through ongoing intra-regional meetings and negotiations, consultations with international organizations such as the EC, UNDP, UNEP and others. In addition, direct dialogues between private sector, scientific and academic experts, non-governmental interests, and governmental representatives in the region will be an important aspect of the program, to generate undertakings with tangible results. This process can mobilize technical expertise and private capital, and stimulate cooperative action including contracts, which address the key issues facing the Caspian.

The European Union's Technical Assistance for the Commonwealth of Independent States (Tacis) Program has allocated resources for the Caspian environment, to support the regional Program Coordination Unit and

Caspian Regional Expert Centers, as well as identify and prepare investment projects in cooperation with the World Bank. Collaboration with national bilateral programs and private sector initiatives operating in the Caspian region is also anticipated. Funds have also been provided to prepare a proposal for the Caspian Environment Program, to be implemented by UNDP.

Finally, public–private partnerships will help to ensure concerted and harmonized environmental activities by the littoral states to create transnational networks, take actions in the stakeholders' mutual interest and to enhance the sea's sustainable development and protection. In this context, the role of oil companies operating in the Caspian region is important. They can work with the CEP to help ensure the adoption of environmental management systems (e.g. ISO 14000), with which the oil companies are familiar, by government bodies and others to minimize waste and prevent pollution in their various operations in the Caspian (exploration, extraction, refining, shipping); develop emergency preparedness and response systems; take a proactive role to improve the environmental provisions in concession agreements under negotiation and express their views on the feasibility of regulations under consideration by the Caspian governments (i.e., engage in regulatory negotiations).

Representatives of international caviar trading companies could also be encouraged to participate in and contribute to the CEP to help prevent the collapse of the wild sturgeon fishery. For example, specific measures could include practical advice regarding implementation of the export and import certification and inspection regime for sturgeon products that took effect in April 1998. Non-governmental organizations (NGOs) can also play an important and constructive role in the environmental management systems of the Caspian, particularly with regard to monitoring of the environment and informing the public of any violations of environmental standards, and working with local fishermen, to ascertain if environmentally sound methods used in other locales would be relevant to their situation.

The priority investment needs of the cooperative program are: the restoration of fisheries, with the sturgeon as the top priority; the protection of other biodiversity (which requires a sound database and an adequate knowledge of natural processes); the establishment of basin-wide tourism opportunities; and the establishment of environmental research, monitoring and data collection capacity. All this will have to be built up in stages because funding remains a major constraint. Most importantly, the programs need to have national ownership and commitment if they are to succeed.

## Mismanagement of water resources in the Aral Basin

### Causes of environmental deterioration

The over-expansion of irrigation in the Aral Basin during the twentieth century echoes similar episodes two to three millennia earlier. During the years

1910–70 the irrigated area doubled, rising at a fairly stable rate, but then it jumped by a further 75 per cent during 1970–90 even as signs of over-use proliferated. Table 10.1 shows that after fluctuating for decades around 65,000 km², the surface area of the Aral Sea contracted by almost half during 1960–90, while the volume of water shrank by two-thirds and the water level fell 15m. Meanwhile, 60 per cent of the water from the Amudarya (which accounted for two-thirds of the Aral inflow in 1960) is estimated to be lost through canal seepage and evaporation.

Pollution is chronic because the shrinking volume of water in the river basins has had to cope with increasing volumes of waste dumped by the expanding riparian communities. Moreover, subsidies under central planning encouraged state farms to make excessive use of chemicals, water and other inputs with adverse impacts on water quality and health. Barely one-quarter of the watercourses in the region are classed as having water quality that is satisfactory or better, and two-fifths are classified as 'bad'. The latter rivers support ten million people or half the total population of the river basins in question (Spoor 1998: 423). Additional pollution problems arise from wind erosion from more than 40,000 km² of recently exposed saline seabed, which deposits salt hundreds of kilometers away (Beisenova 1998). One of the worst affected places is Karakalpakstan in the Amudarya delta where infant mortality is three times the national average, at 60/1,000 (World Bank 2002a: 21). Life expectancy is below 60 years in regions of Kazakhstan adjoining the Aral Sea (Zviagelskaia and Naumkin 1999) compared with a national average of 65 (World Bank 2002b).

Yet pressure on water resources continues to intensify. Uzbekistan and Turkmenistan take just over one-half and one-fifth, respectively, of the available Aral Basin water (World Bank 1996) and both recently expanded irrigated grain production (by 50 per cent and 300 per cent during 1990–95), with only modest contraction in the cotton area. This reflects efforts to boost food self-sufficiency and maintain the sizeable rents which the governments extract from irrigated agriculture (see Chapter 5). However, such levels of rent extraction accelerate the deterioration of the irrigation and drainage system, transport network and the environment (O'Hara and Hannan 1999), even as the transition shock increases the number of workers who depend on

*Table 10.1* Contraction of Aral Sea 1960–2000

| | *Average level (m)* | *Average area (km²)* | *Average volume (km³)* | *Average salinity (g/l)* |
|---|---|---|---|---|
| 1960 | 53.4 | 66,900 | 1,090 | 10 |
| 1971 | 51.1 | 60,200 | 925 | 11 |
| 1980 | 45.4 | n.a. | 602 | n.a. |
| 1990 | 38.6 | 36,500 | 330 | 30 |
| 2000 Forecast | 32.4 | 24,155 | 183 | 67 |

*Source:* Spoor 1998: 417.

farming. Levels of salination are especially severe in the middle and lower reaches of the Amu Darya and Syr Darya, ranging from 60 to 90 per cent and requiring substantial extra water for periodic leaching (Spoor 1998: 421). A recent World Bank (2003a: 21) field study concludes that parts of the irrigation system do not merit restoration.

### Can Uzbek agriculture yield true natural resource rents?

Rents have been squeezed from the agricultural sector in an unsustainable fashion, which represses incentives, fails to maintain infrastructure and intensifies damage to the environment and public health. The rents so extracted are estimated at 5–10 per cent of GDP annually, but the capital cost of rehabilitating the neglected waterway network alone is estimated at 2.5 per cent of GDP annually for the next fifteen years (World Bank 2003b). The energy sector is similarly squeezed to subsidize households and industry at the cost of system maintenance. As the STEX model predicts, the rents from agriculture and energy support an over-expanded public sector, which preys on private firms, and also an uncompetitive manufacturing sector, which is capital-intensive and whose factories either run well below capacity or close down (World Bank 2003c). The growth in public debt intensifies the non-sustainability of Uzbekistan's development strategy. Using the indicative exchange rate (which combines the official, commercial and curb market rates), the share of public debt in GDP quadrupled to 63 per cent during 1996–2001 while debt service tripled to 27 per cent of exports. To prevent debt service from spiraling out of control requires a GDP growth rate of at least 6 per cent, a level double the recent rate (World Bank 2003c: 7 and 10).

Yet the gradual reform that Uzbekistan claims to pursue has not created a dynamic market-driven farm sector as it did in China and Vietnam (Yao 2000). This is mainly because the East Asian reforms liberalized farm incentives, whereas Uzbek reformers have been reluctant to do so (Table 8.2). The critical question is therefore: can the Uzbek government rationalize agricultural incentives to allow increased productivity to generate revenue that covers the full costs of production (including a risk-related return on investment, adequate remuneration for farm labor, payment of 'normal' rates of taxation and maintenance of the infrastructure and environment), and also produces true natural resource rent? A tentative answer is provided by the World Bank (2003a) field study, which concludes that more than 80 per cent of the Uzbek irrigation system can be efficiently maintained at world prices. However, that study omits charges for water and environmental damage because it was unable to measure them. It also assumes, not unreasonably, a low opportunity cost for labor (farm wages in Uzbekistan are less than one-third of the mean non-agricultural wage), whereas we wish to determine whether rents can be generated without exploiting rural workers.

Table 10.2 attempts to estimate the potential rent on Uzbek cotton for typical world fiber prices during the past five years. It draws largely upon costs in the World Bank (2003a) field study but makes four modifications regarding wages, water charges, taxation and environmental charges. First, rural wages are doubled to lift them from barely one-quarter of the non-agricultural mean to around half (a typical ratio in CEE countries). Second, a charge for water is added, based on recent estimates of the total delivered cost of water cited by Spoor (1998: 423), which range up to $8.64/1,000 m³. The rate adopted is $6.33/1,000 m³, as proposed by the Irrigation Research Institute, which gives a charge of $57/hectare on the assumption that improved practices reduce water absorption by one-third from the 13,000 m³ per hectare reported by Spoor (1998). Charging for water requires provision of metering and formation of local water councils. Third, in line with a World Bank (2003b) survey of Uzbek agriculture, a land tax is levied, which is three times the existing (frequently unpaid) level. Finally, following Cai *et al.* (2003), a salt tax is imposed as an incentive to deploy water more effectively and to provide revenue to compensate those who reside downstream, whose

*Table 10.2* Estimated potential rent from reformed Uzbek cotton production

| Descriptor/input | | Value | Assumptions |
|---|---|---|---|
| Growth: Labor[a] | | 39 | 1/3 labor = 215 man-hours at $0.18/mh |
| | Machinery[a] | 140 | 95% machinery applied to growing |
| | Seed[a] | 27 | |
| | Fertilizer[a] | 85 | |
| | Pesticide[a] | 53 | |
| | Water[b] | 57 | Efficiency gain: 9,000 m³/ha at $6.33/ 1000 m³ |
| | Water pump electricity[a] | 15 | |
| Harvest: Labor[a] | | 77 | 2/3 labor = 430 man-hours at $0.18/mh |
| | Machinery[a] | 7 | 5% machinery applied to harvest |
| Levies: Land tax[c] | | 27 | Three times current level |
| | Environment tax[d] | 50 | Salinity tax only |
| Total farm cost ($/ha) | | 577 | Yield 2.4 tonnes raw cotton/ha |
| Farm gate cost ($/tonne cotton fibre) | | 721 | 3 t. raw cotton/ 1 t. cotton fibre |
| Transport farm → gin[e] | | 5 | |
| Ginning[f] | | 150 | Net of by-products |
| Transport from cotton gin → border[e] | | 5 | |
| International transport ($/tonne)[e] | | 180 | |
| Delivered price ($/tonne fibre) | | 1061 | |
| Rent: world fibre price $1,000/t | | (61) | |
| Rent: world fibre price $1,500/t | | 439 | |

*Sources:* a World Bank 2003a: Table A4.2; b: Spoor 1998; c: World Bank 2003b; d: Cao *et al.* 2002; e: World Bank 2003a: Table A4.1; f: IMF 2003 51.

crop yields and health are adversely affected by upstream water users. The proposed $50/hectare levy almost certainly underestimates the true cost of the environmental and health damage inflicted by the irrigation system, which should reflect compensation for the loss of Aral Sea fisheries as well as for pollution-related illnesses among downstream residents (measured in terms of medical bills, work-days lost and personal suffering). Based on the assumptions set out in Table 10.2, the generation of true rent from irrigated cotton would require world prices in excess of $1,050, just above the lower level of world prices in the past five years.

However, a liberalized agriculture would allow farmers to adjust to new incentives to become more productive by changing crop combinations. For example, Pastor and van Rooden (2000) estimate returns from sun-dried tomatoes in Turkmenistan could be 15–24 times higher than returns for growing wheat under the state procurement system (Table 10.3). The ratio for dried fruit (raisins) is seven times higher than wheat and 4.5 times higher than cotton grown under the state procurement system. In addition, both sun-dried tomatoes and raisins are much more labor-intensive so they are well-suited to de-regulated farming, which will be much more labor-intensive, given the ten-fold rise in real machinery prices since the transition shock. Moreover, farmers are consumers as well as producers, so that a sizeable rural population with rising personal and aggregate incomes will generate strong demand multiplier effects for other economic sectors, as Yao (2000) reports for China and Vietnam. Finally rising rural incomes will strengthen demand for a cleaner environment, while generating the resources with which to achieve that goal. So what are the obstacles to achieving environmental improvements, aside from the inefficient rent extraction system?

### Repairing Aral Basin mismanagement

Although the rate of contraction of the Aral Sea has decelerated since the mid-1980s, further measures are required to prevent the sea from effectively drying up by 2020 (Spoor 1998). Yet, as with the Caspian Basin, the first decade of independence has brought much talk about environmental

*Table 10.3* Alternative crops: value added and inputs, Turkmenistan 1999 (1,000 manat/ha)

|  | Wheat | Cotton | Sun-dried tomatoes | Raisins |
|---|---|---|---|---|
| Revenue[a] | 2.954 | 5.304 | 34.320 | 13.585 |
| Raw material + inputs | 1.040 | 0.962 | 4.342 | 0.840 |
| Value added | 1.914 | 4.342 | 29.978 | 12.745 |
| Value added/ 1,000 manats inputs | 1,840 | 4,514 | 6,904 | 15,173 |

*Source:* Pastor and van Rooden 2000: 16.

*Note a:* Based on world prices at 5,200 manat/US$, after deducting costs of transport.

improvement but little action. A regional water management system was agreed in 1994, with each of the five Central Asian states pledging to sub-scribe 1 per cent of its GDP, a target that they came nowhere near meeting. Three years later an overall regional water management council (ICWC) was set up alongside state-level ministries and two Basin Water Management Organizations (BVOs) that were established for each main tributary in 1986. However, both BVOs accept the historical pattern of water allocation, which is unsustainable, while states refuse to contribute funds in proportion to their withdrawal of water (Bedford 1996). By 1998, the International Fund for Saving the Aral Sea was established and also the Interstate Council of the Central Asian Economic Association. All these bodies are ineffective and water conflicts continue to be resolved through bilateral deals between states, despite frequent failure to comply and severe sanctions levied by aggrieved parties (Olcott 2000: 136–8).

Micklin (2000) advocates focusing on the initially more modest task of securing recovery of the northern Aral Sea, where salinity levels could be kept sufficiently low to restore fishing and permit ecological recovery. Cai *et al.* (2003) develop a model that seeks to meet the legally required flow into the northern Aral Sea of 7 $km^3$ annually, which is based on the average flow of the Syr Darya during 1960–75. Their scheme requires the withdrawal of 10 per cent of the irrigated land from cultivation and cuts the share of the irrigable area in 'thirsty' crops like cotton and rice from 60 per cent to 40 per cent while the share of wheat and maize rises from 10 per cent to 32 per cent. The model raises irrigation efficiency by 25 per cent and extends drainage to 80 per cent of the area, with notable improvements in the central region. Overall, it lifts water delivery to 85 per cent of the target (twice the status quo level) while reducing land degradation and salination. The cost is estimated at $300 million annually. However, the scheme boosts farm profitability by 25 per cent to $2.5 billion annually, allowing up to 80 per cent of the annual investment to be recouped through an annual tax on crops of $10 per tonne. Finally, a salt tax levied at $50 per tonne significantly reduces salt discharges and improves water quality in the middle and lower reaches of the basin.

Such potential gains cannot be achieved, however, in the absence of inter-state agreements on basin infrastructure investments, which could also include Afghanistan and Iran, as well as the five central Asian countries. Afghanistan, Kyrgyzstan and Tajikistan are 'net exporters' of water and Uzbekistan and Turkmenistan the principal 'importers'. As discussed in Chapter 6, both Kyrgyzstan and Tajikistan have plans to reduce their external dependence upon energy by completing unfinished hydro schemes, thereby retaining more water upstream (Nurkhanov 2001). Kyrgyzstan already con-trols the bulk of the water flowing along the Syr Darya and during summer re-stocks water in its reservoirs, the biggest of which has 14 $km^3$ of capacity (one-eighth of the entire Aral Sea flow), in order to boost annual power generation. This denies water to Uzbek farmers in the Ferghana Valley, while still further downstream, Kazakhstan complains about insufficient water and high levels of pollution and salinity (Cai *et al.* 2003). Yet, simulations suggest that the returns to water used for irrigation exceed those used for hydro so downstream states can compensate Kyrgyzstan for releasing more water during the summer cropping season and generating less hydroelectricity in winter (ibid.). Meanwhile, additional water allocation conflicts have arisen between the two most dependent users, Uzbekistan and Turkmenistan, concerning the volume of water diverted into the Karakum Desert and also between Uzbekistan and Kazakhstan over water allocation north of the Ferghana Valley.

As Kyrgyzstan has found with regard to trade reform (see Chapter 9), the expected benefits of rational policy changes, water and land use allocation in this case, may be severely curtailed if neighboring countries fail to reform or to cooperate. The unsustainable nature of economic development throughout the CCA region, but especially in the resource-rich countries, is shown in Table 10.4, which estimates the genuine or true saving rate. This index of sustainability is the residual saving after deducting the depreciation of natural resource consumption and environmental damage from the net national saving rate. A negative rate connotes non-sustainability. Unfortunately, the preoccupation of governments within the region with narrow sectional interests severely restricts the prospects for capturing the benefits from policy reform, so that external intervention may be essential to broker agreements for environmental improvement.

## Conclusions

This chapter has demonstrated the importance of cooperation between the CCA states in solving environmental problems. In the light of the massive economic and social problems they face one can understand why they are not moving as fast as one would wish in this area, but to ignore it can have serious consequences. Moreover, these consequences will not take long to materialize; indeed we are already seeing some of the social and economic impacts of the environmental degradation. It is also inappropriate to think that these losses can be made up by increased oil and gas revenues (for those who have access to these resources). The exploitation of oil revenues may benefit the national economy, but it does not generally provide enough for the poor local communities that depend on the natural resources of the Caspian for their livelihoods.

The international community must help to promote environmental cooperation within the region. The CEP provides an example of the kinds of things that need to be done. More resources will be needed, however, to achieve the goal of sustainable development and perhaps more can come from the oil companies. They have a long-term stake in the region and corporate responsibility on their part should extend to wider support for the whole eco-system, not just the direct implications of oil extraction and transportation. The countries too can, and should, allocate more funds for the

Table 10.4 Sustainability indices, CCA countries 2000 (% GNI)

| Country/group | Gross national saving | Fixed capital consumed | Education expenditure | Energy depletion[b] | Mineral depletion | Net forest depletion | $CO_2$ damage | Adjusted net saving |
|---|---|---|---|---|---|---|---|---|
| Resource-poor | | | | | | | | |
| Armenia | 2.5 | 8.2 | 1.8 | 0.0 | 0.0 | 0.0 | 1.1 | −5.0 |
| Georgia | 9.1 | 16.1 | 2.5 | 0.6 | 0.0 | 0.0 | 1.0 | −6.1 |
| Kyrgyzstan | 4.8 | 8.0 | 5.5 | 1.5 | 0.0 | 0.0 | 3.6 | −2.9 |
| Tajikistan | 15.0 | 7.2 | 2.0 | 0.6 | 0.0 | 0.0 | 4.1 | 5.2 |
| Resource-rich | | | | | | | | |
| Azerbaijan | 24.5 | 9.5 | 3.0 | 56.2 | 0.0 | 0.0 | 5.3 | −43.5 |
| Kazakhstan | 21.5 | 10.1 | 4.6 | 28.7 | 0.0 | 0.0 | 5.1 | −17.8 |
| Turkmenistan | 29.1 | 9.4 | 4.0[a] | 63.2 | 0.0 | 0.0 | 5.8 | −45.3 |
| Uzbekistan | 13.9 | 7.9 | 7.8 | 33.4 | 0.0 | 0.0 | 9.6 | −29.2 |

Source: World Bank 2002b except: a  Educational expenditure for Turkmenistan estimated at 4% GNI.
b  Hydrocarbon rents for resource-rich countries from Table 5.2.

sustainable development of the region. But most importantly, they should develop joint programs that coordinate action and see that no one tries to 'free ride' on the good actions of the others.

## Notes

1   Of course even national governments cannot coerce their citizens in these matters – some degree of broad acceptance is required. But it is materially different from a problem where there is an international dimension.
2   In the economics literature this distinction is that between agents who operate under the 'Cournot-Nash Assumption' (if I change my behavior others will carry on doing the same thing) and the 'Kantian Assumption' (if I change my behavior others in the same position will also change theirs).
3   We do not discuss here the risks of oil spills but the consequences of normal operations. Oil spills are reviewed separately later.
4   Brown 2002. He states that BP and Statoil have sold their stakes in this field on account of these problems.
5   It was not possible to get figures for production in the Caspian shelf from Iran and Russia.

## References

Aguero, M. and Zuleta, A. (1994) Management options for transboundary stocks: the Peruvian-Chilean pelagic fishery in Loayza, E.A. (ed.) Managing Fishery Resources, *World Bank Discussion Paper* 217, Washington DC: World Bank.

Bedford, D.P. (1996) Institutional water management in the Aral Sea Basin, *Water International* 21, 63–69.

Beisenova, A.S. (1998) Environmental problems in Kazakhstan, in: Akiner, S., Tideman, S. and Hay, J. (eds.) *Sustainable Development in Central Asia*, London: Curzon, 159–166.

Brown, P. (2002) Oil money threatens to make killing fields of Kazakhstan, *Guardian*, December 4.

Cai, X., McKinney, D.C. and Rosegrant, M.W. (2003) Sustainability analysis for irrigation water in the Aral Sea region, *Agricultural Systems* 76, 1043–1066.

Hardin, G. (1968) The tragedy of the commons, *Science* 162(1), 243–248.

IMF (2003) *Republic of Tajikistan: Selected Issues and Statistical Appendix*, IMF Country Report 03/05, Washington DC: International Monetary Fund.

Markandya, A. *et al.* (2002) *Environmental Economics for Sustainable Growth*, Cheltenham, UK: Edward Elgar.

Micklin, P. (2000) *Managing Water In Central Asia*, London: Royal Institute of International Affairs.

Nurkhanov, D. (2001) Tajikistan, Kyrgyzstan seek to bolster power generating capacity, Eurasianet, August 7.

O'Hara, S. and Hannan, T. (1999) Irrigation and water management in Turkmenistan, *Europe-Asia Studies* 51, 21–41.

Olcott, M.B. (2000) Regional cooperation in Central Asia and the South Caucasus, in: Edel, R. and Menon, R. (eds.) *Energy and Conflict in Central Asia and the Caucasus*, London: Rowman and Littlefield, 123–144.

PADECO (2002), *The Ecotoxicology Study: Investigation into Toxic Contaminant*

*Accumulation and Related Pathology in the Caspian Sturgeon, Seal and Bony Fish*, Washington DC: World Bank.

Pastor, G. and van Rooden, R. (2000) Turkmenistan: The burden of current agricultural policies, IMF Working Paper 00/98, Washington DC: International Monetary Fund.

Speer, L., Lauck, L., Pikitch, E., Boa, S., Dropkin, L. and Spruill, V. (2000) Roe to ruin, http://www.caviaremptor.org/contents.html.

Spoor, M. (1998) The Aral Sea basin crisis: Transition and environment in Former Soviet Central Asia, *Development and Change* 29, 409–435.

Tacis (1998) Report on World Bank Mission to the Russian Federation from 12 March until 18 April 1998, World Bank/ Tacis.

United States Energy Information Administration (EIA) (2000) 'Caspian Sea Region: Environmental issues', http://www.eia.doe.gov/emeu/cabs/caspenv.html.

Williot, P. (1998) Conservation of Caspian Sturgeon: Some questions and suggestions, in Dumont, H., Wilson, S. and Wazniewicz, B. (eds.) Caspian Environment Program: Proceedings from the First Bio-Network Workshop, Bordeaux, November 1997, Washington DC: World Bank.

World Bank (1996) *Developing a Regional Water Management Strategy: Issues and Work Plan*, Washington DC and Tashkent: World Bank.

World Bank (2002a) *World Development Report 2003: Sustainable Development in a Dynamic World*, Oxford: Oxford University Press.

World Bank (2002b) *World Development Indicators 2002*, Washington DC: World Bank.

World Bank (2003a) *Irrigation in Central Asia: Socio-economic and Environmental Considerations*, Washington DC: World Bank.

World Bank (2003b) *Agriculture and Rural Sector Background Report: Uzbekistan Country Economic Memorandum*, Washington DC: World Bank.

World Bank (2003c) *Uzbekistan Country Economic Memorandum*, Washington DC: World Bank.

Yao, S. (2000) How important is agriculture in China's economic growth? *Oxford Development Studies* 28(1), 33–49.

Zviagelskaia, I.D. and Naumkin, V.V. (1999) Non-traditional threats, challenges and risks in the former Soviet South, in: Menon, R., Fedorov, Y.E. and Nodia, G. (eds.) *Russia, the Caucasus and Central Asia: The Twenty-first Century Security Environment* Vol. 2, London: M.E. Sharpe, 226–247.

# 11 Regional threat perceptions and risks of military conflict

*Roy Allison*

This chapter is divided into two main sections. First, the core threat perceptions of local states and elites in the South Caucasus and Central Asia are identified. Second, the most likely risks of military conflict in the overall region are analyzed. The chapter reveals the diversity of thinking about security policy between the eight countries concerned. It also highlights the deep divisions that fracture the South Caucasus as a region, specifically between Armenia and Azerbaijan, and that also create antagonisms in Central Asia especially around the Ferghana Valley and when rivalry surfaces between Kazakhstan and Uzbekistan. With these differences it is hardly surprising that regional efforts to coordinate defense and security policy, through mechanisms for multilateral cooperation, have made little progress to date. The chapter concludes by outlining a number of broad constraints and obstacles that have limited such defense and security cooperation, as well as limiting the broader cause of regionalism.

There exist two basic challenges for the formation of 'national security' thinking in the South Caucasus and Central Asia. The first is internal. Security policy is being developed in the countries of the region in conditions of fragile sovereignty, where political power is contested but where democratic processes have not taken root to allow for mediation between powerful interests, regional power brokers and the population at large. It is hardly surprising, therefore, that the concepts of national security or national interest proclaimed by political leaders and elites in the South Caucasus and Central Asia have tended to reflect the exigencies of 'regime security' or temporary political expediency rather than the idea of security as a public good. This is relatively less the case in the South Caucasus since the mid-1990s than for Central Asia. But threat perceptions remain highly politicized throughout the CCA states, which fuels the risks of intra-state and inter-state conflict and militates against regional multilateral efforts at defense cooperation.

The second challenge is external. Despite the phrasing of their official documents on security questions, several CCA states have continued to view Russian 'overlordship' as a security threat, which reflects a reality of the Soviet past as well as their experience in the first half of the 1990s. This perception has weakened since the late 1990s in response to the more pragmatic focus of

Russian policy under President Putin on resolving outstanding disputes bilaterally and on shelving coercive efforts to reintegrate these states into some Russian-led CIS structure. However, those states that feel most strongly the gravitational pull of alternative security links with Turkey, Western states and NATO – Georgia, Azerbaijan and Uzbekistan – remain wary of entanglements in Russian-led security frameworks.

It is important to acknowledge the regional diversity of the CCA states. The South Caucasus forms part of a Caucasian security complex, whereby intricate interactions occur across the frontiers of South Caucasus states and North Caucasus autonomous republics and regions in the Russian Federation. To some extent the South Caucasus states also form part of a wider Black Sea security constellation, which includes Turkey and Ukraine. But they have less in common with Central Asian states, except in their joint need to contend with certain soft security challenges which relate to the flow of human traffic and goods from Central Asia through a Caucasian corridor westwards. Central Asia in turn finds that its security and threat environment is determined by internal challenges within the complex Ferghana Valley region, the stability of Tajikistan and cross-border influences from Afghanistan, which threaten the stability of local states and their regimes.

Between the South Caucasus and Central Asia it is difficult to identity the parameters or content of a common 'Caspian' security zone, except in terms of the need to secure and manage the production and evacuation of hydrocarbon resources. However, the controversial issue of the demilitarization of the Caspian Sea and risks associated with the failure to agree on the territorial delimitation of the sea does impact on adjacent South Caucasus and Central Asian states in common.

## Threat perceptions in the South Caucasus

The strategic culture in the South Caucasus has been powerfully influenced by the experience of inter-state, if in part proxy, warfare between Azerbaijan and Armenia over Nagorno-Karabakh in the early 1990s, around which other security interests have pivoted (see below). The prospects for this political and military standoff will determine the long-term potential for a reinvigoration of the South Caucasus region. The military balance between Baku and Yerevan continues strongly to favor Armenia and the Karabakh Armenian forces, but this could change if Azerbaijani oil wealth eventually supports the creation of significantly stronger military forces. In this event Azerbaijan, despite having some fifth of its territory occupied, will no longer represent the military underdog and Armenia may be thrown into a more defensive military posture.

Nagorno-Karabakh has been the most important example but is only one of several separatist challenges which have strongly influenced threat perceptions in the South Caucasus, particularly where these have had external sponsorship, which has acted to internationalize internal challenges to state cohesion. The Russian role has been particularly controversial. Georgia and Azerbaijan wrested their independence from Soviet control in an atmosphere of confrontation and their perceptions of Russian strategic objectives in the Caucasus in the 1990s continued to be decisively influenced by perceived Russian support for separatism in their states.

The course of Russian–Abkhaz relations and the retrenchment of the separatist leadership of the Abkhaz republic on the Georgian Black Sea coast, despite the presence in the region of Russian peacekeeping forces, explain the persistent belief of many Georgian politicians that Russia represents the main external danger to their country.[1] The impasse in discussions over the withdrawal of Russia's remaining bases on Georgian territory and Russia's insistent demands for joint Russian-Georgian military operations to eradicate Chechen militants in the Pankisi Gorge have ensured that the Georgian population, alone among the CCA states, still views Russia as an imminent threat. In a survey conducted in September 2002 most Georgians named either Russia (54 per cent) or Chechnya itself (16 per cent) as the principal threat to Georgia's security.[2] These perceptions are unlikely to have changed much since then, despite an improvement in Georgian–Russian official relations in spring 2004 after Georgia, under its new president Mikheil Saakashvili, regained effective control of its Ajaria region from the formerly Russian-supported local ruler Aslan Abashidze.

Azerbaijan has effectively normalized its relationship with Russia since Putin's visit to Baku in January 2001.[3] This was facilitated by a more even-handed Russian approach to the Nagorno-Karabakh conflict (upholding the principle of the territorial integrity of Azerbaijan), the overarching perceived source of threat for Azerbaijan. Russia and Azerbaijan have also reached a basic agreement on the principles for Caspian Sea delimitation. In contrast, clashes between Azerbaijan and Iran over territorial delimitation in the Caspian Sea have revived underlying Azerbaijani fears of Iran as a possible military threat (see Chapter 12).

Armenia in turn still perceives Russia as a strategic guarantor in a hostile geostrategic environment, particularly since Armenian–Turkish relations still verge on hostility. Russian military facilities in Armenia are welcomed as providing Yerevan with a guarantee against potential future Turkish military pressures. But the growing Russian–Turkish rapprochement is discouraging the political leadership in Moscow from characterizing its military relationship with Armenia in these terms. This relationship has been complicated by the fact that Yerevan still connects its security policy interests closely with the provision of security for the Karabakh Armenians (in the enclave of Nagorno-Karabakh). In fact Armenia can no longer expect from Putin's Russia the same kind of partisan, albeit often clandestine, Russian support for this cause which it received at times in the 1990s.

In official thinking high-level threats, particularly the proxy warfare between Azerbaijan and Armenia, still overshadow concerns about immediate non-traditional security threats, and define the way some of the latter are understood, such as terrorism. However, the broad challenges which face the South Caucasus countries overall are identified in various draft security concepts produced by the Georgian parliament, in the views of the military-political department of the Georgian foreign ministry, the Academy of Sciences and various NGOs. These pay special attention to separatism, the relative strength of ethnic self-identification, the country's relatively weak military potential in comparison to neighboring countries, its poorly protected frontiers, the uncontrolled transit of drugs and weapons, and the role of organized crime in society.[4]

This broad agenda of threats has increasingly been discussed in bilateral and multilateral contexts with regional states as well as the EU, OSCE and NATO Partnership for Peace. The South Caucasus states accept that it requires specific and often new defense and security/intelligence responses. At the same time they perceive 'new threats' as often connected with or enabled by unresolved conflicts in the region, including Chechnya. Georgia, Azerbaijan and Turkey have concluded joint agreements on security cooperation against such threats and Russian–Azerbaijani bilateral cooperation on security and intelligence has been upgraded.

## Threat perceptions in Central Asia

Official threat perceptions in Central Asia now focus on transnational non-traditional security challenges – religious extremism, terrorism, separatism, drug trafficking, illegal arms trade and organized crime – although the interpretation of these phenomena and the appropriate responses to them have varied between the five regional states.[5] However, possible threats from powerful regional states – Russia and China – remain a background concern (though rarely discussed directly by officials) and the fear of the escalation of disputes between the Central Asian states themselves is a serious issue, especially for Uzbekistan's smaller neighbors. The geopolitical rivalry between Kazakhstan and Uzbekistan is a crucial constraint on regionalism but more a source of dissension than active threat.

Threat perceptions among the leaderships of the new Central Asian states have been far less defined than in the South Caucasus by fears of Russian hegemony. These states were all strong advocates of defense integration with Russia until at least the mid-1990s and Kazakhstan even explored the option of developing a joint military doctrine with Russia. The trio of Kazakhstan, Kyrgyzstan and Tajikistan still rely on some aspects of defense coordination with Moscow through CIS structures. Russia has not been perceived fundamentally as militarily threatening by leaders of these states but rather as part of a collective effort to ward off possible Taliban incursions into Central Asia from Afghanistan (during 1996–2001) or as providing a form of existential deterrence in the medium term against Chinese military power (see below, page 202).

Kazakh leaders, nevertheless, have felt it necessary to remain wary about any indications of unofficial Russian nationalist irredentist claims on the ethnic Russian populated parts of northern Kazakhstan. But this sensitive issue, which surfaced periodically during the 1990s, has not been expressed in the Kazakh defense posture or official statements: Kazakh forces have not been redeployed north and no northern military district has been created. A second phase of Russian–Kazakh discussions on the delineation of their joint border began in May 2002 and frictions arising from border controls have been contained. Kazakh fears of Russian irredentism have been allayed with Putin's new emphasis on creating long-term Russian commercial and energy relationships with Kazakhstan and the sidelining of the more egregiously nationalist Russian politicians in Russian political life. Moreover, Kazakhstan's active multilateralism and its new bilateral defense ties with the United States raise the international stakes of any challenges by a regional state on Kazakhstan's territorial integrity in the future.

Fears in Kazakhstan, Kyrgyzstan and Tajikistan about Chinese pressures or future intentions have been alleviated by effective progress on border demarcation for almost all stretches of the Chinese–Central Asian borders. Most notably, in May 2002 China and Kazakhstan signed a protocol on the demarcation of their common border. This enabled Kazakhstan to relocate troops from its Eastern Military District, which could not anyway provide effective security against the powerful military contingents in China's neighboring Lanzhou Military Region, which are almost three times the size of all Kazakhstan's forces. Security coordination in the Shanghai Cooperation Organization and new bilateral security assistance programs with the United States have also lessened though not eliminated the anxieties of Central Asian countries about the proximity of China.

The new Central Asian states have no experience of the region being fractured by direct interstate warfare between themselves, or of large-scale violent separatist conflict comparable to that of Nagorno-Karabakh. However, there are two important qualifications to this comparison. First, until 1997 Central Asian leaders sought for years to avoid a regional spillover of the effects of the civil war in Tajikistan, which was essentially a struggle between local power holders rather than one between central government and separatists. Second, throughout the post-Soviet era Uzbekistan's Central Asian neighbors have nursed deep anxieties about Tashkent's regional aspirations and conduct. Worries about Uzbek efforts to seek compliance on various issues from its neighbors permeate the security thinking of the smaller Central Asian states and hamper their efforts to respond to other possible local sources of military threats. They have observed the strengthening of the Uzbek armed forces in recent years with concern.[6] However, the broad regional rivalry between the Kazakh and Uzbek leaderships has proved to be containable and bears no resemblance to the entrenched Armenian–Azerbaijani hostilities.[7]

During 1996–2002 a possible incursion into Central Asia by Taliban forces featured prominently in official regional threat perceptions (see below, page 207). Since 1999, and significantly linked to cross-border threats from Afghanistan, the threat perceptions of the Central Asian states have increasingly been focused more diffusely on catalysts of low intensity or local conflicts – insurgent movements, terrorism, religious extremism, arms and drugs trafficking. This spectrum of perceived threats remains in place after the overthrow of the Taliban at the end of 2001.

The military doctrine of Uzbekistan issued in February 2000 identified the two main threats to national security simply as 'terrorism and religious extremism'. Tashkent has been at the forefront of efforts in Central Asia to conflate these two phenomena and associate them with the Islamic Movement of Uzbekistan as well as non-insurgent radical Islamic organizations such as Hizb-ut-Tahrir. Until 2000 Kazakhstan was more relaxed about the threat it faced from religious extremism deeper in Central Asia, but since then has become increasingly concerned about radical Islamic organizations trying to operate in the country, as has Kyrgyzstan.[8] However, Central Asian leaders have remained divided over the appropriate means to manage Islamic opposition movements and the threat they represent. These differences have caused serious tension since they have become entangled with a variety of local grievances between Uzbekistan and its Central Asian neighbors.

## The risks of military conflict in the South Caucasus and Caspian Sea

The risks of conflict in the South Caucasus and Caspian Sea fall into three main categories. First, the risk of a reactivation of the 'frozen conflicts' in Nagorno-Karabakh and Abkhazia, which might happen as the result of a general deterioration of the 'soft security' environment. Second, the danger of new military clashes arising from ethnic disputes, or from the spillover of the intractable Chechnya conflict. Third, the risk of clashes arising from contesting views of Caspian Sea delimitation. In each case one can envisage scenarios according to which regional states are drawn into the dispute either because of their ties with one or other party or through geographic proximity and the escalation of local incidents.

The Nagorno-Karabakh 'frozen' conflict continues to pose regional risks. The links between Karabakh Armenian forces and Armenia proper transposes the local conflict into a thinly veiled international confrontation between Azerbaijan and Armenia. Although the Karabakh military forces have a separate command structure, they are heavily dependent on Armenian equipment and soldiers and is it implicitly understood that the Armenian defense minister has overall responsibility.[9] In negotiations on the conflict Armenia has insisted on security guarantees to the people of Karabakh, which would include a right of Armenia to intervene militarily in defense of Karabakh. The conflict has drawn Turkey and Russia into counterposing proxy military relationships with Azerbaijan and Armenia respectively. As noted above, this may be moderating as a result of a new Turkish–Russian rapprochement. However, the 1997 Russian–Armenian friendship treaty (which provided for mutual assistance in the event of a military attack to either party) was bolstered in January 2003 by a new bilateral military-technical cooperation agreement.

There remains a risk of open conflict over Karabakh between the local adversaries. The continued occupation by Karabakh Armenian forces of 9 per cent of Azerbaijani territory in addition to Karabakh itself (a total of 15 per cent of Azerbaijan) sustains a sense of embittered frustration and prompts bellicose statements in Baku by officials competing to prove their nationalist credentials.[10] After OSCE-mediated negotiations reached an impasse in spring 2001 the Azerbaijani armed forces and those of the Karabakh Republic carried out a series of large-scale military exercises near the location of the cease-fire line. That autumn Azerbaijani President Heidar Aliyev talked of the growing mood in Azerbaijan in favor of a military solution.[11] His son, Ilham Aliyev, who succeeded him in autumn 2003, has similarly suggested that Azerbaijan would consider resorting to force if the negotiating stalemate over Karabakh is not broken soon. However, any new offensive is deterred by the fact that the Karabakh military remain the most powerful in the South Caucasus and they control most of the strategic heights along the Line of Control. No diplomatic progress could be expected in negotiations on Karabakh before the presidential elections in 2003 in Armenia and in Azerbaijan. But even after this the negotiating positions of the two sides have been essentially unchanged and it seems unlikely that the impasse over Karabakh will be overcome in the medium term.

The frozen conflict over the Georgian territory of Abkhazia on the Black Sea, which borders Russia to the north, also has the potential for serious regional destabilization No resolution to the conflict appears close. The Abkhaz separatist leadership rejects all initiatives that stipulate that Abkhazia is part of Georgia. Yet the Abkhaz separatists are neither able nor wish to extend their operations beyond the province of Abkhazia itself. There has been no real danger of major powers such as Russia and Turkey clashing militarily over this territory, although Russian retains a significant military involvement in Abkhazia, through its military base in Gudauta and a Russian-led CIS peacekeeping force. However, if Russia provides arms to the Abkhaz, as some unconfirmed reports claim, while Georgia receives US and Turkish bilateral military assistance and is an active member of the NATO Partnership for Peace program, then there exist catalysts for a possible broader destabilization in the region. This danger may have risen since the commencement in spring 2002 of an American program to train Georgian anti-terrorist forces, which Georgia could try to use (against American wishes) for future operations in Abkhazia.

The former Georgian President Shevardnadze resisted calls by Georgian politicians to take direct military action in response to Abkhaz intransigence. Domestic pressures for the Georgian government to resort to force are counteracted by the limited Georgian military potential (notwithstanding the US training program). However, general instability around Chechnya could provoke renewed conflict in Abkhazia. This was indicated in October 2001 when Abkhaz fighters clashed with guerillas operating out of the Kodori Gorge near Abkhazian-controlled territory in north-west Georgia.[12] The combination of Georgian partisans and Chechen fighters in the clash confirmed the difficulty of sealing off the South Caucasus from insurgency in the North Caucasus. It even prompted Russian anxieties, so far unfounded, about the possible commencement of hostilities in the mountains of Karachaevo-Cherkessia and other nearby Russian republics and regions.[13]

The risk of a military overspill from the Chechnya conflict and the impact of this on the cohesion of Georgia was one reason behind the US decision to initiate counter-terrorist and counter-insurgency training for Georgian rapid-deployment battalions. Tensions around the Pankisi Gorge on Georgia's northern border with Chechnya (in the Kakheti region's Akhmeta district) during 1999–2001 threatened to escalate into a serious international crisis. This risk has been moderated since 2002 by Georgian security operations in the region (which have restored Georgian authority here) and the new US military presence, but it still exists on several levels.[14]

First, there is a danger of inter-communal and inter-ethnic violence from frictions between the ethnic Georgian, Ossetian and Kist-Chechen communities in the Pankisi Gorge. Second, any retreat of Chechen fighters seeking sanctuary in the region risks a localized extension of the zone of military operations from Chechnya to Georgia. Interstate military clashes occurred in 2000 and 2002 as a result of Russian cross-border operations. Third, Georgia could become a direct party in the Chechnya conflict if it were to accede to periodic Russian pressures for it to establish a so-called 'joint' Russian-Georgian military operation against 'Chechen and international terrorists'. This could turn northern Georgia into a theatre of war and re-ignite the Chechen–Georgian conflict that occurred during the 1992–93 Chechen intervention in Abkhazia.[15]

Among other effects, the psychological impact of Georgian–Russian animosities over the Pankisi issue has impeded the development of any framework for regional security cooperation involving Russia and Georgia. These animosities moderated in the first half of 2004 when the new Georgian President Mikheil Saakashvili established working relations with his Russian counterpart. But Saakashvili's high-risk strategy of confronting the secessionist regions of Georgia could ignite serious conflict in the future.

In the South Caucasus, as in Central Asia, future local conflicts may originate from the lack of effective control by central governments over their territories (as in the case of the Pankisi Gorge) or be driven by inter-ethnic or intercommunal grievances over access to resources or status. Such conflicts become regional threats if neighboring states or regional powers define an interest in the dispute and become an active party in it. However, there may be good practical reasons for neighbor states to avoid actions that could destabilize regions on their borders. For example, tensions have been contained in the Javakhetia region in the south of Georgia, which borders Armenia and contains most of Georgia's ethnic Armenian population as well as a controversial Russian military base. Armenia has consistently avoided official support for demands for an ethnic Armenian autonomous district in Akhalkalaki, demands which surfaced at times in the 1990s and were heard again in street rallies in the region in spring 2002. Armenia has been aware that any conflict in the region would significantly increase its economic isolation since a sizeable part of its trade moves through Javakhetia and onward via Georgian ports.

The Caspian Sea represents a different kind of risk of conflict. This arises from the failure to reach an overall agreement on the principles for the territorial delimitation of the sea, the growth in naval strength of the littoral countries and the high commercial stakes involved as exploration for oil and gas fields proceeds. To Moscow's growing frustration, Iran still rejects the formula for delimitation of the Caspian Sea on the median line principle that Russia has agreed bilaterally with Kazakhstan and Azerbaijan.

The risks were dramatized in July 2001 when Tehran threatened military force against Azerbaijani research ships working in the southern portion of the sea. Kazakhstan has been building up the infrastructure of its Western Military District in response to 'new threats stemming from the lack of legal status of the Caspian Sea, the appearance of new sources of oil, and hot spots approaching western Kazakhstan'.[16] However, the main danger for all the Caspian Sea littoral states is a clash between Russia, which has some forty naval craft based at Astrakhan and Makhachkala, and Iran which has nearly fifty at Bandar-e Anzali.[17] Russia has renounced the goal of the demilitarization of the sea, which Iran still promotes. Iranian proposals for a Caspian Sea Cooperation Organization, first presented in the early 1990s, and aimed at excluding the influence of extra-regional actors, have made no progress.

In August 2002 Moscow conducted the largest joint maneuvers in post-Soviet history of its army, airforce and Caspian Flotilla, the 'Sea of Peace – 2002 anti-terrorist military exercises', which included a joint Russian-Kazakh component.[18] Russian Defense Minister Sergei Ivanov subsequently described Kazakhstan as part of a so-called 'Caspian grouping', and Russian officials suggested that Azerbaijan might also enter such a grouping. However, the Kazakh Defense Minister, General Mukhtar Altynbayev, considered that there was no urgent need 'to set up a military grouping similar to the [CIS] Collective Rapid Reaction Forces in the Caspian with Russia', though he accepted it would be beneficial to have a small joint group.[19] Russia, Azerbaijan and Georgia have conducted joint command-staff exercises of border guard services in the Caspian Sea. The US meanwhile has begun to supply Azerbaijan as well as Kazakhstan with naval defense equipment and since June 2003 has effectively called for the overthrow of the current Iranian regime. Against this background, in the absence of any agreed confidence building measures among the Caspian Sea states, small incidents could escalate into serious clashes and further undermine the potential for cooperative management of disputed issues.

## The risks of military conflict in Central Asia

As noted above, the Central Asian states share a great deal in their official threat perceptions and descriptions of the risk factors for military conflict. But they are understandably reticent or non-specific about the potential for internecine conflict between themselves. This is reflected, for example, in documents on the Kazakh National Security Strategy for 1999–2005 and Kazakhstan's military doctrine, adopted in February 2000. These defined national military policy in response to three challenges: 1. 'existing and potential sources of armed conflict in close proximity to the border of the state'; 2. 'possible infiltration of the territory of the country by armed formations of extremists and international terrorists'; and 3. 'the appearance of new nuclear powers in the region'.[20]

The first concern could refer to low-level insurgency inspired by opposition or Islamist groups and aggravated by effects of the civil war in Afghanistan at that time. But for Kazakhstan, Kyrgyzstan, Tajikistan and Turkmenistan it could equally well reflect the existence of disputes with Uzbekistan over border demarcation and border regimes, the treatment of ethnic diaspora and the management of water resources. The emphasis on national military construction in Kazakhstan (especially its Southern Military District) and in Uzbekistan is driven at least partly by tensions between these two states themselves.

The second concern, which has become a dominant element in Central Asian conflict assessments, explicitly expresses fears of insurgent and hit-and-run attacks by opposition or Islamist groups. The third concern, the new nuclear capabilities of India and Pakistan, encourages the Central Asian states to pursue negotiations to create a Central Asian Nuclear-Weapon Free Zone, but it does not suggest a scenario of conflict for Central Asia itself.

There has been one well-publicized risk of a violation of Central Asian borders from outside the CIS set of states – the threat of Taliban cross-border raids, for example when Taliban forces approached the Tajik border in northern Afghanistan in summer 1998.[21] However, there is no compelling evidence that Taliban commanders wished to carry out raids or pursue an Islamist campaign in the CIS Central Asian states at any time before their overthrow at the end of 2001. Turkmenistan did not share the perception of the Taliban as a threat, despite its long and insecure border with Afghanistan; Ashgabat maintained political links and trade relations with north-west Afghanistan. The Uzbek leader Karimov in turn criticized Russia for seeking to inflate this threat to secure Tajik agreement for a Russian base with a long-term lease in Tajikistan.[22]

Moscow used the putative threat of the Taliban as a focus to rally the Central Asian states behind general Russian-led collective military efforts in a

CIS framework. But this was never fully convincing. In May 2000, when an aide of President Putin stated that Russia might use preventive air-strikes on Afghanistan, the Kazakh president said that there was no need for such air strikes and Uzbekistan also dissociated itself from this option. The defeat of the Taliban, and the destruction of part of the insurgent Islamic Movement of Uzbekistan (IMU), has not moderated Russian interest in developing collective rapid deployment forces with Central Asian states. This suggests that Russia has political interests in exaggerating the risk of such externally inspired conflict in Central Asia.[23]

The risk of insurgency against the incumbent regimes in Central Asia was dramatically expressed by the infiltration during summer 1999 and 2000 of IMU fighters from Tajikistan into Kyrgyzstan and Uzbekistan, having taken advantage of northern Afghanistan as a hinterland. Their well-trained and equipped hit-and-run attacks could in no sense either threaten the overthrow of the Uzbek regime or inflict significant damage to its security forces, although such strikes could be destabilizing for weaker Kyrgyzstan. However, they created an urgent demand to create low-intensity counter-insurgency military and internal security capabilities, which began in earnest in Uzbekistan, Kazakhstan and to a lesser extent in Kyrgyzstan.[24]

These attacks also confirmed the need for the Central Asian states to try to work collaboratively to manage a cross-region threat. Yet Uzbekistan harshly criticized Tajikistan for ostensibly harboring such militants on its territory, and claimed that the presence of Islamic party representatives in the Tajik government (an outcome of the peace treaty in 1997 that ended the Tajik civil war) was linked to this. This revealed significant differences between the Central Asian states about the interpretation of the events in summers 1999 and 2000, which have also been reflected to some extent in responses taken by specialized forces, border troops and internal security forces. The risk here is that insensitive acts can inflame local tensions, regional socio-economic disparities and underlying ethnic disputes, especially in the mosaic of the Ferghana Valley divided between Uzbekistan, Kyrgyzstan and Tajikistan, and result in new clashes.[25]

The destruction of a significant part of the IMU at the end of 2001 during fighting in northern Afghanistan has been followed by claims that the remaining IMU militants are working to re-establish and expand their insurgent networks. They have reportedly merged with other regional radical Muslim groups and with Chinese Uighur separatists to form the Islamic Movement of Central Asia.[26] This movement could be capable in the future of sporadic small-scale attacks on government targets or even US military targets in Central Asia. The support and clandestine activities of the radical Islamist group Hizb-ut-Tahrir, especially in the Ferghana Valley, are also reported to be growing. Since this group advocates the non-violent overthrow of existing governments in Central Asia and the establishment of an Islamic caliphate in the region, it will not in itself be the originator of violent conflict in at least the medium term.

President Karimov blamed a series of bombings and shootings in Uzbekistan in March 2004, the most violent incidents suffered by the country since several bomb blasts in Tashkent in February 1999, on the IMU and an international terrorist conspiracy. But these attacks have not been conclusively explained and some specialists have argued that they bear the hallmarks of an indigenous revolt against Karimov's administration.[27] At the end of July 2004 attacks by suicide bombers targeted the US and Israeli embassies and the Uzbek prosecutor-general's office in Tashkent. Further incidents of this kind could provoke a strong security response in Uzbekistan, which in turn could be regionally destabilizing.

In response to the July 2004 attacks in Tashkent Kyrgyzstan and Kazakhstan tightened their border controls. This could increase the risks of border clashes between the Central Asian countries and the escalation of such clashes has already posed a serious risk of military conflict.[28] Kazakhstan's southern border with Uzbekistan has been bolstered on both sides by additional border troops and facilities since a serious border incident in January 2000 when Uzbek troops began unilaterally to demarcate the common border. Since 1999 there have also been tensions over Uzbek borders with Tajikistan, Kyrgyzstan and Turkmenistan. The existence of ethnic enclaves on either side of common border regions has threatened to turn border wrangles into bitter inter-ethnic clashes.

A landmark bilateral agreement was signed in November 2001 on the demarcation of most of the Kazakh–Uzbek inter-state border and in September 2002 a further agreement finalized the demarcation.[29] However, after analyzing all the borders between the Central Asian countries one scholar has concluded that only the Kazakh–Turkmen and Kazakh–Kyrgyz borders are consistently conflict free. The Uzbek–Kazakh, Uzbek–Turkmen and Kyrgyz–Tajik border relations were characterized by latent conflict, while Uzbek–Tajik and Uzbek–Kyrgyz border relations expressed 'elements of clear crisis' and a lack of political readiness by the parties to search for long-term solutions based on compromises.[30]

In current conditions tensions over disputed borders in Central Asia can become intermeshed with broader inter-state frictions and can stimulate ethnic antagonisms in border areas. For example, in December 2002 as part of a broader crisis in Uzbek–Turkmen relations, the two countries built up their armed forces on their common border. A couple of months later, observing this standoff, Russia media sources even speculated about the threat of the first officially declared war between two former republics of the USSR.[31]

The growth of American security policy ties with Central Asian states since autumn 2001 may have served to encourage a certain rapprochement between Uzbekistan and Tajikistan over border and other issues. But it has had little effect on dampening down other local disputes. Early in 2003, for example, clashes occurred between Kyrgyz and Tajik villagers over disputed frontier areas, Uzbekistan imposed a harsh border regime for its border with

Kazakhstan and a deterioration of Uzbek–Kyrgyz relations over border issues did not augur well for talks on demarcating their border.[32] In September that year Kazakh officials went so far as to describe the tendency of Uzbekistan's border troops to use excessive force as 'taking on a systemic nature' and complained that Uzbekistan showed no desire to address border issues.[33]

The potential for conflict between Central Asian states is increased by the failure to reach an effective and sustainable agreement on the use of water resources between the main supplier and user states. The upper and lower reaches of the principal rivers are located in different countries. It can be argued that the need to work cooperatively in the management of such an important shared resource is essential and unavoidable. But it is equally possible that the unequal distribution of water supplies will aggravate other areas of friction between the local states, be used to exert leverage in bilateral relations or serve as a direct catalyst for conflict in the future.[34]

## Obstacles to regional, multilateral defense cooperation

The record of over a decade of inter-state diplomacy in the South Caucasus and Central Asia has registered little progress towards the objective of securing an effective and sustainable framework for multilateral defense cooperation or conflict prevention in either region, let alone for the eight states concerned together. The analysis in this chapter reveals significant variations and differences between the local states in their threat assessments, in their management of border disputes and in their views on responses to new security challenges. These differences have been an important impediment to the development of common military/security structures, to the implementation of common military projects or the discussion of such issues as joint border delimitation. Turkmenistan, moreover, has opted to remain outside all such multilateral initiatives on the grounds of its adherence to 'permanent neutrality'.

However, these differences reflect a number of underlying structural factors, which have retarded and counteracted regionalism and the formation of regional frameworks and institutions for defense and security, especially those which only include the local states of the South Caucasus and Central Asia. Five key factors help to explain this outcome.[35]

First, the South Caucasus and Central Asia remain deeply divided by historical competition. In the case of the South Caucasus this is expressed in the frozen conflict around Nagorno-Karabakh, which so far has precluded any kind of multilateral cooperation on defense issues or the development of a regional security identity. In Central Asia the more diffuse rivalry between Kazakhstan and Uzbekistan, as well as many lesser axes of tension, are sufficiently well entrenched to reinforce the inhibitions against multilateral regional projects arising from the authoritarian mindset described below.

Second, the existence of the CIS structure has had a distorting effect. As in other parts of the world, regionalism or sub-regionalism[36] in the South Caucasus and Central Asia in the 1990s was promoted by the decentralization of the international system and the removal of superpower hegemonic control mechanisms. However, former Soviet controls were not wholly eradicated since the CIS organization continued to act as a Russian mechanism of supranational regional management for much of the 1990s. It still retains the institutional trappings of this ambition under President Putin, although he has increasingly emphasized bilateral over multilateral diplomacy in relations with CIS states.

The CIS structure has not expressed a real multilateral convergence of interests and it has impeded multilateral efforts that exclude Russia. Peace-support operations in the South Caucasus and Tajikistan, despite their CIS designation, have been dominated by Russia.

In response to core security challenges originating from outside the former Soviet region, Armenia and most of the Central Asian states, at least before 2001, felt it preferable to bandwagon with Russia, rather than to rely on alternative but still incipient regional mechanisms.

Third, multilateral regional projects have been limited politically, especially in Central Asia, by strong presidential or authoritarian regimes.[37] Fearful of the implications of regionalism for their own sovereignty and power base, local rulers have been unwilling to invest regional structures with any real institutional content, or to create mechanisms to make agreements binding. They have no more wished to surrender power to a regional structure than to a rival organization within the state itself. Their focus has been on regime security rather than on security as a public good.

There are parallels in this respect between the Arab Middle East and Central Asia.[38] For example, the focus of the Gulf Security Council on internal security rather than external defense is replicated in various new groupings in Central Asia. In each region authoritarian rulers fear that structures for regional cooperation may resemble structures for regional intervention. Concerned about this for their own control they have deprived such structures of any institutional coherence.

Fourth, the states concerned are likely to continue to rely heavily for their defense on the development of well-organized national military forces, rather than investing energies in developing multilateral defense and security relationships. This comprises part of the ongoing process of establishing state and national identities, and reflects a reluctance to depend too much for security on groupings or frameworks that are poorly institutionalized and could be transient phenomena in a period of rapid transition. The paradox of multilateral regional security cooperation among CIS states in the South Caucasus and Central Asia is that the more serious the defense concerns have been for a group of states, the more unlikely they have been to engage in significant defense and security cooperation with each other. Cooperation has mostly involved issues that are secondary rather than core security or defense interests. As noted above, it has been more likely also to concern issues of domestic or internal security rather than traditional forms of external defense.

Therefore such defense cooperation has emphasized small-scale and relatively inexpensive practical measures, particularly plans to form joint peacekeeping battalions and officer training, and some coordination over security policy in wider international organizations. The various plans for peacekeeping battalions have represented a desire to be seen to be pooling some military assets on a regional or sub-regional basis and to be contributing to United Nations or NATO Partnership for Peace (PfP) security policy agendas, rather than a commitment to tackle intractable regional conflicts. The joint Uzbek-Kazakh-Kyrgyz battalion (Centrasbat), the only one of this kind formed, has never been used in combat. It has carried out exercises in or on the borders of the CIS region, but played no role against the insurgency of summer 1999 and 2000.

Finally, as a reflection of their concerns outlined above, the leaders of the South Caucasus and Central Asian states have given priority in their external defense policies and planning to building bridges bilaterally to powerful regional states. These regional patrons include Turkey (particularly for Georgia and Azerbaijan), Russia (for Armenia, Kazakhstan, Kyrgyzstan and Tajikistan) and the United States. Such bilateral security assistance and defense agreements have been viewed by the local states as more effective than the creation of joint military assets or defense programs that exclude regional powers and the assets or guarantees they can provide.[39]

However, to the extent that such bilateral ties assist the construction of military forces in certain countries that look threatening to their neighbors this can encourage the formation of counterposing alliances or blocs. At the least this can feed perceptions of vulnerability and suspicion that impede the spirit of regional cooperation. In this sense it may be illusory for outside powers to expect that the process of strengthening military security ties bilaterally with given states may be part of and eventually lead to the formation of an overarching multilateral security environment for the region.

## Notes

1 David Darchiashvili and Tamara Pataraia, 'Returning to Europe? Georgia's security policy priorities', *Central Asia and the Caucasus*, 1(7), 2001, pp. 59–61. For a summary of the various points of tension in current Russian–Georgian relations see Sergei Blagov, 'Military issues block Russia–Georgia détente', *Eurasia Insight*, 6 January 2003, www.eurasia.net.org (and as in subsequent references).

2 'Russia remains central to Georgia's security, but US seen as "best friend" ', *Opinion Analysis*, Office of Research, Department of State, Washington DC, 6 November 2002, p. 2. The other countries or territories listed by respondents as thought to pose the greatest threat to Georgia were the Islamic world (6 per cent), Abkhazia (5 per cent), and Turkey (4 per cent). Paradoxically, despite their misgivings about Russian troops on their soil, when asked whether Georgia should seek closer relations primarily with Russia and the CIS or with the US and other western countries, more and more have chosen Russia in surveys between 1998

and 2002. Evidently, Russia is viewed as so big and powerful that Georgia must try to have good relations with it; ibid., p. 3.

3 See the text of the Baku Declaration between Azerbaijan and Russia, in *BBC Summary of World Broadcasts, Former Soviet Union* (henceforth SU) 4046 F/1–3, 17 January 2001.

4 For the threats and strategic priorities identified in Georgian documents, see David Darchiashvili, 'Trends of strategic thinking in Georgia: Achievements, problems and prospects', in Gary K. Bertsch *et al.*, eds, *Crossroads and Conflict*, London, Routledge, pp. 66–74.

5 For a Central Asian assessment of the challenges of drug trafficking, organized crime and illegal arms trade, see Orozbek Moldaliev, ' "Non-traditional" threats to security in Central Asia', *Central Asia and the Caucasus*, 1(7), 2001, pp. 28–36.

6 Russian analysts have been rather alarmist in arguing that the strengthening of Uzbekistan's military potential upsets the existing balance of forces in the region and could encourage the illusion that Tashkent can resolve its disputes with neighbor states by the use of force, which would create new sources of tension and could possibly spill over into open military conflict. For example, Mikhail Kholarenok, 'Novaya rol' Uzbekistana', *Nezavisimoe voennoe obozreniya*, 12, 12–18 April 2002.

7 This rivalry in its many dimensions is analyzed in Dmitry Trofimov, 'Regional preeminence in Central Asia', *Prism*, Jamestown Foundation, February 2000, vol. vi, parts 3 and 4.

8 For a detailed analysis of religious extremism and terrorism from a Kazakh perspective, see A.G. Kosichenko *et al.*, eds, *Sovremennyy terrorizm: vzglyad iz Tsentralnoy Azii*, Almaty, Dayk-Press, 2002.

9 Razmik Panossian, 'Informal politics: Armenia–Nagorno Karabakh relations', *Analysis of Current Events* 13(3) (September 2001), p. 3.

10 Clare Doyle, 'Azerbaijani bluster masks military weaknesses', *Eurasia Insight*, 13 December 2002.

11 BBC Monitoring *Inside Central Asia*, issue 395 (1 October–7 October 2001); issue 400 (5 November–11 November 2001).

12 Akaky Mikadze, 'Abkhazia war threatens to destabilise Caucasus', *Moscow News*, 42, 17–23 October 2001, p. 3.

13 Reports in *Nezavisimaya gazeta*, 5, 13, and 17 October 2001, and *Izvestiya*, 15 October 2001.

14 For a full analysis, see Tracey German, 'The Pankisi Gorge: Georgia's Achilles' heel in its relations with Russia?', *Central Asian Survey*, 23(1) (March 2004), pp. 27–39.

15 See note issued by the Russian Foreign Ministry on 18 September 2001, Jamestown Foundation, *Monitor*, vii(173) (21 September 2001); Mikhail Vignansky, 'Georgian "terrorist" dilemma', Institute of War and Peace Reporting, *Caucasus Reporting Service*, 98 (19 September 2001).

16 Statement by first deputy chief of the Kazakh General Staff, Major General Malik Saparov, *Panorama* (Almaty), 19 January 2001.

17 For a detailed breakdown of military and naval assets around the Caspian Sea, see Alexander Plotnikov, 'Kaspiyskiy gorodovoy', *Novye izvestiya*, 11 August 2001.

18 Igor Plugatarev, *Nezavisimaya gazeta*, 1 August 2002; BBC Monitoring, *Inside Central Asia*, issue 439 (12–18 August 2002); Igor Torbakov, 'Russia to flex military muscle in the Caspian Sea with an eye on future energy exports', www.eurasianet.org 31 July 2002. Iranian officials were restrained in their response to these exercises, however, and some suggested they were directed against any NATO involvement in the Caspian Sea; Ardeshir Moaveni, 'Iran largely silent on Russian-led Caspian Sea military exercises', *Eurasia Insight*, 8 August 2002.

19 *Inside Central Asia*, BBC, issue 439, 12–18 August 2002.

20  Statement by President Nazarbayev, reported in BBC Monitoring, *Inside Central Asia*, issue 337 (31 July–6 August 2000); and Kazakh Defense Minister Sat Tokpakbayev in *Kazakhstanskaya pravda*, 6 May 2000.

21  For example, Leonid Bondarev, 'Voennye ugrozy bezopasnosti Tsentral'noy Azii', *Tsentral'naya Aziya: Politika i ekonomika*, 1(3), January 2001, pp. 33–34.

22  *Monitor*, Jamestown Foundation, 26 September 2000, vi(178); *Inside Central Asia*, BBC, issue 344, 25 September–1 October 2000.

23  See Roy Allison, 'Strategic reassertion in Russia's Central Asia policy', *International Affairs*, 80(2) (March 2004), pp. 277–293.

24  For the subsequent military reform plans and efforts of the Central Asian states, see Roy Allison, 'Central Asian military reform: National, regional and international influences', in Sally Cummings, ed., *The Caspian States: Energy, Geopolitics and Governance*, London, Routledge, 2003.

25  For a Kazakh assessment of the socio-political preconditions of conflicts within these countries, of the course of military operations during summer 2000, and of the consequences of such conflicts for the geopolitical situation in Central Asia, see Ye. T. Karina, ed., *Voenno-politicheskie konflikty v Tsentral'noy Azii*, The Central Asian Agency of Political Studies, Almaty, 2000. For the report of a conference on the causes of local conflicts in the region, possible measures to avert them and the risks of local conflicts expanding into a regional war, see 'Lokal'nyy konflikt ili regional'naya voyna?', *Tsentral'naya Asiya: politika i ekonomika* (Almaty), 1(3), January 2001.

26  Ibragim Alibekov, 'IMU reportedly expands, prepares to strike Western targets', *Eurasia Insight*, 29 October 2002.

27  Olivier Roy, as cited in 'US failure to comprehend Islamic radical motivations undermines democratization hopes for Middle East, Central Asia', *Eurasia Insight*, 13 May 2004. See also Esmer Islamov, 'Bombings and shootings rock Uzbekistan', *Eurasia Insight*, 30 March 2004.

28  For a thorough analysis see *Central Asia: Border Disputes and Conflict Potential*, International Crisis Group, Asia Report no. 33, Osh/Brussels, 4 April 2002. For potential scenarios for conflict between states involved in border disputes, see pp. 6–7.

29  *Inside Central Asia*, BBC, issue 401, 12–18 November 2001; *Radio Free Europe/ Radio Liberty Central Asia Report* (henceforth *RFE/RL Central Asia Report*), 2(35), 13 September 2002.

30  Dmitry Trofimov, 'Ethnic/territorial and border problems in Central Asia', *Central Asia and the Caucasus*, 1(13), 2002, p. 63.

31  *Inside Central Asia*, BBC, issue 457, 16–22 December 2002, 16 February 2003.

32  'Kyrgyz-Tajik border riots highlight building inter-ethnic tension in Central Asia', *Eurasia Insight*, 8 January 2003; *Eurasia Insight*, 'Uzbek border row introduces new element of tension in Central Asia', *Business and Economics*, www.eurasianet.org, 27 January 2003; *RFE/RL Central Asia Report*, 3(11), 13 March 2003.

33  Ibragim Alibekov, 'Kazakhstan, Uzbekistan clash over border policy', *Eurasia Insight*, 29 September 2003; BBC Monitoring, *Inside Central Asia*, 28 September 2003.

34  See Stuart Horsman, 'Water in Central Asia: Regional cooperation or conflict?', in Roy Allison and Lena Jonson, eds, *Central Asian Security: The New International Context*, Brookings/RIIA, Washington DC and London, 2001, pp. 69–86.

35  Here I draw on my analysis 'The limits of multilateralism', *NBR Analysis* (National Bureau of Asian Research, Seattle), 14(3) (October 2003), pp. 23–40. For a fuller assessment of the weaknesses of security-related regionalism in Central Asia, see Roy Allison, 'Regionalism, regional structures and security management in Central Asia', *International Affairs*, 80(3) (May 2004), pp. 463–483.

36 If the OSCE is a regional arrangement in the sense of Chapter VII of the UN Charter then 'subregional' could refer to a geographically and/or historically reasonably coherent area within the OSCE space as a whole. See, Andrew Cottey, 'Introduction', in Andrew Cottey, ed., *Subregional Cooperation in the New Europe: Building Security, Prosperity and Solidarity from the Barents to the Black Sea*, Macmillan, London, 1999.
37 Annette Bohr, 'Regionalism in Central Asia: New geopolitics, old regional order', *International Affairs*, 80(3) (May 2004), pp. 498–501.
38 See Charles Tripp, 'Regional organizations in the Arab Middle East', in Louise Fawcett and Andrew Hurrell, *Regionalism in World Politics: Regional Organization and International Order*, Oxford, Oxford University Press, 1995, pp. 283–309.
39 Roy Allison, 'Subregional cooperation and security in the CIS', in Renata Dwan and Oleksandr Pavliuk, *Building Security in the New States of Eurasia: Subregional Cooperation in the Former Soviet Space*, Armonk NY, M.E. Sharpe, 2000, pp. 170–173.

# Part V

# Assessing the strength of external leverage on the CCA political economy

# 12 Prospective impacts of Russia and Iran

*Mark N. Katz*

Earlier chapters in this volume have concluded that political and economic reform are essential for sustained economic development to occur in the greater CCA region. Other chapters have also discussed the many obstacles to political and economic reform within the greater CCA region in order for sustained economic development to occur. The policies of external powers, though, also affect the prospects for political and economic development in the region. Two of the most important of these for the greater CCA region are Russia and Iran.

This chapter examines the prospective impacts of Russian and Iranian policies and perspectives on developments in the greater CCA region. The roles played by these two countries in the greater CCA region could, of course, be considered separately. But since their perspectives on the region are often similar, and since their differences over it are tied up in the overall Russian–Iranian relationship, the roles played by Russia and Iran in the greater CCA region will be considered here together. Table 12.1 compares the recent economic performance and military statistics for Russia and Iran.

## Russian and Iranian priorities

Moscow and Tehran currently share several priorities related to the greater CCA region in the economic, political, and security spheres. These include:

- *A common desire to limit American influence in the greater CCA region.* Iranian hard-liners – who retain control of the Islamic Republic's foreign policy – continue to see the United States as their principal opponent. They see any increased American influence in this region as serving to limit their own influence in it, and so want to exclude Washington from the CCA region as much as possible.[1] While Moscow has much better relations with the USA than does Tehran, Russia too sees increased American influence in the CCA region as limiting its own there. Moscow, though, is more willing than Tehran to tolerate some American presence in the region, as demonstrated by President Putin's acquiescence in the deployment of American troops to Central Asia and (to a lesser extent)

*Table 12.1* Russia and Iran: comparative economic and military statistics

|  | Russia | Iran |
|---|---|---|
| Population 2002 (millions) | 146.1 | 65.5 |
| Population growth 1980–2002 (%/yr) | 0.2 | 2.3 |
| GNI 2002 (US $ billion) | 306.6 | 112.9 |
| GNI 2002 (US $ PPP billion) | 1,165.0 | 438.0 |
| GNI per capita (US $) | 2,130 | 1,720 |
| GNI per capita 2002 (US $ PPP) | 8,080 | 6,690 |
| PCGNI growth 1998–2002 (%/yr) | 4.6 | 2.9 |
| Petroleum as % of exports 1998–2002 | 48.1 | 84.8 |
| Army (personnel) | 321,000 | 325,000 |
| Navy | 171,500 | 18,000 |
| Air force | 184,600 | 52,000 |
| Paramilitary | 409,100 | 40,000 |
| Revolutionary Guards | N/A | 125,000 |

*Sources:* World Bank (2004) *World Development Indicators 2004*, Washington DC: World Bank; International Institute for Strategic Studies (2002) *The Military Balance, 2002–2003*, Oxford: Oxford University Press/IISS, 88–94, 103–105.

Georgia after 9/11.[2] There are many in Moscow, however, who begrudge this American presence and who are determined to prevent it from increasing.[3]

- *A common desire to limit Turkish influence in the region.* Because Moscow and Tehran both see Turkey as an ally of the USA, both see expanded Turkish influence as being undesirable since this would further American influence there too. But even if Turkey was not allied to the USA, both Russia and Iran would oppose any attempt by Ankara to expand its influence in the region. The Azeris, most Central Asians (except the Tajiks), and many North Caucasians and other Muslims in Russia are related to the Turks by cultural/linguistic ties. Many in Moscow and Tehran fear the rise of a 'pan-Turanianism' which would link the Turkic-speaking peoples of the former USSR and Iran with Turkey, even though such a project is not now being attempted and would face enormous challenges even if it were.[4]

- *A common desire to prevent secession in the region.* Moscow is actively fighting against Chechen secession. It does so partly out of the fear that if Chechnya did become independent, other Muslim 'nations' in the Russian Federation (including the North Caucasus) would attempt to follow suit. Some of these regions – most notably Tatarstan – contain significant petroleum reserves, which Moscow does not want to lose. Similarly, Tehran fears that the loss of any of its non-Persian border-lands would lead to the break-up of Iran. It is especially concerned that Iranian Azeris – who outnumber those in independent Azerbaijan – will seek either independence or unification with their cousins north of the border. Neither Moscow nor Tehran supports secessionist movements operating in each other's territory.[5] If one of them did so, the other could retaliate in kind.

- *Common interests vis-à-vis Azerbaijan and Armenia.* Both Moscow and Tehran favor Armenia in the unresolved Azeri–Armenian dispute over Nagorno-Karabakh. Tehran fears that a peaceful, prosperous Azerbaijan would increase the desire of Iranian Azeris to join them in a Greater Azerbaijan, while a partially occupied, poor Azerbaijan is far less attractive to them. In addition to Russian public opinion favoring Orthodox Christian Armenia over Muslim Azerbaijan, the Russian government regards Armenia as an ally since it willingly allows Russian troops to be stationed on its territory. Despite some recent improvement in their relationship, Azerbaijan is regarded by Moscow with suspicion and distrust both for its unwillingness to host Russian troops and its apparent desire to increase its links with the West and Turkey, and thereby reduce Azeri dependence on Russia. Tehran also prefers Russia to the West and Turkey as the dominant external power in Azerbaijan.[6]

- *Similar attitudes toward the Baku–Ceyhan pipeline.* This pipeline, of which Washington has strongly supported the construction, would allow for the export of Azeri (and, if a trans-Caspian link is built, Kazakh) oil across Georgia and Turkey to the Mediterranean coast. Because this route will bypass both Russian and Iranian territory, neither Moscow nor Tehran will reap the revenues from oil transiting the Baku–Ceyhan line rather than going through their territories. The Baku–Ceyhan pipeline also reduces Russian and Iranian ability to control the export of oil from Azerbaijan, which dependence on routes through Russian and Iranian territory would have allowed (this, of course, was one of the primary incentives for Azerbaijan and its western partners to construct this pipeline route). While the Baku–Ceyhan pipeline appears well on the way to completion, its operation may still be subject to disruption by Russian-backed opponents of both the Georgian and Azeri governments.

- *A common fear of Sunni Islamic fundamentalism.* Except for the Azeris (who are mainly Shia), the Muslims of the former USSR are predominantly Sunni. It is readily understandable, then, why Moscow fears the rise of Sunni fundamentalism among Russia's large Muslim population, within the former Soviet republics of Central Asia, and on the periphery of the former USSR. One of the motives for Russia's fierce campaign in Chechnya is the fear that an independent Chechnya would be ruled by Islamic fundamentalists who would then attempt to spread their rule throughout the North Caucasus and other Muslim regions of Russia.[7]

Although Iran is an Islamic Republic, the Shia clergy ruling Iran (along with the predominantly Shia population) also have reason to fear the rise of Sunni Islamic fundamentalism. This is because Sunni fundamentalists, in addition to being hostile toward the West and toward secular Muslims, are usually also hostile to Shi'ism (which they regard as a form of apostasy). The spread of Sunni fundamentalism, Tehran realizes, will not lead to the spread of Iranian influence. Worse still, Sunni fundamentalist regimes may well attack Iranian interests or Iran itself (war almost broke out between Iran and the Taliban regime in Afghanistan in 1998). Finally, there exists the specter of external forces fomenting opposition within Tehran's sizeable Sunni minority. This is probably a challenge that Tehran could contain, but which it does not want to have to deal with.[8]

Russia and Iran, then, have adopted similar policies designed to contain or suppress Sunni Islamic fundamentalism in the region. Both support the continued rule of secular authoritarian governments that have suppressed their Islamic opponents. Both supported a settlement of the 1992–97 Tajik civil war, which gave a greater share of power to the ex-communists than to their Islam-oriented opponents. Both supported the opponents of the Taliban in Afghanistan long before the United States intervened there in October 2001. Both are wary of Pakistan, which (despite its close ties to the USA) still supports Sunni fundamentalists. Both are friendly toward Hindu India – Pakistan's arch rival.[9]

In addition to their many shared interests and priorities, however, there are also areas where Moscow and Tehran have important differences. First, there is a *continuing inability to agree upon the division of the Caspian*. The three new littoral states (Azerbaijan, Kazakhstan and Turkmenistan) that emerged after the break-up of the USSR soon realized that oil and/or gas deposits lay off their Caspian coasts, and so favored a territorial division of this inland sea. Apparently not having such deposits off their coasts, Russia and Iran both initially called for the natural resources lying under the Caspian Sea (which they declared to be a lake) be shared by all the littoral states in common. Once, however, Russia discovered that it had significant oil deposits off its coast, it too switched to favoring a territorial division of the Caspian.[10]

Since then, Moscow has championed the division of the Caspian according to a 'modified median line' which would give each littoral state the same percentage of the Caspian seabed as its percentage of the Caspian shoreline. Russia has signed agreements with its two Caspian neighbors, Kazakhstan and Azerbaijan, agreeing upon just such a boundary. Kazakhstan and Azerbaijan have also signed an agreement with each other based on this principle of division. If this principle were used to establish the remaining maritime boundaries, Iran would receive approximately 13 per cent of the Caspian – which would be up from the 11 per cent that Stalin assigned it during the Soviet era.[11]

Iran, though, has not accepted this principle of division. While Tehran would prefer that the five littoral countries share equally in all the undersea resources of this inland sea, it insists that if the Caspian is to be divided on a territorial basis, each of the five littoral states should obtain an equal 20 per cent of it. And as luck would have it, while there appear to be only limited oil deposits in the 13 per cent of the Caspian Iran would be entitled to using the modified median line, there are substantial deposits just beyond it in the area Azerbaijan would own using this principle of division but which Iran would own if it received the 20 per cent share of the Caspian that Tehran claims.[12]

Russia's position on the division of the Caspian clearly favors the development of Azerbaijan's offshore oil fields while Iran's position blocks it. On the other hand, the Russian position that pipelines cannot be built along the Caspian seabed without the agreement of all five littoral countries prevents Kazakhstan from building a pipeline that links up with the Baku–Ceyhan pipeline.[13] Despite years of diplomatic efforts aimed at resolving this dispute, fundamental differences remain on this issue between Russia, Azerbaijan and Kazakhstan on the one hand and Iran on the other (Turkmenistan's policy on this issue has not been clear[14]).

Second, as major oil producers, *Russia and Iran have competing oil interests.* While Iran is a member of the Organization of Petroleum Exporting Countries (OPEC), Russia along with the CCA producers is not. As an OPEC member, Iran has agreed to limit its oil exports to an assigned quota in order to keep up oil prices. While Iran (like many other OPEC members) may 'cheat' somewhat on this quota and export above it to some degree, it is not believed to do so excessively. Russia and the CCA oil producers, by contrast, are not bound by OPEC quotas, and have been aggressively seeking to expand both their production and their exports. OPEC members (more or less) limiting production see this expanding Russian and CCA production as encroaching on their market share. Thus, OPEC members (including Iran) would like to see Russia and the CCA producers join OPEC and adhere to its production limits. Neither Russia nor the CCA oil producers, however, have been willing to do this. This, of course, does not just affect Iran, but OPEC as a whole.

There is one oil question over which Russia and Iran have starkly diverging interests. As was mentioned above, neither Moscow nor Tehran favors the Baku–Ceyhan pipeline as an export route for Caspian Basin oil, since this bypasses both Russian and Iranian territory. On the other hand, *Moscow and Tehran favor different export routes for CCA petroleum.* Moscow clearly has an interest in Caspian Basin oil being exported via Russian territory, while Tehran would prefer to see it exported via Iranian territory. Because of continued Iranian–American hostility, Washington has acted to block financing for export routes via Iran.[15] As a result, far more Caspian Basin petroleum has up to now been exported via Russia than via Iran. Russia, then, has benefited from continued Iranian–American hostility in this regard.

## The impact of Russia and Iran on CCA region political and economic reform

Neither Russian nor Iranian policies toward the CCA region encourage political and economic reform there. This is true both in those instances where Moscow and Tehran agree, and where they disagree. The Russian and Iranian desire to prevent reform in the CCA region is most evident in their common desire to limit American influence in the region. There does not appear to be any instance in which Russia or Iran, much less both, are doing anything to promote reform in the region. True, both Moscow and Tehran wish to prevent the spread of Sunni fundamentalism in the region. Both, however, prefer to work with existing authoritarian regimes to prevent this and not with democratic forces. Indeed, the USA and the West in general have adopted a similar approach.

That said, however, the 'Rose Revolution' in Georgia showed that neither Moscow nor Tehran was able to prevent the strong democratization movement there from displacing either the authoritarian regime of Eduard Shevardnadze or Moscow's client Abashidze in Ajaria (one of Georgia's Muslim regions). Iran, of course, did not have the ability to prevent democratic revolution in this predominantly Christian country, which it neither borders, nor has much influence in. Russia, though, could have done far more than it did to prevent the Rose Revolution. Not only does Russia border Georgia, but it also has an enormous concentration of military force just to its north in Chechnya. Russia even has troops in Georgia itself. But instead of bolstering either Shevardnadze or Abashidze, Moscow acted to facilitate their being ousted and prevent conflict.[16]

Would Russia and Iran be as accommodating if strong democratic movements managed to rise up elsewhere in the CCA region? The question appears moot for the five Central Asian republics, since there do not appear to be strong democratic movements in any of them. Democratic movements do exist in Armenia and Azerbaijan, but the authoritarian governments there have been able to keep them in check – so far. The game is not completely over in Georgia either, where Moscow can do much to thwart Tbilisi's efforts to re-establish control over the breakaway provinces of South Ossetia and Abkhazia, both of which border Russia.

President Putin's reported comments to the acting president of Georgia shortly after the Rose Revolution indicate that both he and the authoritarian leaders of other CIS states fear the spread of the Rose Revolution to other undemocratic ex-Soviet republics.[17] His actions in Georgia, though, suggest that Moscow will not act to suppress a powerful democratic movement elsewhere in the CCA even if it is supported by the USA (as was the case in Georgia). Iran, with still less ability and access to most of the CCA region than Russia, is even less likely to attempt this. The one CCA country where a strong democratic movement would make Tehran nervous is Azerbaijan, since a successful democratic revolution there could prove attractive to

Iranian Azeris, and perhaps even affect the balance between reformers and hard-liners in Tehran. Any effort by Iran, though, to prevent democratization in Azerbaijan risks both stirring up Iranian Azeris and provoking a response from the USA.

While their policies during Georgia's Rose Revolution suggest that Russia and Iran will not act to block strong reform movements in the CCA, neither Moscow nor Tehran is acting to support reform elsewhere in the region where the indigenous demand for it is weak or absent. Are there circumstances, though, which might lead Russia or Iran (or both) to more vigorously promote reform efforts in the CCA region? For this to happen, significant change may first have to occur in either Russia or Iran. The type of change that might lead one or both of them to promote reform in the CCA region includes an Iranian–American rapprochement and the revival of democracy in Russia. Each of these possibilities will be considered next.

## The impact of an Iranian–American rapprochement

Predicting whether or how an Iranian–American rapprochement might occur is beyond the scope of this chapter. That it might occur, though, must be taken as a serious possibility. Rapprochements, after all, occurred between the USA on the one hand and seemingly hostile regimes in Moscow and Beijing during the Cold War. After years of poor relations, a sudden rapprochement occurred between the USA and Libya in 2003–4. If this could happen with a regime that had been as anti-American as that of Colonel Qadaffi, the possibility that a rapprochement between Washington and the ayatollahs has to be taken seriously.

One dramatic impact of an Iranian–American rapprochement would be the end not only to American economic sanctions against Iran but also to US efforts to block the construction of pipelines to carry Caspian Basin oil through it to the Persian Gulf and Indian Ocean. If Washington dropped its opposition to construction of these pipelines through Iran, it is highly likely that they would soon be built. It is commonly acknowledged that pipeline routes through Iran would be the cheapest means of exporting most Caspian Basin oil partly because the distances to the sea are shorter than other routes and partly because there is already a pipeline infrastructure in Iran.[18]

If these pipeline routes through Iran do get built and much of the Caspian Basin's oil flows through them, one impact is that the fees Moscow might have earned if this oil had gone through Russia's much longer (and often unreliable) pipeline system will go instead to Tehran. But in addition to this economic loss, the flow of Caspian Basin oil (and gas) through Iranian pipelines would also lead to what the Russians would consider to be a loss of political influence within the CCA region. The ability of Azerbaijan, Turkmenistan and Kazakhstan to export their petroleum resources southward would not only benefit them economically, but would also enable them to reduce their political dependence on Russia. Of course, Moscow could continue to exert its influence through playing the role of a spoiler: it could, for example, do even more to assist Armenia against Azerbaijan or stir up the large Russian population in northern Kazakhstan. Doing so, however, would only encourage these states to move closer both to the United States and to an Iran allied to it.

In addition, an Iranian–American rapprochement could have an impact on the dispute over the division of the Caspian. Iran has proven unwilling to compromise with Russia on this issue even though Tehran has poor relations with Washington and regards Moscow as a friend against it. If Iranian–American relations become warm, Tehran may prove even less willing to compromise with Russia on this since it will then no longer need a 'strategic partnership' with Moscow against Washington. The US government may prove far more sympathetic than it is now to the Iranian position on the Caspian issue after an Iranian–American rapprochement. This, of course, might strain both Azerbaijan's and Turkmenistan's ties to the USA. But instead of turning to Moscow for help against the USA and Iran, either or both may seek Washington's assistance in mediating their disputes with Tehran – without reference to Moscow at all. Although Moscow would object to this, the fact that Russia has reached agreement about its own maritime borders with Azerbaijan and Kazakhstan might actually facilitate this process: Tehran could argue (if it changed its own position) that since Moscow established the principle of Caspian maritime borders being agreed to bilaterally between neighboring states, the remaining sets of Caspian neighbors (Iran-Azerbaijan, Iran-Turkmenistan, and Azerbaijan-Turkmenistan) are free to establish their bilateral borders without the input of the other littoral states but with American involvement if any two neighboring states seek it.

If an Iranian–American rapprochement were accompanied by increased democratization in Iran, this could serve to increase the prospects for democratization in the CCA region as a whole. On the other hand, democratization in Iran and closer Iranian–American ties could induce the authoritarian regimes of the CCA to cling to Russia for protection against what they might perceive as increased pressure to reform.

## The impact of a democratic revival in Russia

As with the possibility of an Iranian–American rapprochement, predicting whether or how a democratic revival will occur in Russia is beyond the scope of this chapter. The possibility that it might occur, though, needs to be taken seriously. In his book *The Third Wave*, Samuel Huntington noted that progress toward democracy can occur in fits and starts. Democracy does not always 'take' the first time it is attempted and authoritarianism re-emerges. Renewed authoritarianism, though, can be followed by a renewed democratization which is more successful for having learned from the mistakes made the first time around.[19]

The revival of democracy in Russia could have a strong impact on the CCA region. Whereas the Putin administration now acts to bolster the region's authoritarian governments, a more democratic Russian government – just by its existence – would serve to undermine their legitimacy and encourage forces seeking reform in them. A Russian government unwilling to defend authoritarian CCA regimes against rising democratic forces might encourage the sort of regime crises that allow such forces to come to power. And the presence of troops from a democratic Russia in a country experiencing this sort of regime crisis might be able to positively affect its outcome. If, for example, Moscow had indicated that Russian troops in Armenia would protect the democratic opposition, which challenged the authoritarian Kechorian regime in mid-2004, the attempt at democratic revolution there might not have failed.

Of course, a democratic revival in Russia will not necessarily lead to democratization in the CCA region. Where the prospects for democratization appear weak (as they do in the Central Asian states), a democratic Russia might prefer to support existing authoritarian regimes rather than risk their being replaced by hostile Islamic fundamentalist ones. This is the approach that the USA and other western democracies have taken. On the other hand, a democratic Russia and the USA together might be able to more successfully push authoritarian CCA regimes to undertake reforms than the USA has been able to do so far without Russian cooperation.

## Conclusion

Despite their differences, Russia and Iran share certain views about the CCA region which are different from those of at least three of the smaller states. While the Russian and Iranian governments are wary of the prospects for an increased American role in the CCA region, Azerbaijan, Georgia and Kazakhstan would all welcome this in order to reduce the ability of Russia and/or Iran to influence them. Armenia would welcome increased American influence if Washington sided with it in the ongoing dispute over Nagorno-Karabakh, but not if, in the more likely case, this meant closer US–Azeri cooperation over oil. Turkmenistan's idiosyncratic ruler does not appear to want an increased American presence in the region (a more normal government there, though, might welcome this as a counterweight against Russia, Iran and Uzbekistan).

This difference in perspective regarding what role the USA should play in the region has caused a certain amount of tension. Russia and Iran have been particularly concerned about the smaller countries playing the role of 'Trojan Horse' for Washington. But while fears about this ran high in Moscow and Tehran some years ago, they seem to have become less of a concern more recently. This appears to be the result of three factors.

First, there appears to be a realization in both Moscow and Tehran that there are certain problems in the CCA region – such as the rise of Sunni

Islamic fundamentalism, terrorist activity and general criminality (especially associated with the illegal narcotics trade) – which can be more readily addressed with an American presence than without one. Hence Russia cooperated with and Iran acquiesced in American military intervention to overthrow the Taliban, which both Moscow and Tehran regarded as a threat.

Second, while Washington now plays an important role in the CCA region (including in the military realm), it is hardly in a position to displace Russia and Iran there. The 2003 American-led military intervention in Iraq has, among other consequences, shown that the CCA region is not America's only – or its highest – priority.[20] Despite their hopes to the contrary, Washington is neither willing nor able to relieve the smaller states of the region of the necessity of dealing with Moscow and Tehran.

Third, while a few of the smaller CCA states have some of the trappings of democracy, all of them have basically authoritarian governments. Even those smaller states which most want an American presence in the region do not want pressure from the USA to democratize. By contrast, neither Russia nor Iran (both of which have embarked upon democratization, but both of which have strong authoritarian elements in their governing structures) is pushing the smaller states of the region to democratize. All the governments of the region are satisfied with the more-or-less authoritarian status quo, and do not wish to see this disrupted by the USA.

More optimistically, an Iranian–American rapprochement and/or the revival of democracy in Russia could have a strong positive impact on the prospects for reform in the CCA region. Yet while both of these developments are possible, neither seems likely to occur any time soon. That being the case, neither Russia nor Iran appears likely to actively promote reform in the CCA region at present. As Georgia's Rose Revolution showed, however, neither seems actively opposed to a strong internal reform movement in this case. If this same pattern holds true for how Russia and Iran relate to other CCA countries, then neither Moscow nor Tehran will pose an obstacle to strong internal reform movements that might rise up elsewhere.

A final comment is in order regarding the growing tensions between Washington and Tehran since mid-2003 as a result of US government charges that Iran is seeking to acquire nuclear weapons. Tehran has denied these accusations, but they were fueled first by its unwillingness to sign the IAEA Additional Protocol (which would permit nuclear inspections anywhere in Iran), and later by unwillingness to implement it. While the prospects for improved relations between the USA and the Islamic world have virtually disappeared, the prospects for either an American or Israeli attack on Iran's nuclear facilities, as well as heightened internal opposition, appear to have increased.

As with the lead-up to the American-led intervention in Iraq, Moscow cannot seem to decide between supporting and opposing the Bush administration. For example, while British Prime Minister Tony Blair reported a pledge by Putin that Moscow would not ship nuclear fuel to the atomic energy reactor Russia is building for Iran at Bushehr until Tehran signed the IAEA additional protocol, both the Russian foreign minister and energy minister denied that any such link had been made.[21]

If tension mounts, Washington will press the smaller CCA states for various forms of support. Azerbaijan and Georgia are highly likely to cooperate militarily with the USA since the presence of large numbers of American troops on their soil would result in a rapid diminution of Russian influence over them. Armenia, pressed by the Armenian-American diaspora, would probably also cooperate with the USA just so that Baku does not become more important to Washington than Yerevan. Kyrgyzstan and Kazakhstan are also likely to cooperate with Washington, though the American military's need for them *vis-à-vis* Iran will be less than its need for the South Caucasus. Turkmenistan, under its present leadership, will attempt to remain neutral.

If all this transpires (and it is not completely clear yet that it will), the rise of American influence in the CCA region will lead to the further decline of Russian influence there. But while Moscow may not support any American military action against Iran, it certainly will not defend Iran either. Indeed, none of the smaller CCA states will risk siding with Tehran in any Iranian–American confrontation; whether they approve of an American intervention against Iran or not, each is likely to calculate that there is nothing to be gained from allying with the losing side. Thus, if the Iranian–American crisis becomes exacerbated, Iran is likely to lose whatever influence it has in the CCA region until a regime change occurs in Tehran.

## Notes

1 Brenda Shaffer, *Partners in Need: The Strategic Relationship of Russia and Iran* (Washington, DC: Washington Institute for Near East Policy, 2001), pp. 36–37.
2 See articles reprinted in 'Russia Responds to Terrorist Attack on U.S.,' *Current Digest of the Post-Soviet Press* (hereinafter referred to as *CDPSP*), October 10, 2001, pp. 1–6; and articles reprinted in 'Russia's Position on Own Role, Central Asia Evolves,' *CDPSP*, October 17, 2001, pp. 4–6, 12.
3 See, for example, articles reprinted in 'Is U.S. Crowding Russia Out of Central Asia?' *CDPSP*, January 30, 2002, pp. 1–4.
4 Negative Russian views of Turkey are noted in Dmitri Trenin, *The End of Eurasia: Russia on the Border Between Geopolitics and Globalization* (Washington, DC: Carnegie Endowment for International Peace, 2002), p. 281. Negative Iranian views of Turkey are discussed in Shahram Chubin, *Whither Iran? Reform, Domestic Politics and National Security* Adelphi Paper #342 (London: International Institute for Strategic Studies, 2002), pp. 43–44.
5 Thus the Iranian government has not supported the secession of Muslim Chechnya from Russia; A. William Samii, 'Iran and Chechnya: Realpolitik at Work,' *Middle East Policy* 8(1) (March 2001), pp. 48–57.
6 Shaffer, *Partners in Need*, pp. 46–48.
7 On Russian fears about the rise of Islamic fundamentalism, see Trenin, *The End of Eurasia*, pp. 167–200, 279–282.
8 On Iranian fears about the Sunni fundamentalist Taliban in Afghanistan and Osama bin Laden, see Chubin, *Whither Iran?* pp. 44–45. On Sunni fundamentalist

hostility toward Shi'ism, see Fandy, *Saudi Arabia and the Politics of Dissent*, pp. 172–173.

9 Shaffer, *Partners in Need*, pp. 53–57; Natalia Yefimova, ' "New Era of Friendship" with Pakistan,' *The Moscow Times*, February 7, 2003, p. 1; and Stephen Blank, 'The Indian-Iranian Connection and its Importance for Central Asia,' *EurasiaNet*, March 12, 2003.

10 Mark N. Katz, 'Russian-Iranian Relations in the Putin Era,' *Demokratizatsiya* 10(1) (Winter 2002), pp. 71–73.

11 Ibid. See also Michael Lelyveld, 'Iran: Azerbaijan-Kazakhstan Caspian Accord Irks Tehran,' Radio Free Europe/Radio Liberty, December 5, 2001.

12 For a discussion of this by a leading expert on the Caspian in Tehran, see Abbas Maleki, 'What Happened in the South Caspian?' International Institute for Caspian Studies, August 17, 2001. According to one estimate, one field in this area was believed to contain oil reserves of 4 billion barrels. 'Gunboat Diplomacy in the Caspian?' *The Economist*, August 3, 2001.

13 Ruslan Dzkuya and Anatoly Gordiyenko, 'No Success in Overcoming Caspian Disagreements,' *Nezavisimaya Gazeta*, April 7, 2004, p. 5 (*CDPSP*, May 5, 2004, p. 18).

14 Viktoria Panfilova, 'Long Conversations by the Sea: Latest Meeting of Caspian Nations' Diplomats Is Fruitless,' *Nezavisimaya Gazeta*, August 1, 2002, p. 5 (*CDPSP*, August 28, 2002, p. 19).

15 On the export of oil and gas from the Caspian Basin via Russia, see Amy Myers Jaffe and Robert A. Manning, 'Russia, Energy and the West,' *Survival* 43(2) (Summer 2001), pp. 141–143.

16 Mark N. Katz, 'Ivanov's Pursuit of Russian National Interests,' *In the National Interest*, June 2, 2004.

17 Putin reportedly told acting Georgian President Nino Burdzhanadze that as a result of the Rose Revolution in Georgia, 'leaders all over the CIS were "shitting in their pants." ' Peter Bouckaert, 'The Chances of Domino Democracy,' *The Moscow Times*, January 29, 2004, p. 8.

18 This viewpoint has been argued strongly by one of Iran's leading experts on the Caspian: Abbas Maleki, 'Iranian Approaches to the Division of the Caspian Sea,' International Institute for Caspian Studies, January 31, 2001. Western analysts, though, concur. See Laurent Ruseckas, 'Caspian Oil Transportation: Insights from a Commercial Perspective,' *Caspian Crossroads* 3(2) (Fall 1997), p. 13; and Bruce R. Kuniholm, 'The Geopolitics of the Caspian Basin,' *The Middle East Journal* 54(4) (Fall 2000), p. 553.

19 Samuel P. Huntington, *The Third Wave: Democratization in the Late Twentieth Century* (Norman, OK: University of Oklahoma Press, 1991).

20 Konstantin Parshin, 'Iraq War Prompts Most Central Asian Leaders to Reevaluate US Ties,' *EurasiaNet*, April 4, 2003.

21 Sergei Blagov, 'Russia Backs Iran's Nuclear Program Despite International Concern,' *EurasiaNet*, June 9, 2003.

# 13 China, Russia and energy in the CCA region and East Asia[1]

*Charles E. Ziegler*

## China's growing demand for energy imports from diversified stable suppliers

China seeks diversified and reliable energy supplies to fuel its rapidly growing economy, which expanded at 10.3 per cent annually 1990–2000, giving a doubling rate of just under seven years. Rapid economic growth continued into the twenty-first century, with the country posting a 9.1 per cent increase in GDP in 2003. In 1971 China's share in the world's primary energy demand was a mere 5 per cent (with 23 per cent of the world's population). By 2020, the International Energy Agency estimates that China's share of global primary energy demand will be 16 per cent, while its share of global population will have shrunk to 19 per cent.[2] In 2002 alone China's energy demand grew by nearly one-fifth.[3]

Since 1994 China has become a net importer of energy, and while Beijing is promoting the exploration of new oil and gas fields within the PRC, specialists are in agreement that imports will constitute an increasing share of the country's energy consumption. In order to combat air pollution, China's energy strategy calls for decreasing the share of coal in the energy balance from 77.9 per cent in 1995 to around 62 per cent by 2015.[4] Oil and natural gas consumption are expected to rise dramatically, along with nuclear and hydroelectric power (the Three Gorges dam). But China's domestic deposits of oil and gas are limited. Consequently, China's oil companies since 1997 have embarked on an aggressive campaign to secure properties and rights to oil and gas around the world, including in Russia, Kazakhstan and Azerbaijan, as well as Sudan, Indonesia, Iraq, Iran, Venezuela and other countries.

Caucasus and Central Asian and Russian energy resources could help China reduce its dependence on Middle Eastern oil, and thus enhance its security. Pipelines, after all, are a more reliable form of transportation than tankers. At the present time virtually all of China's imported oil and natural gas comes via ocean-going tankers, and their supply routes could be interdicted either at the source (the Strait of Hormuz) or in transit, at the Strait of Malacca.[5] However, the probability of a disruption in deliveries resulting from a conflict or instability in the Middle East is greater than deliberate interference. Fully 50 per cent of China's oil imports come from the Persian Gulf states, making that volatile region vitally important to China. Like the United States, China is seeking to reduce its dependence on Middle Eastern energy. America's strategic domination of the Middle East constitutes an additional vulnerability for China. Beijing's frequent calls for a more multi-polar world order are understandable in the context of the country's vulnerable energy situation.

CCA and Russian fuels are potentially important to China's energy strategy, but Beijing's planners are considering many alternative sources. For China, the Middle East will remain in first place as a supplier of crude oil for the indefinite future. This region has by far the largest reserves, combined with low production costs: $2.50 a barrel compared with $6–10, or even as much as $12 in some areas, for Russian oil.[6] China's foreign policy seeks to preserve amicable relations with the Middle Eastern oil-producing states, while courting additional suppliers who would not impose the Asian surcharge of $1–1.50 per barrel.

CCA and Russian oil occupy the second tier in Chinese priorities. These regions have substantial energy reserves (Table 13.1), and China views the development of these resources as key to its energy security, as a 'strategic backup' or reserve. As Tables 4.2 and 4.5 show, the costs of extraction and transportation of oil are considerably higher for Central Asia than for the Middle East. More importantly, Russia and the Caspian states combined account for less than 8 per cent of the world's reserves, compared with the Middle East's two-thirds. Russia and Central Asia do have a key advantage in natural gas, though, since their reserves, at 31 per cent of the global total, far exceed those of the Persian Gulf states. At present gas accounts for only a small fraction of China's energy needs, but as environmental pressure to use cleaner fuels intensifies and pipelines come on-stream this will change. Russia will likely provide an increasing share of China's energy needs. But in the more distant future, China is also looking to import gas from Turkmenistan, Kazakhstan and Uzbekistan. As Russian and Central Asian gas becomes available via pipelines, it could displace more expensive liquid natural gas (LNG) imported from Indonesia and Australia.[7]

*Table 13.1* Estimated recoverable oil and gas reserves, selected countries 2003

| Country | Oil (billion bls) | Natural gas (trillion m³) |
| --- | --- | --- |
| Azerbaijan | 7.0 | 0.85 |
| Kazakhstan | 9.0 | 1.90 |
| Turkmenistan | 0.5 | 2.90 |
| Uzbekistan | 0.6 | 1.85 |
| Russia | 69.1 | 47.00 |
| China | 23.7 | 1.82 |
| World | 1147.7 | 175.78 |

*Source:* BP (2004) *Statistical Review*, London: BP, 4 and 20.

Chinese energy officials have been hedging their bets over the past few years by acquiring oil and gas properties in South-east Asia, Africa, and Latin America. Projects of varying sizes have been concluded with Central Asian states and Azerbaijan in recent years. Chinese foreign policy favors greater economic regional integration, and envisages the construction of a land bridge linking Central Asia, Russia and China that, unlike the Persian Gulf, would not be hostage to US Naval forces.[8] Energy deals are an important component of regional integration. In 1997 China proposed to invest $9.5 billion to update the Uzen oilfield in Kazakhstan and construct a 3,200 km pipeline from the western province of Aktobe into western China. However, it was unclear whether the Kazakh fields held reserves that would justify such a huge investment, and the Chinese National Petroleum Corporation (CNPC) put the project on hold in 1999.

Reportedly, during Nazarbaev's December 2002 visit to Beijing the Chinese proposed reviving the project. Kazakh energy minister Vladimir Shkolnik stated that construction of a pipeline system that could eventually supply China with up to 1 mbpd of crude was continuing.[9] In May 2004 the Kazakh and Chinese governments signed a $700 million agreement to construct an oil pipeline from Atasu in central Kazakhstan to Xinjiang, with a proposed capacity of 200,000 bpd. Kazakhstan's approach is to divide the 3,000 km route into sections, with the 1,240 km Atasu stretch capable of being linked to the western oil (the Kenkiyak–Atyrau pipeline) at some point in the future. This stage, which is being carried out jointly by KazMunaiGaz and CNPC, will cost only US$700–850 million. When completed (by the end of 2005, if all goes as planned) the pipeline would carry 200,000 bpd to Xinjiang. China then plans to pipe Kazakh crude further eastward to regions that have an energy deficit.[10]

In March 2002 the Chinese company Gun 1 signed a contract with Kyrgyzneftgaz to rehabilitate over 100 idle oil wells, investing $10 million in return for 65 per cent of the oil produced.[11] In 2002 CNPC purchased a share in Azerbaijan's Kursangi and Karabagli oilfields from the EBRD for $52 million, and an additional 20 per cent share from Delta Hess, giving CNPC a 50 per cent share in the Salyan Oil operating company. These fields are estimated to have reserves of 0.75–1.1 billion barrels. SOCAR (the State Oil Company of Azerbaijan) owns the remaining 50 per cent. China plans to invest some $80 million to rehabilitate these old onshore oil deposits, drilling new wells and expanding existing ones.[12] Early in 2003 CNPC announced it would acquire a substantial share in Azerbaijan's onshore project Canub-Qarb Qobustan.[13]

China's interest in the CCA region has been welcomed, albeit a bit warily, by the region's leadership, but Russian and western oil companies are less enthusiastic. Efforts by the China Petroleum and Chemical Corporation (Sinopec) and China's National Offshore Oil Company (CNOOC) to acquire a 16.67 per cent share in the North Caspian Sea PSA foundered in May 2003 when five of the six partners – Shell, Exxon-Mobil, France's TotalFinaElf,

Conoco Phillips and Italy's ENI – exercised their pre-emption rights to purchase shares from British Gas. Had the Chinese companies succeeded in their bid, they would have acquired a significant share in one of the world's largest fields, which includes the huge Kashagan oilfield in addition to several others.

Reportedly, the Kazakh government enthusiastically supported China's involvement in the project.[14] When the Chinese bid was stymied the Kazakh government signaled its intention to purchase the British Gas stake, asserting that Kazakh law trumped the consortium's right of first refusal. The Kazakh government is seeking greater control over its energy resources, by raising the share of the state oil and gas company KazMunaiGaz in the country's production. At present KazMunaiGaz controls only 20 per cent of Kazakhstan's oil output. In addition, the government wants more diverse outlets for its oil, and favors routes through Iran despite opposition from the United States and Russia.[15]

Natural gas is a resource that has the potential to link China more closely with Central Asia, Russia and its own western frontiers. Natural gas is important to China's development plans, but less so than oil. As of 2002, only 3.1 per cent of China's energy balance was accounted for by gas (compared with 24.5 per cent for oil), but that share is expected to nearly double by 2010. China has significant domestic gas reserves (estimated at 53.3 Tcf in 2004), and the government plans to supplement this with imported pipeline gas and LNG.

China inaugurated the domestic West-to-East Pipeline in July 2002 as one of several major projects that Beijing is promoting to increase the supply of natural gas flowing to power generation plants in the more populated and developed coastal areas. Originating in the Xinjiang-Uighur autonomous republic, the pipeline will cover some 4,000 km en route to Shanghai, and is estimated to cost $8.9 billion. China's domestic companies PetroChina and Sinopec hold 50 per cent and 5 per cent stakes respectively in the project, and Russia's Gazprom had a 15 per cent stake in the venture. The Chinese were at first opposed to Gazprom's participation in the project, but then relented. Royal Dutch/Shell and ExxonMobil also have substantial shares in the pipeline. Russian companies may anticipate linking into the pipeline at some point in the future in order to expand the export market for Siberian natural gas, but such integration is presently a low priority for Chinese planners.

Exporting gas to China is a good long-term bet for Russia, but it may also be feasible for Central Asia. Russia has the reserves to supply China for decades, and Chinese demand will continue to grow. The BP Kovykta gas pipeline would supply both south-eastern China and South Korea at a total cost of $10–12 billion. In this context, Chinese specialists often refer to Central Asia as a 'strategic backup' to present suppliers. A gas pipeline from Turkmenistan would cost roughly the same, but without major foreign investors it may not be feasible in the near future. Chinese companies are more interested in small-scale joint ventures in Turkmenistan: in early 2003 there were nineteen Chinese projects valued at $210 million in the Turkmen oil and gas sectors.[16]

Regional trade outside the field of energy is also important to China. For example, in 2000, 76.3 per cent of China's imports from Kazakhstan consisted of metals, while crude oil accounted for only 16 per cent.[17] Xinjiang imports raw materials such as cotton, fertilizer, metal and ores from Central Asia, while the Central Asian states, particularly Kazakhstan, provide a lucrative market for Chinese finished goods.[18] Rail and road links are being expanded in an effort to build a new Silk Road. Integrating China's western regions into the Central Asian regional economy is part of Beijing's strategy to develop the poorer periphery. Moreover, as Chapter 9 argues, such trade offers the most immediate economic benefits for the Central Asian countries. Although trade between China and Central Asia tripled in the decade after the collapse of the Soviet Union, it remained below US$2 billion, or less than 0.5 per cent of China's total annual trade turnover. Some two-thirds of this is border trade with Xinjiang province. Limitations on economic integration include low levels of regional development, poor infrastructure and forbidding terrain.[19]

Securing reliable and diversified energy supplies will be central to China's security in coming decades. As a net energy importer, China has a stake in the stability of neighboring oil and gas producing regions. China's leaders are determined to maintain economic growth rates and maintain domestic stability. However, the development of energy resources in Xinjiang-Uighur Autonomous Region could exacerbate the already tense relations between Uighurs and Han Chinese, as more of the latter migrate into Xinjiang in connection with energy projects. In addition, increased reliance on Central Asian energy, together with trade in foodstuffs, clothing and minerals, and the opening of road and rail links, also raises the risk that destabilizing influences will seep into China from émigré Uighur communities.[20] China's strategic interests therefore act as a constraint on Central Asian policies.

China's primary concern in the Central Asian region is to prevent destabilizing factors such as terrorism, separatism, religious extremism, weapons smuggling and narcotics trafficking from affecting China internally. The Muslim Uighur population in Xinjiang, numbering eight million, has connections to Uighurs living in Kazakhstan and Kyrgyzstan, and China fears talk of the re-creation of a Greater East Turkestan. China's strategy seems designed to establish a 'social contract' in western China (as in the other border provinces) to promote economic development in exchange for political quiescence. Closer economic integration with the Central Asian states in the form of rail, road and air links, oil and gas pipelines and electrical grids is part of this strategy.[21]

## Russian interests and Chinese–CCA relations

Geographically, Russia is ideally positioned to exploit the huge energy reserves in its eastern lands, but must struggle to control the flow of oil and gas from the south. Along its eastern borders are the energy-consuming economic powerhouses China, Japan and South Korea; to the south are energy producers Kazakhstan, Azerbaijan and Turkmenistan. Competitors toward the east are scarce, while the south is awash in hydrocarbons. The energy mix in East Asia provides a strong imperative for functional integration, which is missing in the CCA region.

Russia is one of the world's largest exporters of crude oil and natural gas. After a sharp decline in production and exports resulting from the Soviet break-up, Russian oil exports increased from 3.2 mbpd in 1993 to 4.8 million bpd in 2001. In 2002 Russia's overall production approached that of Saudi Arabia and averaged about 8.4 million bpd in 2003.[22] This shift partly reflected the fall in domestic consumption, which halved from 1991 to 2003 (2.5 million bpd).[23] In addition, demand for oil is strong in Western Europe and supplies are limited; Russia consequently provides about one-fifth of the region's oil. Russia has for years supplied one-quarter of Western Europe's natural gas needs.

Revenues from oil exports were key to Russia's improved economic performance during 1999–2004. The Putin administration attaches high priority to using Russia's natural resources and technological capabilities efficiently, to enhance economic growth and modernization. Since energy resources are a major source of revenue, the government is seeking to maximize exports, and bring domestic prices more in line with world market prices. Moreover, Moscow is reinvigorating the country's nuclear energy program, which stalled after Chernobyl. By supplying a larger percentage of its domestic demand for electricity from nuclear power, Russia can free up more oil and natural gas for export.[24] The government's nuclear energy program, adopted in May 2000, calls for $15 billion of investment in the nuclear power sector by 2010, and an increase in the Ministry of Atomic Energy's (Minatom's) share of electricity production from 15 per cent to 40 per cent.

Energy exports are critical for the Russian government – energy accounted for approximately 40 per cent of the country's export earnings in 2001, rising to fully half in 2002. According to the World Bank, Russia's oil and gas sector generated about 20 per cent of real gross domestic product, far more than the 9 per cent attributed to it by official Russian statistics.[25] These ratios confirm the status of Russia as a mineral economy, with all the risks that poses. The UN's Economic Commission for Europe, for example, warned that Russia is susceptible to 'Dutch Disease,' with ruble appreciation poised to harm the competitiveness of domestic manufacturers.[26] In the long term, Russian policy seeks to diversify and modernize its energy structure, to avoid the pitfalls of excessive dependence on raw materials. Economics Minister German Gref's blueprint for sustainable growth calls for increased taxes on energy exports and promotion of finished commodities in Russia's trade structure.[27]

In a shorter time frame, Russia must capitalize on high energy prices and uncertainty in the Middle East and other oil-producing regions to establish the infrastructure for further exports. This means building pipelines to China, and finding alternative pipeline routes and terminals in the western part of the Russian Federation. Consequently, a major component of Russia's energy strategy is to expand the network of oil and gas pipelines running east and west, in order to maximize the country's export earnings and sustain the recent momentum of positive economic growth rates.

### The pipelines west

Russia under Putin has followed a policy of attempting to control the flow of oil and gas from the CCA region westward, using possession of the post-Soviet pipeline infrastructure and the landlocked status of Central Asian nations as leverage. The United States favors Central Asian/Caspian pipelines that skirt Russia if possible, and is adamant that oil and gas should not run through Iran. American and other western companies have the greatest resources to invest, and their financial leverage is backed by the military capabilities of the United States. China cannot match the infrastructure or the military strength of Russia and the West, but it does have increasing amounts of disposable capital to invest. Moreover, China provides an alternative market that is attractive to Central Asian and Caspian regimes. However, it would be misleading to suggest that the interests of the major actors – Russia, China, the USA and the Central Asian states – are solely competitive.

For example, the Caspian Pipeline Consortium illustrates the degree to which the economic interests of Russia, Kazakhstan, the United States and other western firms are linked. Construction of the CPC, involving a total capital investment of $3.5 billion, is the biggest single foreign investment project in Russia. It was built between May 1999 and October 2001. By the end of 2002 some 0.26 mbpd was flowing through the pipeline to the terminal in Novorossiysk, with plans to increase the flow to 0.6–0.7 mbpd by the end of the decade. The pipeline is 1,504 km long, starting at the Tengizchevroil facility in Kazakhstan and running north of the Caspian Sea, passing through southern Russian, and terminating in Novorossiysk on the Black Sea. CPC utilized and upgraded the existing pipeline from Tengiz to Komsomolsk, building the additional section from Komosomolsk to Novorossiysk (Figure 13.1). The pipeline system uses the latest SCADA (Supervisory Control and Data Acquisition) technology. Fiber optic cables buried along the pipeline allow remote monitoring from the central control facilities in Novorossiysk, with backup controls at the Kropotkin pumping station, to ensure safe operation and prevent tampering with the pipeline.[28]

The CPC is a complex multinational project, originally made up of

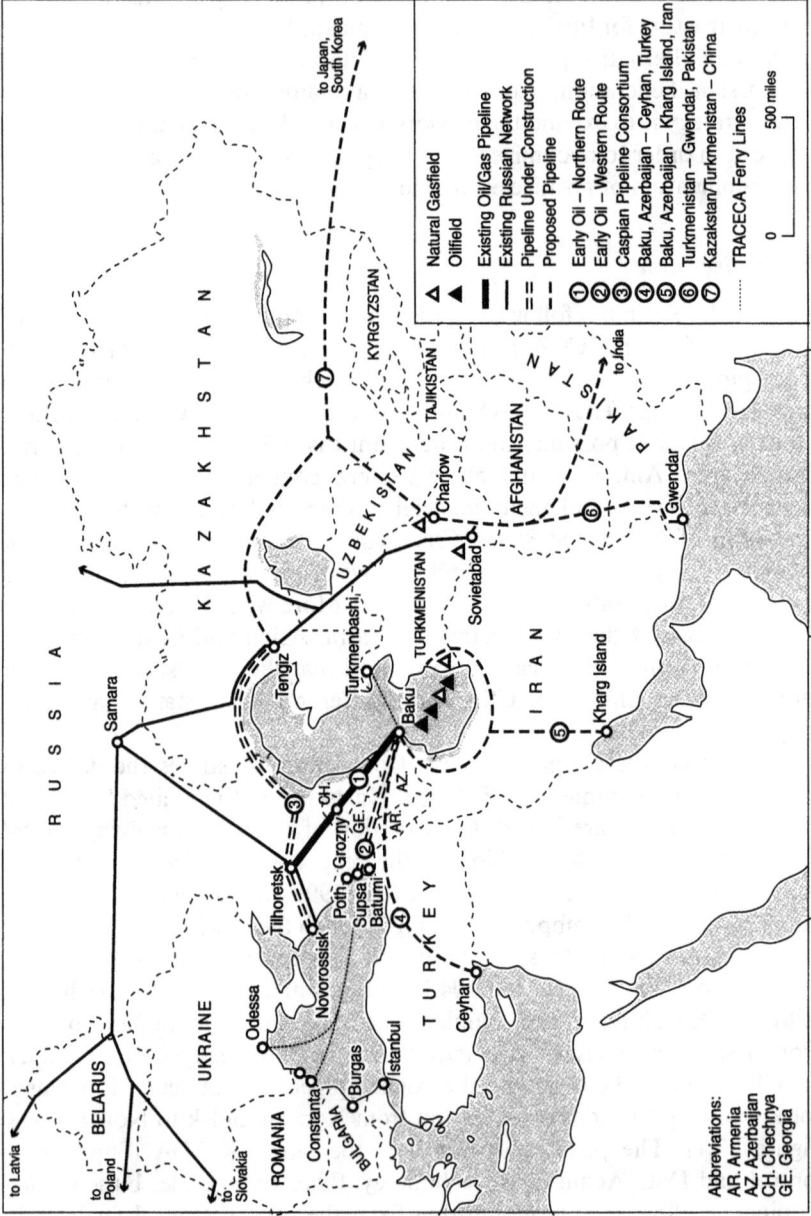

*Figure 13.1* Oil and natural gas export infrastructure of the Caucasus and Central Asia.

three governments and ten companies.[29] For Russia, the CPC provides a much-needed source of revenue. It is expected that the CPC will generate over $20 billion in taxes over the next 40 years.[30] While no Russian oil at present is being exported through the CPC, plans are eventually to transport some 0.144 mbpd of Russian oil through the pipeline, by linking a Samara-to-Kropotkin spur. In addition, Karachaganak's KIO consortium, made up of British Gas, Agip, ChevronTexaco and Lukoil, is investing $3.5 billion to raise output in this northern Kazakh field, and plans to build a new 600 km pipeline spur southward to hook up with the CPC pipeline. This would raise Kazakh deliveries to 0.36 mbpd.[31]

Problems arose: in November 2002 ChevronTexaco and the Kazakh government were involved in a dispute over a $3 billion expansion project at Tengiz. ChevronTexaco, which owns 50 per cent of the Tengiz venture (ExxonMobil owns 25 per cent, KazMunaiGaz 20 per cent and LukArco 5 per cent ) announced suspension of the planned expansion because of the partners' inability to agree on a funding plan.[32] In 1999 the Kazakh government had enacted legislation revising conditions for extracting mineral resources; Tengizchevroil was simply the most visible of some 200 contracts affected by that legislation.[33] Western observers speculated that the furor would damage the investment climate in Kazakhstan, which has attracted the largest foreign investment in Central Asia. Still, the stakes were high enough that the two sides reached an accommodation by January 2003, with the consortium agreeing to pay an additional $810 million in taxes and help KazMunaiGaz finance its share of expansion costs. The expansion is planned to increase production from 260,000 bpd to about 460,000 bpd by mid-2006.[34]

While the Russian central government welcomed the CPC project, the regional population was skeptical. Attitudes in Kazakhstan were likewise skeptical about Tengizchevroil. Much of the difficulty in both countries stems from the central government's reluctance to include local and regional governments in planning and operations. Security-conscious CPC officials and workers were secretive about the construction process. The area is seismically active, and there are fears a major earthquake could rupture the pipeline.[35] The CPC terminal was constructed to the west of the city, in the popular resort area of Iuzhnaia ozerka. Consortium officials declined to consider running the pipeline to the port of Novorossiysk, where the Sheskharis (Chernomorsktransneft Black Sea Oil Transport Company) state-owned oil facilities are located, preferring instead to exercise full control over the operation.

Russia is able to maintain a foothold in the CCA region by virtue of its energy links and its security ties to the region. Putin has played on these strengths. One example is Moscow's support for Gazprom, which has managed to consolidate control over virtually all gas exports from the region. Another example is Moscow's efforts on regional security through the Shanghai Cooperation Organization (SCO). In June 2004 the leaders of the six member nations – Russia, China, Kazakhstan, Uzbekistan, Kyrgyzstan and Tajikistan – met in Tashkent to inaugurate the group's Regional Anti-terrorist Center, to be located in the Uzbek capital. Putin emphasized the extent to which Russia was rebuilding its ties with Central Asia, and specifically Uzbekistan, the country most affected by Islamic terrorism.

But China has also used the SCO to extend and consolidate its influence in Central Asia, perhaps even more effectively than has Russia. Chinese President Hu Jintao spent a total of five days in Uzbekistan, and signed ten separate agreements with Uzbek President Islam Karimov. The Chinese side reportedly promised US$1.25 billion in economic assistance to Uzbekistan, the largest aid package ever granted to any country at one time.[36] Like Russia (and for that matter the United States), China is determined to preserve stability in the region. For Beijing, the chief worry is Uighur separatism in Xinjiang province, and their supporters in Central Asia. In 2003 the SCO staged its first anti-terrorist exercises in Kazakhstan and China.

However, China views Russia as a power in decline in Central Asia, and seems to be positioning itself to challenge Russia there. Shortly after the SCO summit CNPC signed a cooperation pact with Uzbekneftegaz, Uzbekistan's national oil and gas company, to conduct exploration work within the country.[37] China has also moved to broaden its participation in Kazakhstan energy projects, by purchasing the entire North Buzachi oil and gas field from Chevron Texaco, and acquiring 63 per cent of the Aktobe field. While Chinese companies are moving aggressively to secure contracts, officials in Beijing, concerned above all with promoting stability, are moving cautiously on the political front.

Central Asia's oil and gas are important for China to maintain its high levels of economic growth and thus to maintain stable development. For China, the Shanghai Cooperation Organization is one means of accomplishing its goal of securing Central Asian support for China's integrity, both in Xinjiang and in Taiwan. Central Asian, Russian and Chinese leaders have stressed the role of the Shanghai Cooperation Organization as a forum to contain the threat of Islamic terrorism. But since multilateral institution-building has proved difficult, China still attributes importance to its relationship with Russia. Beijing's Russia policy, while not without tensions in Central Asia and the Caspian, is vital to China's foreign policy goals, chief among them balancing US influence in that part of the world. To the extent that Russian and Chinese presence in Central Asia stabilizes the region, there is no reason why either should seek to deny the other a role.

### The pipelines east

East Asia's growing demand for energy makes it a natural market for Russian oil and gas. The eastern Siberian fields near Irkutsk, which can also be linked into the west Siberian fields, are prime candidates for exploitation to develop exports eastward.[38] Russia currently supplies a limited amount of crude oil to

China. Yukos exported about 105,000 bpd by rail in 2003, a substantial increase from the 27,000 bpd exported in 2002.[39] At the July 2001 Sino-Russian summit the two sides pledged to construct a 2,400 km pipeline from Angarsk to the Daqing oil center by 2005 (Figure 13.2). But the political troubles of Yukos with tax evasion charges in 2004 have put the project on hold indefinitely.

The Daqing route would have given Moscow much-needed geostrategic clout with China, but it reduced Russia's options and made its potential earnings hostage to developments in a risky environment.[40] North-east China is a logical termination point for the pipeline, since the infrastructure (particularly refineries) and labor force are already in place. This variant would also have significantly strengthened the regional economies of Irkutsk and Chita oblasts, and the Buriat Republic. One estimate predicted the creation of around 3,000 construction jobs and 1,700 specialist positions. And the combined annual revenue for the federal and local budgets from the project was estimated at $1.5 billion.[41]

However, construction of the Daqing pipeline would have done little to ease the chronic energy shortages in the Russian Far East, as long as domestic prices remain artificially low, nor would Russia have been able to market the oil to any country other than China. The route that Moscow seems close to approving is a 4,000 km oil pipeline from Angarsk to a terminal in Perevoznaia Bay near Nakhodka (Figure 13.2). The Perevoznaia route would fuel development in the Russian Far East, and thus fits nicely with Putin's goal of raising the standard of living in depressed areas. It also provides Russia with greater marketing flexibility, since the oil could be loaded on to tankers and then be exported to Japan, South Korea, Taiwan or the United States. To placate the Chinese, Putin has indicated that a spur would be constructed to Daqing.

This route is expensive, but Japan has offered to underwrite much of the cost. At a peak capacity of one million barrels of oil per day, the pipeline would allow Japan to reduce its dependence on Middle Eastern oil by 10 per cent or more, from its current 90 per cent. Japan would also avoid the $1–1.50 Asian premium that is usually charged by Middle Eastern producers.[42] In addition to providing great energy security for Japan, the Japanese hinted that Russia should choose the longer route as a means of counterbalancing China's growing power in East Asia.

On the natural gas front, Russia and China are planning a major pipeline to run from the Kovykta field north of Irkutsk eastward to the Pacific coast. The Kovykta field, reportedly the largest gas condensate deposit in the world, will be developed by a joint venture led by Russia Petroleum, a private company with controlling shares held by the BP/TNK venture. Described as one of the largest gas projects in the world, the huge distances involved, through rugged terrain and inhospitable climate zones, will make construction of the pipeline expensive. BP has estimated the project will command a total investment of $10–12 billion.[43]

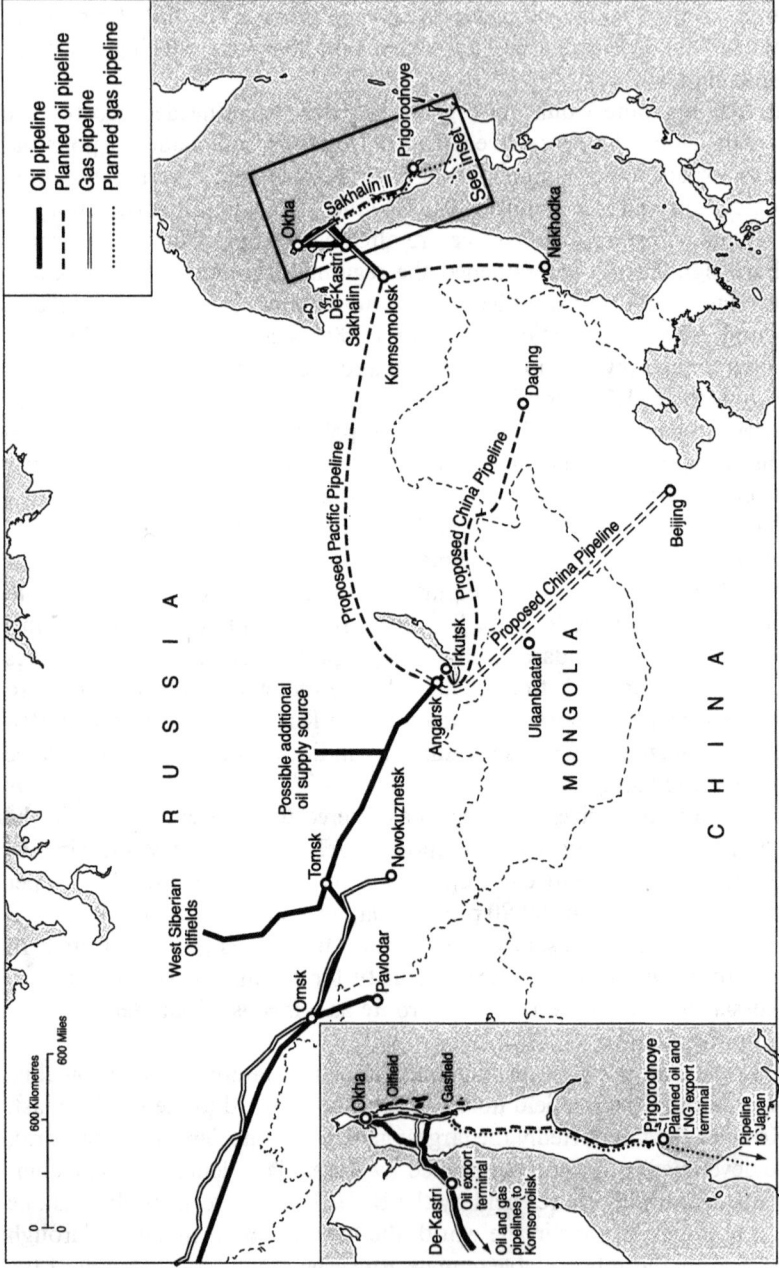

*Figure 13.2* Selected existing and proposed oil and gas infrastructure in Russia's Far East.

Complications over pipeline routes and a perceived breach of promise angered Beijing and undercut promises of 'strategic partnership' between the two countries. Moscow's peremptory treatment of China has made Russia appear to be an unreliable oil supplier. Central Asian-Caucasus energy resources have therefore become more attractive to Beijing, and may in part explain China's renewed interest in bringing the Kazakhstan pipeline to completion.

## Chinese and Russian economic influence on the CCA region

Chinese policy towards Central Asia is more coherent than that of Russia, although the central government does not appear fully to control the country's oil giants, whose interests are more short-term and profit-driven than those of the government. These internal divisions, and the competitive tension among China, Russia and the United States, give the smaller resource-rich states considerable leverage, assuming the leaders are skilled enough bargainers, or not totally venal. But unfortunately regional officials may be both: Niyazov's twenty-five year contract to provide Russia and Ukraine with natural gas at concessionary rates is a prime example.[44]

Central Asian officials welcome Chinese trade and investment in their economies, and view China as a factor for economic growth in the region. They also promote a regional security role for China through the SCO. And yet many in Central Asia are wary of China's growing influence. Perhaps the greatest potential threat is to Kazakhstan, which shares a long border with China (over 1,700 km), has by far the largest territory in the region and the greatest store of raw materials, and is the most sparsely populated. While much has been written about the impact of Central Asia's Muslim resurgence on Xinjiang, few scholars have considered the impact of a massive influx of Chinese into Central Asia. Kazakhstan has a population of only 15 million, of which about eight million are ethnic Kazakh, so Chinese immigrants could quickly alter the cultural balance in this new nation. The number of Han Chinese in Xinjiang province, for example, increased from 5.3 to 7.5 million in just eighteen years, from 1982 to 2000. Pipeline projects and other forms of economic cooperation could bring large numbers of Chinese into Central Asia, leading to ethnic tensions.[45]

The resource-poor states in the region – Armenia, Georgia, Tajikistan and Kyrgyzstan – have little to offer their larger neighbors other than military basing rights, and so are in a much weaker position than Kazakhstan, Turkmenistan or Uzbekistan. Moreover, as described in Chapter 11, Russia has a clear strategic interest in the Caucasus region, and a record of manipulating conflicts there (in Nagorno-Karabagh, South Ossetia and Abkhazia) to its advantage. China's interests in the Caucasus appear to be purely economic and limited largely to Azerbaijan, and their investments there are modest. In the Caucasus Russia carries far more weight, for better or worse, than does China.

Both Russia and China are actively pursuing a policy of integration into the international economy. Russia is committed to an active, multifaceted foreign policy in which economics is a top priority.[46] Like China, Russia is trying to overcome the isolationist legacy of its communist past. Joining the World Trade Organization and opening up to foreign investment in various spheres, particularly energy, will be critically important in domestic development and in foreign economic relations. Increasing cooperation in both the Caspian and East Asia will help develop the economic potential of Russia's less prosperous southern and eastern regions.

In Russia's relations with the CCA oil and gas producing states there are both competitive and cooperative elements. More than a decade of efforts to reintegrate the former Soviet space through the Commonwealth of Independent States has largely failed, whether along political, security or economic dimensions.[47] Energy development in the CCA region is not likely to lead to cooperation as in East Asia. Russian oil companies will benefit from increased production to the extent that they partner with Westerners and Central Asians, as in the CPC or the North Caspian Production Sharing Agreement. State monopolies and the Russian government will benefit from increases in Caspian production if they can ensure that oil and gas pipelines are routed northward. Gazprom, for example, negotiated natural gas transit agreements with each of the Central Asian countries in 2002–3 as part of its strategy of controlling the flow of gas from Central Asia to Europe. These moves strengthen Russia's political influence in the region, while padding the state treasury.

Expanded and more diversified energy supplies favor China's interests, as they do those of the United States. Consequently, Russia finds itself in fierce competition for a market – the Mediterranean littoral – that has ample supplies of oil and natural gas. In the Caspian region Russia is both a supplier, and a transit country. In some cases, most notably the Caspian Pipeline Consortium, Russia has found ways to turn Caspian regional energy production to its advantage. In other cases – the Baku–Tblisi–Ceyhan pipeline is the prime example – the Russian government and oil interests have vigorously opposed efforts to marginalize Russia's role.

Beyond the oil issues, Russia and China, and the United States, have common interests in keeping the CCA region politically and economically stable. The threat from radical Muslim organizations in the region may have been temporarily curtailed by the US military campaign in Afghanistan, but Chechnya and Xinjiang remain serious problem areas for Moscow and Beijing, respectively. With the US move into Central Asia, Moscow and Beijing have seen their influence in the region diminished. Moscow's position is relatively stronger, given Putin's close cooperation with Washington on terrorism, but opposition from both countries to a US-led invasion of Iraq may be interpreted as resistance to American encroachment, and fear of further regional destabilization. The new Treaty Organization on Collective Security, comprised of Russia, Armenia, Belarus, Kazakhstan, Kyrgyzstan and Tajikistan, should be interpreted as a Russian effort to constrain US influence in the region, notwithstanding the organization's overt mandate to counter terrorism and narcotics trafficking.[48]

China and Russia prefer to handle terrorism and other threats to the central Eurasian heartland through multilateral forums. However, neither Moscow nor Beijing has addressed the repressive domestic policies being pursued by all Central Asian leaders, which, in the long term risk strengthening the hands of Islamic militants and jeopardizing the productive development of regional energy resources. Succession crises may well prove to be the most destabilizing events in Central Asia and the Caucasus, but there is little evidence that Russian or Chinese leaders recognize the problem, or are willing to deal with it.

## Notes

1 Research for this chapter was supported in part by a grant from the International Research and Exchanges Board (IREX) with funds provided by the National Endowment for the Humanities, the United States Department of State through the Title VIII Program, and the IREX Scholar Support Fund, which supported a research trip to Russia in October–November 2002 and Kazakhstan in 2003. None of these organizations is responsible for the views expressed. Additional support was provided by a University of Louisville IRIG grant. I would also like to thank the following for their kind help with this project: Sergei Chugrov, Tatiana Klepikova, Olga Musikhina, Oleg Voronin, Sergei Lounev, Zha Daojiong, Kazbek Kazkenov and Ambassador Bolatkhan Taizhan. I am greatly indebted to Richard Auty for his incisive editorial comments.
2 *China's Worldwide Quest for Energy Security*, International Energy Agency, 2000, 14.
3 *Economist*, 21 June 2003.
4 Gao Shixian, 'China,' in *Rethinking Energy Security in East Asia*, Paul B. Stares, ed. (Tokyo: Japan Center for International Exchange, 2000), 48.
5 Sergei Troush, 'China's Changing Oil Strategy and its Foreign Policy Implications,' CNAPS Working Paper, Fall 1999.
6 Mark N. Katz, 'Big Decisions Loom for Russian Oil Production,' EurasiaNet.org (26 November 2001). (http://www.eurasianet.org/departments/business/articles/eav112601.shtml). Middle East producers, however, do add a $1–$1.50 per barrel surcharge to oil shipped to Asia.
7 Shell Vice President F.K. Lung calculates that pipeline gas is generally cheaper if the distances involved are less than 3,000 km. Between 3,000 and 9,000 km LNG and gas offer similar prices, depending on construction costs, and beyond 9,000 km LNG is cheaper than piped gas. F.K. Lung, 'Clean Fossil Energy – Roles for Natural Gas and Coal,' (http://apec-egcfe.fossil.energy.gov/7thtech/p206.pdf).
8 Amy Meyers Jaffe, 'The Potential of Energy as a Geopolitical Binding Factor in Asia,' *Post-Soviet Geography and Economics* 42(7) (2001), 499.
9 Interfax-Kazakhstan, in Global News Wire-Asia Africa Intelligence Wire (29 January 2003). The perception that a Kazakhstan to China pipeline would eventually be constructed was reinforced by a series of interviews conducted in Kazakhstan in June 2003.
10 Michael Lelyveld, 'Kazakhstan, China Revive Pipeline Deal,' *Middle East Economic Survey* 47, 19 July 2004 (http://www.mees.com/postedarticles/oped/a47n29d01.htm).

11 Caspian News Agency (22 March 2002), http://www.caspian.ru/cgi/eng/article.cgi?id=5508.
12 Turan News Agency, in BBC Monitoring Asia Pacific – Political (13 February 2003); Global News Wire (13 February 2003).
13 BBC Monitoring International Reports (28 January 2003).
14 Dan Roberts, 'Western Oil Majors Flex Their Muscles,' *Financial Times* (10 May 2003); Lina Saigol, 'Battle Lines Drawn for Caspian Oil,' *Financial Times* (8 May 2003); AFX European Focus (7 and 12 May 2003). The sixth partner in the joint venture, Japan's Inpex, declined to increase its stake.
15 Ibragim Alibekov, 'Kazakhstan Asserts State Interests in Kashagan Oil,' Eurasianet.org (http://www.eurasianet.org/departments/business/articles/eav070904.shtml).
16 ITAR-TASS (16 February 2003).
17 Calla Wiemer, 'The Economy of Xinjiang,' in S. Frederick Starr, ed., *Xinjiang: China's Muslim Borderland* (Armonk, NY: M.E. Sharpe, 2004), 185.
18 Kazakhstan accounts for just over half of Xinjiang's two-way trade; Kyrgyzstan for an additional 7.6 per cent. Wiemer, 182. Xinjiang has growth rates above China's national average, and the province currently sends half its production to other parts of China. Xinjiang also has surplus refinery capacity. Spechler, 'Crouching Dragon, Hungry Tigers.'
19 Chien-Peng Chung, 'The Defense of Xinjiang: Politics, Economics and Security in Central Asia,' *Harvard International Review* (Summer 2003), 56–62; Bates Gill and Matthew Oresman, *China's New Journey to the West: China's Emergence in Central Asia and its Implications for U.S. Interests* (Washington, DC: CSIS Press, August 2003), 28–30.
20 See Martin C. Spechler, 'Crouching Dragon, Hungry Tigers: China and Central Asia,' *Contemporary Economic Policy* 21 (April 2003), 270–280.
21 Kyrgyzstan is seeking Chinese and Russian investment to complete several hydro-electric projects started during the Soviet era. Power would be exported to Western China and Siberia, and possibly Pakistan, earning Kyrgyzstan valuable foreign currency. Kyrgyz television, in BBC Global Newswire – Asia Africa Intelligence Wire, 29 August 2002; Interfax, 24 April 2003.
22 Russia Country Analysis Brief, Energy Information Administration, US Department of Energy (http://www.eia.doe.gov/emeu/cabs/russia.html).
23 Testimony of Edward C. Chow before the Senate Committee on Foreign Relations Subcommittee on International Economic Policy, 30 April 2003 (Federal News Service).
24 Charles E. Ziegler and Henry B. Lyon, 'The Politics of Nuclear Waste in Russia,' *Problems of Post-Communism* 49 (July–August 2002), 38.
25 The discrepancy is caused by transfer pricing, where Russian companies sell product to offshore trading companies at below-market prices. The trading companies then resell the oil at world market prices, avoiding taxes and ensuring the full value of the resource is not included in national accounts. Russian Economic Report, February 2004 (www.worldbank.org.ru).
26 Economic Survey of Europe 2004 No. 2, United Nations Economic Commission for Europe (http://unece.org/press/pr2004/04gen_p12e.htm).
27 Victoria Lavrentieva, 'Gref Says It's Time to Squeeze Big Oil,' *The Moscow Times* (20 February 2003). Putin's more pragmatic approach led to an effective resolution of the problem in 2001, with Russia agreeing to restructure the debt and Ukraine agreeing to end illegal siphoning.
28 I am indebted to Brian Isert, Technology Manager at the CPC terminal in Novorossiysk, for a tour of the facilities in November 2002.
29 Russia, Kazakhstan and ten private companies comprise a consortium

that owns the pipeline. The companies that own the field are ChevronTexaco, KazMunaiGaz, ExxonMobil and LukArco.

30 *Pipeline News Notes*, Vol. 2 (21 June 2001), www.anvilpub.com/2q2001.htm

31 *Financial Times*, 'Survey – Kazakhstan: Substantial Quantities of Oil Could One Day Worry OPEC,' 17 December 2001 (http://surveys.ft.com/kazakhstan2001/). Personal interview with Amanbay Kassanov, Operational Excellence Lead Consultant for Project Operations, Tengizchevroil, Kazakhstan, 12 June 2003.

32 Mark Berkiner, 'A Troubled Project Holds Warnings for Kazakhstan's Oil Sector,' Eurasianet.org (www.eurasianet.org/departments/business/articles/eav111902_pr.shtml).

33 Personal interview with K.S. Maulenov, Almaty, 5 June 2003. Also, see K.S. Maulenov, *Neftianoe pravo respubliki Kazakhstan i zarubezhnyikh stran* (Almaty: Daneker, 2003), 57–67.

34 Eduard Gismatullin, 'Chevron Ends Kazakh Dispute,' *Financial Post* (28 January 2003).

35 In November an earthquake registering 5.0 on the Richter scale shook the region, but there was no damage to the pipeline. Personal communication from Brian Isert.

36 BBC Monitoring International Reports, 1 July 2004, citing *Nezavisimaya gazeta* 30 June 2004.

37 *Financial Times* (21 June 2004).

38 Russia is also counting on alternate routes westward, primarily the Baltic Pipeline System, which will terminate at Primorsk on the Gulf of Finland. However, discussion of the BPS is beyond the scope of this chapter.

39 Lelyveld, 'Kazakhstan, China Revive Pipeline Deal.'

40 Workers in the declining Daqing oilfields held massive protests over layoffs, reductions in pensions, and low wages in spring 2002. A steady inflow of Russian crude oil would reinvigorate the regional economy by supplying China's refineries, which now have excess capacity, and by promoting domestic stability would be of great value to Chinese officials.

41 Dmitrii Karpov, 'Rossiisko-Kitaiskii nefteprovod: ne tol'ko biznes, no i bol'shaia politika,' *Nezavisimaia gazeta* (16 September 2002).

42 *Financial Times* (11 January 2003), 7; AFP (11 and 15 January 2003); James Brooke, 'Koizume Visits Energy-Rich Russian Region,' *The New York Times* (13 January 2003), 3.

43 Proekt postavok Kovyktinskogo gaza v severo-vostochnyiu Aziiu, nd. Official report of the consortium. I am indebted to Peter Henshaw, VP of British Petroleum-Russia, for a copy of this report. BP's decision to invest $6.75 billion in a joint venture with TNK is an indication of the company's long-term commitment to the Russian energy sector. Catherine Bolton, 'BP Strikes Record $6.75 Bln TNK Deal,' *The Moscow Times* (12 February 2003).

44 The fixed price agreed to was $44 per thousand cubic meters, well below the world market price of $100–110, but well above Russia's price of about $16. Russia's strategy is to sell the cheaper Turkmen gas domestically while exporting its own gas to Europe. Marat Gurt, 'Niyazov Pitches $1 Bln Gas Line to Russia,' *The Moscow Times* (14 April 2003).

45 These concerns were raised in discussions with Kazakh officials in 2003 and 2004.

46 Igor S. Ivanov, *The New Russian Diplomacy* (Washington, DC: The Nixon Center and Brookings Institution Press, 2002).

47 Martha Brill Olcott, Anders Aslund, and Sherman W. Garnett, *Getting It Wrong: Regional Cooperation and the Commonwealth of Independent States* (Washington, DC: Carnegie Endowment for International Peace, 1999).

48 Ibragim Alibekov and Sergei Blagov, 'Novaia organizatsiia bezopastnosti mozhet usilit' vliianie Rossii v Srednei Azii' (2 May 2003), (www.eurasianet.org/r ... tments/insight/articles/eav043003ru.shtml).

# 14 The effectiveness of western leverage
## IFI projects and programs

*Robinder Bhatty and Richard M. Auty*

Although there have been instances during the transition to market where western financial assistance has elicited economic and, occasionally, political reform within the CCA region, the momentum has tended to flag and the political regimes have regressed, with one or two exceptions. This is so, even though the leverage of the international financial institutions (IFIs) strengthened in several of the Central Asian countries as a consequence of sharply rising external debt. Chapters 7 and 8 have argued that opposition to reform is rooted in a combination of the general absence of serious challenges to the political power of the incumbent elite and the legacy of dependent social capital from central planning within the FSU. This combination has helped to consolidate authoritarian regimes, which maintain their power through long-established patronage systems built on loyalty to family and regional associates rather than to national welfare. One consequence is a disconnection between the aims of the central, oblast and local governments on the one hand, whose prime goal is to capture and redistribute rent, and on the other hand the aims of the IFIs, with their long-term vision of economic and political reform towards global integration. Even if a central government were prepared to incur the wrath of disappointed clients as well as patrons at lower tiers of government by espousing reform, it would struggle to implement it. Under such circumstances, efficiency gains from reform tend to be diluted at best and at worst, reform stalls in a twilight of the plan, which combines relatively high levels of economic intervention by the state with limited competition to maximize scope for rent-seeking (Aslund 2000).

Some grim truths regarding western prospects for promoting reform must therefore be acknowledged at the start. First, and most importantly, no amount of international pressure for reform of public administration and the economy can substitute for strong domestic incentives to pursue such reforms; and such incentives have been lacking in the CCA region. Dismissing the patronage system as mere corruption does it small justice, ignoring its historical roots and minimizing the scale of the challenge western donors take on when they undertake anti-corruption efforts as part of their development agenda. Within the CCA region there is no tradition of honest public administration, as the term is understood in the West. Institutionalized administrative corruption and state capture were features of Soviet, Imperial Russian and Imperial Persian rule dating back many centuries. Moreover, corruption is not an unalloyed evil, for it performs a vital social insurance function by enabling some redistribution of wealth, as well as permitting some version of state administration to continue functioning in the absence of sufficient public revenue. Throughout the CCA region the current national and regional elites do not favor extensive reforms because they believe that reform will disrupt their rent-seeking activity and thereby destabilize the regimes within which they thrive. However, the patronage system privileges some groups over others and the STEX model shows that its inefficiency incurs high economic costs over the long term.

Second, the political capital available from western powers for investment in the CCA region is limited. Unfortunately, the world is not short of under-developed regions suffering from economic stagnation and political corruption, and many of these have a claim on the attention and sympathy of the international community, which is as strong as, or stronger than, that of the CCA region. The apparent unwillingness of the region's governments to effectively address reform saps the determination of external agents to intervene to change local preferences. Indeed, respect for national sovereignty requires respect for central government unwillingness to reform.

Third, even if the political willingness to intervene exists on the part of the outside world, the tools available, mainly the IFIs and individual national development agencies, are flawed. Although the number of such agencies active in each country is not large in absolute terms, they have difficulty coordinating their programs. In addition, they often have no way of judging whether or not progress is being made; indeed, organizational structures and incentives emphasize maintaining programs and beginning new ones, but penalize officials who seek to terminate existing programs on the grounds of corruption or ineffectiveness. A desire to maintain good relations with host governments frequently takes precedence over policing the uses of aid money or pointing out failures by partner governments to meet their obligations. Consequently, whether involved as purveyors of loans and grants to recipient governments, or as financiers of private sector infrastructure projects – such as oil pipelines – there are limits on the ability of IFIs to play a constructive role. Furthermore, it is unfortunately the case that international aid and reform programs have frequently been perceived locally to have destructive effects on living standards and to promote an explosion of highly visible corruption that has de-legitimized national governments in general and reformers in particular.

This chapter assesses western prospects for re-igniting economic and political reform, bearing in mind these constraints and the failures in regional cooperation reviewed in Chapters 9–13. The chapter argues that the absence of market-supporting institutions (most critically: developmental political states, autonomous civic associations (to give voice) and the rule of law) together with flaws in the IFIs, present formidable obstacles to reform. The next section examines recent theoretical and empirical evidence regarding external leverage on domestic reform, while the third section (pages 254–257) then evaluates current prospects for changing domestic reform incentives. The fourth section (pages 257–261) proposes reform strategies where such change is not forthcoming. The concluding section (pages 262–263) argues that faster reform requires the IFIs to: (1) demonstrate that wealth creation offers superior prospects for dynastic survival to rent redistribution; (2) encourage a dual-track reform strategy to channel rent-seeking toward wealth creation and away from wealth redistribution; (3) promote grass-roots support for reform by encouraging micro-level reform projects; and (4) make use of the economic and political shocks that temporarily strengthen IFI leverage to accelerate reform.

## Theoretical and empirical constraints on external leverage for reform

This section integrates recent empirical work with theoretical thinking about IFI conditionality to provide a conceptual framework with which to evaluate the scope for IFI leverage to sustain reform. It confirms that IFI intervention faces daunting constraints in the CCA region and provides a rationale for the multi-pronged reform strategy presented in the rest of the chapter.

### *The limitations of conditionality*

Mayer and Mourmourus (2002) formulate the efforts of IFIs to influence domestic policy in terms of game theory in a way that has resonance within the CCA region. The starting premise is that political support for the government depends on either the general welfare of its people or the financial support from special interest groups, or some combination of the two. The special interest groups are assumed to be in the private sector, but Drazen (2000) usefully identifies special interests within government that may veto reform. Such 'within government' special interests are likely to include the ruling family and oblast leaders (Jones Luong 2002) as well as powerful central ministers, which the government prefers to keep within its tent.

Mayer and Mourmourus (2002) suggest that if the government successfully implements reforms to remove economic distortions, it acquires greater political support, but only indirectly and over the long term as the benefits of greater efficiency in resource use feed through in terms of rising social welfare. But if the government maintains or increases economic distortions, then special interest groups enhance their political support for the government directly and more immediately. It follows that reform is likely to generate immediate opposition from special interests, which may threaten the government's hold on power, and only muted enthusiasm from the general public. This outcome has clear potential to bias the stance of the government towards either gradual reform or else stalling reform in order to maximize rent-seeking options.

Dalmazzo and de Blasio (2001) concur, but they note that autocratic governments are more likely to engender such an outcome than governments with a wider set of encompassing interests, such as a diffusing oligarchy (see Chapter 8). They argue that autocratic governments maximize their revenue by appropriating rent, which they extract directly either from natural resource wealth or by taxing business activity onerously in order to secure contrived rent. We might add that foreign aid (or geopolitical rent) affords a third opportunity for rent capture and distribution. The rent extraction system is threatened by effective reform. This is because economic reform enhances competition, which curbs state intervention and thereby reduces the ability of autocratic governments to appropriate rents, while political reform constrains rent extraction by boosting transparency.

The presence of natural resource rents boosts the attraction of rent appropriation compared with wealth creation and nurtures autocratic governments, as the STEX model explains. The large immediate gain from the rent extraction effect outweighs the lagged and less direct wealth creation effect of expanded business activity generated by reform. Consequently, this diminishes the incentive for authoritarian governments, especially those in resource-rich countries, to help business other than special interest groups. It also imparts a bias against SMEs and in favor of larger, often state-owned, enterprises. This is consistent with the fact that the rent-rich CCA countries experienced tardy reform, as shown in Chapter 3.

Non-conditional foreign aid can have a similar negative effect on reform to that of natural resource wealth. In combination with the degraded social capital of the CCA region it can offset the pro-reform bias that the CIEN model predicts for resource-poor countries (see Chapters 6–8). The development literature confirms that such geopolitical rent can be large in relation to GDP. For example, Svensson (2000) cites World Bank estimates that foreign aid accounted for 54 per cent of central government expenditures in the fifty most aid-dependent countries during the period 1975–95. This also implies, however, that if conditions can be attached to the supply of geopolitical rent, it can exert effective pressure for change and help to constrain authoritarian trends. But, although foreign aid transfers some decision-making to the donor, recent research suggests that the effectiveness with which foreign aid is deployed varies substantially.

Burnside and Dollar (1997) find that aid has a strong positive effect on low-income countries pursuing policies that are sound with regard to the fiscal balance, inflation and trade openness (i.e. countries governed by developmental political states) but that it has no discernible effect on countries with maladroit policies. Elsewhere, Boone (1996) reports that foreign aid does not increase the investment rate in recipient developing countries, because it goes mostly into expanding consumption and serves to boost the scale of government. He finds that for the period 1971–90 aid did not increase the rate of investment and that while it did raise consumption, it did not benefit the poor. The result was the same whether Boone studied predatory, redistributive or 'laissez-faire' political states: the political elite benefited and basic indicators of poverty reduction like primary school enrolment and infant mortality were unaffected. Easterly (2001) concurs and argues foreign aid should be concentrated upon those countries that demonstrate they can use it effectively. This conclusion has clear policy implications for the CCA region.

As shown in Table 6.6, the level of aid to GDP for the resource-poor CCA countries was orders of magnitude higher than that in the resource-rich ones and it increased during the first decade of the transition. Such geopolitical rent appears to be partly responsible for the initial easing of political repression, first in Kyrgyzstan and then in Tajikistan (Table 8.1). But a perceived weakening in the political strength of the center may also be a factor in these two countries (Jones Luong 2002). More recently, donors have made efforts to link aid to curbing corruption throughout the CCA region, but although some government officials have been fired as a consequence, any overall improvement may be slight.

Mayer and Moumourus (2002) compare the returns from different forms of IFI intervention for the major parties involved. They suggest that conditional assistance (i.e. a more rigidly prescribed reform program, of which the 'big bang' associated with the CEE countries is a more extreme variant) lowers economic distortions and is a superior strategy for the IFIs and their financial backers than the polar opposite strategy that offers unconditional assistance. However, according to the model, conditionality does not guarantee that the inhabitants of the recipient country are better off. Moreover, the *absence* of conditionality always secures greater political support for the recipient government. These two propositions strengthen the motive for developing country governments to resist any extension of conditionality.

Somewhat more optimistically, however, Dalmazzo and de Blasio (2001) argue that credible conditionality regarding the provision of aid can lead to the adoption of reform policies. The intervention of IFIs can change government incentives, so it can tip the balance in favor of maintaining reform momentum. Most importantly for the present analysis and consistent with the STEX model, empirical evidence suggests that IFIs can reduce economic distortion proportionately more during difficult times than they can during easier times. This is because imposing conditionality on external assistance is most effective during crises (Bruno and Pleskovic 1997). A common form of crisis that is particularly relevant to the transition economies is one that is triggered when an abrupt decline in social welfare (i.e. a growth collapse) is accompanied by an increase in the damage inflicted on the public by distortions favoring special interest groups. A second relevant form of crisis arises where a substantial increase takes place in a country's cost of external borrowing. Chapter 10 suggests that in 2004 Uzbekistan faced the possibility of both forms of crisis. The country's erstwhile reluctance to pursue economic and political reform could therefore change abruptly if a growth collapse brought exogenous democratization.

### Domestic constraints on IFI reform

Attacking corruption should utilize a combination of shaming tactics combined with the mobilization of pressure groups and the recruitment of supportive officials within the ruling regimes themselves. International actors can fund and encourage efforts to gather information about the extent of corruption, the identities of corrupt officials and the networks through which funds raised from graft are channeled and redistributed among officials and political actors. Monitoring of customs posts can be performed, and persons who have just passed through border crossings can be interviewed about their experiences, with the proceedings publicized. Even as corrupt officers are identified and named, honest officers can be rewarded with public praise and material benefits. The creation of civic associations like trade groups, business associations, automobile associations and farmers' unions can accelerate social capital formation and allow individuals targeted by corrupt public officials to share information and be informed as to their rights when confronted with demands for bribes. Georgia showed in 2003 that if a critical mass of such civic associations can be formed, they make control of administrative corruption a serious political issue.

A second approach is to enlist government officials who display an interest in, and support for, clean government. Although most public officials will have paid in order to win their posts, this does not mean that they are blind to the benefits of honest administration. Identifying such officials and rewarding them – for example, channeling development funds into the districts and provinces they control – could offer significant political payoffs. Not only could such men (they are almost all men) serve as salesmen for reform, but if their districts can be made to thrive, then a politically useful 'demonstration effect' will be created by which other officials may perceive a link between relatively clean administration and greater economic growth, which would lead in turn to higher revenues (including for the officials themselves).

As in all reform efforts, the political aspects of anti-corruption are key to the success of the program. The goals must be clear, and progress towards them must be measurable using reliable and valid indicators. This may require adopting modest goals, and very focused efforts (for example, limiting anti-corruption efforts to a few special enterprise zones (SEZs) and provinces run by forward-looking governors, or one or two customs posts). International actors must emphasize the importance of reform in public and private. Resources should be focused on customs reform in particular because this form of corruption corrodes respect for and the legitimacy of the state and steals sorely needed public funds.[1]

All of the CCA states are crippled by shortages of trained personnel able to develop policies for consideration by decision-makers. They also have a very limited ability to monitor and enforce the implementation of such policies when they are adopted. Most importantly, perhaps, all of the countries lack viable and independent judiciaries and police forces, which makes the defense of property rights problematic and so constitutes a major barrier to the development of the national economies. Without able and honest bureaucracies capable of monitoring and enforcing professional standards within their own ranks, any gains made in combating corruption in the customs services, fighting predatory taxation and improving the effectiveness of the judiciary will be transitory at best.

Addressing these deficiencies is in one sense straightforward; civil services must be streamlined and professionalized, with their members receiving enough pay on a regular basis in order to make honesty a viable choice. Talented officials must be induced to remain in government, and officials at all levels must be offered credible guarantees of secure, fixed tenures in their posts, in order to discourage rent-seeking arising from employment instability. However, it is also the case that these reforms will require considerable amounts of funding and have the potential to be highly explosive. As Figure 7.1 shows, 'streamlining' the civil service is difficult for any government if it means dumping personnel into a domestic economy already suffering from high unemployment. Funds to offer higher salaries to officials are often not available, and CCA governments not infrequently balance their budgets by allowing pay to public servants to fall into arrears for months.

Having established the grass-roots constraints on conditional assistance, we now examine the options available to the IFIs and western governments in this light.

## Policies to boost IFI leverage by changing domestic incentives

The basic difficulty confronting IFIs and other international donors is that further reform is almost impossible without challenging the vested interests controlling the CCA states, which in turn may jeopardize good relations with those states and might also – depending upon how forcefully international pressure was applied – risk their destabilization. Yet, without reform, the public sector will be denied the revenues it needs to pay adequate wages and thereby curb petty corruption and provide the public goods that wealth creation requires. Moreover, in the absence of reform SMEs will continue to be repressed and fail to make the major contribution to economic diversification and employment creation of which they are capable.

### *Adjusting domestic political incentives for reform*

An informed and rational leader with dynastic ambitions has an interest in sustaining GDP growth. The STEX model shows why failure to competitively diversify the economy heightens its vulnerability to shocks and a growth collapse. The model also suggests that the events leading to a growth collapse are associated with increasing authoritarianism because the shrinking size of the rent stream relative to GDP requires governments to concentrate the rent upon a smaller number of its most critical supporters and to use repression to control the losers. The risk of a political challenge therefore intensifies, while the actual growth collapse discredits the regime in power and renders it vulnerable to replacement. A regime may be able to sustain its power in such circumstances, especially an autocratic one (Smith 2004), but the leadership most likely will not and its ejection from power could be violent (Ross 2001).

However, even gradual reform will change the nature of dynastic power. The CIEN model shows that sustained rapid growth in PCGDP strengthens three basic sanctions against anti-social governance, namely political accountability, civic associations and rule of law. This propels the political state towards a consensual democracy via a diffusing oligarchy as the social groups co-opted into the political process steadily widen. The model also suggests that although a dynasty can survive such trends, it can only do so by ceding some authority. Yet, an astute dynasty might enjoy considerable *political* longevity, based on the legitimacy conferred by delivering sustained PCGDP. The empirical evidence suggests that citizens of countries experiencing sustained rapid PCGDP growth are prepared to trade increased political accountability for rapidly rising material living standards. For instance, political accountability is far less strongly and positively linked to rising PCGDP among countries pursuing the CIEN trajectory than either voice or the rule of law (Auty 2004). This acceptance of lagged political accountability extends the margin for a dynasty to peacefully diversify from authoritarian political power to economic power during the diffusing oligarchy phase.

More specifically, informed and rational leaders with dynastic ambitions in the CCA countries can take advantage of the current economic booms, whether fed by rising energy prices, inflows of geopolitical rent or worker remittances to embrace economic reform, if not yet political reform. Moreover, this need not precipitate an immediate clash over loss of rent because, as Khan and Jomo (2000) argue on the basis of post-war East Asian experience, rent-seeking activity is not incompatible with competitive diversification of the economy and sustained GDP growth. What is required is tighter control of rent-seeking to channel it away from rent extraction and distribution and into wealth creation in order to curb its repressive effects on economic growth and reward the use of rent that promotes efficient use of scarce economic resources.

### Re-channeling rent-seeking effort: dual-track or gradual reform

The gradual reform strategy (or, more accurately, dual-track reform) of China offers a practical means of changing rent-seeking incentives. The basic idea is to create, alongside the moribund plan sector, a dynamic market sector in which post-reform (i.e. world class) levels of infrastructure, incentives and institutions immediately apply. This would be the likely path in the CCA countries, but in China, it initially entailed agriculture, which responded so swiftly to the adoption of personal incentives during 1978–84 that increased output caused food prices to fall and made it necessary to extend wealth-creating incentives to manufacturing. This was achieved in Special Enterprise Zones (SEZs), which subsequently propelled much of that country's rapid GDP growth (Lau *et al.* 2000).

It is interesting to note that two successful resource-rich countries also nurtured SEZs (or Export Processing Zones (EPZs)). The Malaysian government consciously developed EPZs from 1971 after disappointing results from experiments with the then more fashionable import substitution strategy. Indonesia stumbled into a similar policy of promoting efficient export-oriented firms because its oil rent deployment bred two forms of manufacturing enterprise. One set of firms took the rent conferred by higher prices from infant industry protection in terms of reduced levels of effort and efficiency whereas the other set of firms took the rent in terms of high profits that were ploughed back into expanded investment (Flatters and Jenkins 1986). In both countries efficient firms were able to compete on international markets when oil prices fell in 1985. They rapidly restructured the economy from rent-driven growth to manufacturing-driven growth.

In fact, recent research on industrial reform in Morocco suggests that export-oriented firms are most likely to be new entrants rather than existing firms. Fafchamps *et al.* (2001) conclude that export firms thrive by what they term market learning (meeting discerning demand) rather than production learning (reducing costs). This is yet further evidence against the once fashionable policy of industrialization by import substitution, which Uzbekistan and more recently Kazakhstan have mistakenly embraced. Fafchamps *et al.* (2001) also report that manufacturers that export usually do so within a short time of the start-up of the firm. In addition, the export firms are productive from the outset, although exporting does not appear to further boost their productivity. Foreign ownership is strongly and positively associated with exporting, the exported products are labor-intensive and export propensity is inversely related to the age of the firm.

EPZs can rapidly and positively transform small economies like those of the CCA countries. Ireland shows most dramatically how FDI can rapidly accelerate the industrial diversification of a relatively small economy. Key prerequisites for the success of FDI in Ireland were fiscal reform to stabilize the public finances, stable and low levels of taxation, access for labor-intensive exports in a large dynamic market (the EU) and improving supplies of infrastructure and educated labor (Barry and Bradley 1997). These could all be provided in EPZs supported by IFIs, if access to the markets of large near neighbors improves. The rate of FDI into Ireland jumped from 0.9 per cent of GDP 1985–91, which was below the EU average and reflected failing inward-oriented policies (Barry 2000), to 2.8 per cent of GDP by 1995–96 when it was more than twice the EU average (Gorg and Ruane 2000). Within just one decade, FDI accounted for almost 50 per cent of employment in

Irish manufacturing and the bulk of the country's manufactured exports. The latter particularly concentrated on weightless export products that exhibit low transport costs (vital for the land-locked CCA states) and also the localization economies provided by clustering in enclaves as well as economies of scale arising from access to larger regional markets.

This dual-track version of gradual reform is quite different from that espoused by Uzbekistan, which conforms more closely to the STEX model because it extracts rents from a potentially competitive sector (agriculture) in a way that damages its long-term growth prospects in order to support protected infant industry that cannot compete on international markets. The Uzbek strategy transfers agricultural rents to the elite, which opposes reform. The genius of the Chinese dual-track strategy is that the dynamic market sector not only builds an economy that can absorb labor from the moribund low-productivity plan sector, while also generating foreign exchange, efficient investment and taxes, but it also builds a political coalition that acquires a vested interest in sustaining economic reform and the capacity to buy off the losers from reform within the plan sector.

## Advancing reform without changed domestic rent-seeking incentives

Reform is still possible even if CCA governments cannot motivate themselves to shift rent-seeking incentives towards wealth creation.

### Local reform experiments

Local reform projects offer an alternative way of avoiding head-on conflict with the vested interests that are associated with top-down reform. Development aid might be refocused towards local partners, cutting out national government agencies wherever possible. To the extent that this involves existing authorities, it is possible that the local nature of the challenges will keep them from being perceived as threats by the national rulers, and so crushed or subverted.[2] This approach also gives scope for a cadre of capable leadership candidates to be developed who would push forward reforms if and when their careers took them to higher office.[3] Local reform need not immediately threaten either central or regional interests. Over time, it can therefore build a constituency for change among the losers from distortions, notably the smaller farmers, SMEs and exporters identified in earlier chapters. Like dual-track reform, local reform provides those who presently benefit from economic distortions and rent-seeking (i.e. government officials, state-backed importers and protected state firms) with time to adopt a more viable and socially desirable way of earning a living.

The CIEN model implies that *regional* reform efforts may be more practical if they are applied in resource-poor oblasts where the absence of rents and FDI means that the leadership has most to gain from improving economic efficiency. In fact, anecdotal evidence does suggest that some localities and regions are more ready to promote SMEs than others (Jones Luong forthcoming). Moreover, there is clear evidence from recent research (Desai *et al.* 2003) that fiscal decentralization in Russia during the 1990s was associated with strengthened lower-tier government incentives to promote both wealth creation and new firms. Here too, China has lessons to offer because when the central government decentralized tax revenues and autonomy, it strengthened political supervision in order to limit rent-seeking abuses. But there were important exceptions to regional wealth creation in Russia in the form of oblasts that were either resource-rich or heavily dependent on transfers from the center. In other words, regional governments dependent upon rents proved more likely to pursue rent-seeking activity than wealth creation.

Azerbaijan provides examples of possible local reform experiments. Auty (1999) suggests pilot projects that establish 'efficiency environments' in which businesses immediately enjoy post-reform (i.e. world class) levels of infrastructure, economic incentives and institutions. Importantly, given the description of non-tariff barriers to trade in Chapter 9, 'efficiency' transport routes would also be required to guarantee unimpeded access for inputs and outputs, as well as reliable deliveries of critical inputs like power or irrigation water. The specific local efficiency environments might take the form of farming sub-districts and even ministerial departments. The objective is to replicate on a local scale the conditions that the Azerbaijan International Oil Corporation (AIOC) claims to have negotiated thanks to the position of strength that it derived from its large size and consequent importance to the country's economy. AIOC targets, and secures, a 17 per cent risk-related return on its investment. In contrast, field surveys (Auty 1999) suggest the necessary target return is four times as much for firms surviving in the corrupted economy outside an efficiency environment.

One pilot project considered in Azerbaijan strives to replicate the successful oilfield equipment refurbishment partnerships negotiated by AIOC with sub-units of state-owned AzNefteKhimMash. This involves applying the basic principles of the AIOC joint venture contracts to the machinery sub-sector with a view to establishing clear rules for each side. The intention is to sustain and enhance the skill base in oil service activity by insulating the firms from the adverse effects of petty corruption. The proposed agreement initially aims to attract 20–30 respected MNCs, each investing $10–16 million ($200–400 million in total) and hiring 50–100 hand-picked workers from AzNefteKhimMash to produce oilfield products to the highest specifications for domestic, FSU and global demand (ibid.). AIOC claims that Azeri workers can match North Sea efficiency levels provided they secure the equipment, management and markets which they currently lack.

Efficiency environments might also be created in rural areas by encouraging lower-tier governments that support local farmers (rather than exploit them) to use the local social network as an agent of change. They call for civic associations to improve the prospects for success by repulsing opposition to reform by local vested interests. The formation of co-operatives may help reduce the risk to individuals of engaging in these pilot projects and so improve the likelihood of success. Suitable prospects include negotiation of efficiency environments between cotton gins, and their cotton supply hinterlands and the regional administrative sub-district. Finally, some local departments within central government ministries may be singled out for experiments with efficiency environments, paying higher salaries to public officials in exchange for the efficient delivery of public services. Those government departments that deliver services to experimental efficiency environments like tourism, as well as agriculture and manufacturing, might be suitable choices.

The geographically diffused micro reform strategy set out above will yield both successes and failures. The successes will build up support for market reform and also provide a demonstration effect to adjacent areas. The diffusion of reform will require management to ensure that the demonstration effect is transferred to other regions that are carefully selected because they exhibit promising pre-conditions. The NGOs can play a useful role in promoting these efficiency experiments. Moreover, industrial donor countries with an interest in the promotion of social capital, such as Denmark and Norway, might help fund such experiments and thereby further strengthen the political attraction of successful experiments, whose promotion is a more economically wholesome form of regional patronage. Competition might emerge between different oblasts, acting as a spur to the lagging ones, as is occurring between states in India.

Both the dual-track and local reform strategies would benefit from infrastructure projects, which invariably entail such large capital investment that they depend on international finance. Dalmazzo and de Blasio (2001: 18) argue that, 'When international aid can provide some infrastructure, the costs of good policies are reduced, while their gains remain in tact. Furthermore, this type of aid can also circumvent the problems associated with financial constraints that prevent governments from borrowing and investing.' In other words, well-targeted infrastructure investment (for example east–west transportation links in the Caucasus, improved road and rail access to near-neighbor economies and irrigation rehabilitation in Central Asia) can compound the benefits from effective reform. Such schemes are highly capital-intensive and entail long-term investment commitments on a scale that strains the financial resources of even an oil-rich country.

However, such mega-projects are vulnerable to transformation into rent-dispensing mechanisms because they can be allocated to favored companies, which raise their margins and engender cost overruns to produce the required rents (Murphy 1983). Caution is also required because building infrastructure without also improving the ability of the recipient state to maintain the new structures will do little to advance responsible governance. For example, the state-owned railways in Georgia and Azerbaijan report rapidly growing levels of profitability in recent years due to increasing volumes of Kazakh and Turkmen crude oil being transported to Georgian ports for shipment to Europe. However, this increasing profitability has not translated into increased investments in rolling stock or better maintenance. In fact, accidents have been increasing, as have delays due to worn out infrastructure and shortages of locomotives and other items. The reason appears to be rent-skimming by railroad employees and managers at all levels, but particularly senior management.

A further problem is that large infrastructure projects rely heavily on the ability of the international partner, whether an IFI or a national aid agency, to effectively monitor the scheme and respond to the behavior of its local partner. To date, the IFIs appear to lack this ability. Although *conditionality* has become increasingly widespread through the 1990s, it is widely perceived as flawed even within the IFI community itself (Collier 1997; World Bank 1998). The prospects for accelerating reform can therefore be strengthened if the IFIs themselves undergo some reform. Critics of the IFIs argue that they do not cancel loans or access to future credits for borrowers who fail to comply with conditions. The IFIs fail to do this because of the internal need to lend in order to meet lending targets. For example, the World Bank needs to demonstrate its activity and success, which it measures not in terms of actual progress in development – which as noted above is notoriously difficult to ascertain – but in terms of disbursements. Bank staff who oppose loans may be subjected to pressure from country managers concerned about maintaining their budgets and protecting their careers, and may also be threatened by criticism from host governments, which may demand that the Bank remove the offending staff member or even declare him or her *persona non grata* (Aslund 2003; Thomas 2003). Recipient countries have also proved adept at playing off the IFIs against other donors who also need to disperse funds.

### Comprehensive reform for faltering economies

A continued squeeze on resources leading to a growth collapse may be a prerequisite for comprehensive national/macro reform in some CCA countries. Vietnam provides a classic case of a reluctant reformer that was forced to accelerate reform in response to a threatened growth collapse no fewer than three times between 1979 and 1998. In each case a macro-economic crisis triggered partial reform that brought a GDP growth surge, which subsequently faltered because reform was incomplete. The first cycle commenced in 1979 after reunification efforts boosted inflation and cut economic growth. The modest reform stimulated production, but the unreformed SOEs sustained deficits that aborted stabilization, forcing the government to reform with its Doi Moi ('renovation') programme in 1988 when growth flagged again after the loss of Soviet aid. But the SOEs remained problematic and a third set of reforms was forced through after the 1998 Asian financial crisis, albeit after a lag that reflected deep disagreement among the Vietnamese leadership.

An economic crisis and its associated political destabilization increase the risk that the political elite will lose power by force. Consequently, some elements within the elite may come to accept the need to share power (i.e. to expand the encompassing interest of the state) to salvage some political influence. Jones Luong (2002) persuasively argues that this was the option that faced many elites in Eastern Europe at the onset of the transition, making democracy a more appealing option for them than seeking to cling to power.

In negotiating adjustment to a growth collapse, the government requires external financial support to stabilize the economy and then IFI loans to foster economic restructuring. As noted earlier, interests diverge regarding the appropriate extent of conditionality, with governments pushing for limited conditions and the IFIs preferring a more controlled package. Erbas (2003) argues from IMF experience that governments are likely to prefer 'split' conditionality, in which future options remain more flexible, even if this concession is won at some cost in terms of reduced efficiency, as opposed to compact conditionality in which prior agreement is given for comprehensive (big bang) reform. Moreover, with regard to the latter, governments may well be ingenuous during negotiations in order to secure assistance and then renege on conditions, effectively seeking to follow a split conditionality route by dissembling and subterfuge. Erbas therefore concludes that split conditionality, in which the reform process is implemented in stages, has a greater chance of securing 'national ownership' and therefore of being successfully implemented than does compact conditionality.

In the event of a growth collapse in Uzbekistan, the IFIs may wish to negotiate first a stabilization program and subsequently a staged structural adjustment program under split conditionality. A structural adjustment program for Uzbekistan would include sustained investment of around 2.5 per cent of GDP annually to rehabilitate the rural water and communication networks (see Chapter 10), but only in conjunction with a comprehensive agricultural privatization program in order to create the required dynamic market sector. In addition, investment in EPZs aimed at trade with the CCA region and near neighbors should attract FDI to rapidly expand non-farm employment. This would permit state-protected manufacturing, overstaffed ministries and subsistence agriculture to release surplus labor and become more productive. Of course, the Uzbek government may opt to retain power by further repression, but with sufficient flexibility on the part of the elite to exploit the country's strategic location and emulate the survival strategy of an Egypt or an Algeria, rather than slipping into the isolationist route of a North Korea and a Myanmar.

## Conclusions

Successful economic and political reform within the CCA region is severely constrained by the threat such reform poses to the patronage systems upon which the authoritarian political states of the region depend. There is a disconnection between the IFIs' outward-looking, efficiency-promoting reform agenda and the inward-focused patronage-broking behavior of the central, regional and local governments. Consequently, even if a central government wished to pursue a coherent reform strategy, it would be hard-pressed to execute it. At best, this mismatch between the objectives of external agents and those of the grass-roots administrators diminishes the gains from a reform program and at worst it negates them entirely. The economic outcomes range from a sub-optimal growth performance to a high probability of a growth collapse, albeit in the long term for energy-rich countries, but only then in the absence of price shocks.

The IFIs should argue the case for national economic and political reform under non-crisis conditions. The oil-rich countries may be receptive because the probability of the central government retaining power after reform is stronger with a booming economy like that of Kazakhstan than with a failing economy like that of Uzbekistan. A rising rent stream engenders optimistic economic prospects, which provide a strong platform on which to campaign. Moreover, the experience of developing market economies like Malaysia suggests the government, as well as a majority of the governed, can benefit from the sharpened incentives to use rents more efficiently, spurred by increasing political accountability. Finally, Chapters 2 and 4 warn oil-rich states that inefficient deployment of depleting energy rents undermines the long-term survival prospects of governments. The experience of the developing market economies reveals a significantly higher risk of violent overthrow for such regimes (Ross 2001). In reassuring contrast, the political elite in diamond-rich Botswana displays enviable longevity, which it has earned through the prudent deployment of mineral rents under conditions of political accountability.

The CCA countries are conspicuously deficient in the institutions required to sustain reform and raise welfare by promoting competition and economic growth. Faster reform requires the IFIs to encourage a multi-pronged attack on the obstacles to reform inherent in the CCA patronage systems. Based on the rent-driven political economy models that reflect the experience of the developing market economies, this study argues that wealth creation offers superior prospects for dynastic survival to rent redistribution. Those CCA governments in countries enjoying an economic boom can take advantage of these conditions to promote reforms to sustain rapid PCGDP growth, while building alternative *economic* power bases to support dynastic ambitions as political power dissolves under a diffusing oligarchy. If successfully executed, such a strategy may extend political power for one or two decades.

This reform strategy entails re-channeling rent-seeking toward wealth creation and away from wealth redistribution. An important means of achieving this under booming economic conditions is through the dual-track gradual reform strategy, which nurtures a dynamic market sector of wealth-creating activity that absorbs labor from the moribund plan sector while also building a political constituency for sustained economic reform.

Even if progress in adjusting domestic incentives is hampered or stalled, the IFIs and NGOs can promote local reform experiments in favorable environments, and the demonstration effect of such experiments can spread in a way not dissimilar to that of the national dual-track reform strategy. In effect, grass-roots support for reform can be built in instances where top-down reform is blocked, without alarming vested interests. At the same time, local reform affords such vested interests a chance to adapt to the economy-wide changes necessitated by the long-term switch from wealth extraction and redistribution to wealth creation.

Finally, if recommendations for reform go unheeded so that a growth collapse occurs, IFI conditionality can be brought more strongly into play, despite the very real practical constraints that IFI conditionality faces. IMF experience suggests that its policy leverage is most effective during times of crisis because at such times the threat to the continued power of the elites invites a widening of the encompassing interest of the state to salvage some of their threatened political power. Such crises are associated with a growth collapse or a shock that renders debt service impractical. Uzbekistan currently faces a high probability of encountering both, so it could yet become an unlikely catalyst for re-igniting economic and political reform within the CCA region. The conditional reform strategy would make finance available for economic stabilization on condition that a multi-stage reform program commences that is designed to restructure the economy to strengthen its capacity to create wealth.

A last note of caution is in order. Realistically, reform within the CCA region must be viewed as a long-term effort, which may require the passage of another decade, and the rise of a new generation of post-transition CCA leaders that is genuinely committed to reforming society. The possibility must also be acknowledged, however, that such leaders may never arise, and without them, the long-term prospects of the region are bleak indeed. No matter how committed the international community and its agents such as the IFIs may be, development will fail without committed local partners. Providing incentives to encourage such partners must therefore become a major theme shaping IFI involvement in the region.

## Notes

1   The scale of the funds generated through graft in customs administration is aston-ishing. In Georgia alone, one estimate of the illicit revenues pocketed by customs officers put the take at approximately 1 billion lari – a sum equal to the national budget. Quoted in M. Specter, 'Letter from Tbilisi: Rainy Days in Georgia', *The New Yorker*, 18 December 2000.

2   Significant efforts are already underway in this direction. See 'Strategy for

Activities in 2002–2003', *Local Government Brief*, Open Society Institute, Spring 2002: 63.
3 This notion should not be pushed too hard, however. Power in all the CCA states is held by small, relatively cohesive elites which offer little in the way of upward mobility or openness.

# References

Aslund, A. (2000) Why has Russia's economic transformation been so arduous?, in: Pleskovic, B. and Stiglitz, J.E. (eds.) *Annual World Bank Conference on Development Economics 1999*, Washington DC: World Bank DC, 399–424.

Aslund, A. (2003) Sizing up the Central Asian economies, *Journal of International Affairs* 56(2), 75–87.

Auty, R.M. (1999) Why is the diversification of manufacturing not occurring in Azerbaijan? Background paper prepared for ECSPE (Azerbaijan CEM), Washington DC: World Bank.

Auty, R.M. (2004) Patterns of rent-extraction and deployment in developing countries: Implications for governance, economic policy and performance, Paper presented at the Poverty Reduction and Economic Management Unit (PREM) Seminar, World Bank, Washington DC, April 27th 2004.

Barry, F. (2000) Convergence is not automatic: Lessons from Ireland for Central and Eastern Europe, *The World Economy* 23(10), 1379–1394.

Barry, F. and Bradley, J. (1997) FDI and trade: The Irish host-country experience, *The Economic Journal* 197, 1798–1811.

Boone, P. (1996) Politics and the effectiveness of foreign aid, *European Economic Review* 89(1), 22–46.

Bruno, M. and Pleskovic, B. (1997) *Annual Bank Conference on Development Economics 1996*, Washington DC: World Bank.

Burnside, C. and Dollar, D. (1997) Aid policies and growth, World Bank Research Working Paper 1777, Washington DC: World Bank.

Collier, P. (1997) The failure of conditionality, in Gwin, C. and Nelson, J. (eds.) *Perspectives on Aid and Development*, Washington DC: Overseas Development Council.

Dalmazzo, A. and de Blasio, G. (2001) Resources and incentives to reform: A model and some evidence in sub-Saharan African countries, IMF Working Paper 01/86, Washington DC: International Monetary Fund.

Desai, R., Freinkman, L.M. and Goldberg, Li. (2003) Fiscal federalism and regional growth: Evidence from the Russian Federation in the 1990s, World Bank Policy Research Working Paper 3138, Washington DC: World Bank.

Drazen, A. (2000) *Political Economy in Macroeconomics*, Princeton: Princeton University Press.

Easterly, W. (2001) *The Elusive Quest for Growth*, London: MIT Press.

Erbas, S.N. (2003) IMF conditionality and program ownership: A case for streamlined conditionality, IMF Working Paper 03/98, Washington DC: International Monetary Fund.

Fafchamps, M., El Hamine, S. and Zeufack, A. (2001) Learning to export: Evidence from Moroccan manufacturing, Working Paper, Washington DC: World Bank.

Flatters, F. and Jenkins, G. (1986) Trade policy in Indonesia, mimeo, Cambridge MA: Harvard Institute for International Development.

Gorg, H. and Ruane, F. (2000) European integration and periphery: Lessons from Irish experience, *The World Economy* 23(3), 405–421.

Jones Luong, P. (2002) *Institutional Change and Political Continuity in Post-Soviet Central Asia: Power, Perceptions and Pacts*, Cambridge: Cambridge University Press.

Jones Luong, P. (Forthcoming) Economic 'decentralization' in Kazakhstan: Causes and consequences, in: Jones Luong, P. (ed.) *The Transformation of Central Asia: State-Societal Relations from Soviet Rule to Independence*, Ithaca NY: Cornell University Press.

Khan, M.H. and Jomo, K.S. (2000) *Rents, Rent-Seeking and Economic Development*, Cambridge: Cambridge University Press.

Lau, L.J., Qian, Y. and Roland, G. (2000) Reform without losers: An interpretation of China's dual-track approach to transition, *Journal of Political Economy* 108, 120–143.

Mayer, W. and Mourmouras, A. (2002) Vested interests in a positive theory of IFI conditionality, IMF Working Paper 02/73, Washington DC: International Monetary Fund.

Murphy, K.J. (1983) *Macroproject Development in the Third World: An Analysis of Transnational Partnerships*, Boulder CO: Westview Press.

Ross, M.L. (2001) Does oil hinder democracy? *World Politics* 53: 325–361.

Smith, B. (2004) Oil wealth and regime survival in the developing world, 1960–1999, *American Journal of Political Science* 48(2), 232–246.

Svensson, J. (2000) Foreign aid and rent seeking, *Journal of International Economics* 51, 437–461.

Thomas, M.A. (2003) *Can the World Bank Enforce Its Own Conditions?* College Park, MD: Center for Institutional Reform and the Informal Sector, University of Maryland, 6–7.

World Bank (1998) *Assessing Aid – What Works, What Doesn't and Why*, Washington DC: World Bank.

# Part VI
# Conclusion

# 15 Conclusion

## Lessons not learned by the CCA countries?

*Richard M. Auty[1]*

### A tale of two scenarios

The so-called 'resource curse', which appears to have inflicted such damage upon the growth prospects of each of the four main categories of the resource-abundant developing market economies during the final quarter of the twentieth century (Table 2.2) is not a deterministic law. If the governments of the CCA countries learn the lessons from that experience then natural resource rents can facilitate the transition to a market economy. Natural resource rent can confer three principal benefits. First, it can increase the rate of investment and thereby speed up the restructuring of the economy into competitive activity that will accelerate the sustainable rate of PCGDP growth. Second, it can expand the capacity of the CCA region to import those capital goods that the restructuring of their economies requires and that the region cannot supply. Third, the rent can cushion the social hardship associated with economic restructuring by increasing social assistance to those least able to fend for themselves.

This book has applied the CIEN and STEX rent-driven models of political economy, which are rooted in the experience of the developing market economies, to analyze the progress with, and the prospects for, transition to a market economy within the CCA region. The scale of the *potential* rent from energy resources within the region has been substantial, measuring 30–60 per cent of GDP. Even by a conservative estimate using the price of oil prevailing in the early 2000s, the Caspian Basin energy rents promise a gift from Nature that will quickly rise to around $20 billion annually and persist for a generation or more. Such an annual windfall is equivalent to almost half the nominal GDP of the CCA region at the start of the millennium, and equivalent to almost the entire GDP of the two main oil-exporters, Azerbaijan and Kazakhstan, at that time (World Bank 2002). Sound management of energy rents on such a scale could quadruple per capita GDP within the CCA region in twenty years (see Table 1.1).

The CIEN model also suggests that sustained rapid PCGDP growth will propel existing autocratic regimes incrementally towards consensual democracies, via diffusing oligarchies. This is because rapidly rising PCGDP strengthens three key sanctions against anti-social governance as, first, the switch away from commodity taxes towards income, profits and sales taxes increases pressure for political accountability in public expenditure; second, the bridging and linking social capital associated with competitive markets strengthens civic associations and voice; and, third, proliferating competition constrains scope for state intervention and rent-seeking while emerging private businesses lobby for secure property rights and the rule of law. Within a generation, sustained rapid economic growth would therefore confer on an increasing number of CCA countries not only the living standards currently enjoyed by countries on the southern and western fringes of the EU, but also the political freedoms.

Yet although the policies required to sustain rapid and relatively egalitarian economic growth and to reduce poverty and environmental damage in both resource-rich and resource-poor economies are widely known, the STEX model shows that effective execution of such policies requires a developmental political state and market-friendly institutions. Unfortunately, such political states remain largely absent from the CCA region. Consequently, there is a substantial risk that history will repeat itself, so that, as with the developing market economies and the Soviet Union during the 1974–78 and 1979–81 oil booms, the natural resource (and geopolitical) rent proves to be a curse rather than a blessing, by being used to consolidate brittle authoritarian regimes that postpone efficiency-enhancing economic reform and repress the associated political dissent.

It is the basic thesis of this book that the recent strong transition rebounds in seven of the eight countries (Uzbekistan is the exception, with a much weaker rebound) are not sustainable and that without further economic reform, all eight countries face the eventual prospect of a growth collapse from which recovery is likely to prove protracted and cannot be guaranteed. The principal obstacle to reform and economic restructuring is the patronage system of rent extraction and deployment with which the regional elites sustain their power. We propose that western governments and agencies should pursue a four-pronged strategy to circumvent this obstacle and accelerate economic reform. The next four sections amplify this thesis by explaining: the risk of growth collapses; the principal constraints on economic reform; the scope for beneficial regional policy cooperation; and the potential contribution of external agents to sustaining improvements in regional social welfare.

## Why the recent transition rebound is unsustainable

De Melo *et al.* (1996) establish a strong positive relationship between the onset and strength of the transition GDP rebound and the speed and comprehensiveness of reform, based upon a comparison of the CEE and CIS countries through the mid-1990s. They argue that swift and comprehensive economic reform (a 'big bang') sustains the rapid growth in PCGDP that the CIEN model suggests will de-politicize the economy. Yet subsequent research (de Melo *et al.* 2001) shows that variations among transition countries in their initial conditions constrain the choice of reform strategy. Among the main groups of formerly centrally planned economies the CCA countries had the least propitious combination of four key initial conditions for transition reform. First, their long exposure to central planning left a legacy of relatively high macro-economic distortion and minimal market-friendly institutions. Second, the CCA countries are extremely remote from dynamic market economies, albeit less so in the case of the western Caucasus, so that the appeal of democracy and the inflow of FDI (other than for resource extraction) with which to expedite broad-based economic re-structuring are both weak.

The third initial condition, the natural resource endowment, is the main differentiating factor within the CCA region. Its effect is compounded by being positively linked to the fourth initial condition, which is the scale of GDP compression. The two are therefore discussed together here. The resource-poor countries experienced the greatest GDP compression. Compared with a decline in GDP of less than 30 per cent in the CEE countries, the mean decline in the energy-rich CCA countries was 44 per cent and that of the resource-poor CCA countries was two-thirds. All four resource-rich countries deployed their exceptionally high natural resource rents to cushion the transition shock by providing selective subsidies to the populace and state enterprises, and also to ease pressure for economic reform that threatened the patronage systems. Progress with reform is slowest in Turkmenistan and Uzbekistan, whose governments were able to extract sizeable rents without heavy reliance on external capital. Reform also flagged in oil-rich Azerbaijan and Kazakhstan once the IOCs had committed large sunk capital investments, although the recent creation of oil funds is a positive step.

The CIEN model suggests the resource-poor countries, notably those closest to Western Europe (Armenia and Georgia) have more favorable conditions for economic and political reform, especially if they attract geopolitical rent that is well targeted by donors. Certainly, despite the severe civil strife that afflicted three of the four resource-poor countries, as a group they made most progress with economic and political reform. Moreover, there is some evidence that the oligarchies in Georgia, and possibly Armenia, may be near a tipping point beyond which they may diffuse toward more pluralistic political systems. However, the potentially positive impact on incentives for efficient investment, which the CIEN model suggests can arise in the resource-poor countries, are offset in the case of the CCA countries by the negative impact of the very severe decline in their GDP. Chapter 6 explains how this has shortened time horizons and boosted corruption in the resource-poor countries so that their social capital exhibits similar levels of patronage and corruption to those of the resource-rich countries. Moreover, economic reform decelerated in the resource-poor countries in the late 1990s in the face of the more difficult second stage reforms.

The recent robust transition rebounds in seven of the eight CCA countries are sustained by either rising energy prices or expanding geopolitical rent or increasing inflows of worker remittances. These growth stimuli cannot persist indefinitely, so further economic reform is required to sustain rapid PCGDP growth. Although small farmers, SMEs and exporters are potentially the most dynamic economic agents for promoting the required investment, economic restructuring and employment creation, they fare poorly. This is so even in the resource-poor countries because their faster reform has failed to translate into an enabling business environment. This has come about because small businesses offer regional and local officials an easy target to exploit for raising revenues to balance budgets and feed patronage networks. The repressing effects of such rent extraction on long-term wealth creation are disregarded. Growth in the resource-poor countries therefore depends strongly on inflows of geopolitical rent, averaging around 10 per cent of GDP annually, and worker remittances. Moreover, the rapid accumulation of external debt in recent years, especially in Kyrgyzstan and Tajikistan, imposes an additional constraint on sustained economic recovery.

The rapid GDP growth in the energy-rich countries is also fragile because it relies on rising energy revenues. The energy-rich countries exhibit evidence of Dutch disease effects, which reverse the competitive economic diversification that is required to sustain rapid GDP growth. Uzbekistan and Turkmenistan, in particular, have made limited progress with economic reform and the associated competitive diversification that is required to avoid falling into the STEX (staple trap) development trajectory. Moreover, as in the resource-poor countries, the degraded social capital starves small farmers, SMEs and exporters of credit and imposes high transaction costs on them. Access to financial and other resources is skewed towards large capital-intensive enterprises, whether in the private or state sector, which frequently function as rent recipients and inefficient providers of employment within the patronage systems.

Despite some recovery in levels of capital investment, the combination of a large investment backlog from the collapse of central planning and continuing inefficient domestic allocation of resources means that basic infrastructure continues to degrade in most countries. This occurs because the process of rent extraction and distribution is liquidating the infrastructure upon which the rent depends. This is especially critical for Uzbekistan, which is already struggling with high debt and lackluster GDP growth. The Uzbek strategy of gradual reform does not emulate the successful East Asian gradual reformers, which created a dynamic market sector by liberalizing agriculture (China and Vietnam) or rapidly expanding manufactured exports via FDI (Cambodia and Laos). Rather, the Uzbek government extracts rents from both its irrigation and energy sectors without adequate provision to maintain their physical assets. It transfers the rent to non-viable manufacturing that runs at low capacity or shuts down. The Uzbek economy is therefore a classic case of the STEX model and the genuine saving coefficient shows that its economy is far from sustainable (Table 10.4). At best the Uzbek economy is an inefficient rent-generating mechanism and at worst it exploits and represses rural workers to support an elite in a manner that is not sustainable.

Nevertheless, the CCA countries have made some progress with trade and price reform, asset redistribution, government elections and institution building. The potential emergence of a diffusing oligarchy in Georgia, which reflects the existence of stronger social voice in the South Caucasus, offers some optimism regarding political change. But for the CCA region as a whole, the patronage systems of authoritarian regimes are incompatible with the expansion of the competitive markets that is required to create wealth and sustain GDP growth. Yet retarded reform also increases the risk of a growth collapse that will discredit the ruling dynasty.

## How dependent social capital and authoritarian states slow economic reform

The two principal causes of faltering reform within the CCA countries emanate from the region's dependent social capital and the authoritarian governments that sustain it through their patronage systems. This dependent social capital is an unfortunate legacy of the USSR. It encourages individuals to bond and co-operate for mutual advantage, but only in relatively small groups and secretively because central planning discouraged the formation of autonomous associational networks. Facing weaker social pressure for change than their CEE counterparts, the CCA political elites continued to pursue their mutual interest after the expiry of central planning, often at the expense of the public good (Jones Luong 2002). The CIEN and STEX models show that economic development requires such bonding social capital to give way to the regional linking and bridging social networks that nurture civic associations and voice. It also requires the strengthening of formal institutions such as property rights and the rule of law in order to protect the returns to wealth creation.

The deficiencies of dependent social capital were amplified by the unusual severity of GDP compression, which in all the CCA countries slashed public sector wages and social entitlements well below the levels required for subsistence. The squeeze on revenues fostered petty corruption as civil servants abused the provision of public services in order to compensate for their diminished official income. A pair of interlinking vicious circles is created that locks in corruption and rent-seeking. First, illicit imposts deter private investment, thereby stifling the growth of the private sector jobs that are required to pull excess labor from the public sector so that real wages in that sector can rise. Second, the imposts elicit requests from businesses for tax exemption, which, if granted, reduce government revenue and make it more difficult to raise public sector wages to adequate levels. The resulting predatory government forms a parasitic sector along with cosseted state enterprises and well-connected privatized firms that receive rents in exchange for political favors. The growth of the parasitic sector absorbs and deploys resources inefficiently at the expense of potentially more dynamic economic agents in agriculture, SMEs and exports whose incentive to invest is repressed so that many seek to lower their profile by entering the gray economy. The literature confirms that corruption is associated with the misallocation of public and private investment and slower GDP growth.

Yet, the CIEN model suggests that the resource-poor CCA countries might be expected to progress faster with endogenous democratization. Levels of freedom and voice are indeed higher in Armenia and Georgia, and both countries may be close to the tipping point that propels them through a diffusing oligarchy, but this promising outcome is by no means assured. Moreover, despite being the fastest economic and political reformer, Kyrgyzstan shows the strong countervailing forces exerted by severe GDP compression, inadequately controlled rent-seeking and uncooperative neighbors. Kyrgyzstan also shows that even if the central government espouses economic reform, a fractured oligarchy lacks sufficient control over lower tiers of government to implement it. Moreover, the tariff and non-tariff barriers to trade imposed by neighboring countries, notably Uzbekistan, negate the benefits of Kyrgyzstan's rapid trade and price liberalization. Yet the small size of Kyrgyzstan's economy makes increased trade and the associated scope for specialization particularly critical for sustained GDP growth. Kyrgyzstan and Tajikistan may not be viable countries, especially the latter, whose leaders have even less control over lower tiers of government than their Kyrgyz counterparts.

Turning to the resource-rich countries, the STEX model suggests that high rents are likely to nurture predatory governments that deploy the rent in ways that distort the economy and lead to a growth collapse. The events preceding a growth collapse increase political repression. This is because rents eventually shrink relative to the burgeoning rent-dependent parasitic sector and thereby force the regime to concentrate the remaining rent on strategic supporters and to repress those who lose out. Yet the STEX model also suggests that a growth collapse provides scope for major political change if external conditions are favorable, notably the presence of external loans to assist economic recovery and also regional neighbors that tolerate political pluralism. Such exogenous democratization is likely not only to be abrupt, but also to require a lengthy period of consolidation, during which it is vulnerable to regression. The political science literature supports the expectation that democratization frequently requires external intervention to promote it.

The political economy models imply that rapid PCGDP growth is in the interests of informed and rational elites with dynastic ambitions, as well as being in the interests of the population at large. This is because the misallocation of investment as a result of uncontrolled rent-seeking will lead to a growth collapse in the absence of economic reform, and a growth collapse is likely to discredit the leadership, if not the regime. Consequently, the longevity of the elite depends on its capacity to make the transition from reliance on political power to reliance on economic strength. This requires increased control of rent-seeking in order to constrain its depressing effects on economic incentives and to channel rents into wealth-creating investment. A dual-track reform strategy offers a politically astute way of achieving this critical objective because it eases the political obstacles to the transition to markets by creating a dynamic market sector that allows the gainers from reform to compensate the losers. The CIEN model suggests the political transition will be incremental and that the population at large, if compensated by rapid increases in the standard of living, will accept a lag in increased political accountability relative to voice and rule of law.

An additional motive for the elite to promote economic reform applies to moribund economies, like Uzbekistan, and arises from the recent divergence in GDP growth rates. If recent economic growth rates persist for a further five years, then during 2004–10 the GDP of Kazakhstan will double to $38 billion, whereas that of the more populous Uzbekistan would be barely $8 billion. Divergence in economic growth on this scale and at this speed threatens the geopolitical balance in Central Asia and strengthens the incentive of the Uzbek elite to raise the efficiency of resource use. Finally, the gains from economic reform would be compounded by increased regional cooperation.

## Prospective gains from regional synergies and why they remain elusive

As relatively small, landlocked economies, remote from dynamic markets and surrounded by stronger neighbors with the power to facilitate access to global trade and to destabilize domestic politics, the eight CCA countries might have been expected to cooperate in defense of common interests, building on their shared experience of independence from the USSR. In fact, the priority accorded to regime security has tended to work against regional coordination for the common good. Consequently, low priority has been given to opportunities to increase regional welfare through cooperation to: facilitate intra-regional trade and improve access to distant markets; manage common environmental resources in a sustainable fashion; combat international criminal and terrorist gangs; and build institutions for resolving political and military disputes. Worse, the pursuit of narrowly focused national and sub-national interests has caused some corrosion of the already limited initial scope for trade. It has also accelerated natural resource depletion and heightened ethnic tension, notably in the Ferghana Valley and southern Caucasus.

The CCA countries appear to have much to gain from economic cooperation because small and landlocked states are especially disadvantaged if their neighbors are hostile or have moribund economies. Dynamic neighboring markets create buoyant demand for, say, energy exports that incur far lower transport costs (and higher profit margins and/or rent) than markets outside the region. In addition, a strengthening of the real exchange rate in the booming energy-rich countries creates opportunities for the resource-poor countries to use their lower real wages to export perishable agricultural produce and high weight/value manufactured goods to their energy-rich neighbors.

Yet, although the actual magnitude of trade among the Central Asian countries is relatively low, this may be due to the common shared dependence of these countries on a relatively narrow range of primary products, a situation that is likely to persist through the medium term at least. The level of inter-country trade is two-thirds of the level predicted by gravity models, so barriers to inter-country trade among the eight CCA countries impose only modest trade loss with each other. However, trade with near neighbors such as Russia, China, Iran and Turkey is substantially lower than would be expected. Chapter 9 suggests that increased trade with near neighbors will boost economic diversification more effectively than either intra-regional or global trade, at least through the medium term. In addition, dropping down from the macro level to the micro level, increased scope for trade by mid-sized firms within Central Asia would be especially beneficial because such firms are a potential catalyst for the competitive restructuring of the economy. Here again, Uzbekistan is especially deficient.

The very high costs of accessing the markets of near neighbors impose substantial penalties in terms of trade opportunities foregone, however. Yet tariffs are a relatively unimportant obstacle to trade, compared with institutional inefficiency and corruption. The pursuit of autarkic transportation policies during the first decade of transition has routed roads inefficiently to avoid border crossings and left the potential economies of scale from sharing infrastructure projects largely unrealized. In addition, transport costs are further boosted because truckers cannot lower their operating costs by securing return loads; and also because of border delays and official and unofficial imposts. Moreover, these conditions inflict severe costs at the grass-roots level through the arbitrary closure of borders, which encourages smuggling and retreat into the gray economy.

The region's largest economy, Kazakhstan, appears to have little to gain from local trade and this, combined with the autarkic trade policy of Uzbekistan, the region's second-largest economy, may explain the lack of enthusiasm for regional trade integration. Any benefits from trade reform will be asymmetric, with Kazakhstan profiting least and Tajikistan and Kyrgyzstan the most. Yet, as Kyrgyzstan confirms, going it alone with unilateral rapid accession to the WTO confers few benefits because the non-member Central Asian countries protect their own producers from global goods by blocking goods from Kyrgyzstan, which they view as a Trojan horse for the products of global business. More optimistically, however, if Russia and Kazakhstan join the WTO in the near future, the smaller countries can capture the benefits of further trade reform while Uzbekistan would have little recourse against anti-dumping action or other measures if it too were not a WTO member.

The neglect of environmental concerns by the central planners persisted through the transition because the decline in real incomes created more immediately pressing problems than did the environment. Although numerous official bodies have been established to arrest and reverse environmental deterioration, environmental issues continue to attract little interest from the region's governments. More than $40 million has been expended to date on studying the region's environmental problems, but precious little has been spent on their solution. The regional cooperation required to resolve shared problems such as the allocation of mineral rights in the Caspian Basin and water allocation in the Aral Sea Basin remains unforthcoming. Moreover, until economic reform correctly prices inputs like water, energy and fertilizer (at marginal cost or world prices) it will be difficult to encourage either the efficient use of energy and farm inputs, or to impose taxes that reflect the cost of environmental damage and thereby discourage pollution. Consequently, conditions in the Caspian Sea and Aral Basin are likely to continue to deteriorate. The even more ambitious task of attempting to clean up the backlog of environmental damage seems to lie far in the future. It requires not only further economic reform to raise incomes and generate more resources for environmental improvements but also political reform to strengthen civic voice in support of environmental improvements and create more robust mechanisms for regional environmental cooperation.

As with regional cooperation on economic, environmental and social issues, only limited progress has been made towards an effective framework for multilateral conflict prevention or defense cooperation in either the South Caucasus or Central Asia, let alone for both regions together. In the case of the South Caucasus the frozen conflict around Nagorno-Karabakh precludes any kind of multilateral cooperation on defense issues or the development of a regional security identity. In Central Asia authoritarian regimes along with the rivalry between Kazakhstan and Uzbekistan, as well as many lesser axes of tension, also militate against multilateral regional projects. Local rulers are unwilling to strengthen regional organizations or to create mechanisms to make agreements binding, for fear of loss of sovereignty.

The CCA states are therefore likely to continue to rely heavily for their defense on the development of well-organized national military forces, rather than looking to develop multilateral defense and security relationships. Paradoxically, multilateral regional security cooperation among the CCA countries is less likely to elicit significant defense and security cooperation the more serious the defense concerns are for the states as a group. The CIS structure has also exercised a distorting effect by acting as a Russian mechanism of supranational regional management during the 1990s. The CIS structure tends to impede multilateral efforts that exclude Russia.

As a consequence of these problems, the CCA leaders have given priority in their external defense policies to building bridges bilaterally to powerful regional states. The regional patrons include Russia (for Armenia, Kazakhstan, Kyrgyzstan and Tajikistan), Turkey (particularly for Georgia and Azerbaijan), and more recently the United States. China and Iran also play an active role. Yet to the extent that such bilateral ties may assist the construction of military forces in certain countries that look threatening to their neighbors this can encourage the formation of counterposing alliances or blocs.

## The prospective role of external agents in CCA reform

Russia and Iran have common interests in the west of the CCA region, including the desire to exercise greater control on the flow of competing energy resources from the CCA countries to global markets. However, they hold conflicting views regarding the allocation of Caspian Sea resources, with Russia backing Azerbaijan and Kazakhstan (likely to be joined by Turkmenistan) against Iranian claims, which has nevertheless effectively blocked oil exploration in the southern Caspian. There are also mutual tensions between Russia and Iran fuelled by suspicions about their future relations with the United States.

Despite shared concern for the increased presence of the US within the region, both Russia and Iran appear to recognize that there are certain problems in the CCA region, like the rise of Sunni Islamic fundamentalism, terrorist activity and general criminality (notably the narcotics trade), which can be more readily addressed with an American presence than without one. Hence Russia cooperated with, and Iran acquiesced in, American military intervention to overthrow the Taliban, which both Moscow and Tehran regarded as a threat. Unfortunately, neither Russia nor Iran (both of which have embarked upon democratization but still retain strong authoritarian elements in their governing structures) is pushing the smaller states of the region to democratize. Most governments in the CCA region are satisfied with the drift towards an authoritarian status quo, and do not wish to see this disrupted by the US.

Nor, in the east of the region, is China likely to welcome the strengthening of democracy. China's key regional interests lie in diversifying its long-term energy supplies and guarding its problematic north-west provinces against secessionist forces. Yet, the rapid growth of the Chinese economy creates substantial opportunities for expanding CCA energy exports (and other forms of trade), as China seeks to diversify its energy supplies away from the Middle East and also away from its heavy reliance on polluting coal. This makes Russia and the CCA countries rival energy suppliers to China, although strategic considerations are likely to ensure that China seeks to avoid dependence on any one supplier. There is also scope for Russia and the Central Asian states to cooperate in sharing the investment burden of constructing the scale-sensitive infrastructure required to reach the Chinese market.

China also has concerns about poverty and secessionist movements in its poor and remote western regions, concerns which create shared interests with the Central Asian states in stimulating regional trade to boost living standards and curb Islamic fundamentalists and international crime. China and Russia would prefer to handle terrorism (other than within their own territories) and additional threats to the central Eurasian heartland through multilateral forums like the Shanghai Cooperation Organization, or the United Nations. However, neither Moscow nor Beijing, nor Washington for that matter, has addressed the risk that the repressive domestic policies being pursued by all Central Asian leaders might in the long term strengthen the hands of Islamic militants and jeopardize regional security.

In contrast to China, Iran and Russia, the western democracies do have a clear interest in furthering political reform within the region and the CIEN and STEX models help to explain the political economy constraints within which this goal must be pursued. The western democracies can play a pivotal role in accelerating economic and political reform. One important lever is the supply of capital to facilitate the restructuring of the CCA economies. Low population density in the CCA region combines with vast distances from markets to make the expansion, rehabilitation and re-orientation of regional infrastructure an urgent priority, but it is also a highly capital-intensive one. Sizeable inflows of FDI will be required to upgrade the stock of infrastructure, and the prosperous democratic countries of the North Atlantic and North Pacific are in a position to provide these inflows. Such funding should be made conditional on being accompanied by economic reforms designed to sustain rising productivity.

Yet, whereas conditional loans have proved effective in securing macro-economic stabilization, there is doubt about their effectiveness in the more long-term process of economic restructuring due to institutional flaws and reform fatigue. Although public accountability frameworks are still evolving, it is not always possible to account for public funds, which poses a dilemma for the IFIs. The interests of the owners of IFIs (i.e. the G7 countries) do not always permit imposition of the conditionality necessary to accelerate institutional development and improve governance. This difficulty can be compounded by the presence of donor development agencies, which need to disburse grant money, sometimes in competition with the IFIs. CCA governments can exploit this competition in order to reduce the collective leverage of donors. Consequently, recipient governments with weak legitimacy and low transparency can end up being supported in ways that propagate rent-seeking mechanisms.

In this context, this book proposes a four-pronged strategy for the IFIs and western governments to promote faster economic reform, which also sows the seeds of political reform, as explained by the STEX and CIEN models. First, the IFIs and other extra-regional agencies should tirelessly explain why wealth creation offers superior prospects for dynastic survival in the CCA region than continued rent redistribution. Second, although rent-seeking cannot be changed overnight because it is so deep-rooted, the current growth rebound in seven of the eight CCA countries can be used to tighten control of rent-seeking in order to progressively reduce its negative impacts on wealth creation and to deflect it to investments that will competitively diversify the economy. The dual-track reform strategy offers a practical means of doing this. It creates a dynamic market economy by establishing early reform zones in which post-reform standards of infrastructure, incentives and institutions immediately apply, alongside the partially reformed plan economy. Dual-track reform also helps build a pro-reform political constituency. Consequently, and third, IFIs, NGOs and donor governments can promote the required grass-roots experimental reform projects, which pose no immediate threat to national elite patronage systems. Finally, economic and political shocks that temporarily strengthen IFI financial leverage can be used to accelerate reform by making the loans conditional on staged economic reform.

Ironically, a growth collapse in the most populous country, Uzbekistan, might provide the catalyst required to halt the regional drift towards authoritarian rule and ossified economic reform. In mid-2005, Uzbekistan appeared vulnerable to a growth collapse due to the cumulative misallocation of investment that has failed to either grow a dynamic market sector or to maintain the basic infrastructure upon which rent extraction depends. A growth collapse would force the Uzbek elite to renegotiate power, recognizing that the state must embrace a wider set of encompassing interests in order to maintain security and accelerate wealth creation. So far the Uzbek elite has accepted the need to share rent reductions as economic performance has faltered, and it may be prepared to share political power with other groups, should that prove unavoidable. A post-collapse Uzbek government would also require substantial capital to rehabilitate the country's neglected infrastructure and sustain economic growth, which capital it could not generate domestically. Herein lies an opportunity for western governments to promote political change to strengthen voice and political accountability, and also attract the capital with which to rehabilitate and restructure the economy. In this way a growth collapse might offer scope for one of the CCA regions autocracies to lead a drive to renew economic and political reform.

Paradoxically, therefore, an extreme adverse event may help the CCA region to achieve the welfare-enhancing potential offered by energy-driven growth. However, Uzbekistan may yet evade a growth collapse, so that, more fundamentally, CCA regional elites must be urged to heed the lessons for effective resource rent deployment from the developing market economies. The basic lesson is that those dynasties thrive that boost social welfare by effectively deploying the rent to provide public goods and incentives for private economic agents to use inputs efficiently. The resulting rising incomes elicit a tolerance for controlled rent-seeking that minimizes the distortion of the economy, as shown by both Malaysia and also Indonesia during 1965–95. Western governments should support this policy because it will not only boost broad-based social welfare, but also encourage the leadership to acquire political legitimacy and/or economic security incrementally as it steadily aligns its interests with those of the majority. The clear gainers (society at large) compensate the apparent losers (the elite), but in fact all parties gain from this compromise, including the global community.

## Notes

1 The author is especially grateful to Cevdet Denizer, Richard Pomfret and Martin Raiser for very helpful comments on an earlier draft of this chapter. All errors remain the responsibility of the author.

## References

De Melo, M., Denizer, C. and Gelb, A. (1996) Patterns of transition from plan to market, *World Bank Economic Review* 10, 397–424.
De Melo, M., Denizer, C., Gelb, A. and Tenev, S. (2001) Circumstance and choice: The role of initial conditions and policies in transition economies, *World Bank Economic Review* 15, 1–31.
Jones Luong, P. (2002) *Institutional Change and Political Continuity in Post-Soviet Central Asia: Power, Perceptions and Pacts*, Cambridge: Cambridge University Press.
World Bank (2002) *World Development Indicators 20002*, Washington DC: World Bank.

# Index

For Product Safety Concerns and Information please contact our EU
representative GPSR@taylorandfrancis.com
Taylor & Francis Verlag GmbH, Kaufingerstraße 24, 80331 München, Germany

www.ingramcontent.com/pod-product-compliance
Lightning Source LLC
Chambersburg PA
CBHW060151280326
41932CB00012B/1713